ATLANTA
1847–1890

ATLANTA
1847–1890

City Building in the Old South and the New

James Michael Russell

LOUISIANA STATE UNIVERSITY PRESS

Baton Rouge and London

Designer: Sylvia Loftin
Typeface: Electra
Typesetter: The Composing Room of Michigan, Inc.
Printer: Thomson-Shore, Inc.
Binder: John H. Dekker & Sons, Inc.

Library of Congress Cataloging-in-Publication Data
Russell, James M. (James Michael). 1944–
    Atlanta, 1847–1890 : city building in the Old South and the New /
James M. Russell.
        p.   cm.
    Bibliography: p.
    Includes index.
    ISBN 0-8071-1413-8
    1. Atlanta (Ga.)—Politics and government. 2. Atlanta (Ga.)—
Economic conditions. 3. Atlanta (Ga.)—Social conditions. 4. City
and town life—Georgia—Atlanta—History—19th century. I. Title.
F294.A857R87 1988
975.8'231—dc19   87-29946
                                                                CIP

Portions of this study were first published as "Politics, Municipal Services, and
the Working Class in Atlanta, 1865 to 1890," *Georgia Historical Quarterly,* LXVI
(Winter, 1982), 467–91. Dun & Bradstreet permitted citation from credit reports
collected by its predecessor, R. G. Dun & Co. All photographs are courtesy of
the Atlanta Historical Society.

The paper in this book meets the guidelines for permanence and durability of the
Committee on Production Guidelines for Book Longevity of the Council on
Library Resources.∞

To my Mother

and the Memory of my Father

CONTENTS

ILLUSTRATIONS

Following page 29

Following page 140

ACKNOWLEDGMENTS

This book has had such a lengthy germination that I am in danger of forgetting to mention someone whose assistance was vital. If I commit such a blunder, I hope that the individual or individuals involved will believe that I am grateful for their help all the same.

Like most people engaged in historical research, I have accumulated a mountain of debts to the staffs of several libraries and archives. The bulk of my time was spent at the Atlanta Historical Society and the Georgia Department of Archives and History. The personnel of those institutions always handled my requests competently and courteously. I would like to express my special thanks to three members of the staff at the Atlanta Historical Society: Gene Craig, Dick Eltzroth, and Lee Alexander (who has since transferred to Trevor Arnett Library, Atlanta University). Other research institutions where I spent at least a week include the New York Public Library, the National Archives, the American Missionary Association Archives at Dillard University, and the Baker Library at Harvard University. The director of the AMA Archives, Clifton Johnson, helped me enjoy New Orleans and generously assisted my scholarly interests. Robert Lovett at the Baker Library rendered me the courteous service that he has given to so many others who have delved into the R. G. Dun & Co. credit reports. Other libraries and archives to which I paid briefer visits include the Robert R. Woodruff Library, Emory University; the Ilah Dunlap Little Memorial Library, University of Georgia; the Southern Historical Collection, University of North Carolina, Chapel Hill; the William R. Perkins Library, Duke University; and Trevor Arnett Library, Atlanta University. The staffs of all these places were universally pleasant and helpful. I would also like to thank several Atlantans and managers of local business firms who let me see records and papers in private possession.

I have nearly as many debts to members of the academic community as I have to the staffs of research centers. Sheldon Hackney gave conscientious guidance. John Shy urged me to study population persistence, advice I ultimately accepted. Several scholars read portions of earlier versions of material that was eventually incorporated into this work and offered their expert advice. These incisive critics included Carl Harris, Blaine Brownell, Howard Rabinowitz, and Ken Jackson. The two men to whom I owe the greatest intellectual debt are David Goldfield and Don Doyle, who both read more than one version of the entire manuscript. Don Doyle shared research material with me and offered penetrating and useful criticism. I also owe much to Franklin Garrett, the staff historian at the Atlanta Historical Society. He also shared his research materials and answered extremely detailed questions about individuals and institutions in Atlanta history that probably no one else on earth could answer.

Financial assistance, so welcome in the course of lengthy research, was provided by two institutions. Through the National Endowment for the Humanities, I attended Ken Jackson's Summer Seminar in American Urban History in 1983. Besides becoming acquainted with one of this country's finest urban historians, I could use the resources of the New York Public Library. In the following academic year, on sabbatical from the University of Tennessee at Chattanooga, I completed a first draft. Without this free time, I doubt that I could have finished the book. I was also fortunate to have two earlier research grants and a summer fellowship from the University of Chattanooga Foundation.

Family and friends have also done their part in bringing this project to fruition. Relatives in Atlanta—my mother while she still lived in the city and later Harry and Lucille Crawford—provided housing and good company. My departmental secretary, Elke Lawson, typed portions of the manuscript. The one person who helped me more than anyone else was my wife, Kathy. She typed parts of various drafts, drew all the maps, entered most of the quantitative data into the mainframe computer, and wrote programs to help process that data. Fortunately, I purchased a microcomputer in time so I could type most of the final draft. While I appreciate deeply all her help, I want my wife to see in print a promise that I will never put so many burdens on her again in connection with my scholarly endeavors.

I need also to express my appreciation to all the professionals at Louisiana State University Press. I would like to thank especially Margaret Fisher Dalrymple, Catherine F. Barton, and Barbara O'Neil Phillips. Ms. Dalrymple was the senior editor in charge of the manuscript from the time it arrived until bestowal of a contract. I

ACKNOWLEDGMENTS

appreciate her encouragement and interest. The managing editor, Ms. Barton, reviewed the manuscript thoroughly and saved me valuable time. Ms. Phillips did exactly what any sensible author wants a good copy editor to do. She demanded dozens of clarifications of confusing items in the text and helped me to write in plain English.

As is customary with acknowledgment of assistance from others, I will end by stating that whatever flaws remain in this book are my responsibility alone.

ABBREVIATIONS

AHB	*Atlanta Historical Bulletin*
AHJ	*Atlanta Historical Journal*
AHS	Atlanta Historical Society
CM	Minutes of the Atlanta City Council
Ga. Laws	*Acts of the General Assembly of the State of Georgia*
GDAH	Georgia Department of Archives and History, Atlanta
GHQ	*Georgia Historical Quarterly*
JEH	*Journal of Economic History*
JSH	*Journal of Southern History*
JUH	*Journal of Urban History*
SSH	*Social Science History*
UGA	Ilah Dunlap Little Memorial Library, University of Georgia, Athens

ATLANTA
1847–1890

INTRODUCTION

Ours, gentlemen, is indeed a wonderful city! So much so, that its rapid growth and prosperity have always been considered by many persons to be a profound mystery. And when we take into consideration the fact that it is situated in a country comparatively poor . . . it is not strange that those who have watched its rise and progress from the beginning have been truly astonished at the rapid strides it has made towards greatness. . . . How is all this to be accounted for? It is owing, I suppose, mainly to the energies of its citizens.

—Mayor William E. Ezzard's Inaugural Address (1870)

The Chinese at one time believed that China was the center of the world, but . . . it has lately been discovered that Atlanta is. . . . If all the newspapers in Atlanta say is true, and of course they would not say so if it were not, everything about the place is in the superlative degree. Their rocks are the hardest, and their mud is the softest; their thunder the loudest, and their rain the wettest that was ever known.

—Milledgeville *Federal Union* (1854)

The first quotation is from a man who served as mayor of Atlanta before and after the Civil War; the second is from a newspaper editor irritated by Atlantans' ambitious efforts to move the state capital from his city to theirs. Together they evoke the main themes of this book. The first implies a continuity between the Old and New South in Atlanta and raises questions about the origins of New South men and ideas. Both speak of the importance of entrepreneurship and urban boosterism in Atlanta, familiar themes in the history of nineteenth-century cities in the United States. Finally, they suggest (though the newspaper writer would have conceded it grudgingly) that Atlanta was somehow "different" from the rest of the South. This notion persisted in the writings of visitors to the city not only throughout the nineteenth century but in modern times as well. Such an impression arose partly because Atlanta always appeared to be remarkably prosperous for a city located in the southern upcountry, a region long noted for its poverty and economic underdevelopment. Through the years the conclusion that many outsiders reached was that Atlanta's "progressive" qualities could only be explained by a population, leaders, and values that were somehow "unsouthern."

Continuity between the Old and New South and the related issue of the origins of New South men and ideas have been subjects of considerable debate.[1] The older interpretation was best expressed by C. Vann Woodward, who detected several discontinuities in southern history. Woodward saw the Civil War as one of the major dividing lines in the region's past: the South's political and economic leadership changed dramatically after 1865.

While Woodward identified numerous antebellum planters who survived the war and entered the ranks of the New South's political and economic elite, he emphasized the emergence after 1865 of a new middle class, which was a product of the region's urban and industrial growth. "The 'victory of the middle classes' and 'the passing of power from the hands of the landowners to manufacturers and merchants,'" Woodward wrote of the New South, "which required

1. A good synopsis of the issues can be found in Dan T. Carter, "From the Old South to the New: Another Look at the Theme of Change and Continuity," in Walter J. Fraser, Jr., and Winfred B. Moore, Jr. (eds.), *From the Old South to the New: Essays on the Transitional South* (Westport, Conn., 1981), 23–32.

two generations in England, were substantially achieved in a much shorter period in the South." Woodward was less than sympathetic to many of these new men such as Joseph E. Brown and John B. Gordon of Georgia, both descendants of the upcountry farmer class that had been overshadowed before the war by the plantation aristocracy. In his work, such individuals often bear a striking resemblance to the rapacious Snopes clan in William Faulkner's novels. Although Woodward's writings are full of subtle ambiguities and qualifiers, he clearly believes that the war undercut the antebellum planters' control of the region.[2]

Historian Jonathan Wiener and sociologist Dwight B. Billings have advanced a very different interpretation of the character of the New South. Both see far more continuity between the Old and New South than does Woodward, and the continuity involves the persistence of the planter class. Wiener found that the landholding aristocracy in Alabama had little trouble weathering the economic disasters caused by the Civil War and that descendants of antebellum planters still directed the state's political and economic development at the end of the nineteenth century. For Wiener's persisting planters, country store merchants and Birmingham industrialists (about whose origins he is noticeably vague) were annoying but powerless and were easily subjugated. Wiener sees Alabama planters in the New South era as resembling Prussian Junkers, a landholding aristocracy that overwhelmed a capitalist bourgeoisie and controlled an industrial movement so that it did not threaten aristocratic values and power. New South Alabama also followed a "Prussian road" to industrialization and urbanization, and its merchants and manufacturers were subservient to a tenacious planter class. Wiener subsequently extended his thesis beyond Alabama and the nineteenth century. The entire South from the end of the Civil War through the mid-twentieth century followed the Prussian road to modernization. Thus, he concludes, its economy was at the mercy of northern capitalists, and its society was dominated by landlords who had overwhelmed a weak bourgeois class.[3]

Dwight B. Billings' study of North Carolina industrialization after

2. C. Vann Woodward, *Origins of the New South, 1877–1913* (Rev. ed.; Baton Rouge, 1971), 29, 140–74; Woodward, *Tom Watson: Agrarian Rebel* (New York, 1938), 56–63.
3. Jonathan Wiener, *Social Origins of the New South: Alabama, 1860–1885* (Baton Rouge, 1978); Wiener, "Class Structure and Economic Development in the American South, 1865–1955," *American Historical Review*, LXXXIV (1979), 970–92.

the Civil War embraces wholeheartedly Wiener's hypothesis and stresses even more than Wiener planter persistence in the New South. While Wiener's Alabama planters faced challenges from Birmingham industrialists, their North Carolina counterparts, according to Billings, did not have similar problems. Resting his argument on a shaky methodological assumption, Billings reveals that planters and their sons were dominant members of boards of directors of upcountry textile mills. Thus resilient planter aristocracy thwarts the rise of a new middle class. The state's economic destiny is charted by men who reject the capitalistic ideal of a free and competitive economy for one characterized by authoritarian paternalism, low wages, and intensive labor. [4]

Studies by David Carlton and Lacy Ford have attacked Wiener and Billings and once again have argued for the newness of the New South. Carlton maintains that those who led the textile mill movement in South Carolina's upcountry after the war came from that part of the state and were not descended from lowcountry planters. Carlton's textile mill owners were part of an emerging middle class, and the direction of the New South's industrial economy was not significantly influenced by representatives of Old South values. Ford points out that commercial revolutions always precede industrial revolutions. The commercial revolution in South Carolina's upcountry occurred because railroads were built there after the war, because farmers shifted from subsistence and foodstuffs agriculture to cotton production, and because the destruction of slavery and the cotton factorage system weakened the economic power of lowland plantation districts. Ford concludes that town merchants in the upcountry, who arranged the sale of the area's cotton crop and its shipment to markets, became the leaders of the textile mill movement that followed this commercial transformation. [5]

Two additional works by Paul Escott and Laurence Shore indirectly support the arguments of Carlton and Ford, but also stress continuity between the Old and New South. Escott's analysis of

4. Dwight B. Billings, *Planters and the Making of a "New South": Class, Politics, and Development in North Carolina* (Chapel Hill, 1979). Billings assumed that the "prominent agrarians" he found in an 1869 business directory were planters. He did not define planters by the acreage they held or by any of the usual quantitative measures (pp. 62–65).
5. David L. Carlton, *Mill and Town in South Carolina, 1880–1920* (Baton Rouge, 1982); Lacy K. Ford, "Rednecks and Merchants: Economic Development and Social Tensions in the South Carolina Upcountry, 1865–1900," *Journal of American History*, LXXI (1984), 294–318.

power and privilege in North Carolina during the second half of the nineteenth century identifies several prominent antebellum textile mill leaders, who helped to revive that industry in the state after 1865. Escott concedes that many of these men had agricultural investments before and after the war, but he avoids labeling them planters and asserts that North Carolina was never "marked by a distinctive planter ethos." According to Escott, there were also many "new men"— merchants, bankers, and professionals in interior towns—who played prominent roles during the postbellum era in establishing textile mills in the state, just as Carlton's "town people" did in South Carolina.[6]

Laurence Shore's study of the ideological origins of the New South also emphasizes overlap between the pre– and post–Civil War South. Many of the region's most prominent spokesmen for slavery and the old order, Shore maintains, became converts to the New South creed after 1865, and crusaded for industrialization and new attitudes toward labor. While Shore traces the social origins of several of these ideologues to the antebellum planter aristocracy, he eschews the neo-Marxist approach of Wiener and Billings. Moreover, his work does not undercut Escott's findings, since it mostly deals with the spokesmen for rather than the business leaders of the New South.[7]

My interpretation of the origins of New South men and ideas parallels more closely the views of Paul Escott than those of the other scholars whose works I have briefly summarized. I will argue that Atlanta's economic leaders after the war shared many of their predecessors' social characteristics and city-building ideas. Moreover, several of the antebellum leaders survived the war and renewed their urban promotive schemes in the city after 1865. Both ante– and post–Civil War business elites had few ties to the planter class and consciously rejected its culture, though Henry Grady and others occasionally toasted Cavalier ideals. New South ideologies and an urban middle-class leadership in Atlanta were thus anticipated in the era before the Civil War.

This continuity between the Old South and the New likely existed in other southern interior cities, which were, after all, the real head-

6. Paul D. Escott, *Many Excellent People: Power and Privilege in North Carolina, 1850–1900* (Chapel Hill, 1985), 199.
7. Laurence Shore, *Southern Capitalists: The Ideological Leadership of an Elite, 1832–1885* (Chapel Hill, 1986).

quarters of the New South movement. Unfortunately, little research on these cities has dealt with the origins of New South men and ideas and none of it has considered the possible overlap of ante- and postbellum urban leaderships and city-building creeds. Don H. Doyle's excellent biography of Nashville, for example, does not deal with that city's career before 1880. A study of Richmond stresses the conservatism of that city's leadership after 1865, but does not systematically evaluate its relationship to antebellum patterns.[8]

I will also argue that a repressive and persistent landholding aristocracy did not significantly hinder Atlanta's postbellum economic leaders in implementing New South urban promotive ventures. Wiener implies that Alabama's planters consistently attempted to use their political power to retard Birmingham's industrial development, which they saw as incompatible with their need for a docile labor supply for their plantations. But he cites only two concrete examples—a battle fought in the state legislature over the route of what became the South & North Railroad and the landholders' success in 1884 in persuading Alabama's congressional delegation to vote against a bill to raise iron tariffs (a bill naturally favored by Birmingham industrialists). The eventual outcome of both contests was defeat for the planters. The South & North was absorbed into the Louisville & Nashville system, which furthered Birmingham's industrial development, and Congress passed the tariff bill over the objections of the Alabama delegation. Wiener is much more persuasive in arguing that the real enemy of Birmingham's business leaders was not the state's planter class but rather the northeastern industrial community, which had no intention of allowing factories in Birmingham to grow at the expense of their own.[9]

Whether Alabama planters were committed to slowing Birmingham's industrialization, there is ample evidence that Georgia's landholding aristocracy was unable to restrict Atlanta's economic growth during the postbellum period. The city's business leaders successfully lobbied the state legislature in 1868 to move the capital to Atlanta from Milledgeville, which was within the upper plantation belt. A series of bills passed by the Georgia legislature and the U.S.

---

8. Don H. Doyle, *Nashville in the New South, 1880–1930* (Knoxville, 1985); Michael B. Chesson, *Richmond After the War, 1865–1890* (Richmond, 1981).
9. Wiener, *Social Origins of the New South*, 162–227.

Congress between 1873 and 1875 made Atlanta a port of entry and authorized the construction of a customshouse there.[10] These legislative actions were detrimental to the interests of importers in Savannah, the seaport most closely identified with the state's lowland rice and cotton planters. They also symbolized the growing political power of Atlanta's business leadership in post–Civil War Georgia.

One indication of the true balance of political power between the old order and the new was the 1877 constitutional convention, which was to replace the document drawn up during Reconstruction. A dominant figure was Robert Toombs, former Confederate statesman, planter, and ultimate symbol of Old South values. Toombs was determined to eliminate state bond endorsement of railroad construction and to take other steps to regulate the railroads. A spokesman for rural interests, Toombs was not alone in lobbying for these provisions in the new constitution. Delegates from Atlanta voted with him on every key railroad issue. Further, the president of Atlanta's chamber of commerce introduced one of the more radical resolutions, one that called for the prohibition of railroad pools. Toombs hated railroads as agents of modern corporate capitalism, but Atlanta businessmen wanted regulation to protect their own commercial and industrial interests. Thus, an Old South planter and businessmen from the state's leading New South urban center eagerly cooperated. This series of events resembles more closely the New South described by Woodward than that portrayed by Wiener.[11]

Investigation of the New South creed and its origins in Atlanta leads into a broader theme, urban boosterism. Industrial development, railroad growth, new business elites, and other economic and social developments associated with the era of the New South were essential ingredients in the urban promotive activities of the region's cities during the period. Urban boosterism was at the heart of the New South creed, whose most prominent spokesmen were city dwellers.[12] Although most noticeable during the New South era, boost-

10. *Ga. Laws, 1875*, pp. 153–54; *Congressional Globe*, 42nd Cong., 3rd Sess., Vol. III, Pt. 3, Appendix, p. 240; *Congressional Record*, 43rd Cong., 1st Sess., Vol. III, Pt. 2, p. 1095, Vol. IV, Pt. 1, p. 915.
11. Ulrich B. Phillips, *The Life of Robert Toombs* (New York, 1913), 269–72; *Journal of Constitutional Convention of Georgia, July 11, 1877–August 25, 1877* (Atlanta, 1877), 9, 436, 649; Woodward, *Tom Watson*, 54–55.
12. The most penetrating analysis is still Paul Gaston's *The New South Creed: A Study in Southern Mythmaking* (New York, 1970).

erism was, in fact, a pervasive ideology in southern cities throughout the nineteenth and early twentieth centuries.[13]

Urban boosterism has also long been a favorite theme of historians of nineteenth-century American cities outside the South. Scholars have been especially interested in assessing the relative importance of entrepreneurial versus geographic and other factors in the location and growth of American cities. Adherents of Walter Christaller's central place theory and other econometric variations with an aura of "environmental determinism" have offered relatively rigid and impersonal models.[14] Several excellent case studies have pointed out that geography alone did not guarantee growth and also that the quality of entrepreneurship was not the same in the nation's cities during the nineteenth century and even later.[15]

Such debates concerning Atlanta's past have usually focused on the contribution to the city's growth that railroads (mostly financed by outside capital and built to the city mainly because of geographic factors) made as compared to that of local entrepreneurs who organized urban promotive ventures. Their respective economic power will be assessed herein. Certainly urban boosterism in its economic manifestation has been central to Atlanta's history, and ignoring it would not be wise.[16] My analysis, however, emphasizes the social,

13. Blaine A. Brownell, "The Idea of the City in Southern History," in Derek Fraser and Anthony Sutcliffe (eds.), *The Pursuit of Urban History* (London, 1983), 146–48.

14. The term is from Burton W. Folsom, *Urban Capitalists: Entrepreneurs and City Growth in Pennsylvania's Lackawanna and Lehigh Regions, 1800– 1920* (Baltimore, 1920), 5. A good introduction to central place and other location theories is in Ralph Tomlinson, *Urban Structure: The Social and Spatial Character of Cities* (New York, 1969), 117–41. Applications of central place theory to nineteenth-century American urbanization include: Kenneth Weiher, "The Cotton Industry and Southern Urbanization, 1880–1930," *Explorations in Economic History,* XIV (1977), 120–40; Roger F. Riefler, "Nineteenth Century Urbanization Patterns in the United States," *JEH,* IX (1979), 961–74; and Francis X. Blouin, *The Boston Region, 1810–1850: A Study of Urbanization* (Ann Arbor, 1980).

15. In addition to Folsom's *Urban Capitalists,* see Julius Rubin, *Canal or Railroad: Imitation and Innovation in the Response to the Erie Canal in Philadelphia, Baltimore, and Boston* (Philadelphia, 1961); Wyatt K. Belcher, *The Economic Rivalry between St. Louis and Chicago, 1850–1880* (New York, 1947); James W. Livingood, *The Philadelphia-Baltimore Trade Rivalry, 1786–1860* (Harrisburg, Pa., 1947); J. Christopher Schnell, "Chicago Versus St. Louis: A Reassessment of the Great Rivalry," *Missouri Historical Review,* LXXI (1977), 245–65; and William D. Angel, Jr., "Zenith Revisited: Urban Entrepreneurship and the Sunbelt Frontier," *Social Science Quarterly,* LXI (1980), 434–45.

16. Dana F. White and Timothy J. Crimmins, "How Atlanta Grew: Cool Heads, Hot Air, and Hard Work," in Andrew M. Hamer, Jr. (ed.), *Urban Atlanta: Redefining the Role of the City* (Atlanta, 1980), 25–44; Charles Paul Garofalo, "The Sons of Henry Grady: Atlanta Boosters in the 1920s," *JSH,* XLII (1976), 187–204; and Garofalo, "The Atlanta Spirit: A Study in Urban Ideology," *South Atlantic Quarterly,* LXXIV (1975), 34–44.

cultural, and political consequences. Entrepreneurial explanations of a city's growth and prosperity, such as the one offered by Atlanta mayor William Ezzard, were often in themselves an intellectual result of urban boosterism. Self-congratulatory pats on local entrepreneurs' backs, public expressions of such theories often initiated a call for financial and moral support of some new or long-standing project, always deemed indispensable to the community.

Historical studies of urban boosterism have often ignored these and similar manifestations of a phenomenon that permeated the social, cultural, and political institutions of ninteenth-century American cities. Much of this scholarly indifference (and in some cases barely concealed hostility) is at least partially attributable to the city booster's image as Babbitt in twentieth-century popular culture. It is also probably a reaction to and ironic revenge on nineteenth-century authors of urban biographies, which mostly chronicled the entrepreneurial success of wealthy Americans who happened to live in cities.

In any case, the modern historiographical bias against the "city-building mania" needs to be replaced by careful examination of an ideology that—as Daniel Boorstin's pioneering work on boosterism in the urban West suggests—had a profound impact on American behavior and social values during the nineteenth century. Even American language, Boorstin indicates, was affected: *businessman*, invented to replace the older English phrase, *man of business*, came into use as the term for those who built "instant cities" in the West. Unfortunately, only a few scholarly works on nineteenth-century American cities thus far have made use of and extended Boorstin's insights.[17]

One finding in the scanty literature on the social aspects of urban boosterism helps to explain why the ideology was so pervasive: the city booster was unable to separate the community's welfare from his own. The urban promoter assumed that what was good for him was good for his town and vice versa. Usually both propositions were indeed correct. Nineteenth-century American towns began essentially as real estate speculations in which urban promoters invested

17. Daniel J. Boorstin, *The Americans: The National Experience* (New York, 1965), 113–68. Valuable insights on the social and intellectual aspects of urban boosterism can be found in Robert R. Dykstra, *The Cattle Towns* (New York, 1968); Carl Abbott, *Boosters and Businessmen: Popular Thought and Urban Growth in the Antebellum Middle West* (Westport, Conn., 1981); and Don Harrison Doyle, *The Social Order of a Frontier Community: Jacksonville, Illinois, 1825–1870* (Urbana, 1978).

heavily. Anything a promoter could do to augment his town's population increased land values and consequently his own personal fortune.[18]

Believing in both the possibility of and the imperative for urban growth, entrepreneurs in nineteenth-century cities created and used a variety of social, political, and economic institutions for booster purposes. In Atlanta, evidence of the booster's fundamental credo— that the city's economic welfare should be the overriding concern of all citizens—was particularly noticeable in the expenditures and policies of municipal government, which local businessmen regarded as an auxiliary engine for speeding up the city's growth. Analysis of another pertinent but generally neglected topic in American urban history—municipal services—offers especially vivid insights into the connections between urban boosterism and city governments.[19] The distribution of services in nineteenth-century cities can be a map of the goals of municipal policy makers. There were those, it should be noted, who objected to boosterism in local government. But, as long as there was the slightest chance for urban growth, the booster was ready to seize power in city hall or any other agency he could use to promote his city.

Of all the diverse techniques of promoting urban growth in nineteenth-century Atlanta, the most frequently practiced and probably most successful was fabricating images of the city as "energetic," "progressive," and "wide-awake." These characteristics, together with salutes to the unity and daring of the city's economic leaders, were publicized as elements of the famous "Atlanta spirit"—indisputably local boosters' most widely advertised product then and later. Newspaper editors, public officials, local historians, spokesmen for the chamber of commerce, and many others churned out innumerable publications, all extolling that spirit and all designed to attract more capital and more people to the city. Especially dramatic proof was the city's remarkable recovery from devastation during the Civil

18. *Daily Atlanta Intelligencer*, October 26, 1867; Leslie E. Decker, "The Great Speculation: An Interpretation of Mid-Continent Pioneering," in D. M. Ellis (ed.), *The Frontier in American Development: Essays in Honor of Paul Wallace Gates* (Ithaca, 1969), 357–80; Michael J. Doucet, "Urban Land Development in Nineteenth Century North America: Themes in the Literature," *JUH*, VIII (1982), 299–342.

19. For suggestive comments on this topic, see by Jon C. Teaford, "Finis for Tweed and Steffens: Rewriting the History of Urban Rule," *Reviews in American History*, X (1982), 133–49; and Teaford, "Technology, Expertise, and Municipal Services, 1860–1940," *JUH*, X (1984), 319–28.

War. Time and again during the nineteenth century and later, Atlanta boosters invoked the fable of the phoenix as a metaphor for that economic and physical resurrection. To permanently fix this metaphor in the minds of all, Atlanta's city government in 1887 changed its official seal. The representation of a locomotive was replaced with a picture of the phoenix and the inscription "Resurgens—rising, ever rising."[20] This substitution of symbols was official notice that the war was chiefly remembered in the city as a useful demonstration of the resiliency and power of the Atlanta spirit.

The intensity and success of such advertising campaigns were one reason why visitors to nineteenth-century Atlanta frequently commented on the city's allegedly nonsouthern values and characteristics. But the city's recovery from the Civil War was not the only factor in creating such impressions. Outsiders generally described the city before and after the war as not typical of the South. Popular writers and journalists still express similar opinions.[21] Visitors from the North and elsewhere in the United States have usually cast those nonsouthern attributes in positive terms, but southerners have been more negative. "Georgia Yankees" was at one time popular among lowland southerners as a synonym for Atlanta residents. Scholars have shown little interest in exploring the origins and accuracy of such terms. Until recently, historians have generally spent more time documenting the similarities between northern and southern cities than in identifying what was southern and unsouthern about urban life in Dixie.[22]

The impression nevertheless persists in the popular culture that Atlanta was and is somehow different and unsouthern. My examination of this question will attend to the historical evidence concerning social values and economic life. In addition, there are statistical analyses of Atlanta's general population and leadership, its receptivity to outsiders (measured by occupational mobility, wealth holding,

20. John B. Goodwin and James A. Anderson (comps.), *The Code of the City of Atlanta* (Atlanta, 1891), sec. 304. See also Ivan Allen, *The Atlanta Spirit* (Atlanta, 1948); and Allen, *Atlanta From the Ashes* (Atlanta, 1928).
21. See, for example, William Ellis, "Atlanta, Pacesetter City of the South," *National Geographic*, CXXXV (1969), 247–80; and *Christian Science Monitor*, May 6, 1986.
22. Blaine A. Brownell, "If You've Seen One, You Haven't Seen Them All: Recent Trends in Southern Urban History," *Houston Review*, I (1979), 63–80; David R. Goldfield, *Cotton Fields and Skyscrapers: Southern City and Region, 1607–1980* (Baton Rouge, 1982); William H. Pease and Jane H. Pease, *The Web of Progress: Private Values and Public Styles in Boston and Charleston, 1828–1843* (New York, 1985).

and other standards), the geographic mobility of its population before and after the war, and other relevant topics that can be developed quantitatively. Comparative historical and quantitative perspectives can provide a firmer fix on a nebulous but intriguing concept than journalistic commentary can.

These interrelated themes will be pursued from Atlanta's origins until 1890, when the city was well on its way to becoming the leading metropolis of the Southeast. We can then better understand the historical forces that still have an impact on this city of more than two million people (in 1980), the sixteenth largest standard metropolitan statistical area in the United States.[23] Although there will be no attempt to depict Atlanta as representative of the entire South, its history, if for no other reason than the city's economic and political importance, provides valuable insights into the region as a whole.

23. *The World Almanac & Book of Facts, 1985* (New York, 1985), 251.

1

BEGINNINGS
The Railroad Matrix

Everyone will admit . . . that the Railroad and locomotive are in this age of the world the main means . . . by which prosperous towns and communities are built up, and by which old towns are protected from Decay.

—*Daily Atlanta Intelligencer* (1858)

Rival towns and cities have exhausted all their devices and ingenuity to depreciate the importance of our city as a commercial point. Their influence with the Banks and Railroads of the country have been exerted to cripple . . . the trade and commerce of Atlanta. . . . But the day of righteous retribution is not far ahead. . . . The sympathies of the upcountry are with us, as soon as we can successfully bid defiance to our oppressors, our Rail Road city will arise and shine with unrivalled splendor.

—*Daily Atlanta Intelligencer* (1858)

Atlanta's origins are directly related to railroads, which began to penetrate the southern backcountry during the 1830s. The rise of interior cities portended striking changes in the economic and social structure of the South, but was relatively unnoticed during the antebellum period. The South in 1860 contained only eleven cities of ten thousand or more inhabitants, and only two (Nashville and Memphis) were at any distance from the seacoast. On the eve of the Civil War, interior cities such as Atlanta and Chattanooga were still far behind the older southern seaports in population and economic significance.[1] Building railroads in the southern upcountry—especially during the 1850s, when the region's miles of track roughly quintupled—foreshadowed the day, however, when "new" cities would eclipse their seaboard rivals.[2] Distant from plantation districts in the southern lowlands, these cities even in their infancy manifested social and economic characteristics that sharply distinguished them from the coastal cities.

Railroads made possible the growth of cities all across the nation, with or without access to water transport. Atlanta, in fact, could not have existed without railroads. The river closest (seven miles away) to the city was the Chattahoochee, which was not navigable above Columbus, Georgia. That sort of liability was rare for nineteenth-century American cities: only Denver and Indianapolis, of all cities with 100,000 or more residents by 1890, were not situated on navigable waterways. But, as one newspaper editor commented, the "old belief" that "rivers or seaports were essential to the growth of large cities" was obsolete in the age of railroads, which made urban growth feasible anywhere.[3]

In view of Atlanta's location and origins, the attitudes of local citizens—especially during the antebellum era, but also later—toward the railroads terminating in the city were surprisingly ambivalent. Although Atlanta promoters, like their counterparts in Kansas

1. E. Merton Coulter, *The Confederate States of America, 1861–1865* (Baton Rouge, 1950), 409; Howard N. Rabinowitz, "Continuity and Change: Southern Urban Development, 1860–1900," in Blaine A. Brownell and David R. Goldfield (eds.), *The City in Southern History: The Growth of Urban Civilization in the South* (Port Washington, N.Y., 1977), 93.

2. Computed from table on page 79 in George Rogers Taylor, *The Transportation Revolution* (New York, 1951).

3. Adna F. Weber, *The Growth of Cities in the Nineteenth Century: A Study in Statistics* (1899; rpr. Ithaca, 1967), 173–74; Atlanta *Constitution*, March 3, 1888.

City, Chicago, and other nineteenth-century railroad centers, bragged about their city's strategic location, they were more prone than others to see railroads as hostile agencies restricting prospects for urban growth. The root cause of this paranoia was local promoters' recognition that Atlanta, as U. B. Phillips accurately said, was the "incidental result of the building of [rail]roads intended exclusively for the benefit of other towns." Many boosters of antebellum Atlanta echoed this idea in newspapers and pamphlets. As one local writer commented in 1858, the city had grown "in spite of the power of Railroads, wielded against her by older and rival cities."[4] Although they exaggerated the railroads' hostility toward Atlanta, local promoters were correct in arguing that these roads were not constructed or operated to benefit their city. Antebellum railroads were truly weapons of economic warfare during an era of intense urban rivalries, which occasioned many of the railroad policies Atlantans protested.

Railroads and the Founding of Atlanta

The demand for railroads in the antebellum South grew out of two transportation requirements that were common to all the Cotton Belt states: a means of importing western foodstuffs (chiefly wheat, corn, whiskey, bacon, lard, and butter) and a means of shipping cotton harvested in the interior to coastal markets.[5] According to many antebellum southerners, railroad communication with the West— vaguely defined as the Ohio and Mississippi valleys—was the more crucial need.[6] But, as cotton agriculture spread rapidly into the interior after the War of 1812, the calls for internal improvements to satisfy both requirements became strident.

4.   Ulrich Bonnell Phillips, A History of Transportation in the Eastern Cotton Belt to 1860 (1908; rpr. New York, 1968), 391; Charles N. Glaab, Kansas City and the Railroads (Madison, 1962); J. Christopher Schnell and Katherine B. Clinton, "The New West: Themes in Nineteenth Century Urban Promotion, 1815–1880," Bulletin of the Missouri Historical Society, XXX (1974), 83–87; Daily Atlanta Intelligencer, November 11, 1858.

5.   Phillips, Transportation, 16–20; James A. Ward, "A New Look at Antebellum Southern Railroad Development," JSH, XXXIX (1973), 409–20; Milton S. Heath, Constructive Liberalism: The Role of the State in Economic Development in Georgia to 1860 (Cambridge, Mass., 1954), 254–92.

6.   What antebellum southerners meant by West becomes important in discussing the agricultural self-sufficiency of the South. Usually, South during this period referred to the southern Atlantic states, and West meant states in the Ohio and Mississippi valleys. See, for example, John C. Calhoun's 1845 definition of the regions in Herbert Wender, Southern Commercial Conventions, 1837–1859 (Baltimore, 1930), 57–58. See also William K. Wood, "The Georgia Railroad and Banking Company," GHQ, LVII (1973), 544–61.

The evolution of a transportation system in Georgia began in 1826, when the state legislature passed a law creating the Board of Public Works. In March, 1826, Governor George M. Troup and seven other persons, one chosen from each congressional district, entrusted the board with a plan carefully designed to prevent sectional jealousy and urban rivalry in the development of the state's transportation network—which was to consist of turnpikes, canals, or railroads. There was to be a canal from the head of navigation on the Oconee River in northern Georgia, or possibly from the head of navigation on the Ocmulgee, to the Tennessee River, by which western produce could be shipped via steamboat to Georgia. From a point in the center of the state on the Oconee, canals were to be constructed to the Chattahoochee in the west and the Savannah in the east.[7]

The Board of Public Works' initial proposal depended chiefly upon whether a canal could be built through the northern portion of the state, which was mountainous and densely forested. The board appointed Wilson Lumpkin, an energetic former U.S. congressman, to inspect this region. In late spring of 1826, Lumpkin began his walking tour from the Oconee River toward the Tennessee line. That summer he wrote to Governor Troup from the foot of Lookout Mountain in Tennessee about his survey. He was reluctant to pass judgment on the feasibility of a canal, but he noted that "the country over which we have passed would admit of an excellent road, either Rail or Turnpike." Further investigation revealed, however, that "the ridge of mountains on the Northern boundary of Georgia—which divide and separate the Western from the Atlantic waters—may justly be considered a formidable breastwork of nature calculated to defy the ingenuity of man to connect . . . [these] Waters." At this point in his career, Lumpkin, to whom much credit should be given for the completion of antebellum Georgia's railroad system, became convinced that railroads, even ones with wood rails and the cars drawn by mules or horses, were preferable to any canal through northern or middle Georgia.[8]

Obstacles even more insurmountable than topography delayed until the 1830s the final working out of the board's 1826 proposal. The most immediate was that the Creek and the Cherokee were

7. Fletcher M. Green, "Georgia's Board of Public Works, 1817–1826," *GHQ*, XXII (1938), 121, 131–33.
8. Wilson Lumpkin to Governor George M. Troup, June 6, 20, 1826, both in Wilson Lumpkin Papers, GDAH, Atlanta.

living in northwestern Georgia. According to Alexander H. Stephens, a staunch advocate of internal improvements, the construction of canals to link "the navigable waters of the great North-West with the Waters of the Southern Atlantic Coast" occupied "men of thought and public spirit in the State, long before the Indian title to the intervening Territory had been extinguished." The treaties of Indian Springs had removed most of the Creek from the area in 1825, but the Cherokee remained. Wilson Lumpkin had found them bitterly determined to assert their rights. He attempted to persuade the "leading men of the Cherokee nation" to prepare themselves for "an entire removal from the limits of Georgia to lands west of the Mississippi," but the Cherokee leaders proved intransigent. Annoyed, Lumpkin decided as early as 1826 that the Cherokee were "ready to deny, before they are solicited."[9]

The removal of the Cherokee from Georgia, justly called a national dishonor, came about for several reasons. The discovery of gold in 1829 near Dahlonega in northern Georgia played a major role, as did white settlers' hunger for new farming lands. The connection between Indian removal and the construction of Georgia's pioneer antebellum railroads has been ignored by most historians, however, and definitely underestimated as a cause of the Indians' forced departure.[10] Lumpkin's public career emphasizes the significance of that connection.

In the fall of 1826, following his survey for the Board of Public Works, Lumpkin was elected to Congress. At his own request, he was appointed to the Committee on Indian Affairs. On December 13, 1827, he introduced the first resolution ever calling for the removal of the Cherokee from Georgia. Although he won some support, Lumpkin was unable to persuade Congress to act. When his term expired in March, 1831, he returned home and was conveniently elected governor in October of the same year. As the state's chief executive, Lumpkin finally had the authority he needed to oust the Cherokee. On December 2, 1831, he ordered an immediate survey of all the lands held by the Cherokee. Their protests were in vain. On November 6,

9.   Alexander H. Stephens, "The Western & Atlantic Railroad," in William R. Hanleiter's *Atlanta City Directory for 1872* (Atlanta, 1872), 174–80; Wilson Lumpkin, *Removal of the Cherokee Indians* (2 vols.; New York, 1907), I, 18–40.

10.   Otis E. Young, "The Southern Gold Rush, 1828–1836," *JSH*, XLVIII (1982), 385–86; Fletcher M. Green, "Georgia's Forgotten Industry: Gold Mining," *GHQ*, XIX (1935), 101–108; Louis Filler and Allen Guttman (eds.), *Removal of the Cherokee Nation: Manifest Destiny or National Dishonor* (Lexington, Mass., 1962).

1832, he proposed to the state legislature that these lands should be divided into counties, subdivided into lots, and then distributed by public lottery. By May, 1833, all the Cherokee lands had been partitioned and assigned to white settlers. Shortly after Lumpkin left the governor's office, the Treaty of New Echota legalized in 1835 what he had already accomplished by force. The treaty authorized the state to take possession of all Cherokee lands in northwestern Georgia. By December, 1838, the entire Cherokee nation had left their homes there. Thus was removed the first obstacle to the transportation system proposed by the Board of Public Works.[11]

During his time as governor, Lumpkin had encountered a growing urban rivalry, another hindrance to the board's plan. Indeed, the quarrel between the citizens of Darien and Savannah over which seaport would become the eastern terminus of the canal system had been the chief cause of the board's demise. When Lumpkin revived the basic ideas of the board's project in his speeches to the legislature in the 1830s, he dealt gingerly with the seaports. His annual message of 1833 proposed a "central railroad," which "should begin at the best emporium on the coast . . . in a direction best calculated to benefit the largest portion of our population [and proceed] to the base of the mountains." Lumpkin was careful to leave unspecified the identity of the "best" seaport—it might be Brunswick, Darien, or Savannah. To conciliate the interior towns, he added that the railroad should be so placed as to facilitate building branch lines to other cities in the state.[12]

Lumpkin's efforts to appease the growing ambitions of the cities were not successful. But in 1833 the state chartered three separate railroad companies, each designed to benefit a particular city. The Central of Georgia was authorized to build a line from Savannah to Macon. Although originally organized by Macon factors and merchants, this company quickly fell under the domination of their counterparts in Savannah. The second was the Georgia, which could construct a road from Augusta to some undesignated point in the state's interior. After the Georgia had finished its main line, it could send branch lines to Eatonton, Madison, and Athens at its discretion, even though cotton mill owners in Athens had first devised the proj-

11. Lumpkin, *Removal*, I, 44–90, 101, 106; Ulrich Bonnell Phillips, *Georgia and States Rights* (Washington, D.C., 1901), 85–86; E. Merton Coulter, *A Short History of Georgia* (Chapel Hill, 1960), 235–37.
12. Green, "Georgia's Board of Public Works," 135; Lumpkin, *Removal*, I, 137–39.

ect. Much to their irritation, Augusta businessmen quickly assumed control. The third company was the Monroe, which was granted the right to build a road between Macon and Forsyth. Thus Macon promoters hoped to gain some measure of independence from their Savannah rivals.[13]

None of these railroads was actually proposed as a part of a transportation system. Organized separately, each could satisfy only one of the state's requirements—that of bringing cotton from the interior regions to urban markets. None could fulfull the more ambitious plan to import western foodstuffs. In the incorporation of these three railroads, cities showed a tendency toward uncooperative individualism. A changing situation, however, forced them to work together.

In 1834, General E. P. Gaines wrote to Wilson Lumpkin, announcing the incorporation of another railroad company, the Atlantic & Mississippi, later called the Memphis & Charleston. The line would run from Memphis via Decatur, Alabama, to Athens, where it would connect with the Georgia, which in turn was linked with the South Carolina to Charleston. This chain would effectively cut Georgia's seacoast off from the Mississippi Valley trade, a threat Lumpkin took seriously. The governor expressed qualified admiration for the project, but also warned that Georgia would be better served by a railroad running through the center of the state to Savannah or "some other seaport." Unless Gaines would consider this route, Lumpkin remarked, the state would probably build a line from the coast to a point of intersection with the Atlantic & Mississippi in western Georgia.[14]

Almost simultaneously a second threat materialized in the form of the Charleston & Cincinnati, a project of John C. Calhoun, Robert Y. Hayne, and others. This railroad would also have passed through the northeastern part of the state, connecting with the Georgia Railroad at Athens. If the state took no action, its seaboard cities might be deprived of Ohio Valley produce—even if the Atlantic & Mississippi were never completed.[15]

13. *Ga. Laws, 1833*, pp. 238–52, 256–68; Thomas Gamble, *History of City Government of Savannah* (Savannah, 1901), 167–70, 172; Max Dixon, "Building the Central Railroad of Georgia," *GHQ*, XLV (1961), 1–2; John C. Butler, *Historical Record of Macon and Central Georgia* (Macon, 1879), 101; C. E. Jones and Salem Dutcher, *Memorial History of Augusta* (Syracuse, 1890), 37–38, 178; Phillips, *Transportation*, 221, 224, 238.
14. Phillips, *Transportation*, 305; Wilson Lumpkin to E. P. Gaines, March 3, 1834, June 18, 1835, both in Governors' [of Georgia] Letterbooks, GDAH.
15. Phillips, *Transportation*, 168–71, 174–202.

Fortunately, the Georgia, the Central, and the Monroe, as alarmed as Lumpkin was, decided that the time was ripe for cooperation. Through their influence, politicians, railroad officials, and interested businessmen met in Macon in November, 1836, to consider a system of internal improvements "whereby the commercial cities of Georgia" would have access to the Tennessee River, "thereby opening to trade . . . the whole Valley of the Mississippi and Ohio." The system they advocated closely resembled the 1826 plan of the Board of Public Works. The state was invited to construct a railroad from Ross's Landing on the Tennessee River (which eventually became the site of Chattanooga) to some point on the Chattahoochee River in De Kalb County, Georgia. From the terminus, wherever it might be, branches could be built to the Georgia Railroad, the Monroe Railroad, Milledgeville, and Columbus. Each of these lines was to be financed privately.[16]

The Georgia General Assembly adopted that plan in December. The governor signed the act on December 21, 1836, incorporating the Western & Atlantic Railroad. The state would build a line from Ross's Landing on the Tennessee River to some point on the southeastern bank of the Chattahoochee. Surveys indicated that the terrain close to that bank was unsuitable for the construction of branch roads. An amendment to the charter of the Western & Atlantic in 1837 consequently authorized an extension up to eight miles from Montgomery's crossing. However, the terminus, not sited until 1842, was at a point seven miles from the Chattahoochee. The zero milepost became the exact center of Atlanta, which at that time was an uninhabited spot called simply "Terminus."[17]

Although the Georgia and the Monroe railroad companies did not know precisely where the Western & Atlantic would end, they obtained charters in 1837. The Georgia could extend a branch from Madison to the state road, and the Monroe could build one from Forsyth.[18]

Construction of all these railroads was delayed by various problems, especially the depression that began in 1837 and lingered until

16. Milledgeville *Southern Recorder*, November 15, 1836.
17. *Ga. Laws, 1836*, pp. 214–18; *Ga. Laws, 1837*, pp. 210–12; Stephen H. Long to Governor George R. Gilmer, November 7, 1837, in Western & Atlantic Railroad Archives, GDAH; Hollis Edens, "The Founding of Atlanta," *AHB*, IV (1939), 277–89; Rupert B. Vance and Sara Smith, "Metropolitan Dominance and Integration," in Vance and Nicholas J. Demerath (eds.), *The Urban South* (Chapel Hill, 1954), 120–21.
18. *Ga. Laws, 1837*, pp. 200–201, 210–12.

the mid-1840s. Severely handicapped by financial problems, the Georgia did not complete its Union Railroad from Augusta to Madison until 1841, and another four years were necessary to complete the branch from Madison to the W & A. The Monroe Railroad went bankrupt in 1845 and was sold to a group of northern capitalists. A reorganized company, the Macon & Western, finally completed the branch from Macon to the W & A in 1846. At one time the finances of the W & A—whose construction took more than half of the state government's revenues during the 1840s—appeared so grim that an 1843 act authorized the sale of the road for only $1,000,000. As Lumpkin's 1826 surveys had revealed, there were numerous topographical obstacles, foremost of which was the Blue Ridge Mountains. After nearly two years' labor, a tunnel—1,477 feet long, 18 feet wide, and 12 feet high—was completed, and James D. B. De Bow called it "one of the grandest achievements that grace the annals of the human family." On May 9, 1850, the first Western & Atlantic train was run between Atlanta and Ross's Landing.[19]

After more than twenty years of planning and construction, the four railroads built in Georgia by 1850 approximated the system proposed by the Board of Public Works. During the antebellum period, these railroads transported cotton in vast quantities from the state's interior to the seacoast. Determining the geographic origins of the truly impressive shipments of foodstuffs enumerated in Table 1 would be useful for shedding light on the heatedly debated issue of the antebellum South's agricultural self-sufficiency.[20] Since north Georgia developed rapidly as a wheat-producing and east Tennessee as a hog-growing region during the 1850s, most of the "western" produce transported by the W & A during those years was probably

19. Peter Wallenstein, "From Slave South to New South: Taxes and Spending in Georgia from 1850 through Reconstruction," *JEH*, XXXVI (1976), 287–90; *Ga. Laws*, 1843, pp. 138–40; Phillips, *Transportation*, 237, 269–70; *Annual Report of the Western & Atlantic Railroad, 1849* (Milledgeville, 1849), 1; *Annual Report of the Western & Atlantic Railroad, 1850* (Milledgeville, 1850), 1; James D. B. De Bow, *The Industrial Resources of the Southern and Western States* (New Orleans, 1852), 357.

20. See William N. Parker (ed.), *The Structure of the Cotton Economy of the Antebellum South* (Washington, D.C., 1970); William K. Hutchinson and Samuel H. Williamson, "The Self-Sufficiency of the Antebellum South: Estimates of the Food Supply," *JEH*, XXXI (1971), 591–612; Forrest McDonald and Grady McWhiney, "The Antebellum Southern Herdsman: A Reinterpretation," *JSH*, XLI (1975), 147–66; Sam Bowers Hilliard, *Hog Meat and Hoecake: Food Supply in the Old South, 1840–1860* (Carbondale, Ill., 1972), 166, 186–92, 229–35; and the essays by Albert Fishlow and Robert Fogel in Ralph Andreano (ed.), *New Views on American Development* (Cambridge, Mass., 1965).

MAP 1   Railroads Terminating in Atlanta, 1860

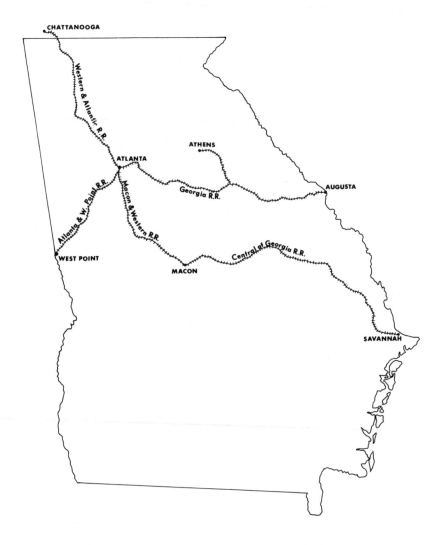

TABLE 1
Principal Articles of Down Freight of the Western & Atlantic, 1849–1860

Fiscal Year Oct. 1 to Sept. 30	Bushels Wheat	Barrels of Flour	Sacks of Flour	Bushels Oats & Corn	Lbs. Bacon, Lard, Tallow, Butter[a]	No. of Hogs & Sheep	Barrels of Whiskey	Bales Cotton
1849–50	28,161	2,535	—	65,512	3,449,048	15,814[b]	—	23,860
1850–51	63,679	2,880	—	130,679	4,033,500	16,913[b]	—	38,826
1851–52	90,141	5,253	6,263	686,493	5,761,447	12,290[b]	—	64,539
1852–53	239,302	18,795	16,194	510,923	6,754,552	29,193[b]	—	65,486
1853–54	327,632	28,654	54,426	755,413	12,191,790	42,056[b]	—	57,833
1854–55	1,039,294	24,759	45,335	98,954	9,720,205	32,450[b]	—	57,892
1855–56	1,176,282	49,220	115,678	938,815	23,305,406	40,016[b]	—	55,658
1856–57	1,506,294	74,758	140,556	530,894	22,070,845	38,939	23,960	47,113
1857–58	959,376	69,295	195,239	356,275	20,759,960	43,715	11,330	35,859
1858–59	535,881	85,436	151,598	340,219	23,252,348	38,543	13,504	42,868
1859–60	320,676	63,940	110,792	909,991	22,516,396	40,865	15,946	52,453

SOURCES: *Annual Reports of the Western & Atlantic Railroad*, 1850–1860.

NOTE: All freight was received at the Atlanta station—*down* means south from Chattanooga.

[a] Before 1857, bacon, lard, tallow, and butter were given separate poundages; these figures were compiled for comparison with later years.

[b] Hogs alone.

southern. But railroad annual reports and other sources document that at least some of the produce coming through Atlanta by rail in the 1850s originated in Louisville, Memphis, Cincinnati, St. Louis, and even more distant points. [21] The W & A's tonnage reports will not permit greater precision about that road's performance as a carrier of western produce.

Railroads and the "Gate City"

In the spring of 1857, a delegation of railroad officials and Memphis businessmen passed through Atlanta on their way to Charleston, where the connection (via a short stretch of the Nashville & Chattanooga) of the Western & Atlantic and the Memphis & Charleston was to be celebrated. The Memphis & Charleston was the most important feeder line to connect with the W & A during the antebellum period. Both Memphis and Charleston merchants were delighted with the prospect of quick transport of Mississippi Valley produce to the southern Atlantic seaboard. It was the fulfillment of an old dream. In remembrance of the canal schemes, the Memphis contingent brought a barrel of water from the Mississippi, which they intended to pour into the Atlantic Ocean.

The Memphis promoters were so pleased with their reception in Atlanta that they invited William Ezzard, Atlanta's mayor, to accompany them to the "Charleston festival." In Charleston, an elegant banquet was prepared, and many toasts were offered to the prosperity of Memphis and Charleston. Finally, toward the end of the evening, someone proposed a toast to Atlanta. Although offered almost as an afterthought, the toast graciously saluted Atlanta as "The Gate City: The only tribute she levies is the affection and gratitude of those who partake of her unbounded hospitality."[22]

Those who built and operated the railroads that terminated in antebellum Atlanta and linked that city with Memphis, Charleston, and other urban centers certainly neither intended nor expected that the Gate City would exact much tribute from them. According to his

21. *Daily Atlanta Intelligencer* cited by Augusta *Constitutionalist*, March 16, 1853; *Daily Atlanta Intelligencer*, February 10, 1856, January 9, 1857. The chief engineer of the W & A reported in 1860 that the wheat crop in eastern and middle Tennessee and northwest Georgia had been poor and that the "bulk of freights over this road for the last few months has been from the far West," principally from Louisville and Memphis (*Annual Report of the Western & Atlantic Railroad, 1860* [Atlanta, 1860], 5).
22. "Recollections of William Ezzard," in William R. Hanleiter, *Atlanta City Directory for 1871* (Atlanta, 1871), 26; *Daily Atlanta Intelligencer*, June 14, 1857.

"prison diary," Alexander H. Stephens, who visited Terminus in 1843, prophesied that "a magnificent inland city will at no distant day be built here." Stephens' vision represented the exception rather than the rule. The W & A's chief engineer in 1846 thought that interior towns would be useful only as small "grain depots," where produce could be temporarily stored before shipment to coastal cities. He also conceded that northern Georgia's "wholesome air, cool waters, and beautiful scenery" might eventually attract a multitude of vacationers anxious to leave "the hot atmosphere of the cities."[23]

Other railroad entrepreneurs who helped to create the village that sprang up around the Western & Atlantic's terminus in the 1840s held similar beliefs about its prospects for urban growth. Richard Peters, a director of the Georgia Railroad and future street-railway magnate in Atlanta, urged one of his associates in 1846 to sell all his real estate in Marthasville (the incorporated town was renamed Atlanta the following year): "The thing is all out for the present, all deadflat. . . . [T]he place can never be much of a trading *city*, yet may be of some importance in a *small* way." Stephen H. Long, the W & A's brilliant chief engineer, and J. Edgar Thomson, the Georgia Railroad's first chief engineer and later president of the Pennsylvania, also had little faith in the town's future. Long, who selected Atlanta's site, sneered that the spot would be "a good place for one tavern, a blacksmith shop, a grocery store, and nothing else." Thomson wrote in 1845 that Marthasville appeared "to be looking up a little, but . . . [as] no person of Capital has located here . . . its progress to greatness will be slow."[24]

Antebellum railroad managers had no incentive to plan for or encourage the growth of Atlanta, whose capitalists invested little in the railroads that terminated in the city. Since municipal governments and entrepreneurs in individual cities often financed railroad construction during the antebellum period, railroads were expected to serve the interests of particular cities. Government financing of

23. Myrta Lockett Avary (ed.), *Recollections of Alexander H. Stephens* (New York, 1910), 460; *Annual Report of the Western & Atlantic Railroad, 1846* (Milledgeville, 1846), 6–7.

24. Richard Peters to Lemuel P. Grant, July 26, 1846, and J. Edgar Thomson to Lemuel P. Grant, September 12, 1845, both in Lemuel P. Grant Papers, AHS; "Recollection of Richard Peters," in Atlanta *Constitution*, February 10, 1889. Terminus was incorporated as the town of Marthasville in 1843 and named by Wilson Lumpkin after his daughter. The principal reason for changing the name to Atlanta was that railway ticket agents complained they had trouble getting "Marthasville" on one ticket. See Nellie Peters Black, Biography of Richard Peters (MS in Nellie Peters Black Papers, UGA), 2–3.

railroads, characteristic of both the South and the West, was especially common in those southern states—such as South Carolina, Louisiana, Kentucky, Virginia, and Georgia—where seaport or river cities sought rail connections with the West. The most striking aspect of this municipal investment was that individual cities could then take over the companies before the Civil War. Locally controlled railroads thus became essential ingredients in urban imperialism.[25]

Municipal investment in antebellum railroads was often costly and risky. In 1836, Savannah invested $500,000 in city bonds in the Central of Georgia project, even though the city's taxable wealth amounted to only $2,357,250. To ease the resulting financial strain, Savannah's city council levied a pioneering municipal income tax of 2.5 percent on commission merchants and professional men. Macon, with a total population of just over three thousand, gave $300,000 in municipal bonds to two railroads and paid for its zeal in 1844 when the city government went bankrupt. Municipal authorities in Milwaukee, Wisconsin, met a similar fate in 1861, after investing $1,614,000 (25 percent of the city's taxable property) in railroads during the 1850s. Given such high levels of investment, railroad managers naturally adopted policies favoring their proprietary cities.[26]

The Georgia city that appeared most likely to profit from railroads during the antebellum period was Savannah, which not only invested more money (about $3,000,000) in their construction than did any other city in the state but also had an excellent harbor. On the eve of the Civil War, the age of great interior cities was just beginning; up to that time, all large cities in the United States either had port facilities or were located on tidewater rivers. Accustomed to thinking about cotton exports to Europe, promoters assumed automatically that railroads would enable southern coastal cities like Savannah to become major grain exporters. Some railroad enthusiasts also believed that westerners who shipped grain by rail to the southern

25. The literature on municipal investment in antebellum railroads is vast. For a useful overview, see Milton S. Heath, "Public Railroad Construction and the Development of Private Enterprise in the South before 1861," *Tasks of Economic History*, Supplement X (1950), 40–53. In Georgia alone, municipal investment in railroads by 1860 totaled $5,380,493.94 (Heath, *Constructive Liberalism*, 277–78).

26. Gamble, *Savannah*, 170–73; Atlanta *Constitution*, March 24, 1871; J. David Griffin, "Savannah's City Income Tax," *GHQ*, L (1966), 173–77; Butler, *Macon and Central Georgia*, 167–69; Douglas E. Booth, "Transportation, City Building, and Financial Crisis: Milwaukee, 1852–1858," *JUH*, IX (1983), 335–63.

Atlantic coast might buy manufactures from southern seaports rather than northern cities. "Savannah and Charleston, with excellent harbors," predicted an advocate in 1838, "may soon become great dry goods markets."[27]

Savannah did approximately double its population between 1840 and 1860, but Charleston probably benefited as much or more from Georgia's western railroad connections. Below Virginia, the only southern railroad in 1860 with access to western cities was the Western & Atlantic, which, in the words of one of its managers, was "like a funnel that almost everything from the West . . . came through to get into Georgia, the Carolinas, and Alabama." More of the down freight shipped from Atlanta by the W & A during the 1850s went to Augusta (linked with Charleston by the South Carolina Railroad) than to Savannah via the Macon & Western and the Central of Georgia. Exceeding even wheat exports from Chicago and Buffalo at roughly the same time, Charleston in 1855 and 1856 exported to domestic cities alone nearly 600,000 bushels and 31,000 barrels of wheat. These impressive exports, according to geographer Allan R. Pred, were primarily due to the completion of the W & A and the Nashville & Chattanooga railroads.[28]

Although Atlanta merchants did not profit as much during the antebellum period as did their competitors in Charleston and Savannah from the produce and other commodities shipped by the W & A, the completion of every new road to the city, extending its railroad connections, spurred economic and population growth. When the Georgia Railroad reached the Western & Atlantic in Marthasville in 1845, the town boasted only two general stores and a dozen families. When the Macon & Western was finished in 1846, Marthasville experienced the first "railroad boom." By 1849, Atlanta's annual trade was estimated at $200,000 and the town then had about 2,000 inhabitants. After the W & A was completed in 1851, the city's trade was valued at $1,017,000. When the Memphis & Charleston via the

27. Griffin, "Savannah's City Income Tax," 173; Edward H. Hopkins to Governor George R. Gilmer, June 1, 1838, in Governor Gilmer's Private Correspondence, GDAH.
28. Quotation from *Letter from Senator Joseph E. Brown to His Excellency John B. Gordon upon the Subject of Betterments Placed by the Lessees upon the Western & Atlantic Railroad* (Atlanta, 1890), 9; Vance and Smith, "Metropolitan Dominance," in Vance and Demerath (eds.), *The Urban South*, 120–21; James E. Vance, Jr., *The Merchant's World: The Geography of Wholesaling* (Englewood Cliffs, N.J., 1970), 152–53; Allan R. Pred, *Urban Growth and City-Systems in the United States, 1840–1860* (Cambridge, Mass., 1980), 113, 214.

Nashville & Chattanooga was linked to the W & A in 1857, Atlanta's annual business in the following year jumped to an estimated $3,000,000. By 1860, Atlanta—which only fifteen years previously had been in the midst of a "howling wilderness"—had 9,554 inhabitants.[29]

The only antebellum railroad built to Atlanta that for a brief period threatened the city's economy was the Atlanta & West Point. One pioneer claimed that the completion of this railroad brought about the "first real crisis in the city's history." The Atlanta & West Point, controlled by the Georgia Railroad and completed in 1854, was originally intended to siphon off western Georgia's cotton harvest from Atlanta and other upcountry markets to Augusta. For a few years, the "wagon trade" of cotton to Atlanta declined markedly, but by 1856 it had risen again and the Atlanta & West Point, ignoring its backers in Augusta, deposited more and more cotton in Atlanta. According to an 1859 estimate, railroads brought to the Atlanta market in that year alone more than 30,000 bales of cotton.[30]

By 1860, Atlanta was beginning to deserve its description at the Charleston festival as a "gate city," albeit in a limited sense. Near the dividing line between the Cotton Belt and the food-producing regions of upper Georgia and east Tennessee, Atlanta was starting its career as a major foodstuffs distribution center for the lower South. To a lesser extent, it also served as an exchange point for upland cotton, though during the antebellum era this trade was toward the southern seacoast rather than directly to northern cities (as became the pattern after the Civil War).[31]

Railroad "Enmity" in Atlanta's Infancy

Atlanta boosters were certainly aware by 1860 that railroads had caused the city to "spring from nothing like a Jonah's gourd," but they were also convinced that the railroads were hostile, or at best indif-

29. E. Y. Clarke, *Illustrated History of Atlanta* (2nd ed., 1879; rpr. Atlanta, 1971), 27–31; George White, *Statistics of the State of Georgia* (Savannah, 1849), 205; Adiel Sherwood, A *Gazetteer of Georgia* (Atlanta, 1860), 69. See Table 1, Appendix A.
30. Quotation from Atlanta *Constitution*, June 12, 1881; Phillips, *Transportation*, 365–66; *Daily Atlanta Intelligencer*, December 11, 1856, September 7, 1858, February 1, 1859.
31. Edward L. Ullman, "A Theory of Location for Cities," in Paul K. Hatt and Albert J. Reiss (eds.), *Cities and Society: The Revised Reader in Urban Sociology* (New York, 1964), 227–29. Gate cities are interchange points for the commodities of contrasting territories. Since little cotton or other products from the lower South passed through the city toward the West, antebellum Atlanta did not really qualify.

ferent, to the city's interests. [32] The most frequently denounced "railroad abuses" were the impact upon Atlanta's physical development, policies concerning various facilities, and especially freight rate and passenger traffic discriminations.

Railroad engineers selected the spot for the Western & Atlantic's terminus, and their choice was unrelated to its suitability as a townsite. The terrain was hilly and irregular, so grading streets was difficult and expensive. The site was the meeting point of three ridges: one leading northwestward across the Chattahoochee River over which the W & A was to pass, and the other two leading southward, convenient paths for the Georgia and the Macon & Western railroads. The land belonged to Samuel Mitchell, a wealthy farmer residing in Pike County, Georgia, and Wilson Lumpkin made a deal with him. Mitchell gave five acres of land lot 77 to the state for depots, roundhouses, and other railroad facilities. In return, Lumpkin, aided by engineer F. C. Arms, promised to lay out the remainder of Mitchell's property as "town lots." Lumpkin fulfilled his part of the bargain in 1842 and also arranged a public auction during which some of those town lots were sold. [33]

Lumpkin's "city plan" contributed to a serious problem that affected the movement of traffic through Atlanta's streets well into the twentieth century. He decided to place Mitchell's town lots in lines perpendicular or parallel to the tracks of the Western & Atlantic. This arrangement had no relationship whatsoever to the public highways (which became McDonough, Peachtree, Whitehall, Decatur, and Marietta streets) already in existence in 1842. As Atlanta quickly outgrew those inadequate dimensions, private landowners and the city government chose to extend and lay out streets on north-south and east-west axes and also in reference to Peachtree and McDonough streets. The legacy of this confusion was a tangle of messy intersections formed by streets meeting at odd angles. As a result, traffic has always flowed unevenly through sections of downtown Atlanta. [34].

32. Herbert A. Kellar (ed.), *Solon Robinson, Pioneer and Agriculturist* (2 vols.; Indianapolis, 1936), II, 468–69.

33. Raymond Stanley Wallace, "The Railroad Pattern of Atlanta" (M.A. thesis, University of Chicago, 1947), 82–85; Wilson Lumpkin to Martha Lumpkin, October 25, 1853, reprinted in Atlanta *Constitution*, September 24, 1894; deed of Samuel Mitchell, reprinted in Franklin M. Garrett, *Atlanta and Environs: A Chronicle of Its People and Events* (3 vols.; New York, 1954), I, 186–87. See also Eugene M. Mitchell, "Atlanta's First Real-Estate Subdivision," *AHB*, III (1930), 7–14.

34. Timothy J. Crimmins, "The Atlanta Palimpsest: Stripping Away the Layers of the Past," *AHJ*, XXVI (1982), 15–26.

Vincent's 1853 map of Atlanta

First Union Passenger Depot, built 1854

West side of Whitehall Street, *ca.* 1864.
Auction & Negro Sales House (*center*);
H. Muhlenbrink's Atlanta Cigar
Manufactory (*right*)

Alabama Street, *ca.* 1864

Another defect of Lumpkin's plan involved a portion of the five acres deeded to the state by Samuel Mitchell. This area was reserved for a "State Square," which was located in the exact center of Atlanta and was to contain the general passenger depot. Streets were opened on three sides of the square, but Wall (later Pryor) Street on the west was only partially opened. To relieve traffic on Loyd Street, the city needed to extend Wall Street across the railroad to connect with Pryor Street. In 1849, Atlanta's city council decided that "there really was a street running parallel with the acres granted to the state square" and asked the railroads to remove all obstructions (including the Macon & Western freight depot). All the railroads terminating in Atlanta countered with an arrogant threat to remove "their entire location of tracks and depots to some other point on one of the connecting roads," unless the city relinquished its "imaginary claim" to Wall Street. Faced with this ultimatum, the municipal authorities withdrew their request and surrendered Wall Street to the railroads.[35]

Atlanta's city government found it imperative to challenge the railroads more forcefully on crossings problems, which seriously hampered the speedy interchange of freight between the railroad depots and mercantile houses and posed a danger to pedestrians. Visitors sometimes complained of standing at street corners for half an hour or longer while locomotives backed to and from the various depots depositing cargoes and boxcars. Occasionally, pedestrians turned these crossings into death traps by crawling beneath moving cars. If the railroads had been willing to construct viaducts or facilities for transshipping, dozens of quarrels and tragic incidents might have been avoided.[36]

Municipal authorities made their first effort to alleviate the most serious crossings problem in the heart of the city in 1852 by constructing a wooden bridge over the Macon & Western line near Whitehall Street. The bridge cost $400, and it had to be replaced in 1858 by a more expensive structure. The entire street tax ($2,700) did not cover the $4,400 for the second Market (later Broad) Street bridge; a special municipal bond issue was necessary to finance the remaining cost. After this bridge was constructed, traffic over the crossing still did not flow properly, because there was too much congestion at the various

35. CM, September 10, 1849; John P. King and others to Jonathan Norcross, June 4, 1851, in James H. Johnston, *Western & Atlantic Railroad of the State of Georgia* (Atlanta, 1931), 173–74. Pryor Street was finally opened in 1865.

36. *Daily Atlanta Intelligencer*, May 18, 1860.

railroad facilities near Market Street. Rather than deal directly with this problem, the city chose to widen Whitehall Street, which cost an additional $4,050 in 1859 for land obtained from a stubborn merchant, Jonathan Norcross, who thought that the Macon & Western depot should be moved rather than his store. Even this measure did not sufficiently improve the Whitehall Street crossing, which was not substantially altered for the better until the city built a wide iron bridge over Broad Street in 1873. The railroads did not contribute a dime to the building of any of these structures.[37]

Not only did the railroads ignore crossings problems, but they also were reluctant to construct and maintain properly some of their depots in Atlanta. These buildings, as one historian has noted, were important physical advertisements of a nineteenth-century city's commercial importance. They served as "city gates," through which visiting businessmen passed to buy and sell goods. Under the direction of superintendent William Wadley, the Western & Atlantic did complete in 1854 a commodious general passenger depot in Atlanta. An engineer of the Georgia Railroad complained that "Wadley appears to be grading off the whole of De Kalb County for his new depot," which he thought was too expensive for Atlanta's commercial needs and prospects. None but Atlanta boosters complained later in the 1850s, however, when the railroads failed to maintain wooden platforms around the depot or provide illumination at night. Even more galling than conditions at the passenger depot was the railroad officials' decision in 1851 to locate the Atlanta & West Point freight depot six miles outside of town at East Point. This action was taken to avoid construction costs in Atlanta; local businessmen protested bitterly, but to no avail.[38]

Even more acrimonious and longer-lived protests against the railroads involved what local merchants regarded as discriminations against the city in regard to passenger and freight traffic. Complaints about passenger schedules—especially the late arrivals in Atlanta and

37.   Atlanta *Republican*, June 17, 1852; *Daily Atlanta Intelligencer*, February 24, April 3, 1859; CM, January 25, 1859; Garrett, *Atlanta*, I, 353–54; Johnston, *Western & Atlantic Railroad*, 191.
38.   Keith L. Bryant, "The Railway Station as a Symbol of Urbanization in the South, 1880–1920," *South Atlantic Quarterly*, LXXV (1976), 499–509; Bryant, "Cathedrals, Castles, and Roman Baths: Railway Station Architecture in the Urban South," *JUH*, II (1976), 195–230; Frederick C. Arms to Lemuel P. Grant, July 29, 1852, in Grant Papers; CM, March 7, 1856; *Daily Atlanta Intelligencer*, January 24, 1860; I. O. McDaniel to John P. King, October 7, 1851, in Grant Papers.

hasty departures—were frequent during the 1850s. The Atlanta & West Point and the Georgia passenger trains did arrive late at night in antebellum Atlanta but early in the day in West Point and Augusta. The solution advocated by Atlanta businessmen was the "market train," a daily excursion train that would have brought well-rested customers to Atlanta markets at convenient business hours. Other Georgia communities such as Augusta, Macon, and Savannah enjoyed the benefits of these excursion trains during the antebellum era. For a brief period in 1860, the Macon & Western did provide Atlanta with a market train, but this service lasted only three months. [39]

Freight tariff discriminations were potentially a much more serious deterrent to Atlanta's economic growth than were unfavorable passenger schedules. Atlanta merchants quickly realized that cities with freight rates lower than their rivals' had a significant advantage in the struggles for trading territories. Throughout the antebellum period, Atlanta businessmen vehemently protested a consistent pattern of rate discrimination that affected all classes of goods coming into and departing from their city. In 1858, local merchants pointed out that it cost twice as much to ship to Atlanta dry goods from Savannah or Charleston (brought there by steamships from New York or other northern ports) as it did to transport the same goods from the seacoast to Nashville, Knoxville, or Memphis. The Western & Atlantic also charged more to carry foodstuffs to Atlanta than it and its tributary roads did to ship them to cities farther south. Freight rates on local transportation (shipments to towns between terminal cities) were also exorbitant. [40]

Many factors—not all of them understood or accepted by Atlanta boosters—were at work. "High and dry" towns in the southern interior like Atlanta lacked water transportation, which was usually cheaper than were railroads. To remain competitive with steamboat companies and to compensate for lost revenue, southern railroads during the antebellum period adopted a "basing point" system— cities with water transportation had low through rates while land-locked cities had high rates. Atlantans' lack of financial control over any of the railroads terminating in the city also accounted for some of

39. *Daily Atlanta Intelligencer*, November 7, 11, 1858, July 11, 1860.
40. *Ibid.*, September 10, November 12, 1858.

the rate discriminations. Antebellum southern railroad managers believed that their policies should favor those cities that invested heavily in their lines. Cities that did not invest could hardly expect sympathetic treatment from lines financed by competing urban centers. The managers also decided that local freight rates should be higher than through rates, since most of the traffic was not local.[41]

Believing that their city's commercial growth was seriously threatened, Atlanta businessmen fought throughout the antebellum period for classification as a basing point—but with little success. The organization of the Southern Railroad Association in 1856 gave frustrated Atlanta merchants a chance to present their arguments against rate discriminations to a large audience of railroad officials. Between 1856 and 1860, the association met several times in Atlanta and heard the pleas of local merchants. The 1860 meeting, attended by the presidents of the South Carolina, the Georgia, the Macon & Western, and the Central of Georgia, did result in a promise that tariffs on goods sent up from the seacoast would be lowered beginning August 1. The reduction was made, but local merchants were outraged when they discovered that it applied only to first-class goods, which represented but one-tenth of the city's commerce. At the same time, there was actually an increase in the tariff on third- and fourth-class goods. These items included hardware and dry goods, which together accounted for three-fourths of Atlanta's trade. The election of Joseph E. Brown, an "upcountry man" from Union County, as governor of Georgia in 1857 raised the hopes of Atlanta merchants that they might at last have a sympathetic ally in their struggle to obtain more favorable freight rates from the Western & Atlantic. While Brown offered sympathy, he did little else, and the W & A's rate structure remained unchanged.[42]

Freight rate discriminations, conflicts about street crossings, passenger schedules that discouraged trade in the city, and various other problems convinced many Atlantans during the antebellum period that the railroads which gave birth to the city were hostile to its

41. Phillips, *Transportation*, 384–85; Maury Klein, "The Strategy of Southern Railroads," *American Historical Review*, LXIII (1968), 1052–68; *Annual Report of the Western & Atlantic Railroad, 1860*, pp. 4–5.
42. *Weekly Atlanta Intelligencer*, December 9, 1858, May 19, 1859; *Daily Atlanta Intelligencer*, December 22, 1858, August 14, 16, 1860; Coulter, *Short History of Georgia*, 264; Phillips, *Transportation*, 384–85.

interests. "Rival and enterprising cities are wielding these . . . un-rivalled weapons of power and prosperity for their benefit in every possible way," one local citizen concluded in 1858. "Atlanta has as yet no weapon . . . for her own protection and defense."[43]

Railroads as the Initial Challenge

Nineteenth-century Atlantans accurately described the origins of their city as an unexpected by-product of antebellum railroad construction. Further, their conspiracy theory depicted these railroads as actively working to limit the city's growth. They equated railroad policies with urban rivalries, especially those between older lowland cities and the new interior towns. This interpretation was obviously paranoiac and myopic. Even Savannah or Charleston, which did have proprietary interests in railroads, complained of "unfair discriminations" by lines that rival cities controlled. Such complaints, whether well founded or not, were universal in an era when railroads were powerful instruments of urban competition.

Assessing the extent to which railroads actually manifested other cities' antagonism to Atlanta's growth is not as important as recognizing what uses Atlantans made of their interpretation of railroads' impact upon the city. As one historian has pointed out, the histories people develop about the cities in which they live may have little correspondence with objective reality but may justify preferred courses of action.[44] For nineteenth-century Atlantans, the city's early experience with railroads was the first chapter in a "challenge-response" narrative. Atlanta was depicted as a besieged city, assailed by economic agencies subservient to older cities in the "unprogressive" plantation districts. Stressing the active enmity of these hostile agencies was a means of eliciting entrepreneurial energies and community action to "make Atlanta grow." Atlanta's troubles with railroads in its infancy were the first obstacle that the town had to overcome before metropolitan status could be achieved. That early experience was described in the same way as was the devastation of the Civil War. Both periods in local history were subsequently seen as proof

43. *Daily Atlanta Intelligencer*, November 9, 1858.
44. Blaine A. Brownell, *The Urban Ethos in the South, 1920–1930* (Baton Rouge, 1975), 191–216.

that with an appropriate dose of the Atlanta spirit, the city's population would always be capable of conquering adversity.[45]

45. This version of Atlanta's railroad history appeared in newspapers and many other published sources before and after the Civil War. For examples, see Atlanta *Constitution*, June 12, 1881; *First Annual Report of the Atlanta Chamber of Commerce for the Year 1885: Historical, Descriptive, Statistical* (Atlanta, 1886); and Jonathan Norcross, *Atlanta, Northern Georgia, and the Great Southern Railroad Pool* (Atlanta, 1886).

2

ORGANIZING FOR GROWTH
Public and Private Enterprise to 1861

Atlanta is destined to be a great city and that at no distant day.
. . . Everything is projected on a large scale and everyone seems
inspired with the growing importance of the place.

—Madison *Family Visitor* quoted by *Daily Atlanta Intelligencer* (1858)

We next saw Atlanta in 1845, and it was a sorry looking . . . town
at that time. Soon, however, it began to take on airs, and its
pioneer citizens adopted the role of bragging on everything it
did, which they have continued to do, world without end. . . .
In our opinion Atlanta succeeds by her "cheek" and supreme
confidence in herself.

—Rebecca Latimer Felton in Cartersville *Courant*,
quoted by Atlanta *Journal* (1885)

Many nineteenth-century observers realized that the urban boosterism flourishing in "New South" Atlanta had taproots in the antebellum era. Local boosters strove to build railroads, attract agricultural fairs, and move the state capital to their city. Entrepreneurs in postbellum Atlanta engaged in the same struggles, often successfully completing or expanding projects initiated before the war. The techniques of urban promotion were also almost identical. Atlanta's economic leaders used public and private funds for urban promotive schemes and adhered to the philosophy that the overriding responsibility of municipal government was to encourage the city's growth.

Researchers investigating the origins of New South urban boosterism in other cities will probably also find more continuity than discontinuity between the ante- and postbellum periods. Promoters in Richmond, Charleston, Galveston, and other antebellum southern towns and cities valued as highly and worked as hard for urban growth as did their Atlanta counterparts.[1] Because of the city's location, booster rhetoric in Atlanta frequently expressed a theme, however, not present in pronouncements from the South's older cities. Atlanta businessmen sought to forge a trading alliance with the "upcountry," so that the city could become a major urban center. One local newspaper editor thus noted in 1858 that "jealous and envious" older southern cities could not prevent Atlanta's growth, as long as the city continued to attract "carts and waggons [sic] laden with cotton and other products of the country . . . and persons here every day, from distant points 50 to 150 miles, in quest of groceries and dry goods which they can purchase here cheaper than any place in the upcountry."[2]

At times the effort to develop the upcountry trade became a social and political crusade against planters and their commercial agents in the lowland South. Atlanta newspaper editors invited their readers in

---

1. See, for example, David R. Goldfield, "Pursuing the American Urban Dream: Cities in the Old South," in Blaine A. Brownell and Goldfield (eds.), *The City in Southern History: The Growth of Urban Civilization in the South* (Port Washington, N.Y., 1977), 52–91; Kenneth W. Wheeler, *To Wear a City's Crown: The Beginnings of Urban Growth in Texas, 1836–1865* (Cambridge, Mass., 1968); Lyle W. Dorsett and Arthur H. Schaffer, "Was the Antebellum South Antiurban? A Suggestion," *JSH*, XXXVIII (1972), 93–100; and Leonard P. Curry, "Urbanization and Urbanism in the Old South: A Comparative View," *ibid.*, XL (1974), 43–60.

2. *Daily Atlanta Intelligencer*, November 2, 1858.

the upcountry to regard the city as the natural home of "crackers" (small farmers whose whips cracked over the oxen drawing country wagons) and the symbol of their joint defiance of the planter class and its trading centers. This rhetoric was an important contribution to the molding of Atlanta's image as more democratic, hardworking, and progressive than were older, rival cities. This image was elaborated and better publicized after the Civil War, but it was already entrenched in the booster creed of antebellum Atlanta.

The Economic Base: Commerce and Industry

As was true in most southern cities, Atlanta's economy was more commercial than industrial throughout the antebellum period. In 1860, about 21.7 percent of Atlanta's working population engaged in commercial pursuits; 15.4 percent had manufacturing jobs. The occupational distribution ten years earlier was even more heavily tilted toward commerce, with 31.3 percent in that area and 16.3 percent in the manufacturing sectors (see Table 2, Appendix A). Only rough estimates are available of the value of the several economic sectors, but they also indicate that commerce dominated. The total value of products manufactured in Atlanta in 1860 was about $414,000; commerce added at least another $2.6 million to the city's trade.[3]

The principal commercial activities in antebellum Atlanta were receiving foodstuffs grown in the upper piedmont region of Georgia and east Tennessee and cotton from Georgia's lower piedmont and selling produce, dry goods, hardware, and agricultural implements to farmers and country merchants in neighboring towns and villages. The trading radius was estimated to be one hundred miles in 1859, but occasionally extended farther. An Atlanta newspaper thus triumphantly reported that the wholesale produce firm of A. K. Seago & A. N. Abbott had sold a "lot of sugar" to a firm in Berzelia, Georgia (about 150 miles from Atlanta), which was "but a short distance from Augusta . . . whose people turn up their noses at the mention of the 'Gate City.'"[4]

The area within the trading radius that more typically defined the

3. Fifteen industries in Atlanta employing 319 workers produced goods valued at $414,366 in 1860. See *Manufactures of the United States in 1860* (1865), 68; and Green B. Haygood, "Sketch of Atlanta," in *Williams' Atlanta City Directory for 1859–1860* (Atlanta, 1860), 11.
4. Haygood, "Sketch of Atlanta," 11–12; *Weekly Atlanta Intelligencer*, January 13, 1859.

limits of Atlanta's commerce included portions of two distinct regions. The upper piedmont or "upcountry" covered all north Georgia to a line approximately thirty-five miles south of Atlanta. The small farmers there were self-sufficient in foodstuffs and had only modest needs for dry goods, hardware, and similar items. The major crop in 1860 was corn; only 10 percent of the cotton grown in the state in that year came from the upcountry. Where the upcountry ended south of Atlanta was the northern edge of the lower piedmont or plantation belt. Cotton was the leading crop, and farmers were more in need of foodstuffs than were their counterparts in the upcountry. *Plantation belt* is, however, a misleading term for the northern portion of the lower piedmont. Although planters and small farmers could be found in every county, the line separating small from large landholders (those with three hundred or more acres) in 1860 stretched across the lower piedmont roughly one hundred miles south of Atlanta. Significantly, all four of Atlanta's principal urban rivals within the state (Macon, Augusta, Savannah, and Columbus) were below that line and were surrounded by counties in which plantations were relatively common. It was this locational factor more than anything else that shaped those cities' economies and social structures and values in ways different from those of nineteenth-century Atlanta. [5]

Although railroads were the principal transportation for goods coming to Atlanta throughout the nineteenth century, the "wagon trade" was important in the expansion of antebellum trade. Twice weekly, long lines of picturesque covered wagons, drawn by oxen or mules with bells on the lead animals, noisily creaked through the city's streets carrying cargoes of cotton, wheat, eggs, "Carolina apples," and other foodstuffs. One observer counted more than 150 such wagons strung out along Peachtree Street one day in the 1850s. Early in that decade, the main item in the wagon trade was cotton—most of the 35,500 bales purchased by Atlanta merchants in 1851 were brought to the city by wagon. Later in the decade, produce from northern Georgia and east Tennessee began to replace cotton in the wagon trade. Local merchants sold most of this produce to store-

5. Steven S. Hahn, *The Roots of Southern Populism: Yeoman Farmers and the Transformation of the Georgia Upcountry, 1850–1890* (New York, 1983), 7–9, 15–28, 147; Enoch Marvin Banks, *The Economics of Land Tenure in Georgia* (New York, 1906), 2–23, 41–43, 135–37.

keepers in towns like Berzelia, south of Atlanta and distant from the food-producing regions.[6]

The creation of a public market provided a special inducement to upcountry farmers to trade in Atlanta. It was intended to provide foodstuffs for local consumers rather than produce for merchants to resell to distant customers. During most of the year, the market was open from one hour before sunrise to seven o'clock in the evening, and farmers could pay a small tax so they could supply fresh meat and vegetables. In 1858 a city council ordinance prohibited anyone from bringing "bacon or produce of any kind into the city by the railroads for sale on the streets" unless the seller had brought a witness "to testify that he grew it or raised it himself." This ordinance was intended to limit the competition of peddlers who were from towns in other regions of the state. Carefully regulated by municipal authorities, the public market became a thriving institution and a great boon to upcountry farmers near Atlanta. Its success also undermines the argument of one historian that antebellum southern urbanization was slowed because small farmers had little interest in trading in urban markets.[7]

Antebellum Atlanta also actively cultivated the wagon trade by offering various amenities. Bored farmers with sufficient means who wished to linger after selling their crops could stay at either Washington Hall or the Atlanta Hotel, both fairly luxurious hotels for the area and capable of accommodating 150 guests each when completed in 1846. Most farmers preferred, however, to camp with their teams of oxen or mules in one of the many "wagon yards." Then there were numerous saloons and grogshops, and liquor could also be purchased by the quart at most provisions stores. For those inclined to seek a higher level of entertainment, the Athenaeum built in 1857 presented lively comedic farces, such as *Toodles, the Gambler's Wife*, acted by a resident company. And sometimes there were special attractions, such as the Campbell minstrels, who were billed in 1857 as "combining in one organization the most pleasing and best vocal-

6. George White, *Historical Collections of Georgia* (Savannah, 1854), 421; Lucy H. Baldwin, Autobiography (MS in Southern Historical Collection, University of North Carolina, Chapel Hill), 1; *Pioneer Citizens' History of Atlanta, 1833–1902* (Atlanta, 1902), 222–23, 233.

7. Quotation from Marshall J. Clarke (comp.), *Acts of Incorporation and Ordinances of the City of Atlanta* (Atlanta, 1860), 36. See Julius Rubin, "Urban Growth and Regional Development," in David T. Gilchrist (ed.), *The Growth of Seaport Cities, 1790–1825* (Charlottesville, 1967), 3–21.

ists & Balladists, the most distinguished and best Instrumentalists and Dancers, at present engaged in the Ethiopian profession."[8]

Finally, another important attraction was the growing number of wholesale and retail provisions, dry goods, and hardware stores. By 1859, there were seventy-seven firms in the city engaged in the sale of produce, dry goods, clothing, furniture, boots and shoes, crockery, and other commodities. Even before the completion of the Memphis & Charleston in 1857, Atlanta was a market for western produce, regarded as a prestigious item for southern merchants to carry. In 1853 the first shipment of groceries direct from St. Louis came down the Ohio and Tennessee rivers to the Western & Atlantic Railroad's northern terminus, and thence to an Irish merchant in Atlanta, Thomas Doonan. Within a year, Doonan claimed to have made such great profits from the western trade that he was able to construct a "fire-proof Ware-House" on Whitehall Street, where cotton from nearby farms and corn (mostly desirable to livestock growers), lard, and bacon from the West could be stored safely. According to one of its newspaper advertisements in 1854, James J. Lynch's produce firm also boasted an ample stock of New Orleans and Cincinnati goods, including "sugar, coffee, syrup, and Provisions generally." Lynch promised that his prices were less than those charged by his competitors in Charleston and Savannah.[9]

In addition, antebellum Atlanta merchants were also able to offer farmers and country store merchants a wide variety of northern dry goods and manufactures. The wholesale and retail dry goods firm of Bartley M. Smith & William E. Ezzard bragged in 1855 that it could sell to the cash buyer everything from "window-glass to dental and surgical instruments." Some of the larger dry goods firms sent agents to New York, where they selected items to sell in Atlanta. In 1853, A. J. Brady, a hardware merchant, spent more than a month in New York, evaluating merchandise. Beach & Lockhart, which purchased much of its stock in New York, stated in 1856 that it could "offer such inducements to merchants, as will convince them that Atlanta is *the* place for dry goods." Claiming to deal only in the cash trade and to

8.   William Stafford Irvine (ed.), "Diary and Letters of William N. White, a Citizen of Atlanta Written 1847," *AHB*, III (1937), 47–48; Thomas H. Martin, *Atlanta and Its Builders: A Comprehensive History of the Gate City of the South* (2 vols.; Atlanta, 1902), I, 45–46; *Daily Atlanta Intelligencer*, June 4, 1857.

9.   Quotations from *Daily Atlanta Intelligencer*, February 10, 1856, January 9, 1857; *Daily Atlanta Intelligencer*, quoted in Augusta *Constitutionalist*, March 16, 1853. Number of firms computed from *Williams' Atlanta City Directory for 1859–1860*.

have a low profit margin, Beach & Lockhart asserted that it had undercut Savannah and Charleston merchants' wholesale trade in the upcountry.[10]

Selling goods "strictly for cash" as did Beach & Lockhart was a policy that antebellum Atlanta merchants said significantly aided their efforts to capture trading territory. It was true that most merchants—especially in cities near the coastal plantation districts but also in upcountry villages—usually offered their customers twelve-month or more credit accounts. Operating on credit rather than cash had the effect of driving up prices for goods. One early historian of Atlanta maintained that the cash trade policy, together with low rents for stores, enabled local merchants during the antebellum period to sell groceries at lower prices than did their competitors in Savannah, Charleston, and Augusta. A local newspaper writer also asserted in 1860 that prices for all classes of goods were 25 to 40 percent lower in Atlanta than "in neighboring cities where credit accounts run for one, two, and three years." Pioneer Atlanta merchants explained that the cash trade system, which they knew to be unusual in the antebellum South, was the product of a shortage of capital and consequent inability to extend credit.[11]

It is impossible to be certain about the extent of the cash trade policy and its impact on Atlanta's antebellum economy. There is sufficient evidence to remove suspicions that claims about it were unsubstantiated rhetoric. One early-twentieth-century diarist who had access to no-longer-extant account books of antebellum Atlanta businesses confirmed the existence of the policy. Credit reports of R. G. Dun & Co. also support the boosters' assertion that no local firms went bankrupt during the 1857 depression. Many said that was because those firms lacked credit burdens. These same reports also indicate that dry goods companies were especially fond of the cash trade. However, firms with high as well as low initial capitalization engaged in the cash trade, which casts doubt on theories connecting

10. Quotations from *Daily Atlanta Intelligencer*, January 20, 1857; Atlanta *Daily Examiner*, July 31, 1857; A. J. Brady to Lemuel P. Grant, July 12, 1853, in Lemuel P. Grant Papers, AHS.

11. Lewis E. Atherton, *The Southern Country Store, 1800–1860* (Baton Rouge, 1949), 8, 14, 47, 52, 131–44; Wallace P. Reed, *History of Atlanta, Georgia* (Syracuse, 1889), 237, 437; I. W. Avery, *Atlanta, The Leader in Trade, Population, Wealth, and Manufactures* (Atlanta, 1885), 16; *Daily Atlanta Intelligencer*, June 18, 1860 (quotation); "Proceedings of Atlanta Pioneer and Historic Society" in William R. Hanleiter, *Atlanta City Directory for 1871* (Atlanta, 1871), 27.

the practice with upward mobility on the part of aggressive but allegedly poor merchants at the start of their careers.[12] It seems reasonable to conclude that Atlanta's remoteness from the plantation districts was more responsible for the evolution of the cash trade than was local merchants' shortage of capital and that the policy must have helped to advance the city's commerce because they could undercut competitors' prices.

By 1860 there were several commercial houses whose business activities were impressive, especially for a city of Atlanta's size. The wholesale and retail dry goods firm of John Ryan & Michael Myers—in 1853 the Dun & Co. reporter described the partners as "Irishmen without visible property"—five years later had an annual business of roughly $300,000 and employed twelve clerks. The dry goods firms of McNaught, Ormond, & Co. and Beach & Root, the wholesale produce company of A. C. Wyly, and several others all had even greater trade volumes by 1860. The growth of such establishments was reflected in physical improvements in Atlanta's business districts during the 1850s. During that decade, larger and more attractive brick buildings replaced the "old wooden hulks" along Whitehall, Peachtree, Decatur, and Alabama streets. During 1859 alone, eighteen two-story brick buildings, several of which had graceful "New Orleans fronts" forged at the local rolling mill, went up in the commercial center.[13]

Although they did not contribute as much as did the mercantile houses to the city's economy, several factories were built in Atlanta during the antebellum period. Industrialization in the city before 1861 proceeded along lines typical of the region. Large-scale manufacturing operations were predominant, with flour milling and metal fabrication overshadowing textiles. By 1860, fabricated metals led Atlanta's industrial economy: 98 percent of the capital invested in manufacturing and 91 percent of all industrial workers were involved.

12. Sarah Huff, "Foundation Families," in Sarah Huff Papers, AHS; Haygood, "Sketch of Atlanta," 12. Examination of the R. G. Dun & Co. credit reports for Fulton County, Ga., revealed only one firm, the Atlanta Rolling Mill, that failed as a result of the panic of 1857. See Volumes XIII and XIV for Fulton County of these reports in the Baker Library, Harvard University, Cambridge, Mass.

13. E. Y. Clarke, *Illustrated History of Atlanta* (2nd ed., 1879; rpr. Atlanta, 1971), 37–38; *Daily Atlanta Intelligencer*, May 28, 1859; Dun & Co. Credit Reports, Fulton County, XIII. A published credit report for 1860 listed fifteen mercantile firms in Atlanta with "A" ratings; Ryan's firm merited only a "B." See J. M. Bradstreet & Son, *Bradstreet's Commercial Reports of the Principal Cities and Towns in the United States and British Provinces*, Vol. VII (2nd ed.; New York, 1860). I am indebted to Don H. Doyle for sharing this source with me.

Like Richmond and Chattanooga, Atlanta benefited from railroad growth during the antebellum period and specialized in factories that catered to the railroads' needs.[14]

The earliest industrial ventures in Atlanta stimulated by railroad growth were several private foundries and the roundhouses and machine shops maintained by the railroad companies themselves. Before the Civil War, the largest foundry was Joseph Winship's Machine Shop & Foundry, built in 1851. Winship, born in New Salem, Massachusetts, employed forty workers by 1854 in his foundry, which concentrated on building railroad cars. After a disastrous fire in 1857 that cost the company more than $30,000, Winship rebuilt and expanded his facilities to make possible the construction of engines, boilers, iron railings, bridge castings and bolts, and parts for heavy machinery.[15]

Not as diversified as Winship's company but even more important to the railroads were the machine shops maintained by the Georgia and the Western & Atlantic. The W & A's shops were the largest and best equipped in the city. John H. Flynn, a native of Philadelphia and former employee of both William Norris' famed locomotive factory and the Phoenixville Rolling Mill in Pennsylvania, was the W & A's master machinist. In 1857, under Flynn's skillful direction, the W & A's machine shops accomplished what most southern foundries could not: they constructed several railroad passenger cars, one of which won a prize at the Southern Central Agricultural Society fair that year. "This car equals any brought from the North," commented one observer. The W & A machine shops also claimed to be capable of building locomotives.[16]

A much larger industrial venture was the Atlanta Rolling Mill,

14. Percentages based on data given in *Manufactures in 1860*, p. 68. See also Lester J. Cappon, "Trend of the Southern Iron Industry under the Plantation System," *Journal of Economics and Business History*, II (1930), 364; Albert W. Niemi, Jr., "Structural Shifts in Southern Manufacturing, 1849–1899," *Business History Review*, XLV (1971), 79–84; Raymond L. Cohn, "Local Manufacturing in the Antebellum South and Midwest," *ibid.*, LIV (1980), 80–91; and Fred Bateman and Thomas Weiss, "Manufacturing in the Antebellum South," in Paul Uselding (ed.), *Research in Economic History: An Annual Compilation* (Greenwich, Conn., 1976), 1–44.

15. White, *Historical Collections*, 422; Franklin M. Garrett, *Atlanta and Environs: A Chronicle of Its People and Events* (3 vols.; New York, 1954), I, 350; *Daily Atlanta Intelligencer*, March 16, 1859, March 4, 1860.

16. *Annual Report of the Western & Atlantic Railroad, 1856* (Atlanta, 1856), 5; *Annual Report of the Western & Atlantic Railroad, 1857* (Atlanta, 1857), 5; Atlanta *Daily Intelligencer and Examiner*, October 29, 1857.

founded in 1857 by Dr. L. A. Douglas of Indiana. He, however, lacked sufficient capital to operate the mill properly, and in 1858 he and Frazier & Co. of Richmond sold it to William Markham and Lewis Scofield, both Connecticut natives. Under their management, the mill specialized in rerolling worn rails for the railroads. The two steam engines that drove the rollers had a combined horsepower of 210. There were also machines to straighten and cut the rails and six large puddling furnaces. In 1859 the mill was deemed capable of producing 18,000 tons of iron rails annually and of giving employment to 150 men. Other than the Tredegar Iron Works in Richmond, no other rolling mill in the South had that capacity.[17]

Despite its impressive facilities, the mill never fulfilled its potential during the antebellum period. From November, 1858, to December, 1859, the mill turned out only 4,339 tons of railroad iron and employed only 75 men. The fundamental cause of its poor record was that the railroads, which had occasioned its existence in the first place, gave the mill only lukewarm support. Although the 1859 convention of the Southern Railroad Association had promised to patronize the mill, the companies continued to import rails from the North and England until the Civil War broke out. Because the mill in its rerolling process added a small amount of "puddle-iron" manufactured from Georgia ore, equal to no more than one-tenth to one-twelfth of the rail's weight, the railroad companies claimed the rails were too brittle and refused to buy them.[18]

One other industrial venture that also had railroad problems was Richard Peters' Steam Flour Mill, built in 1849, the largest one south of Richmond. Its two powerful steam engines, 80 horsepower each, later formed the nucleus of the Confederate powder manufactory at Augusta. In 1857 the mill daily turned out 280 barrels of flour, which was, according to an Atlanta newspaper editor, "a super-excellent article . . . which will compare favorably with the choicest American or British flour." More often than not, however, the grinding stones were idle. Having failed once in 1850, the mill closed permanently in 1858. Its owners said the causes were the railroads' failure to lower freight tariffs on wheat shipped to Atlanta and the success of Mark A.

17. Atlanta *Daily Examiner*, July 31, 1857; *Daily Atlanta Intelligencer*, November 20, 1858, May 18, 1859; *Weekly Atlanta Intelligencer*, November 2, 1858; Stephens Mitchell, "Atlanta: The Industrial Heart of the Confederacy," *AHB*, I (1930), 22.
18. *Daily Atlanta Intelligencer*, February 25, 1860 (citing Charleston *Courier*), May 28, 1859.

Cooper's Etowah Mills, close to the grain districts in northern Georgia.[19]

Although Atlanta had thus not entirely neglected manufacturing, its economy by 1860 was still predominantly commercial. Many explanations of the antebellum South's failure to industrialize have been offered; for cities such as Atlanta, however, they are in some ways misleading. As Allan R. Pred has noted, manufacturing was not a major component of the economy of any large mid-nineteenth-century American city; less than 10 percent of the population of major cities in the United States in 1860 was engaged in industrial activities.[20]

Most important for the history of city building in the South was the attitude of urban promoters: they were—if antebellum Atlanta was typical—lukewarm rather than hostile to industrialization. It is possible that anti-industrial sentiments in Atlanta were muted because the city lacked economic and cultural ties with the planter class, but even in Charleston, which was one of the cities much more in tune with planter values, entrepreneurs worked hard during the 1840s and 1850s to build factories. The chief detriment to the growth of manufacturing in Charleston and other coastal cities was probably not specifically an anti-industrial bias but rather the high rate of return promised by investment in plantation agriculture and the status accorded those involved in it.[21]

Whatever the reason, public opinion in antebellum Atlanta was not explicitly anti-industrial. Those Atlantans who established manufacturing enterprises from iron mills to brick factories were saluted in local newspapers and elsewhere as public benefactors. H. Muhlenbrink's cigar factory, for example, was grandiloquently praised in 1858 as "one of the institutions which . . . is destined to make Atlanta one of the most flourishing cities of the South." Lewis Scofield, co-proprietor of the Atlanta Rolling Mill, was also commended publicly

19.   Nellie Peters Black, *Richard Peters* (Atlanta, 1904), 27; *The War of the Rebellion: A Compilation of the Official Records of the Union and Confederate Armies* (130 vols.; Washington, D.C., 1880–1901), Ser. IV, Vol. I, p. 557; Reed, *History of Atlanta*, 47; Atlanta *Daily Examiner*, August 18, 1857; Augusta *Daily Chronicle and Sentinel*, May 5, 1860.
20.   Allan R. Pred, *Urban Growth and City-Systems in the United States, 1840–1860* (Cambridge, Mass., 1980), 7, 9. The literature on antebellum southern industrialization is vast. For the best available bibliography, see Fred Bateman and Thomas Weiss, *A Deplorable Scarcity: The Failure of Industrialization in the Slave Economy* (Chapel Hill, 1981).
21.   Ernest M. Lander, "Charleston: Manufacturing Center of the Old South," *JSH*, XXVI (1960), 330–52; William H. Pease and Jane H. Pease, *The Web of Progress: Private Values and Public Styles in Boston and Charleston, 1828–1843* (New York, 1985), 43, 122.

as "a practical mechanic, a high-toned gentleman . . . who will make an impress upon the city of Atlanta." Moreover, Atlanta's municipal government passed a series of ordinances between 1852 and 1856 that exempted from taxation machinery attached to any manufacturing plant and capital invested in manufactories (though the land they occupied was still taxable). These steps to encourage industrialization were modest but at least indicated some support for the idea.[22]

A few Atlanta businessmen thought that the city was poised for an industrial takeoff. "The influence . . . which the foundries, work-shops, and Rolling Mill . . . [will] have upon the city . . . cannot yet be estimated," wrote one observer in 1858. "The future alone will . . . [tell whether] our city shall be filled with a population of twenty, thirty, or forty thousand."[23] Most local promoters still thought in terms of commercial development, however, and rarely expressed such visionary notions on the eve of the Civil War.

Public and Private Enterprise

City-building strategies and schemes abounded in antebellum Atlanta, as they did all across urban America, and touched many aspects of the city's economic, political, and cultural life. Local boosters fought unsuccessfully during the 1850s to move the state capital and even the state penitentiary to Atlanta, believing that thus increasing the city's prestige and the number of jobs would attract more immigrants. Knowing that institutions of higher learning could have a positive economic impact, they also tried to persuade the trustees of the University of the South to build in Atlanta, but the trustees chose the more isolated location and less sinful town of Sewanee, Tennessee.[24] The list of such efforts and schemes could proceed *ad infinitum*. Describing a few will show how they often involved a combination of public and private enterprise and how they also reinforced the city's growing self-image as a citadel of upcountry enterprise assailed by the "unprogressive" lowland South. These entrepreneurial ventures were the founding of the city's first bank, the effort to persuade the Southern Central Agricultural Society to hold its fairs in

22. *Daily Atlanta Intelligencer*, November 3, 28, 1858; Atlanta Ordinance Book, April 3, 1852, May 5, 1856, in AHS.
23. *Daily Atlanta Intelligencer*, October 8, 1858.
24. Meta Barker, "Schools and Teachers of Ante-Bellum Atlanta," *AHB*, IV (1939), 31–33; CM, March 31, 1854; *Atlanta Weekly Intelligencer and Cherokee Advocate*, October 12, 1855; *Weekly Atlanta Intelligencer*, December 16, 1858.

Atlanta, and two railroad projects, the Georgia Air Line and the Georgia Western.

Like any other fledgling city, Atlanta needed a bank to advance its commercial economy. One observer commented in 1851 that Atlanta merchants could have doubled their purchases of Tennessee and Georgia produce if only capital had been available. An agent of the Georgia Railroad and Banking Company had set up shop in Atlanta in 1847 and a branch of a Macon bank opened the following year, but these institutions served the interests of the railroads, cotton planters, and merchants in Augusta and Macon. In 1852, several local citizens successfully petitioned the state legislature, therefore, to incorporate the Atlanta Bank for the express purpose of lessening the city's dependence "on the Banks of other places, by whose orders discounts are controlled, and often stopped when they are most wanted and needed . . . to purchase the produce brought to this market."[25]

The Atlanta Bank was nothing more than a legal entity for several months because its sponsors could not assemble the necessary capital to initiate its operations. Suddenly in 1853, a mysterious speculator from Chicago, George Smith, arrived in the city and subscribed $295,000 of the bank's $300,000 total stock issue. Unknown to his new friends in Atlanta, Smith had concocted a daring scheme to gain complete control of the banking systems in Chicago and all Illinois. He intended to flood the Midwest with notes from Georgia banks, which could issue unlimited amounts of currency, and thus drive his competitors to the wall. By the summer of 1853, some of the Atlanta Bank's incorporators realized that Smith was not "going to do the clean thing." "Our man Smith is looking entirely to the West in his operations," wrote Mayor John F. Mims to railroad construction engineer Lemuel P. Grant in June, 1853. "His officers declare and promise to do all the necessary business that this section of upcountry may need, [but] I am watching them *pretty* close."[26]

A powerful attack was soon launched upon the Atlanta Bank. Smith's western competitors sent agents to Atlanta with huge quantities of bank notes to be redeemed for specie. In 1854, two men exchanged $77,000 for gold and silver coin. By February, 1856, the

25. White, *Historical Collections*, 422; Garrett, *Atlanta*, I, 251; *Ga. Laws*, 1852, pp. 39–44.

26. Larry Gara, "The War Against Georgia Wild Cats," *GHQ*, XL (1956), 383–91; John F. Mims to L. P. Grant, June 10, 30, 1853, both in Grant Papers.

Atlanta Bank had redeemed almost $1.5 million in its own notes. Representatives from Augusta, Savannah, and Macon in the state legislature also actively campaigned for withdrawal of the bank's charter. Critics claimed that the bank was a "wildcat" and had issued far more notes in proportion to its capital than was legal. James M. Calhoun, state senator from Atlanta, despite valiant efforts was unable to prevent the revocation of its charter in 1856.[27]

The moral was plain. When another bank, the Bank of Fulton, was founded in the city in 1856, it was locally controlled. Of the $207,600 total stock subscribed by November, 1857, $120,200 was in the hands of Atlanta residents. Two speculators from New York owned another $47,000 of the bank's stock, and the remainder belonged to small investors in the upcountry surrounding Atlanta. During the panic of 1857, Augusta and Savannah banks attempted to force all banks in the state's interior to accept a more burdensome system of exchange.[28] But the Bank of Fulton survived and was firmly established on the eve of the Civil War. After an initial failure, Atlanta businessmen had thus succeeded in creating a stable financial institution to provide capital for various city-building enterprises.

Persuading the Southern Central Agricultural Society to hold its annual fairs in Atlanta was not as critical to the city's antebellum economic development as was establishing a bank. The fairs did serve, however, to advertise the economic potential of both Atlanta and the surrounding farmland and also were one of the city's earliest triumphs over its lowland urban competitors. Organized in 1846, the society tried to call attention to north Georgia's agricultural and mining potential and also to undermine the belief that the plantation belt was the state's only productive region. Its founders were Mark A. Cooper, owner of the Etowah Mining & Manufacturing Company and a leading industrialist, and John W. Graves, proprietor of a hotel at the Stone Mountain depot a few miles east of Atlanta. Between 1846 and 1849, the society held its fairs at Stone Mountain.[29]

27. *Daily Atlanta Intelligencer*, February 1, 1856; Savannah *Republican*, February 2, 1856; Augusta *Daily Chronicle and Sentinel* quoted in Athens *Banner*, December 21, 1854; Augusta *Constitutionalist*, September 20, 1856.

28. R. P. Govan, "The Banking and Credit System in Georgia," *JSH*, III (1938), 177–78; *Ga. Laws, 1855–56*, pp. 66–70; Atlanta *Daily Intelligencer and Examiner*, November 20, 1857.

29. David W. Lewis (ed.), *Transactions of the Southern Central Agricultural Society, from Its Organization in 1846 to 1851* (Macon, 1852), v–viii.

In 1850, Richard Peters, one of the society's directors, successfully led a movement to transfer the society's annual fair from Stone Mountain to Atlanta. Peters, grandson of a prominent Pennsylvania judge and a colorful railroad man who had come in 1834 to work on the Georgia, had settled in Atlanta in the 1840s. He quickly became an enthusiastic booster of the city and seized every opportunity to promote its growth. Peters was also well known throughout the antebellum South as the owner of Belmont, a 1,500-acre model plantation in Gordon County, Georgia, on which he raised exotic livestock and experimented with such unusual crops as millet, oat grass, and Chinese sugarcane. He was the first farmer in the United States to raise Angora goats, which he imported directly from Turkey. His activities clearly showed that the interests of urban promoters and farmers were not irreconcilable, even in the antebellum South. In fact, during the nineteenth century, urbanites across the country organized and crusaded for agricultural and horticultural societies.[30]

After detailing the virtues of the Southern Central Agricultural Society, Peters persuaded Lemuel P. Grant, another Georgia Railroad official and Atlanta resident, to donate a ten-acre lot in the city for the fair. Atlanta's city council also appropriated $1,000 for a building to house the fair's exhibits. When the fair was finally opened to the public in the fall of 1850, it was a great success and attracted ten to fifteen thousand people from all over the region. For four years after this triumph, Atlanta engaged in a tug-of-war with Macon for the honor of hosting the society's fairs, which were held alternately in those cities.[31]

In 1855, Atlanta promoters took steps to have the fairs permanently in their city, which faced competition not only from Macon but also from Savannah and Athens. Atlanta's city council in that year appropriated $3,000 to buy another fifteen acres of land for the society, which was guaranteed the use of the property as long as its fairs took place in the city. The society finally accepted this offer in 1857 and made Atlanta its headquarters until the outbreak of the Civil War,

30. *Dictionary of American Biography*, XIV, 510–11; Fletcher M. Green, *The Role of the Yankee in the Old South* (Athens, 1972), 113–15; Blake McKelvey, *American Urbanization: A Comparative History* (Glenview, Ill., 1973), 46; Atlanta *Constitution*, February 10, 1889; Royce Shingleton, *Richard Peters: Champion of the New South* (Macon, 1985); David R. Goldfield, "Urban-Rural Relations in the Old South: The Example of Virginia," *JUH*, II (1976), 146–68.
31. *Pioneer Citizens' History*, 230–32; Lewis (ed.), *Transactions*, vii, viii; CM, April 5, 10, 1850; Atlanta *Intelligencer* quoted in Augusta *Constitutionalist*, September 18, 1850.

when its activities ceased. By 1860, the society maintained impressive facilities that included "three main buildings, one for ladies' work and fancy articles, another for mechanics and manufactured articles, and the last for fruits, flowers &c." There was also a track for thoroughbred horse racing.[32] The society's success helped to cement Atlanta's trade alliance with the upcountry and emphasized as well the city's growing importance as a market center.

Neither the Georgia Air Line nor the Georgia Western railroad project was as successful as was Atlanta's effort to be the permanent site of the society's fairs. These schemes (eventually completed after the Civil War) were significant, however, because they represented the community's first serious campaign to alleviate freight rate discriminations and also forecast inland rail centers' dominion of the South's urban network.[33]

The Georgia Air Line was originally chartered in 1856 by the state legislature to build a line from Atlanta to Anderson, South Carolina. All its incorporators were Atlanta residents. The leader and the first president of the company was Jonathan Norcross, a native of Orono, Maine, who had settled in Marthasville in 1845 after unsuccessful business ventures in North Carolina and Cuba. Later described by Henry Grady as "the father of Atlanta" and a "hard fighter in everything," Norcross had taken up various occupations, ranging from sawmill operator to Atlanta's mayor, before trying his hand at railroad construction in the late 1850s. The author of numerous pamphlets and articles on railroads for local newspapers, Norcross seized upon the Georgia Air Line as potentially the most important project for Atlanta's economic development.[34]

Norcross and other backers of the railroad presented a number of arguments in favor of its construction. Above all, the Air Line, when connected with other projected railroads through the Carolinas and Virginia, would provide a new route from New York to the southern interior. Steamships from New York would deposit manufactures

32. CM, March 30, 1855, June 10, 1857; Columbus *Enquirer*, June 27, 1857; Athens *Banner*, February 22, 1855; Atlanta *Southern Confederacy*, May 1, 1861; *De Bow's Review*, XXVII (1859), 467–68.

33. Milton S. Heath, *Constructive Liberalism: The Role of the State in Economic Development in Georgia to 1860* (Cambridge, Mass., 1954), 277.

34. Reed, *History of Atlanta*, 106–10; Southern Historical Association, *Memoirs of Georgia* (2 vols.; Atlanta, 1895), I, 879; *Georgia Air Line Rail Road: Charter, Action at Madison Springs, Table of Distances, Engineer's Report, Speeches, Letters &C., Relating to the Same* (Atlanta, 1857); Grady quoted in Atlanta *Constitution*, June 12, 1881.

and dry goods at Norfolk, Virginia, rather than at Charleston or Savannah, and then a direct line of railroads (hence the name "Air Line") would transport these goods to Atlanta. The savings in time and freight costs to merchants in the interior would be enormous. Second, the Air Line route through the Carolinas and Virginia would cross a number of railroads that connected with the grain-growing regions of the South and West. Local merchants happily envisioned the shipments of hogs, grain, corn, and wheat that could come down the Air Line to Atlanta from Tennessee, Virginia, and Ohio without the discriminatory freight rates imposed by the Western & Atlantic. Since the Air Line route was seen as part of a "great national thoroughfare" from New York to New Orleans, Atlanta also had a chance of becoming a distributor of dry goods to the Southwest in competition with New Orleans. The Atlanta & West Point and the Montgomery & West Point were already a portion of the Air Line's natural extension to the Southwest, and local railroad entrepreneurs believed that other links in the chain to New Orleans would be completed shortly. In sum, Atlanta with its strategic location in railroad geography stood to gain more from the construction of the Air Line than did any other city in the southern interior.[35]

The major problem was the Georgia Air Line's projected cost, estimated in 1857 at $1,581,215.26. The rugged, mountainous terrain the road would traverse was less populated and poorer than was the eastern Cotton Belt, which hindered efforts to raise local capital. Stressing the unity of interests between Atlanta and its agricultural hinterland, Norcross and his associates combed the upcountry for investors but had limited success. Since liquid capital was scarce in the region, many subscriptions by individuals and county governments were not in cash but rather real estate or promised labor. A concerted effort by upcountry representatives in the Georgia legislature in 1857 to alleviate some of these financial problems resulted in the submission of a bill granting the railroad state aid for construction costs. After heavy lobbying by the Georgia and the Central of Georgia, which felt threatened by the Air Line, the bill was eventually defeated.[36]

35. *Georgia Air Line Rail Road*, 10–11; Ulrich Bonnell Phillips, *A History of Transportation in the Eastern Cotton Belt to 1860* (1908; rpr. New York, 1968), 322.

36. *Georgia Senate Journal*, 1857–58, pp. 316–17; *Georgia House Journal*, 1857–58, pp. 184–86; Atlanta *Daily Examiner*, August 28, 1857; *Annual Report of the Central of Georgia Railroad and Banking Company for 1858* (Savannah, 1858), 8–9; *Annual Report of the Central of Georgia Railroad and Banking Company for 1857* (Augusta, 1857), 7–8.

Norcross and his company then turned to Atlanta's municipal government as the only other public agency capable of substantial support for the project. In lobbying city hall, Norcross and his colleagues pointed to the financial investments other southern cities had made in railroad construction and stressed that local control of the Georgia Air Line would be necessary to guarantee relief from freight rate discrimination. These arguments apparently convinced Atlanta's city council, which subscribed $300,000 in a series of resolutions between 1857 and 1860. One of these resolutions was overwhelmingly approved—the popular vote was 458 to 98. All taxpayers, whether they voted for or against the Air Line, received stock equivalent in value to the tax they paid. [37]

Before little more than preliminary surveys and rough grading had been accomplished, the sponsors encountered a dangerous adversary in Lemuel P. Grant, who had railroad projects of his own that he believed to be more vital than the Georgia Air Line to Atlanta's future and his own pocketbook. Grant, a native of Frankfort, Maine, had come south in the 1840s to work on the Georgia Railroad as an assistant engineer. In 1844, he began buying extensive tracts of real estate in Atlanta—apparently his only serious interest in the city for several years—and at one time owned more than six hundred acres there. It was a measure of his shrewdness that he was one of the few antebellum southern railroad entrepreneurs to recognize Atlanta's potential for urban growth. Grant was also a member of Fannin-Grant & Co., an Augusta-based railroad construction firm, and that interest at times conflicted with his concern for Atlanta. During the 1830s and 1840s, Fannin-Grant & Co. was one of the most active such firms in the South, building all or parts of the Georgia, the Central of Georgia, the Macon & Western, the Western & Atlantic, and the Atlanta & West Point. [38]

Like many other railroad enthusiasts, Lemuel P. Grant and John T. Grant, the most active partners in Fannin-Grant & Co., turned their attention in the early 1850s to New Orleans' western Cotton Belt

37. Ordinance Book, January 6, 1857, March 5, 1858; CM, May 11, 1860; Atlanta *Daily Intelligencer and Examiner*, January 29, February 9, 1858.

38. See my sketch of John T. Grant for more detailed information on Fannin-Grant & Co. in Kenneth Coleman and Charles Stephen Gurr (eds.), *Dictionary of Georgia Biography* (2 vols.; Athens, 1983), I, 362–64. For information on Lemuel P. Grant, see Reed, *History of Atlanta*, 168–72; Green, *Role of the Yankee in the Old South*, 127–28; Southern Historical Association, *Memoirs of Georgia*, I, 793–95; and W. J. Northern, *Men of Mark in Georgia* (7 vols.; Atlanta, 1912), III, 34–36.

and Mississippi River trade. Beginning in 1853, they became involved in a series of projects to divert that trade to the southern Atlantic seaboard. They first contracted to build the New Orleans, Jackson & Great Northern Railroad and persuaded William Wadley, an able and shrewd railroad manager, to leave his post with the Central of Georgia to become superintendent of the New Orleans line. At the same time, Fannin-Grant & Co. contracted to build the Vicksburg, Shreveport & Texas Railroad and became that road's principal stockholders. The firm also began work on the Southern Railroad in 1852, which was to extend from Vicksburg to the Alabama state line. William Wadley took on the job of superintending the Southern in 1856. To top off these western interests, Fannin-Grant & Co. finally became in 1857 the contractors of the Southern Pacific Railroad, a grandiose scheme to link the Pacific coast with Marshall, Texas. After an initial organization failed, Fannin-Grant took over and Lemuel P. Grant became the Southern Pacific's president in 1858.[39]

There were two routes Lemuel P. Grant saw as possibilities for diverting New Orleans' southwestern trade. One went eastward via Jackson to Atlanta and thence to Charleston and Savannah. Fannin-Grant & Co.'s southwestern railroads would all be links in this lower route. Another possibility was to build a chain of roads from Memphis to Atlanta that was more direct than the existing route of the Western & Atlantic and the Memphis & Charleston. To open up this second possibility, Grant and his associates incorporated in 1854 the Georgia Western Railroad, which was to go from Atlanta to Jacksonville, Alabama. It would thus become the first leg of a new route to Memphis. Although they mainly thought of Mississippi Valley produce in southern Atlantic seaports, Grant and spokesmen for the Georgia Western stressed in letters to local newspapers that better access to that produce might significantly improve Atlanta's commerce. They also noted that the road would tap coal and iron regions in Alabama and thus aid the city's industrial development.[40]

In 1860, after several years' involvement in his southwestern rail-

39. John Hebron Moore, "Railroads of Antebellum Mississippi," *Journal of Mississippi History*, XLI (1979), 74–77; Sarah Wadley, *A Brief Record of the Life of William Wadley* (New York, 1884), 33, 353; Coleman and Gurr (eds.), *Dictionary of Georgia Biography*, I, 363.

40. *Ga. Laws*, 1854, pp. 440–42; *Daily Atlanta Intelligencer*, April 23, 1860; Robert S. Cotterill, "Southern Railroads and Western Trade, 1840–1850," *Mississippi Valley Historical Review*, III (1917), 431.

road schemes, Grant decided that it was time to proceed with the route from Memphis to Atlanta, beginning with the Georgia Western. This decision brought him into conflict with the Georgia Air Line's supporters in Atlanta, who were still anxiously scouring the city for investors. It appeared to Grant and Richard Peters, who joined Grant's campaign for the Georgia Western, that Atlanta could not afford both railroad projects. They therefore began to vilify the Air Line. Grant charged in the summer of 1860 that the line was undercapitalized and had so altered its path, "running hither and thither after driblets of conditional subscriptions," that it could no longer accurately be called an "Air Line."[41]

In a lengthy letter published in a local newspaper, E. M. Seago, an Atlanta merchant and a director of the Georgia Air Line, responded heatedly to Grant's attack. Grant, once a friend of the Air Line, had written a technical paper on its moneymaking potential. Only when his other railroad projects had become too ambitious had Grant turned against the Air Line. The Georgia Air Line, Seago added, was much better capitalized than some of Grant's western railroads; 95 percent of the capital invested in the Southern Pacific consisted of land only.[42]

The quarrel resulted in a premature end for both projects. In April, 1860, Atlanta's city council decided to subscribe $300,000 to the Georgia Western. After hesitating for a few months, a council committee chaired by Richard Peters announced it would revoke the city's subscription to the Georgia Air Line—the company allegedly violated "the rules and conditions on which subscriptions were supposed to be made." After legal battles between the city council and the Air Line's directors, the project was abandoned. But the Georgia Western did not fare much better. Air Line partisans pointed to Grant's ideas about the Georgia Western's potential benefits to southern Atlantic seaports, rivals of Atlanta, and the Georgia Railroad's $250,000 subscription. This counterattack seriously hampered Grant and Peters in raising money for their railroad. They were unable to recover before the coming of the Civil War, which temporarily put an end to the venture.[43]

41. Phillips, *Transportation*, 366–69; Grant quoted in *Daily Atlanta Intelligencer*, June 23, 1860.

42. *Daily Atlanta Intelligencer*, July 17, 1860.

43. CM, May 21, 1860; *Daily Atlanta Intelligencer*, June 26, July 12, September 6, 1860; Clarke (comp), *Acts of Incorporation and Ordinances*, Appendix, 2–3 (quotation); Phillips, *Transportation*, 370–72.

Although belying later rhetoric about the perennial "unity" of Atlanta's economic leaders, the bitter conflict between partisans of the Georgia Air Line and the Georgia Western was only incidental to the failure of both projects. Both ventures were actually far beyond the means of local capitalists and government during the antebellum period. Even when both railroads were eventually completed after the Civil War as Atlanta became the preeminent inland rail center envisioned by entrepreneurs such as Jonathan Norcross, most of the capital for their construction came from nonlocal sources.

Failure as well as success was thus the outcome of city-building activities in antebellum Atlanta. Even botched ventures, such as the Air Line and the Georgia Western, served, however, to buttress Atlanta's image as a "daring," progressive, and new city. Working hard to extend their trade into the upcountry and scorning the values of the lowland South, Atlantans were confident that their visions would soon be fulfilled.

A "Business Government"

Atlanta's municipal government not only helped finance railroads and other entrepreneurial schemes but also approved "routine" expenditures and services with business' needs given priority. Neither partisan nor class divisions among Atlanta's antebellum mayors and councilmen caused any deviation from a philosophy of municipal government in which the city's economic welfare was paramount. The Know-Nothing party and its successor, the American party, waged a fierce war with the Democrats for control of city hall in the 1850s. Roughly 16 percent of Atlanta's mayors and councilmen were manual laborers during the antebellum period and the remainder were white-collar workers. But in decisions on "physical" welfare services (such as fire protection and street maintenance) or social welfare services (such as public relief or education), Democrats, Know-Nothings, merchants, and mechanics never disagreed that the primary concern should be the city's economic development. This concept prevailed in many other towns and cities in the antebellum South and West.[44]

44. Richard C. Wade, *The Urban Frontier: Pioneer Life in Early Pittsburgh, Cincinnati, Lexington, Louisville, and St. Louis* (Chicago, 1964), 77–100; Goldfield, "Pursuing the American Urban Dream," in Brownell and Goldfield (eds.), *The City in Southern History*, 67–83. For more information on partisan affairs and the occupational composition of Atlanta's municipal government, see my "Elites and Municipal Politics and Government in Atlanta, 1847–

In Atlanta, streets were the commercial arteries of the city, so the greatest municipal expenditures (besides special bond issues for railroads and other entrepreneurial ventures) involved street improvements and public bridges. From 1851 through 1860, the city council spent $93,658.31 (35 percent of its total expenditures for the entire period) on streets and bridges alone. To this considerable sum should be added the substantial but incalculable value of free labor obtained through the ordinances requiring all white males between the ages of sixteen and forty-five to perform "road duty" or pay a street tax set at $5.00 in 1852. The city contracted frequently with private citizens to open or repair streets, and these individuals were excused from the street tax in proportion to their service.[45]

Since the unimpaired movement of traffic in certain areas was vital for commerce, the city council's street appropriations were used mostly where the mercantile houses were located. A special focus of municipal attention was streets that led to railroad freight depots— drays had to be able to move back and forth with ease from there to the mercantile houses. These were the only paved streets in town. In 1848, Whitehall Street was first paved with oak planking, which rotted all too rapidly. An 1857 city ordinance required that Whitehall and the "business portions" of Alabama, Marietta, Decatur, and Peachtree streets be paved with "smooth flagstone or burnt brick." Other forms of street upkeep were also confined to the city's business center. An 1851 ordinance required all citizens to lay sidewalks on their property adjacent to any public street within the incorporated limits, but enforcement was lax outside the commercial center. An oak plank sidewalk graced two blocks of Whitehall Street; nowhere else in the city was there such a luxury.[46]

In 1855, Atlanta's commercial district received another blessing from the city council. In return for all the revenues earned from the operation of the gas works for fifty years, William Helme of Philadelphia contracted in March, 1855, to build a coal gas works capable of generating twenty thousand cubic feet of gas daily. Helme raised $30,000 in private subscriptions, to which the city added $20,000 in

1890," in Orville Vernon Burton and Robert C. McMath, Jr. (eds.), *Toward a New South? Studies in Post–Civil War Southern Communities* (Westport, Conn., 1982), 39, 44–45, 56–57.

45. Ordinance Book, April 26, 1852. Statistics on municipal expenditures from city treasurer's reports, presented in January for previous calendar year, in CM.

46. CM, July 30, 1848, May 30, 1857; Clarke (comp.), *Acts of Incorporation and Ordinances*, 87–89.

bonds, and this sum was enough to "brilliantly illuminate the city on December 25, 1855." Since Helme laid only three miles of pipe, there was gas lighting for only the city's business center.[47]

Fire protection was another municipal service that was similarly restricted. After the fire that consumed Winship's foundry and several mercantile houses, the city council passed an ordinance that defined "fire limits" for the first time (Maps 2 and 3). Within these limits, wood buildings and roofs covered with wood shingles were forbidden. Atlanta's four volunteer fire companies (which received funds from the city for equipment and for maintaining their fire halls) were responsible for putting out fires only within that same area. Since the only "fire cisterns" capable of supplying large quantities of water were also all located on streets specified in the ordinance, the volunteers could not have worked outside the city's center, no matter what the ordinance said.[48]

Table 2 and Maps 2 and 3 offer some clues about why protest over these municipal policies was extremely rare during the antebellum period. The maps and the table reveal that working-class (manual laborers) and white-collar white males lived in distinct areas as early as 1860, when Atlanta's corporate limits were formed—the circle had a radius of only one mile.[49] Working-class whites tended to live near the railroad tracks, where the various foundries, railroad machine shops, and the Atlanta Rolling Mill were located. Also, as Table 2 shows, working-class whites were less likely than were white-collar whites to live within the first half-mile circle from the city's center.[50]

47. CM, March 23, 30, 1855; Haygood, "Sketch of Atlanta," 13.
48. CM, March 10, 1851, December 7, 1857; Clarke (comp.), *Acts of Incorporation and Ordinances*, 50.
49. There was actually a 400-by-500-yard protuberance on Atlanta's southwest side, near where the Macon & Western entered the city, that is not represented on the maps. Although this area became part of the city in 1854, it is not depicted on any extant map of Atlanta (see N. J. Hammond [cod.], *Revised Code of the City of Atlanta* [Atlanta, 1866], 5). So that 1854 extension is not included on Maps 2 and 3. However, one individual residence, which appears to be outside the city limits on Map 2, was within that area and is thus recorded within the city limits in Table 2. Some individual residences listed in the table as outside the city limits could not be plotted on the maps because of the scale used.
50. Because of Atlanta's small area during this period, I saw no reason to break down these occupational categories further. Historians and geographers have studied racial but have virtually ignored occupational residential patterns in nineteenth-century southern cities. For the only systematic studies, see John P. Radford, "Race, residence, and ideology: Charleston, South Carolina in the mid-nineteenth century," *Journal of Historical Geography*, II (1976), 329–46; and Radford, "Testing the model of the pre-industrial city: the case of ante-bellum Charleston, South Carolina," *Transactions of the Institute of British Geographers*, IV (1979), 392–410. The only study dealing with occupational residential patterns in the postbellum

MAP 2   Residential Distribution of Sample of White-Collar White Males in
Atlanta, 1859–1860

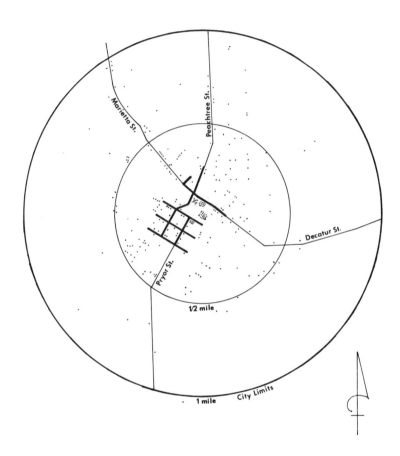

Marietta St.

Peachtree St.

Decatur St.

Pryor St.

1/2 mile

1 mile   City Limits

▬▬▬▬ Fire limits (1857)
One dot represents one white-collar white male

MAP 3   Residential Distribution of Sample of White Working-Class Males in
Atlanta, 1859–1860

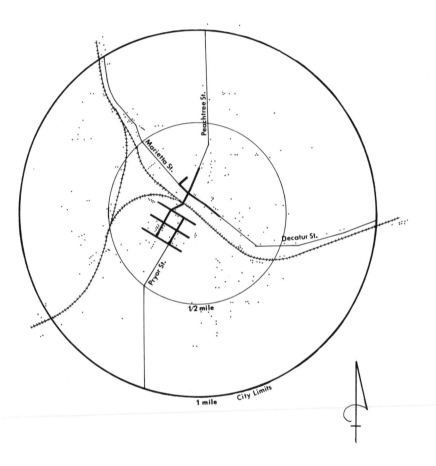

Peachtree St.

Marietta St.

Decatur St.

Pryor St.

1/2 mile

City Limits

1 mile

Fire limits (1857)
One dot represents one white working-class male

TABLE 2
Residential Distribution of White-Collar and Working-Class Whites
in Atlanta, 1859–1860

DISTANCE FROM CENTER OF CITY	% WHITE COLLAR	% WORKING CLASS
0–½ mile	79.3	50.7
½–1 mile	19.6	41.5
Outside city limits	1.1	7.7
Total[a]	100.0	99.9
N	271	272

SOURCE: Sample data drawn from Williams' Atlanta City Directory for 1859–1860 (Atlanta, 1860).
[a]Percentages do not sum to 100 because of rounding error.

This tendency toward a mixture of occupational classes in all areas of the city but with the lower-status occupational groups more likely to reside nearer the perimeter was typical of mid-nineteenth-century American cities and has been called the "commercial city residential pattern."[51]

But, as far as access to municipal services such as fire protection, paved streets, and street illumination is concerned, the real message of the maps is that white-collar workers had negligible advantages over working-class whites. The area of well-serviced streets was so restricted—only within the fire limits were streets lighted and paved—that a merchant and a mechanic were almost equally likely to live in a house on an unpaved, dark street that was beyond the fire companies' range. The fire limits had more to do with the location of business buildings than with the residential distribution of occupational groups. And the city kept the principal business avenues in good repair.

Social welfare services also were administered with Atlanta's economic development in mind. Scarce tax dollars could not be used to subsidize to any significant extent public relief, education, and public

urban South is my "Politics, Municipal Services, and the Working Class in Atlanta, 1865 to 1890," GHQ, LXVI (1982), 467–91.
　51.　Ian Davey and Michael Doucet, "The Social Geography of a Commercial City, ca. 1853," in Michael B. Katz, The People of Hamilton, Canada West: Family and Class in a Mid-Nineteenth-Century City (Cambridge, Mass., 1976), 319–42; John Swauger, "Pittsburgh's Residential Pattern in 1815," Annals of the Association of American Geographers, LXVIII (1978), 265–77.

health, which local businessmen considered only marginally related to the city's economic growth. In 1859 the city council spent, for example, $18,796.41 on streets and bridges but only $1,791.00 on the poor. In the same year, the Inferior Court of Fulton County offered to furnish lodging and firewood in the Alms House if the city would provide food and clothing. "Believing that the city [could] make no better arrangement," the council reluctantly accepted that proposal and thereafter tried to shirk its responsibilities. In 1860, only twenty-four paupers were sheltered at the Alms House. Voluntary associations could not relieve the council's parsimony. The Ladies Union Benevolent Society, the only charitable organization in antebellum Atlanta, raised only $233.55 in 1858, the first year of its existence.[52]

Educating children who were unable to attend the private academies in Atlanta was another public burden shunned by the council. In 1852 local banker E. W. Holland generously leased without charge a schoolhouse for five years to the city, on the condition that tuition would be waived for needy children in accordance with state law. In 1857 the Holland Free School was able, however, to enroll only forty students—more than a thousand children had to be refused admission for want of space.[53]

In 1858, A. N. Wilson, proprietor of a classical academy, organized a movement for a free public school system, modeled on that of Providence, Rhode Island, which he had studied and admired. Unfortunately, the movement encountered strong opposition from several members of the city council and from wealthy citizens. Eventually, municipal authorities diverted the public school movement into the founding of the Atlanta Female College by appropriating $4,000 in city bonds for that purpose in 1859. The college was an adornment for the city, but it was no substitute for public schools. "Why are there so many dirty, mischievous urchines [sic] running at large . . . in our streets?" asked an Atlanta newspaper correspondent who signed himself "Poor Man" in 1860. "It is because we have no free schools in the proper acceptance of the term."[54]

Public health was a municipal service even more neglected than

52. CM, February 18, 1859 (quotation), January 13, 1860; *Daily Atlanta Intelligencer*, April 8, 1859; Eighth Census of Social Statistics for Fulton County, Georgia, 1880, in William R. Perkins Library, Duke University, Durham.

53. CM, November 26, December 3, 18, 1852, March 26, 1858; Meta Barker, "Atlanta's First Public School," *AHB*, I (1930), 31–39.

54. Reed, *History of Atlanta*, 318; *Daily Atlanta Intelligencer*, June 13, 1860.

was education. The Board of Health, which consisted of nine members, was first appointed by the city council in 1848 and reappointed annually until the Civil War. The board's authority extended only to notifying the council of "public nuisances," such as stopped-up gutters, stagnant water, and privies and stockyards needing "a free use of lime and charcoal." But the council could (and often did) ignore the situation. The board lacked the means and the council the will to establish a public hospital or clinic. The council refused to pay the salary of a physician, James Morris, who offered his services to the poor at a reasonable rate in 1858. In that year the Atlanta Medical College at last provided the poor a dispensary and the city agreed to fund only the cost of medicines.[55]

Throughout the antebellum period, Atlanta's city government had thus unabashedly adhered to "business first" in the scope and orientation of municipal services. A rather cavalier attitude toward public welfare prevailed in council chambers. If the lack of protest is any indication of the attitudes of the community as a whole, most Atlantans concurred with this philosophy of municipal government.

Identity Through Enterprise

By 1860, Atlantans had organized a number of entrepreneurial projects supported by public and private resources to encourage the commercial and, to a lesser extent, the industrial growth of their city. They had also administered the "routine" functions of municipal government with the same goals in mind. Although the actual consequences are not measurable, it is clear that by the end of the antebellum period the attempts of local city builders to establish banks and build railroads had helped to develop an image of Atlanta as "progressive." This image was undoubtedly held more firmly by local boosters than by outsiders, but it was not confined to Atlanta. One visitor from a neighboring town in the upcountry in 1859 referred, for example, to the city as "the very personification and embodiment of Progress itself."[56]

Other visitors had similar opinions about the city and recognized

55. CM, July 3, 1848, August 27, 1858; Jethro Manning (comp.), *Code of the City of Atlanta* (Atlanta, 1863), 45–57; Minute Book of the Atlanta Medical College (1855–1873), December 18, 1858, in Emory University Medical School Library, Atlanta; F. Phinizy Calhoun, "The Founding and Early History of the Atlanta Medical College, 1854–1865," *GHQ*, IX (1925), 42.
56. Marietta *Patriot* quoted by *Weekly Atlanta Intelligencer*, February 3, 1859.

an important corollary to Atlanta's "progressive" image. As one somewhat hostile observer said, antebellum Atlanta was a "fast town" with a people characterized by a "go-ahead spirit regardless of consequence," because it was not a part of the older South but rather a bastion of "upcountry enterprise."[57] Let us now turn to an exploration of the social bases of this urban imagery and antebellum Atlanta's entrepreneurial spirit.

57. Milledgeville *Southern Statesman* quoted in *Daily Atlanta Intelligencer*, June 25, 1860.

3

ORIGINS OF THE ATLANTA SPIRIT
Social Structure and Leadership

To understand the spirit of Atlanta since her foundation—the spirit of pluck and push—one must take into consideration the peculiar character of the pioneers who made the country that made Atlanta. In doing so one cannot but be struck by the analogy of her history with that of the average western town. . . . In those days it was a common saying among the restless landless class that "A poor man has no chance in Georgia." The arable lands of the commonwealth were largely in the hands of the large slaveholders. . . . For years before the opening of the Cherokee reservation was accomplished the eyes of thousands of worthy men with little capital but the will and muscle to do, were turned toward the forbidden land. . . . Since these men largely laid the foundation of Atlanta's prosperity, it is well to know something about them.

—Thomas H. Martin, *Atlanta and Its Builders* (1902)

The population of the city is remarkable for its activity and enterprise. Most of the inhabitants came here for the purpose of bettering their fortunes by engaging actively in some kind of business, and this presents the anomaly of having very few aged persons in it; and our people show their democratic impulses by each allowing his neighbor to attend to his own business, and our ladies are allowed to attend to their own domestic and household affairs without being ruled out of respectable society.

—Green B. Haygood, "Sketch of Atlanta" (1860)

Historians and other observers identified a number of distinctive characteristics of nineteenth-century Atlanta's population, leaders, and social values that supposedly explained why the city became an urban embodiment of New South enterprise. A few of these observations pertained only to postbellum Atlanta, but many had to do with the city before the war.

A reasonably complete inventory of theories concerning the social characteristics of antebellum Atlanta's population and leaders includes several sometimes contradictory claims. The residents' geographic origins were frequently cited as the source of the city's vigor and progressive aspects. Others believed that the social values prevalent there allowed young men with little money and unheralded family backgrounds a chance to compete for personal advancement. This ideology of democratic opportunity, it was asserted, was a natural consequence of the city's upcountry location, distant from the plantation districts in which an entrenched landholding aristocracy allegedly stifled the initiative of energetic but relatively impoverished entrepreneurs. Members of antebellum Atlanta's entrepreneurial class, it was further asserted, entered the race for wealth with the "fire and enthusiasm" of "those who turned . . . their faces towards the California wilds," knowing that personal success was readily obtained.[1]

These somewhat romantic theories offer a convenient framework for analyzing antebellum Atlanta's social structure and leadership. Thus we can explore the social distinctions between Atlanta and its lowland urban competitors, the extent to which opportunity and democratic values prevailed in the city, and the characteristics of its population and leaders.

Population Benchmarks

There are two contradictory theories concerning the geographic origins of Atlanta's population. One argues that northerners were especially welcome because their presence encouraged an energetic atmosphere. "A noticeable sprinkling of Northern capital and Northern settlers soon appeared [in Atlanta] and began to add a bustle not characteristic of Southern cities," wrote historian E. Merton

1. *Pioneer Citizens' History of Atlanta, 1833–1902* (Atlanta, 1902), 224.

Coulter. A corollary further specified that natives of New England and Pennsylvania constituted the majority of the pre–Civil War northern population. The other theory attributes Atlanta's entrepreneurial spirit to an influx of settlers born in the mountainous districts of Virginia, the Carolinas, and east Tennessee. "The population of northeast Georgia [including Atlanta] is largely made up of immigrants . . . from the mountain regions of the states lying eastward," wrote Thomas H. Martin. These men were "for the most part of that matchless strain known as Scotch-Irish, possessing those rugged traits of independence, industriousness, and honesty."[2]

The census manuscripts, however, do not support the basic assumptions of either theory. Despite the claim in 1847 that "nearly half the population are northern men," the census returns for 1850 indicate that less than 4 percent of the city's free population were northern born while 92 percent were native southerners (see Table 3 in Appendix A). Pennsylvania and New England did contribute the majority of Atlanta's northern population, but one-third came from New York.[3]

Foreigners were actually slightly more numerous than were northerners in antebellum Atlanta. Four percent of the city's free population in 1850 were foreign born, mostly of Irish or German extraction. But in other southern cities such as Memphis, Charleston, Savannah, and Mobile in 1860, foreigners provided between 20 and almost 50 percent of the free populations. The dearth of foreigners in Atlanta was probably due to the city's remoteness from the two principal routes of foreign immigration into the antebellum South, one along the eastern seaboard and the other via the Ohio and Mississippi rivers.[4]

While the antebellum census returns do not provide sufficient information for answering questions about ethnic ancestry, they do

2. E. Merton Coulter, *A Short History of Georgia* (Chapel Hill, 1960), 260–61; Wallace P. Reed, *History of Atlanta, Georgia* (Syracuse, 1889), 31; Thomas H. Martin, *Atlanta and Its Builders: A Comprehensive History of the Gate City of the South* (2 vols.; Atlanta, 1902), I, 12–13.

3. William Stafford Irvine (ed.), "Diary and Letters of William N. White, a Citizen of Atlanta Written 1847," *AHB*, III (1937), 39–40.

4. Randall M. Miller, "Immigrants in the Old South," *Immigration History Newsletter*, X (1978), 9; Miller, "The Enemy Within: Some Effects of Foreign Immigrants on Antebellum Southern Cities," *Southern Studies*, XXIV (1985), 32–33; Clement Eaton, *The Growth of Southern Civilization, 1790–1860* (New York, 1961), 250; Herbert Weaver, "Foreigners in Antebellum Towns of the Lower South," *JSH*, XIII (1947), 62–67; Richard H. Haunton, "Law and Order in Savannah, 1850–1860," *GHQ*, LVI (1972), 19.

show that the majority of Atlanta's population were born in Georgia rather than states farther north and east in the region. Of the city's free population in 1850, some 68 percent were natives of Georgia and 22 percent had come from Virginia, the Carolinas, and Tennessee. Samples from the 1860 census follow the same trend. The typical free antebellum Atlantan was thus a native Georgian. Since the northern portion of the state was opened to white settlement at about the same time that Atlanta was founded, the vast majority of these Georgia natives could not have been born in its mountainous districts. Theories attributing the city's character to the numerical preponderance of either Yankees or industrious migrants from the southern highlands cannot be substantiated.

On the other hand, assertions about the relative absence of Negroes and planters can easily be verified. Only 20 percent of the city's population in 1850 and ten years later were black. The vast majority of these Afro-Americans were slaves; the city had only nineteen free Negroes in 1850 and twenty-five in 1860. The black populations of cities in the coastal regions were proportionately much larger on the eve of the Civil War.[5] Planters were also scarce in antebellum Atlanta. There was not a single planter in Atlanta in 1850, and only 0.3 percent of the city's working population ten years later were so listed in the census manuscripts. Those who gave their occupation as farmers (which conceivably could have included some planters) were also few in number—only 3 percent in 1850 and 1.4 percent in 1860 were so classified. Planters and farmers were much more visible in Charleston, Richmond, and Savannah and also in small towns such as Lexington, Kentucky, and Athens, Georgia. While the city's upcountry location readily accounts for the absence of planters, the scarcity of farmers (compared, for example, to the population of Athens) is more surprising. The cause was probably the strength of the city's commercial economy and industries, which supported a wide variety of urban occupations.[6]

5. The black populations of Savannah, Mobile, and Charleston ranged between 29 percent and 42 percent. Computed from Richard C. Wade, *Slavery in the Cities: The South, 1820–1860* (New York, 1964), 326–27.

6. Constance McLaughlin Green, *American Cities in the Growth of the Nation* (New York, 1965), 24–26, 67–72; Bernard Mayo, "Lexington: Frontier Metropolis," in Eric F. Goldman (ed.), *Historiography and Urbanization: Essays in American History in Honor of W. Stull Holt* (1941; rpr. Port Washington, N.Y., 1968), 21–25; Emory M. Thomas, *The Confederate State of Richmond* (Austin, 1971), 21, 30–31; Frank Huffman, "Town and Country in the South, 1850–1860: A Comparison of Urban and Rural Social Structures," *South Atlantic Quarterly*, LXXVI (1977), 366–81.

Statistics on slave ownership further confirm the lack of large slaveholders in antebellum Atlanta. This trend was to be expected, since roughly one hundred miles south of Atlanta was the dividing line across the state between the prevalence of small and large (twenty or more slaves) slaveholding units. According to the slave schedules, 139 persons owned slaves in Atlanta in 1850, but only 7 men owned 10 or more slaves. Hotelkeepers Joseph Thompson and James Loyd were the only Atlantans in that year who possessed 20 or more slaves, the traditional minimum required for planter status. Neither Thompson nor Loyd owned plantations; most of their slaves were servants in their hotels. By 1860, the number of slaveholders in the city had risen to 373; of this number, 44 individuals owned 10 or more slaves and 15 possessed 20 or more. The only legitimate planter among those 44 was Benjamin Yancey, brother of the Alabama planter and politician William Lowndes Yancey. He held only 12 slaves in Atlanta, but he owned many more on plantations outside the city.[7] It appears that few antebellum Atlantans were able to build a life of ease on slave labor.

It is difficult to be precise about the impact of planters and slaves on Atlanta's social life and values. Despite the relatively small slave population, Atlanta did share many southern cities' concerns about and conflicts over slavery. Fear of insurrection haunted many Atlantans and was the basis for a lengthy list of municipal ordinances prohibiting slaves from "walking with a cane stick," "smoking a pipe in any street," or leaving their masters' homes after sunset. At times such fears seemed justified. In 1851, Henry Long, "a notorious runaway slave" from Richmond who had been captured and taken to Atlanta, was arrested and tried in the Mayor's Court for "making insurrectionary speeches." In 1854, slaves Leitha and Eunice Allen were arrested for arson, tried, convicted, and severely whipped.[8]

Like many other antebellum southern cities, Atlanta was also plagued with difficulties in regulating the hiring-out system, which

7. Enoch Marvin Banks, *The Economics of Land Tenure in Georgia* (New York, 1906), 23. Statistics based on federal slave schedules for De Kalb and Fulton counties, Georgia, 1850 and 1860 (microfilm copies in GDAH, Atlanta). See sketch of Benjamin Cudworth Yancey in B. C. Yancey Papers, William R. Perkins Library, Duke University, Durham.

8. Atlanta Ordinance Book, April 21, 1851, in AHS; CM, July 29, 1851, February 24, 1854; *Daily Atlanta Intelligencer* quoted in Augusta *Chronicle and Sentinel*, August 2, 1851. Henry Long was the first runaway slave returned to the South in accordance with the provisions of the Fugitive Slave Law of 1850. For more details of his life, see Augusta *Chronicle and Sentinel*, May 13, 1853.

permitted slaves to live away from their masters' residences and supervision. The system was legalized in Atlanta in 1853 and then prohibited in 1855. The practice nevertheless continued after 1855 and was a source of tension, especially among the city's white working-class, which resented the competition of slave labor. Ephraim Ponder, who owned sixty-five slaves on a plantation just outside Atlanta, compounded the problem by frequently sending his skilled male slaves—nearly all of whom were blacksmiths, carpenters, or mechanics—into the city for work. [9]

Although Atlanta was not entirely immune to the actions of planters and the problems of controlling slaves in an urban environment, such influences had a minimal impact on the city's social life and values. One local historian was correct in asserting that "the planter with his semi-feudal ideas and mode of life had little to do with laying the foundation of . . . [Atlanta]." Planters were rarely even seen in upcountry towns such as Atlanta, which lacked the cultural amenities of southern coastal cities and did not satisfy aristocratic criteria for urban resorts. A pioneer Atlantan got to the heart of what many believed was the resulting social atmosphere: "There are not 100 Negroes in this place, and white men black their own shoes, as independently as in the north." Other Atlantans boasted later that their town was "wonderfully New Yorkish in its notions." [10]

One element of antebellum Atlanta's population that promoters did not boast about and that local historians later tended to ignore was its disreputable characters. Like the upcountry villages described in Augustus Baldwin Longstreet's *Georgia Scenes* (1835), Atlanta had many "adventurers" (one local historian's euphemism) among its first settlers. One migrant to the city put matters more succinctly when he suggested that Atlanta's earliest settlers were mostly "whiskey dealers." In a similar vein, a judge summed up young Atlanta as "a typical crossroads village of the old Southern civilization—a place for stump-speeches, barbecues, and fisticuffs." And he added, "A rougher village I never saw." [11]

9. Ordinance Book, May 20, 1853, July 21, 1855; CM, March 5, 1858, January 4, 1861; Henry Ossian Flipper, *The Colored Cadet at West Point* (New York, 1878), 7–9; Fred Siegel, "Artisans and Immigrants in the Politics of Late Antebellum Georgia," *Civil War History*, XXVII (1981), 228.

10. Martin, *Atlanta and Its Builders*, I, 17; Irvine (ed.), "Diary and Letters of William N. White," 40–41; *Daily Atlanta Intelligencer*, June 4, 1860.

11. Atlanta *Constitution*, October 4, 1886, June 10, 1888; E. Y. Clarke, *Illustrated History of Atlanta* (2nd ed., 1879; rpr. Atlanta, 1971), 35–39.

Those who wished to build a city where this "crossroads village" stood had much trouble in controlling its disorderly inhabitants. The first government established in 1843—the town commissioners of Marthasville—failed miserably at raising taxes and enforcing the laws. When the commissioners attempted in 1844 to levy a tax for opening new streets, the rowdier citizens arrogantly invited them "to hitch up their mules and plow them themselves." The renaming and rechartering in 1847 did not noticeably improve the situation. A substantial proportion of the population still refused to pay taxes or to perform road duty and also ignored the new government's ordinances against prostitution, cockfighting, discharging firearms on city streets, and similar activities. Atlanta's city council, whose members were all qualified to serve as justices of the peace, spent much of their time in the late 1840s and early 1850s trying cases involving such offenses.[12]

Most of Atlanta's prostitutes, gamblers, cockfighters, and murderers congregated in Snake Nation and Murrell's Row (named after the notorious Tennessee slave thief and murderer, John A. Murrell). Snake Nation was on the city's southwestern side along Peters Street and the Macon & Western Railroad, on whose tracks murder victims were sometimes placed. Murrell's Row was located on Decatur Street not far from the Union Depot. Its denizens enjoyed rolling hogsheads containing live hogs down hilly streets in the area late at night. Officers of the law usually avoided both neighborhoods at all times.[13]

When Jonathan Norcross, a stern exponent of New England Puritanism, was elected mayor in 1851, he decided that it was time for a showdown between Atlanta's undesirables and its respectable citizens. Norcross made clear early in his administration that he intended to collect taxes and enforce the ordinances against cockfighting and prostitution. Objecting to Norcross' policies, the rougher types, who had organized a political entity appropriately called the "Rowdy party," attempted to frighten the mayor into resigning. They put a loaded cannon in front of his dry goods store. Undaunted, Norcross started a volunteer police force and refused to back down. And some of the town's criminal element emigrated. Two years later, during the mayoralty of John F. Mims, most of the gamblers and toughs were

12. Quotation from *Pioneer Citizens' History*, 19–20; Reed, *History of Atlanta*, 60–61; N. J. Hammond (cod.), *Revised Code of the City of Atlanta* (Atlanta, 1866), 7.
13. Eugene M. Mitchell, "Queer Place Names in Old Atlanta," *AHB*, I (1931), 27–28; *Pioneer Citizens' History*, 181.

driven from Snake Nation and Murrell's Row and their dilapidated shanties torn down. Settlers later recalled this period as a "turning point in Atlanta's history," when it was decided once and for all that the town would become more than a rendezvous for assorted roughnecks and criminals.[14]

Thus the general population did not conform to some ideas developed by local historians and publicists but unfortunately did conform to others that such observers preferred to ignore. The gaps between rhetoric and reality concerning geographic origins and other matters are relatively unimportant, however. More accurate and significant as a description of antebellum Atlanta's social characteristics was the absence of planters and slaves, which was to be expected in an upcountry city. Further, those characteristics undoubtedly had an impact on the city's economic development. Merchants in pre–Civil War Charleston may well have preferred to invest their surplus capital in land and slaves rather than in manufactories because of the status accorded planters, but this cultural ideal was foreign to antebellum Atlanta. The city's businessmen invested most of their profits in their own mercantile houses or industries.[15] An urban promotive creed prevailed.

Indexes of Opportunity

Whether the upcountry way of life translated into opportunity for young men of diverse geographic origins and social backgrounds is a question that can be approached by means of several quantitative indicators. These indexes of opportunity include wealth holding, occupational rank and mobility, and persistence. Urban and social historians have analyzed all these topics in various ways to test the "egalitarian myth" of opportunity in early-nineteenth-century America. Some of the evidence from these studies can be used to place the Atlanta data into comparative perspective.

The distribution of wealth in antebellum Atlanta does not support booster rhetoric about opportunity. The 1850 federal census reveals that wealth was in the hands of a few. In that year only 0.5 percent of the white population eighteen years or older held about 43 percent of

14. Atlanta *Constitution*, July 29, 1888; Franklin M. Garrett, *Atlanta and Environs: A Chronicle of Its People and Events* (3 vols.; New York, 1954), I, 329–31.
15. This statement is based on the R. G. Dun & Co. credit reports for Fulton County, Ga., XIII–XIV, in Baker Library, Harvard University, Cambridge, Mass.

all the real estate reported to the census takers, and 12.6 percent of the white adult population owned *all* the real estate. According to the 1850 census, 80 percent of white adult males in Atlanta did not own any real estate.

Although the census takers in Atlanta in 1860 did such a poor job of recording personal and real wealth that the data for those topics are worthless, an 1858 city tax digest is available to show that ownership of property later was not democratized. According to that digest, 42 individuals held 32 percent of all the real estate and 28 percent of all the taxable property. According to the tax assessors, 55 percent of all the real estate in the city in 1858 belonged to 128 individuals who represented about 1.6 percent of the population.[16]

A popular statistical measure, the Gini Index of Inequality, can be used to compare the distribution of wealth in Atlanta in 1850 with that of other antebellum cities. Zero indicates perfect equality; one, perfect inequality. The figures are .599 for all property owners and a very high .914 for all males eighteen years of age or older (see Table 4 in Appendix A). The Gini score for Jacksonville, Illinois, in 1850 is a little higher, about the same for Charleston in 1860, and lower for Richmond, Milwaukee, Chicago, and the entire United States in 1850. The most interesting feature of these comparisons is that wealth was poorly distributed even in presumably more democratic frontier towns and new cities such as Atlanta, Jacksonville, Chicago, and Milwaukee.[17]

Given the small number of property holders listed in the 1850 census of Atlanta, further statistical analysis of wealth holding is of limited value. The mean wealth of northern-born property holders was higher than that of southern natives, and the mean wealth of foreign-born owners was about the same. This finding probably says less, however, about opportunity for foreigners and Yankees in antebellum Atlanta than it does about the likelihood that immigrants

16. In addition to amusements and the professions, Atlanta taxed real estate, slave property, merchandise, money and solvent debts, capital invested in stocks of various types, and household property.

17. Lee Soltow, *Wealthholding in Wisconsin Since 1850* (Milwaukee , 1971), 9–10; Soltow, *Men and Wealth in the United States, 1850–1870* (New Haven, 1975), 181; Craig Buettinger, "Economic Inequality in Early Chicago, 1849–1850," *Journal of Social History*, XI (1978), 104; Michael P. Johnson, "Wealth and Class in Charleston in 1860," in Walter J. Fraser, Jr., and Winfred B. Moore, Jr. (eds.), *From the Old South to the New: Essays on the Transitional South* (Westport, Conn., 1981), 68; Clyde A. Haulman, "Changes in Wealth Holding in Richmond, Virginia, 1860–1870," *JUH*, XIII (1986), 69; Don Harrison Doyle, *The Social Order of a Frontier Community: Jacksonville, Illinois, 1825–1870* (Urbana, 1978), 263.

from distant places would bring capital with them. Statistical analysis also does not support the controversial thesis of one cliometrician that age variation (the older, according to the theory, the wealthier) largely accounted for inequality of wealth in mid-nineteenth-century America. Occupational rank was the better predictor in Atlanta.[18]

Ranking occupations in categories verifies the claim of local boosters that the "mechanical element prevailed in the city."[19] In 1850 and in 1860, skilled workers represented, respectively, 51 percent and 44 percent of the city's working population, greater percentages in both years than any other occupational category (see Table 6 in Appendix A). Those percentages are high for two reasons. First, there was great demand for their services—the railroad machine shops, foundries, construction firms (which were very active because new housing was a constant need in a rapidly growing city), and related industries all needed such workers. Second, the unskilled labor grouping is artificially small since slaves are not included, thus increasing the percentages of all other occupational categories.[20]

If the vertical occupational categories are used as a scorecard to measure success with high-white-collar and unskilled jobs assumed to be most and least desirable, the resulting data show that southerners, northerners, and foreigners did equally well in Atlanta.[21] The city was open in the sense that job discrimination against outsiders was not evident. In both 1850 and 1860, birthplace was with one exception irrelevant to occupational rank. The exception was that foreign-born citizens in 1850 tended to have higher occupational

18. For the five occupational categories in Table 6 and the age categories in Table 17 in Appendix A, analysis of variance for the value of real estate of property holders in the 1850 census yielded eta² values of, respectively, .092 and .041 (eta² for occupation was significant at the .006 level and not significant for age). A lively debate on the distribution of wealth in antebellum America can be found in the following articles in *Social Science History*: Robert E. Gallman, "Professor Pessen on the 'Egalitarian Myth,' " II (1978), 194–209; Gallman, "The Egalitarian Myth Once Again," V (1981), 223–34; Gallman, "Professor Blumin on Age and Inequality," VI (1982), 381–84; Edward Pessen, "On a Recent Cliometric Attempt to Resurrect the Myth of Antebellum Egalitarianism: Cliometrics and Surmise to the Rescue," VI (1982), 111–28; and Stuart M. Blumin, "Age and Inequality in Antebellum America: The Case of Kingston, New York," VI (1982), 369–79.

19. Green B. Haygood, "Sketch of Atlanta," in *Williams' Atlanta City Directory for 1859–1860* (Atlanta, 1860), 14.

20. On slaves and occupational structures, see Ira Berlin and Herbert G. Gutman, "Natives and Immigrants, Free Men and Slaves: Urban Workingmen in the Antebellum American South," *American Historical Review*, LXXXVIII (1983), 1181–82.

21. This "scorecard" assumption seems justifiable for Atlanta in 1850, since the mean wealth of the five occupational categories used in this study decreased as workers moved down the occupational ladder.

TABLE 3
Vertical Occupational Distribution
of Natives and Foreigners in Atlanta, 1850

	NATIVE	FOREIGNER
High white collar	14.8%	40.0%
Low white collar	23.6	20.0
Skilled	52.8	26.7
Semi-skilled	2.8	2.2
Unskilled	6.0	11.1
Total	100.0	100.0
N	432	45

SOURCE: Manuscripts of the federal population schedules for De Kalb County, 1850.

NOTE: Although the sample analyzed in this table is
identical with that categorized in Table 6 in Appendix
A, N is smaller here. Sometimes the census taker did
not record birthplaces, and those cases had to be discarded from the analysis.

$\chi^2 = 22.460$ with 4 degrees of freedom. Significance $=$
.000

Gamma $= -.311$

ranks did than southern or nonsouthern natives. About 38 percent of
the native population had white-collar jobs in 1850, and 60 percent of
the foreign-born population did (Table 3). This occupational structure was unusual—a study of six antebellum southern cities has
revealed that immigrants were concentrated in the unskilled-labor
categories.[22]

Some studies have indicated that immigrants enjoyed greater occupational mobility in small American cities during the nineteenth
century. But foreign-born citizens' attaining relatively high occupational rankings does not necessarily prove that job opportunities in
Atlanta in 1850 were better for immigrants than for natives.[23] Antebellum Atlanta's occupational patterns more likely reflect the selectivity of the foreign immigration that came to cities in the antebellum

22. Berlin and Gutman, "Natives and Immigrants," 1178, 1183–86; Miller, "The Enemy
Within," 30–41.
23. Joan Underhill Hannon, "City Size and Ethnic Discrimination: Michigan Agricultural Implements and Iron Working Industries, 1890," *JEH*, XLII (1982), 825–45; Gordon
W. Kirk and Carolyn T. Kirk, "The Immigrant, Economic Opportunity, and Type of Settlement in Nineteenth Century America," *ibid.*, XXXVIII (1978), 226–34.

South that were literally off the beaten track. Foreigners who arrived in Atlanta early on presumably had better job skills than did natives. In any case, however, by 1860, there were no significant differences between the occupational rankings of natives and foreigners.

The occupational mobility data, which deal with a very small segment of Atlanta's work force, cannot be used to distinguish between natives and foreigners. Rates were determined only for the sample of white household heads who persisted in Atlanta from 1850 to 1860 (Table 7 in Appendix A).[24] Because these individuals (virtually all of whom were married men with an average age of thirty-seven years) were presumably more successful than were other groups such as single young men, their mobility rates should have been relatively high.

Their rates were not, however, very impressive. About 69 percent of the household heads remained in the same occupational category in 1850 and 1860; some 19 percent improved their ranking and 12 percent declined. The most noticeable improvement was among skilled workers—21 percent of those sampled in 1850 had white-collar jobs ten years later. Many craftsmen moved into proprietorships, such as family-owned grocery stores. While there was small net upward mobility for all occupational ranks in Atlanta during the 1850s, the rates during the same decade for Houston, Poughkeepsie, and Jacksonville, Illinois, were actually higher and were not restricted to household heads. This further undermines booster propaganda about exceptional opportunities for personal advancement in antebellum Atlanta.[25]

One last quantitative indicator—persistence rates—can be used to measure success and opportunity. Persistence is a plausible criterion for judging how successful settlers in Atlanta were, since many studies of nineteenth-century cities have shown that those who prospered tended to remain while those who did not tended to leave. Contrary to the assertions of some settlers, antebellum Atlantans were a little more likely to depart from than stay in the city. Only 45 percent of white male household heads in Atlanta in 1850 were still there a

24. Because the number in the persistence sample was so small, the findings concerning occupational mobility are not statistically significant and should be regarded as tentative.
25. Susan Jackson, "Movin' On: Mobility Through Houston in the 1850s," *Southwestern Historical Quarterly*, LXXXI (1978), 270–72; Clyde Griffen and Sally Griffen, *Natives and Newcomers: The Ordering of Opportunity in Mid-Nineteenth-Century Poughkeepsie* (Cambridge, Mass., 1977), 60–61; Doyle, *Social Order of a Frontier Community*, 262.

decade later (Table 9 in Appendix A). Persistence rates of household heads in five other cities during the same decade ranged between 15 and 53 percent.[26] It seems fair to conclude that prospects for economic advancement were reasonably but not exceptionally attractive to migrants to Atlanta.

Determining the characteristics of those who left and those who stayed offers a way to explore more fully the nature of success and failure in antebellum Atlanta. It is possible that middle-aged or young household heads, for example, were more likely than others to remain in the city. The statistical procedure employed to investigate these possibilities was Multiple Classification Analysis (MCA), which can measure separately the importance of various factors such as age and occupational rank and also their cumulative value in determining the outcome of a dependent variable (in this case, persistence).[27]

Table 4 displays the results of a typical MCA performed on Atlanta household heads. Age, occupational rank, property category, household size, and number of children all seemed to have little impact on persistence.[28] Together, these variables accounted for only 3.5 percent of the differences between those who remained and those who departed.[29] A middle-aged, propertied merchant was thus not much more likely than a young, penniless mechanic to stay in the city. These findings may seem surprising, but recent works on persistence in other nineteenth-century American cities have found that occupational rank and even the ownership of property were not as powerful predictors of persistence as has been argued in older studies.[30]

The results were similar when other variables such as birthplace were plugged into the analysis. In view of the emphasis that E. Merton Coulter, Green B. Haygood, and other historians and ante-

26. For the most recent summary, see Table 2 in Robert G. Barrows, "'Hurryin' Hoosiers and the American Pattern: Geographic Mobility in Indianapolis and Urban North America," *SSH*, V (1981), 203–204.

27. MCA and analysis of variance and covariance are explained in Norman H. Nie *et al.*, *SPSS: Statistical Package for the Social Sciences* (2nd ed.; New York, 1975), 398–433.

28. This statement is based on the low value of the betas for each of the independent variables. MCA in *SPSS* does not generate standardized betas for covariates. I am indebted to Michael Biderman of the University of Tennessee, Chattanooga, for giving me a formula to obtain them.

29. This statement is based on the fact that R^2 equals .035.

30. Michael B. Katz, Michael J. Doucet, and Mark Stern, *The Social Organization of Early American Capitalism* (Cambridge, Mass., 1982), 118–20; Howard P. Chudacoff, "Success and Security: The Meaning of Social Mobility in America," *Reviews in American History*, X (1982), 101–12.

TABLE 4

Persistence of White Male Household Heads in Atlanta,
1850–1860 (Grand Mean = .45)

FACTORS	ADJUSTED DEVIATION	N
Age		
Under 30 years	−.08	78
30–49 years	+.04	159
50 or more years	+.01	31
Property category		
No property	+.02	167
Property holder	−.03	101
Number of children		
None	−.02	54
1–4 children	+.04	161
5 or more children	−.11	53
Occupational rank		
High	+.08	48
Middle	+.00	194
Low	−.12	26

Factor	Eta/Beta
Age	.10/.10
Property category	.02/.04
Number of children	.11/.12
Occupational rank	.12/.10
Covariate	Beta
Household size	.007[a]
R^2 = .035	

SOURCE: Sample data drawn from federal census manuscripts for De Kalb and Fulton counties, 1850, 1860.

NOTE: The grand mean represents the percentage of household heads who persisted. The deviations are from the grand mean. A plus sign indicates a tendency to be more and a minus sign a tendency to be less persistent.

[a]Significant at .05 level.

bellum boosters placed upon youth and birthplace, it is especially interesting that neither variable separated those who left from those who stayed in Atlanta. The one exception was the slight tendency for male southern household heads under thirty years of age to remain in the city.[31] Coulter, however, had argued that Yankees were more

31. This was discovered because of a significant interaction between age and birthplace as independent variables. When independent variables interact, MCA is invalid. For this reason, birthplace could not be included with the variables analyzed in Table 4.

successful in Atlanta than they might have been in other southern cities less hospitable to migrants from outside the region. Persistence patterns, it should be emphasized, do not imply that northerners were less likely than any other nativity group to persist. The conclusion to be drawn from the data is rather that they were no more likely than were household heads from elsewhere in the country with similar or dissimilar ages, occupations, and various other characteristics to find success in antebellum Atlanta.

Quantitative analysis of persistence, occupational rank and mobility, and wealth holding yields several conclusions. Most obviously, the evidence indicates that the structure of opportunity in antebellum Atlanta closely resembled that of most mid-nineteenth-century American cities. In several measurable areas, there were great gaps between democratic rhetoric and reality in Atlanta, as was true of the urban landscape all across the country at this time. Of course, a rapidly growing city such as Atlanta may have acquired an image as a place of great opportunity that even actual experience could not dislodge—outsiders as well as those who decided to settle in the city would hold onto it. These findings, however, apply to antebellum Atlanta's general population or relatively large segments of it and not necessarily to more restricted groups such as the city's economic leadership.

Emergence of Leadership

In Atlanta's economic elite, northern capitalists or men with planter antecedents might well have been overrepresented. Or, as several local historians maintained, young men of small means had the "grit and determination" to seek wealth and economic power.[32] Investigating these and other similar theories can teach us more about antebellum Atlanta's business leaders and how they acquired money and economic power. To identify an elite, several criteria were used that measured wealth and involvement in economic institutions and business associations. Appropriately for a city whose economy was primarily commercial, nearly half of those selected as leaders were merchants, and the others were in six different occupational categories (see Table 12 in Appendix A).[33]

32. Atlanta *Constitution*, August 15, 1880.
33. The occupations summarized in Table 12 in Appendix A are those that individuals had when they were selected as members of the elite. Many economic leaders had several occupations during their careers. Three men are included who were in the city before the war but not fully qualified as economic leaders until 1862.

Only 32 percent of the economic leaders were born in southern states north and east of Georgia, and only 16 percent were known to be of Scotch, Irish, or Scotch-Irish descent, which contradicts ideas about the impact of these population strains (see Table 25 in Appendix A). On the other hand, a much higher percentage of the leaders than of the general population was born outside the South and especially in the northern states, which supports the assertions of Coulter and others about the "noticeable sprinkling" of northern men in antebellum Atlanta. Yankees accounted for 32 percent, foreigners 13 percent, and southerners only 52 percent of the elite (see Table 15 in Appendix A). However, foreigners and Yankees were also overrepresented in the antebellum economic elites of more aristocratic southern cities such as Mobile and Charleston. On the other hand, Mobile's nonsouthern born leaders frequently did not settle permanently in the city. [34]

Another interesting finding is that the majority of Atlanta's economic leaders were born in places where the population was less than twenty-five hundred. As far as can be determined, only 3 percent of the elite from the United States had hometowns with more than twenty-five hundred inhabitants, and none were born in towns with populations of ten thousand or more (see Table 16 in Appendix A). The economic leadership was thus even more of rural than nonsouthern origins. The "hayseed" upbringing confirms a theme in biographical sketches by local historians: many of these men were country boys who left plows and family farms to become clerks in mercantile houses as they began to seek wealth and economic power.

Despite their rural background, the majority of the elite did not have planter antecedents or substantial investments in slavery. As far as can be determined, only one was a planter before coming to Atlanta and only one had a father who was a planter (see Table 13 in Appendix A). Only nine members of the elite owned ten or more slaves. James Loyd and Joseph Thompson had business concerns that made ownership of slaves highly desirable; the same was true of two other large slaveholders, foundry owner Joseph Winship and brick

34. Frederic Cople Jaher, *The Urban Establishment: Upper Strata in Boston, New York, Charleston, Chicago, and Los Angeles* (Urbana, 1982), 338; Harriet E. Amos, "'Birds of Passage' in a Cotton Port: Northerners and Foreigners Among the Urban Leaders of Mobile, 1820–1860," in Orville Vernon Burton and Robert C. McMath, Jr. (eds.), *Class, Conflict and Consensus: Antebellum Southern Community Studies* (Westport, Conn., 1982), 232–62.

manufacturer Julius A. Hayden. This was in sharp contrast to other southern cities such as Charleston, where a majority of the elite were planters or large slaveholders.[35] This trend supports the interpretation offered by Thomas H. Martin and others that Atlanta's origins and antebellum progress were not connected with the plantation aristocracy. The city's business leaders were reared in the country, but they rejected the plantation ideal and sought urban occupations.

Other assertions by promoters such as local lawyer Green B. Haygood about youth and persistence also accurately described the elite if not the general population of antebellum Atlanta. More than half of the economic leaders were less than forty years of age by the time they qualified as members of the elite (see Table 17 in Appendix A). The mean age of the elite was only forty years, and that of white male household heads in the city was thirty-seven years. The decennial persistence rate of the elite was twice that of household heads during the 1850s. About 90 percent of the leaders resided in Atlanta for at least a decade, and almost 82 percent lived there twenty or more years (see Tables 9 and 18 in Appendix A). These figures equal or better the persistence rates of elites in other nineteenth-century American cities.[36]

Except for the rural upbringing, the antebellum elite described thus far does not fit the self-made-men thesis of its origins. Some of the career histories preserved in R. G. Dun & Co. credit reports provide evidence for exploring this thesis more directly. These reports lend credence to the idea that it was indeed possible in a rapidly growing new city for entrepreneurs with "small means" (a common phrase in the reports for capital of $1,000 or less) to launch businesses that earned impressive profits within ten years if not sooner.

This career pattern fitted members of the elite such as Jonathan Norcross, John R. Wallace, and James J. Lynch. Norcross, a dry goods merchant, succeeded in converting his "small means" in 1847 into real estate worth $20,000 in 1857—although his career had ups and downs because of a tendency to speculate in cotton. John R. Wallace, president of the only locally based fire insurance company, left Shelbyville, Tennessee, to become Norcross' clerk in 1852. He opened his own dry goods store the following year and soon was about

35. Jaher, *The Urban Establishment*, 326–27.
36. Richard S. Alcorn, "Leadership and Stability in Mid-Nineteenth Century America," *Journal of American History*, LXI (1974), 685–702; David R. Goldfield, *Urban Growth in the Age of Sectionalism: Virginia, 1847–1861* (Baton Rouge, 1977), 41.

as wealthy as his former boss. By 1857 his firm received the standard salute from the Dun & Co. credit reporter, who advised suppliers to "sell them all you can."[37]

James J. Lynch was one of five brothers born in county Meath, Ireland, all of whom began their working lives in the United States during the 1840s as laborers on the Georgia Railroad. They all left the railroad and settled in Atlanta in 1847. Four of them launched mercantile ventures, and the fifth opened a quarry. With his brother John as his junior partner, James founded a family grocery. The capital of the firm in 1849 was deemed "small" by the Dun & Co. credit reporter, and the brothers were described as having "no business capacity, but eternally industrious . . . misers." Five years later, the report was more favorable, the firm estimated to be worth $8,000 and James and John praised as "industrious men, never speculate." By 1858, James had expanded his business to sell both retail and wholesale groceries and his personal wealth exceeded $33,000. Although he "lost heavily" during the Civil War, his fortune at the time of his retirement in 1874 was estimated at $100,000, an impressive sum for a former laborer.[38]

How typical were the careers of Jonathan Norcross, John R. Wallace, and James J. Lynch? Several bodies of evidence are available to shed light on this question. They include data on the initial wealth of the economic leaders at about the time of their arrival in Atlanta, their occupational histories, and their kinship and support networks.

The data concerning "initial capital" contradict the rags-to-riches theme in local historians' biographical sketches of many of these men. Initial capital, defined as the estimated wealth of individuals within two years of their arrival in Atlanta, was not lacking for a majority of the elite. Only 13 percent began with less than $1,000. About 65 percent started their businesses in Atlanta with $10,000 or more (see Table 19 in Appendix A).

These statistics do not deny the possibility and significance of the careers of men such as Lynch and Wallace, but they suggest the rarity of such success stories. More typical was William McNaught, the first president of the Atlanta Chamber of Commerce. McNaught and his partner James Ormond came to Atlanta from Gadsden, Florida,

37. Dun & Co. Credit Reports, Fulton County, XIII.
38. Garrett, *Atlanta*, I, 255–56; Carol Louise Hagglund, "Irish Immigrants in Atlanta, 1850–1896" (M.A. thesis, Emory University, 1968), 54–56, 58–59; Dun & Co. Credit Reports, Fulton County, XIII.

TABLE 5

*Interval Time by Initial Wealth Category
of Economic Leaders, 1847–1864*

INITIAL WEALTH CATEGORY	INTERVAL TIME (YEARS)	N
Under $1,000	9.0	4
$1,000–4,999	8.4	5
$5,000–9,999	6.5	2
$10,000–24,999	4.5	8
$25,000–49,999	1.8	4
$50,000–99,999	4.5	6
$100,000 or more	1.5	2
Eta = .618[a]		
Eta^2 = .382		

SOURCES: See Appendix B.
[a]Significant at the .05 level.

in 1858 to open a wholesale and retail dry goods store. According to a Dun & Co. credit reporter, the personal wealth of each man then was between $50,000 and $100,000, and within a year they had the "finest storehouse in the state." Besides McNaught and Ormond, six other merchants, manufacturers, and bankers who eventually qualified as members of the elite also began their careers in the city with at least $50,000 capital, and two other men started with nearly that much.[39]

Table 5 gives some indication of how important initial capital was in gaining access to antebellum Atlanta's economic elite. "Interval time" in the table is the number of years between individuals' arrival in the city and their selection as members of the elite. The year of selection is not exact in every case—some men probably deserved the designation sooner. Nevertheless, there is a clear relationship between initial capital and interval time. Those who had the least initial capital took nine years to qualify as economic leaders; those who began with $10,000 to $24,499 took only half that time. Moreover, the amount of initial capital in nearly four out of ten cases determined the time lag between a man's arrival and his entry into the elite.[40] These findings contradict the image of frontier democracy

39. Dun & Co. Credit Reports, Fulton County, XIII.
40. Eta^2 equals .382 in Table 5. This means that 38 percent of the differences in interval time can be accounted for by the amount of initial capital.

that Atlanta embodied as a new city in the southern upcountry. Many of the future economic leaders were surprisingly well heeled on their first day in town. Although money was not the only factor governing access to the elite, it clearly was very important.

The occupational histories of the elite reveal that, to whatever extent their careers manifested significant mobility, most of these men had already risen before they came to Atlanta—74 percent had high-white-collar jobs in the city (see Table 14 in Appendix A). Most of the rest started as clerks, bookkeepers, or family grocers. The one member of the elite who began as a manual laborer was Moses W. Formwalt, a tinsmith. He became Atlanta's first mayor in 1848 and later opened a tin and copperware shop. Formwalt was one of only five men in the city who owned as much as $20,000 in real estate, according to the 1850 federal census. He was murdered in 1852.[41]

The occupational beginnings of the city's economic leaders seem to show that some of these men experienced significant mobility (see Table 13 in Appendix A). There is no evidence that any of them began their working lives in Atlanta. The record of what they did for a living before they arrived in the city is incomplete, but about 26 percent of them are known to have begun as manual laborers. Two of the seven were apprentices and were placed in the unskilled-labor category, which may be too low a rank. A few others who reported that they started out as laborers on family farms were not included in manual-labor categories, because it was assumed that such work did not actually represent the beginning of a career.

The occupational mobility of the seven who started as manual laborers was less substantial than first impressions indicate. Richard Peters and Lemuel P. Grant began as "rodmen" for northern railroad companies, but they were under the tutelage of J. Edgar Thomson with the clear expectation that they would rise much higher. The two apprentices were Sidney Root and Joseph Winship. Root, the son of a Massachusetts farmer, at the age of fourteen was apprenticed to a Vermont jeweler. Four years later, he left New England to become a clerk for William A. Rawson (himself later a member of Atlanta's postbellum elite), a wealthy merchant in Lumpkin County, Georgia. Also the son of a Massachusetts farmer, Winship was an apprentice to a boot- and shoemaker and later moved with his employer to Monticello, Georgia. He was an apprentice for only two years and then

41. Garrett, *Atlanta*, I, 263, 347.

was in quick succession a merchant, tanner, manufacturer of cotton gins, and finally foundry proprietor in various Georgia locations. Given their subsequent occupational histories, it seems doubtful that the apprenticeship of either Root or Winship was seriously intended as training for a lifetime of skilled labor. Only Formwalt, Norcross, and James J. Lynch appear to have had genuine working-class origins.[42]

One other aspect of these men's early careers is their prior residences (see Tables 21 and 22 in Appendix A). All the elite whose places of prior residence are known had lived elsewhere in the South and most of them in Georgia. The majority had lived in villages or towns that had fewer than twenty-five hundred inhabitants; only 3 percent had resided in towns with populations greater than Atlanta's on the eve of the Civil War. What these statistics show is that the economic leaders were an adventurous lot. They began their careers in small southern villages and, after a seasoning experience in various towns, moved to the "big city" to make their fortunes.

Family relationships may have been an important means for Atlanta's well-traveled business leaders to accumulate wealth and gain access to the elite. About 42 percent were related by blood or marriage or both (see Table 23 in Appendix A). Studies of other nineteenth-century American cities indicate that this percentage of marital and familial bonds within their elites was not uncommon. What is difficult to determine is to what extent marriage represented a consolidation of social and economic power and to what extent it was a means of entering the elite. The career of hardware merchant Edward E. Rawson is a good example of this problem. He was a Vermont native who moved from Stewart County, Georgia, to Atlanta in 1857. He married the sister of Sidney Root and was reported by a Dun & Co. representative to have "made some money by selling goods in the country & some by marriage." How much of Rawson's wealth came from his business and how much from his wife's dowry is not recorded. Similar questions exist about other members of the elite.[43]

Specific information on how familial ties and business connections aided the careers of antebellum Atlanta's economic leaders is

42. For sketches of Winship and Root, see Reed, History of Atlanta, 134–37; and Martin, Atlanta and Its Builders, II, 709–10.

43. John N. Ingham, The Iron Barons: A Social Analysis of an American Urban Elite, 1874–1965 (Westport, Conn., 1978), 127–36; Dun & Co. Credit Reports, Fulton County, XIII.

available in only a few cases (see Table 24 in Appendix A). Dun & Co. credit reports indicate that six men had family resources (none of the families were in the local elite) to draw upon. Three others were helped financially by business associates, and one of these patrons was a member of the Atlanta elite. None of those aided by family or business associates started out at the bottom of the economic ladder in Atlanta. There is no evidence that anyone gave financial assistance to any of the four men who began their businesses in the city with less than $1,000. The most likely candidates for self-made men were probably to be found among these four individuals.

Although only a few of antebellum Atlanta's elite were classic examples of self-made men, we should not minimize the factual basis for the widespread belief of residents before and after the Civil War that energetic men could attain wealth. Urban growth opened up real possibilities for a few men. The careers of men such as James J. Lynch were genuinely dramatic. In another more stagnant urban economy during the nineteenth century, not a single laborer rose beyond small farmer status.[44] Moreover, those who invested in real estate (and almost all the antebellum elite did) in a rapidly growing nineteenth-century city such as Atlanta achieved impressive results. At the peak of their careers, 39 percent of the economic leaders had personal fortunes of $100,000 or more (see Table 20 in Appendix A).

A final message implicit in this analysis is how much those leaders had in common. Most had rural or small-town backgrounds and similar work experiences before coming to Atlanta; most were relatively young and overwhelmingly Protestant in their religious affiliations.[45] A good many of them were related by blood or marriage. Most also lived and worked within a few blocks of each other and doubtless saw and met each other almost daily.[46]

What these common experiences and shared points of reference did was breed a sense of unity as Atlanta's economic leaders went about the task of city building in the antebellum South. These were the men who incorporated pioneer banks, organized agricultural fairs, promoted railroad projects, and launched a multitude of other

44. Stephan Thernstrom, *Poverty and Progress: Social Mobility in a Nineteenth Century City* (Cambridge, Mass., 1964).
45. Of those economic leaders whose religious affiliation could be ascertained, about 94 percent were Protestant.
46. All but three lived within the first half-mile circle from the center of the city. About two-thirds lived north and the remainder south of the conjunction of the Western & Atlantic and Georgia railroads.

entrepreneurial ventures to further their city's growth. While they occasionally disagreed about the priority of specific projects, they had enough in common so that their investments of time and money never deviated from the overriding purpose of augmenting both their personal fortunes and Atlanta's economic growth, which were inextricably linked.

New South in the Old?

Like Atlanta's upcountry setting and economic orientation, its antebellum business leadership and society were disassociated from the plantation South. Planters and slaves were uncommon, and the city's cultural values did not correspond with those of the landholding aristocracy. These features of social life, along with the Yankee presence in the economic elite, helped Atlanta evolve as a city that had more in common with the New South than with the Old.

The most striking premonition of the New South was the quick emergence of a vigorous upper-middle-class leadership that showed little interest in the culture of the plantation South. Many of these men resumed their careers and urban promotive efforts in Atlanta after 1865. But the experience of the Civil War changed their concepts of city building. It also tested their determination to survive.

4

THE CIVIL WAR IN ATLANTA
Toward the New South

We are happy to see that in all parts of the South, manufactures are springing up as if by magic. . . . Let the manufacturers extend their limits and facilities . . . until every hamlet shall resound with the clack of the water-wheel or the puff of the steam engine.

—Atlanta *Southern Confederacy* (1861)

The war did us vast evil. It has done good too. It has vastly stimulated Southern ingenuity and industries.

—Atlanta *Constitution* (1871)

Although it has held little interest for students of American urban or southern urban history, the Civil War era has long fascinated historians of Atlanta. They have tended to dwell upon the military events, particularly the awesome devastation that followed General William Tecumseh Sherman's siege. But even this dramatic event is treated in most local histories as insignificant in the city's development. For those writers and most nineteenth-century observers, the city's growth after 1865 made the wartime siege and destruction useful chiefly as a promotional device, a trial by fire from which "New South" Atlanta rose like its official postbellum symbol, the phoenix.[1]

This view, however, ignores the impact of the war on residents of Atlanta and many other southern cities and its connection with the New South urban-industrial creed. Since most scholars have been mesmerized by the military history of the period, only a few have noticed the "revolutionary" effect of the Civil War on southern urbanization and industrialization.[2]

If Atlanta's wartime experience was typical, Emory Thomas and a few others are correct in arguing that the Civil War played a major role in changing southern attitudes toward urbanization. Above all, the war caused southerners to preach and practice the "industrial gospel." Although there was an industrial movement in the antebellum South, wartime demands for ordnance and domestic manufactures greatly intensified southern interest in building factories.[3] Much more frequently than had been the case, these factories were

1. See E. Y. Clarke, *Illustrated History of Atlanta* (2nd ed., 1879; rpr. Atlanta, 1971); Wallace P. Reed, *History of Atlanta, Georgia* (Syracuse, 1889); Thomas H. Martin, *Atlanta and Its Builders: A Comprehensive History of the Gate City of the South* (2 vols.; Atlanta, 1902); and Franklin M. Garrett, *Atlanta and Environs: A Chronicle of Its People and Events* (3 vols.; New York, 1954). See also Samuel Carter III, *The Siege of Atlanta, 1864* (New York, 1973).

2. Emory M. Thomas, *The Confederacy as a Revolutionary Experience* (Englewood Cliffs, N.J., 1971), 87–99; Raimondo Luraghi, "The Civil War and Modernization of American Society: Social Structure and Industrial Revolution in the Old South before and during the War," *Civil War History*, XVII (1972), 244–46; J. W. Mallet, "Work of the Ordnance Bureau of the War Department of the Confederate States, 1861–1865," *Southern Historical Society Papers*, XXXVII (1909), 11; Lester J. Cappon, "Government and Private Industry in the Southern Confederacy," in *Humanistic Studies in Honor of John Calvin Metcalf* (Charlottesville, 1941), 153–54, 168–69; E. Merton Coulter, *The Confederate States of America, 1861–1865* (Baton Rouge, 1950), 199–218.

3. Herbert Collins, "The Southern Industrial Gospel before 1860," *JSH*, XII (1946), 386–402.

located in cities, which linked industrialization to urbanization and gave generals such as Sherman the incentive to destroy southern cities. Confederate military strategy also forced southerners to recognize the importance of cities as distribution centers. That recognition plus the Confederate industrial drive was an important antecedent to the urban-industrial ideology of the New South period.[4] Finally, the Civil War introduced the region to rapid urbanization on a scale it had never experienced before. The Confederacy was a nation of "instant cities." Atlanta's population during the war grew from less than 10,000 in 1860 to almost 22,000 while Mobile nearly doubled and Richmond more than doubled its 1860 population. Cities and towns throughout the Confederacy enjoyed equal or greater growth rates.[5] The residents of these cities received an excellent though unexpected education in the social and economic problems that accompanied rapid urban growth.

Disruption of the Traditional Economy

Although one historian has argued that southern cities became ringleaders of the secession movement to free themselves from economic vassalage to New York, the majority of voters in Atlanta and the region's urban centers opposed secession efforts before Lincoln's election, knowing that separation from the Union would cripple their commercial economies. James P. Hambleton, the fiery editor of a newspaper founded in Atlanta in 1859 named the *Southern Confederacy*, discovered the depth of local merchants' opposition to disunion in early 1860 when he attempted to persuade them to accept the idea of "non-intercourse" with their northern counterparts. In February of that year, Hambleton's "southron" followers attended the first meeting of a mercantile association (Atlanta's first chamber of commerce) to demand that local merchants do business only with southerners. The association rejected the demand in favor of an organized protest against freight rate discrimination. According to the

4. One scholar has argued that the sectionalist controversies of the 1840s and 1850s inspired southerners to strive for urban growth. See David R. Goldfield, *Urban Growth in the Age of Sectionalism: Virginia, 1847–1861* (Baton Rouge, 1977).
5. V. T. Barnwell, *Atlanta City Directory, 1867* (Atlanta, 1867), 24; Thomas, *The Confederacy*, 93–95.

association's charter, its main purpose would be the protection of Atlanta merchants "not only as Southern men but as merchants."[6]

The presidential election results of 1860 in Atlanta were also displeasing to secession advocates. Like their counterparts in Norfolk, Augusta, Richmond, New Orleans, Vicksburg, and other southern cities, Atlanta voters in 1860 cast their ballots for the Unionist candidates (Stephen A. Douglas and John Bell) rather than the secessionist, John C. Breckinridge.[7] Bell received 1,070 votes in Atlanta; Douglas, 345; and Breckinridge, 835. Douglas' total would probably have been higher had he not visited Atlanta shortly before the election and run into a barrage of tough questions from Breckinridge supporters concerning states' rights and secession.[8]

Lincoln's victory in 1860 brought an eventual shift in public opinion in Atlanta toward secession, but there was still resistance to disunion, especially in the city's mercantile community. One Atlanta merchant and a native of England, Samuel P. Richards, wrote in his diary about a month after the election that "the secessionists are chiefly professional men and young squirts who have little or nothing to lose." Another merchant, S. B. Robson, who wrote a financial column for a local newspaper, gloomily commented that "the South . . . has taken a bold step without stopping to inquire as to what pecuniary results may follow." The campaign to elect delegates from Fulton County to a state convention to decide whether Georgia would remain in the Union resulted in the virtual landslide election of three secessionists on January 3, 1861. Although enthusiastic demonstrations, including the burning of Lincoln several times in effigy, took place in Atlanta fifteen days later when the convention voted in

6. Arthur Schlesinger, *Paths to the Present* (1949; rpr. Boston, 1964), 209–10; Henry Thompson Malone, "Atlanta Journalism during the Confederacy," GHQ, XXXVII (1953), 212; *Daily Atlanta Intelligencer*, February 1, 21, 24 (quotation), March 8, 1860.

7. Ollinger Crenshaw, "Urban and Rural Voting in the Election of 1860," in Eric F. Goldman (ed.), *Historiography and Urbanization: Essays in American History in Honor of W. Stull Holt* (1941; rpr. Port Washington, N.Y., 1968), 43–66; Gerald M. Capers, *Occupied City: New Orleans under the Federals, 1862–1865* (Lexington, Ky., 1965), 20–21; Peter Walker, *Vicksburg* (Chapel Hill, 1960), 24. A vote for Breckinridge in 1860 was not necessarily indicative of secessionist sympathies. Nevertheless, a study of the secession movement in Georgia found support for Breckinridge to be "the best single indicator of the vote for secession"(see Michael P. Johnson, *Toward a Patriarchal Republic: The Secession of Georgia* [Baton Rouge, 1977], 71–78, 199–204).

8. *Daily Atlanta Intelligencer*, October 30, November 7, 8, 1860.

favor of secession, several of the city's most prominent merchants and economic leaders privately deplored those actions.[9]

Georgia's withdrawal from the Union created danger for many of the city's merchants and business leaders who had come from the North. About two weeks after the bombardment of Fort Sumter, a "citizens committee" threatened to visit all northern merchants in Atlanta to request that they fly Confederate flags over their stores. Refusal would mean they would "be accommodated to a coat of tar and feathers." Hostility against northerners was chiefly responsible for the organization in 1861 of the Committee of Public Safety and in 1862 of the Vigilance Committee. Like similar organizations in other Confederate cities, these terrorist groups assumed responsibility for ferreting out spies and men of "unsound principles." Northerners who tried to remain neutral also quickly found themselves in trouble. The Confederate draft laws made neutrality difficult. Military manpower demands were heavy in Fulton County, which furnished the Confederacy with 2,660 soldiers during the war.[10]

As pressures mounted on the Confederacy those civilians of known Unionist sympathies in Atlanta, whether born in the North or elsewhere, were often severely punished for their views. James L. Dunning, foundry proprietor and a native of Litchfield, Connecticut, refused to manufacture ordnance for the Confederacy, was arrested, and imprisoned for most of the war. A merchant of Irish ancestry, Michael Myers, was suspected of disloyalty because he declined in 1862 to accept Confederate money in his store. He too was arrested and, during interrogation by Confederate soldiers, was hit over the head "with the butt of a rifle and killed."[11]

Unionists in Atlanta had no choice but to go underground. There were no formal Union Clubs, such as the Peace and Constitution

9. Samuel P. Richards Diary, December 8, 1860, in AHS; Robson quoted in *Daily Atlanta Intelligencer*, December 17, 1860; Ralph Benjamin Singer, Jr., "Confederate Atlanta" (Ph.D. dissertation, University of Georgia, 1973), 42–63; *Daily Atlanta Intelligencer*, January 3, 1861.

10. Atlanta *Southern Confederacy*, April 24, 1861; *Daily Atlanta Intelligencer*, May 9, 1862; Coulter, *Confederate States*, 87–88; T. Conn Bryan, *Confederate Georgia* (Athens, 1953), 138; Walter G. Cooper, *Official History of Fulton County* (Atlanta, 1934), 890–900; Robert Gibbons, "Life at the Crossroads of the Confederacy, 1861–1865," *AHJ*, XXIII (1979), 23, 31–33; Atlanta *Southern Confederacy*, September 5, 1861.

11. Testimony of James L. Dunning, in Claim of Thomas G. Healey, Southern Claims Division, Record Group 217, NA; Reed, *History of Atlanta*, 187–88; Atlanta *Southern Confederacy*, April 17, 1862; Testimony of Cornelius P. Cassin, in Claim of Thomas G. Healey, Southern Claims Division, RG 217 (quotation).

Society that flourished nearby in Alabama. Several Atlanta Unionists—among them, Dunning, banker Alfred Austell, brick manufacturer Thomas G. Healey, shoemaker Christian Kontz, and merchants John Silvey, Michael Lynch, Peter Lynch, William T. Farnsworth, and A. S. Stone—did meet regularly and secretly. Connecticut native William Markham, who was forced to sell his interest in the Atlanta Rolling Mill to the Confederate government at the outset of the war, was the leader of this group. Unionists in Atlanta also contributed secretly in whatever way they could. There was a Confederate prison for Federal soldiers in Atlanta, which contained more than three hundred men in 1864 in an enclosed field of approximately half an acre without fire and shelter. Atlanta Unionists occasionally managed to smuggle blankets and food to these prisoners.[12]

As the war intensified, Atlanta merchants of southern origins and sympathies found it almost as difficult as Unionists to run their businesses. Military invasion and Confederate government policies gradually strangled the trade of Atlanta and other Confederate cities. Their commercial economies were virtually moribund by 1863.

The decision to break away from the Union soon caused serious shortages of northern manufactures in Atlanta, especially in the once thriving wholesale and retail dry goods trade. Most merchants either directly or indirectly purchased their supplies from New York. The war never entirely eliminated smuggling of northern goods into Atlanta and other Confederate cities—such items arrived via Memphis and other Mississippi River cities until mid-1862.[13] The war made obvious, however, the need to obtain manufactures from other sources.

Like their counterparts in other Confederate cities, Atlanta merchants hoped at the outset of the war that direct trade with Europe would largely replace dealings with the North. One of the city's most prominent dry goods merchants, Sidney Root, announced in 1861 that he would "quit the business" if he "had to go back to New York."

12.   Testimony of William Markham and Testimony of William T. Farnsworth in Claim of Thomas G. Healey and Testimony of John Silvey in Claim of Christian Kontz, Southern Claims Division, RG 217; H. M. Davidson, *Fourteen Months in Southern Prisons* (Milwaukee, 1865), 36–38; *The War of the Rebellion: A Compilation of the Official Records of the Union and Confederate Armies* (130 vols.; Washington, D.C., 1880–1901), Ser. I, Vol. XXXII, Pt. 3, p. 629, hereinafter cited as *OR*; Georgia Lee Tatum, *Disloyalty in the Confederacy* (Chapel Hill, 1934), 3–23, 73–79.

13.   Ludwell H. Johnson, "Commerce between the Northeastern Ports and the Confederacy, 1861–1865," *Mississippi Valley Historical Review*, LIX (1967), 30–43; Joseph H. Parks, "A Confederate Trade Center under Federal Occupation," *JSH*, VII (1941), 281–314.

The Atlanta Chamber of Commerce, upon the urging of Root and other hardware and dry goods merchants, organized the Board of Direct Trade to further commerce with Europe. Atlanta merchants, such as Root's partner John N. Beach, went abroad as "correspondents" to major European markets in 1861 and 1862. They took with them circulars composed by Root and others describing Atlanta's advantages and railroad connections. Another Atlanta dry goods merchant, William H. Barnes, founded the "European and Confederate States Advertising Agency" in 1861 to advertise those manufacturers in southern newspapers. Atlanta newspapers also forwarded their weekly editions, which contained local importers' advertisements, to manufacturing cities in England, France, Belgium, and other countries.[14]

The city's establishing and maintaining trade with Europe ultimately depended upon the Confederacy's success in breaching the northern blockade of southern seaports. Several blockade-running companies were formed in wartime Atlanta, where capital invested in shipping rose from only $2,500 in 1862 to about $73,000 by 1864. The Fulton County Export & Importing Company was founded in 1863 by William McNaught, James Ormond, and Jonathan Norcross. This company went out of business in 1864 when its steamer, the *Powerful*, sank off the mouth of the Suwannee River in Florida. A company organized by Richard Peters and two other men earned more than $3 million running the blockade. The success of Peters and his associates was unusual—blockade-runners' ships were rarely used for more than a single voyage. The difficulties in penetrating the blockade were reflected in wartime Atlanta, where by 1864 a pair of lady's shoes cost $500; a felt hat, $150; and a woolen shawl, $600.[15]

Foodstuffs became as scarce as manufactured goods in Atlanta by 1863. Not only were the wholesale and retail grocery and produce merchants likely to go out of business, but an increasingly hungry population was outraged. A multitude of problems contributed to the scarcity. The wheat crops of middle and east Tennessee and north

14. Root quoted in Atlanta *Southern Confederacy*, May 31, 1861; *Daily Atlanta Intelligencer*, June 25, July 14, September 18, 1861, July 10, 1863.
15. Minute Book of the Fulton County Export & Importing Company, May 19, 1863, January 9, 1864, and William McNaught to G. M. Avendano, November 17, 1863, both in William McNaught–James Ormond Papers, AHS; Nellie Peters Black, *Richard Peters* (Atlanta, 1904), 27–31; *Annual Report of the Comptroller-General of the State of Georgia, 1862* (Milledgeville, 1862), 56; *Annual Report of the Comptroller-General of the State of Georgia, 1864* (Milledgeville, 1864), 14; Stanley Lebergott, "Through the Blockade: The Profitability and Extent of Cotton Smuggling, 1861–1865," *JEH*, XLI (1981), 867–88; Reed, *History of Atlanta*, 181.

Georgia were lean from 1859 to 1861. The superintendent of the Western & Atlantic Railroad noted in 1860 that most of the wheat and corn transported by his railroad was "grown on the prairies of the far West." Especially after the Memphis & Charleston fell into Union hands in 1862, it became almost impossible to obtain western foodstuffs in the lower South. Military use of the railroads also affected bringing produce to Confederate cities. An Atlanta merchant in Memphis in 1862 reported that warehouses there contained more freight marked for Atlanta "than half a dozen other cities," but the Memphis & Charleston no longer had enough rolling stock to satisfy both commercial and military needs. When an unusually heavy wheat crop was harvested in east Tennessee and north Georgia in 1862, a sense of frustration prevailed in Atlanta because the lack of rail transport meant that residents could get only a small portion of the crop.[16] Tonnage reports for the W & A indicate that wheat shipments to Atlanta in that year were only 20 percent of what they had been five years earlier. These reports also indicate that, by 1862, shipments of flour, hogs, sheep, and corn had declined between 31 and 77 percent from 1860 levels.[17]

In addition, farmers within Atlanta's market area found it difficult to bring foodstuffs to the city via the wagon trade. The Confederate impressment laws, first enacted in 1861 and modified several times thereafter, allowed "pressmen" (government agents) to seize produce. They claimed military necessity and often did not pay the farmers enough. Thus, many small farmers in north Georgia and elsewhere stayed at home rather than risk encountering pressmen in Atlanta and other cities. Shortages of salt, necessary for preserving meats, also cut down on supplies of beef and pork available to city consumers. As early as 1861, farmers within Atlanta's trading territory were reportedly unwilling to slaughter livestock because they had no salt. Encouraged by the state, which provided free transportation on the W & A, a company headed by Atlanta wholesale produce merchant A. K. Seago established in 1862 an agency in Saltville, Virginia, to arrange

16. Quotations from *Annual Report of the Western & Atlantic Railroad, 1860* (Atlanta, 1860), 4, and Atlanta *Southern Confederacy*, February 8, 1862; *Daily Atlanta Intelligencer*, August 20, 1860, April 10, 1861, July 2, 1863; Robert C. Black III, *The Railroads of the Confederacy* (Chapel Hill, 1952), 139–42.

17. The W & A shipped 299,031 bushels of wheat, 60,375 barrels of flour, 205,058 bushels of oats and corn, and 15,747 hogs and sheep to Atlanta (see *Annual Report of the Western & Atlantic Railroad, 1862* [Atlanta, 1862]). *Cf.* figures in Table 1.

the transportation of salt from the Confederacy's largest mines to Georgia. Shortages continued, however, until the end of the war.[18]

The final blow to Atlanta's commercial economy was the inflation that overwhelmed the entire Confederacy. By the end of its career, the Confederate government had issued treasury notes amounting to $1,554,087,354, more than three times the value of Federal greenbacks issued during the war. Because the Confederacy's inflation rate was the worst in American history (by April, 1865, goods in the eastern Confederacy cost ninety-two times what they had four years earlier), all the paper money the government printed was still insufficient. As the need increased for some medium for transactions in Atlanta and elsewhere in the South, almost every imaginable form of currency appeared. "Shinplasters," notes issued by insurance companies and other businesses, grew "as thick as the frogs and lice of Egypt," according to one local newspaper editor during the summer of 1862. Counterfeit notes also circulated freely in the city in 1862 and 1863. But even all this currency, legal and illegal, could not match the cyclonic inflationary spiral, which devastated Atlanta and the rest of the Confederacy as thoroughly as did the Union armies.[19]

The combination of scarce goods and overabundant paper currency resulted in horrendous price inflation, which made wartime Atlanta notorious as a "nest of speculators." Some individuals deserved the label, especially those who bought large quantities of salt, meat, flour, and other foodstuffs. Lazarus Bendigo, who tried to corner the salt market in Atlanta, was sarcastically described as "one of the most fortunate of our merchant princes . . . [having] accumulated an enormous fortune, bought several blocks of buildings . . . [and] one of the largest and oldest and most influential substitutes in the army." On the other hand, several other Atlanta merchants made determined efforts to avoid being accused. Two Jewish merchants who were potential victims of the Judaeophobia that was a widespread

18. CM, October 23, November 6, 1863; *Daily Atlanta Intelligencer*, December 15, 1861, October 25, 1863; A. K. Seago to Governor Brown, April 19, 1862, in Governor Joseph E. Brown Papers, GDAH, Atlanta; Allen D. Candler (comp.), *The Confederate Records of the State of Georgia* (6 vols.; Atlanta, 1909–11), II, 477–78; Ella Lonn, *Salt as a Factor in the Confederacy* (New York, 1933), 64–65, 97.

19. Richard Cecil Todd, *Confederate Finance* (Athens, 1954), 89–91; Eugene M. Lerner, "Inflation in the Confederacy, 1861–1865," in Milton Friedman (ed.), *Studies in the Quantity Theory of Money* (Chicago, 1956), 170–75; CM, May 1, 1863; Atlanta *Southern Confederacy*, August 27 (quotation), September 2, 1862.

result of the speculator phenomenon, David Mayer and Henry Hirsch, publicly denounced the speculators. A few others made special arrangements for poor customers. Er Lawshe, a produce merchant, offered free molasses to needy families in 1862. A. K. Seago offered salt to the poor families of Confederate soldiers for $10 a sack in 1862, when speculators would have paid him $75.[20]

Few could match the altruism of Lawshe and Seago, and many Atlanta merchants consequently were identified as speculators. The charge was especially applied to the city's wholesale and retail produce merchants. Wholesale prices for foodstuffs climbed to astronomical levels between 1861 and 1863. Many consumers placed the blame squarely upon the grocery and produce dealers. Between March, 1861, and November, 1863, the wholesale price for top-grade flour rose from $6.25 to $110.00 per barrel, the wholesale cost of lard from $0.125 to $3.00 per pound, New Orleans sugar from $0.085 to $3.75 per pound, and ham from $0.115 to $5.00 per pound.[21] These figures indicate that the merchants had allowed prices for their goods to keep pace with inflation. These men were unfairly condemned for a problem not within their control. They had only to buy goods, keep a portion for a month, and then resell at the new, much higher price to be accused of speculation.

Frustrated consumers did not sympathize with the plight of the mercantile community. Outrage over the ridiculously high cost of everything from boots to butter swept through the city as the war continued. Thieves, frequently disguised as Confederate soldiers, raided mercantile houses and homes of wealthy citizens in 1863 and 1864. Although there were guerrillas and refugees coming into the city as Union armies approached Georgia in 1863, some permanent residents showed signs also of losing respect for the institution of private property. The day of reckoning arrived on March 18, 1863, when a mob of hungry war widows rioted and looted Whitehall Street provisions stores of bacon, flour, and other foodstuffs. City marshal J. N. Williford rushed to the scene and quickly dispersed the mob without serious injury to anyone, but not before the women had

20. Atlanta *Southern Confederacy*, January 31, 1864; Bryan, *Confederate Georgia*, 150; *Daily Atlanta Intelligencer*, May 6, October 7, 1862; Richard M. McMurry, "Rebels, Extortioners and Counterfeiters: A Note on Confederate Judaeophobia," *AHJ*, XXII (1978), 45–52; A. K. Seago to Governor Brown, April 17, 1862, in Gov. Brown Papers.
21. Atlanta *Southern Confederacy*, March 5, 1861, November 24, 1863.

succeeded in dramatizing that Atlanta's poor were increasingly class-conscious. Bread riots in Richmond and other Confederate cities in 1863 made the same point.[22]

In addition to manifesting the class conflict that undermined the Confederacy in the latter stages of the Civil War, the 1863 bread riot symbolized the breakdown of Atlanta's commercial economy. Shortages of manufactured goods and provisions, pressure from the Federal blockade of Confederate ports and from Union armies, inflation, and many other problems made merchandising increasingly difficult as the war dragged on. Wartime disasters all but dried up traditional outlets to supplies, revealed the inadequacy of new sources of goods, and rendered traditional business practices ineffectual.

The Industrial Vision

While Atlanta's commercial economy languished, wartime necessities caused many to see Atlanta's economic development in a new light and stress the city's potential for industrialization. "On the hills around Atlanta there might be a dozen large cotton factories, each employing a thousand hands," wrote one visionary on the eve of disunion in 1860. "We question if there is a . . . [better] site that capitalists should select as the great manufacturing centre . . . of the South." William Gregg, proprietor of the famous Graniteville, South Carolina, cotton mills, fueled the confidence of local industrial entrepreneurs when he addressed the first convention of the Manufacturing and Direct Trade Association of the Confederate States held in Atlanta in March, 1861. Atlanta, he said, would soon "become a great centre of manufacturing . . . because of its proximity to the coal regions, its railroad facilities, and its healthy climate."[23]

Atlanta businessmen were supremely confident that they could fulfill Gregg's prophecy. "For a time, we might be subjected to some want of certain manufactured articles," remarked one local optimist in February, 1861, "but necessity, which is said to be the mother of invention, will soon supply us with everything we might need." In view of the city's almost exclusively commercial orientation during the

22. *Daily Atlanta Intelligencer*, March 19, 20, 1863; Atlanta *Southern Confederacy*, March 20, 1863; Emory M. Thomas, *The Confederate Nation, 1861–1865* (New York, 1979), 203–205.

23. *Daily Atlanta Intelligencer*, August 7, 1860; *Proceedings of the Manufacturing and Direct Trade Association of the Confederate States on February 13, 1861 and March 9, 1861* (Atlanta, 1861), 9.

antebellum period, necessity did mother an astonishing array of "inventions" in Atlanta after 1861—everything from ready-made clothing and leather goods to machine and axle grease, alcohol, ink, shoe blacking, and a steel mechanical leg. Local foundries joined with a new type of company, called a novelty iron works, to concentrate on products for domestic consumption, including saddle and harness mountings, bedsteads, plows, buckles, sash weights, and fire grates. Although the production of such items did decline after 1863 when the Confederate government began to restrict supplies of iron ore to all but ordnance manufacturers, one local company—the Atlanta Novelty Iron Works, founded in 1862 by William McNaught and James Ormond—was able to sustain its operations because its furnaces were located in iron-rich Bartow County in north Georgia.[24]

These new ventures and their organizers were each hailed as important contributions to the wartime crusade to make Atlanta a manufacturing city. The enthusiasm for factories, no matter how specialized or trivial their product, was remarkably intense. According to one enthusiast, the manufacture of excelsior, a material used for stuffing chairs and beds and formerly imported from Massachusetts, would "save the city $100,000 annually." Soap manufactured locally, according to the dubious claim of the same observer, would save "millions." Others lauded the achievements of a firm that said it turned out porcelain teeth at the rate of one thousand molars per week in 1863. The praise for local industries plunged to the ridiculous in the same year: two enterprising capitalists had set up a button factory in a field "where all the dead horses and cows had found a resting place for their remains." Anchored in "an unpretending wooden building," the factory's "small steam engine chugged merrily away at these bones," turning them into "beautiful buttons ready to be strung."[25]

There was similar fervor for Atlanta industries that manufactured ordnance. These firms produced a great variety, displaying considerable ingenuity in adapting their machinery to military needs. Bowie knives suitable for "tickling the ribs of the abolitionists" were fab-

24. *Daily Atlanta Intelligencer*, February 1, 1861; J. Withers to H. Valentine, in McNaught-Ormond Papers; Stephens Mitchell, "Atlanta: The Industrial Heart of the Confederacy," *AHB*, I (1930), 20–28; *Daily Atlanta Intelligencer*, August 19, 1861, December 12, 1862.
25. *Daily Atlanta Intelligencer*, May 17, 1861, December 12, 1862, August 21, 1863 (quotation).

ricated at a local blacksmith's shop and saluted as "one more step in the march of independence from our northern enemies." John C. Peck, a sawmill proprietor, overcame numerous technical difficulties in 1862 to turn out approximately 1,000 "Joe Brown pikes," 829 of which were delivered to the Army of Tennessee. These wooden staffs were about six feet long and had retractable sixteen-inch blades— they were, incredibly, considered offensive weapons against an enemy armed with rifles. In 1861 the W & A machine shops adapted four forges to the rifling of gunbarrels, which were manufactured by the Atlanta Machine Works. Under master machinist William Rushton's supervision, the Georgia Railroad machine shops forged two breech-loading cannons, each of which weighed between six and eight hundred pounds. One cannon in October, 1861, lobbed a spectacular shot over nearby Stone Mountain (roughly seventeen hundred feet high) from a distance of one and a half miles.[26]

Other privately owned factories in Atlanta made more significant contributions to the manufacture of Confederate ordnance. The Atlanta Rolling Mill specialized in casting two-inch naval armor plate and provided armor for the ironclads *Merrimack* and *Arkansas*. In May, 1862, the newly organized Atlanta Sword Factory, founded by Kentucky native Hammond Marshall, contracted with the Confederate War Department to deliver 3,000 cavalry and 1,000 artillery sabers. A month later, the factory was busily casting 170 swords weekly. Marshall's firm also designed and forged brass carbines. The most important firearms producer, the pistol manufactory of E. N. Spiller and David J. Burr, had a more checkered career. They had started their company in Richmond but transferred its operations to Atlanta in 1862. They were to supply the Confederacy with 15,000 cavalry pistols by June, 1864. Because of design problems and materials shortages, they had to renegotiate the government contracts several times and fulfilled none of them on time.[27]

26. *Daily Atlanta Intelligencer*, May 29, 1861 (quotation); Atlanta *Southern Confederacy*, August 31, September 10, October 11, 1861; Payroll Book of Employees of the Western & Atlantic Railroad, 1861–1863, in Western & Atlantic Railroad Archives, GDAH; Mary A. H. Gay, *Life in Dixie During the War* (Atlanta, 1901), 320–24; Louise B. Hill, *Governor Brown and the Confederacy* (Chapel Hill, 1939), 65–66.

27. John H. Kennaway, *On Sherman's Track* (London, 1867), 111–12; William N. Still, "Facilities for the Construction of War Vessels in the Confederacy," *JSH*, XXXI (1965), 302; Beverly M. DuBose, "The Manufacture of Confederate Ordnance in Georgia," *AHB*, XII (1967), 18–19; Contract of H. Marshall & Co., May 22, 1862, Chap. X, Vol. 78, Record Group 109, NA; Contract of Edward N. Spiller & David J. Burr, November 20, 1861, in Spiller-Burr

The most impressive ordnance producer in wartime Atlanta was the Confederate government's arsenal, which opened on March 5, 1862. The arsenal, commanded by the energetic colonel Moses H. Wright, began its operations in Nashville in September, 1861, but moved to Atlanta in December after arsonists destroyed most of its facilities. By 1863, the new buildings in Atlanta included a percussion cap factory, a harness and saddle manufactory, a "Pyrotechnic laboratory," and various machine shops for producing all types of ammunition from .57 caliber Enfield rifle cartridges to artillery shells for ten-inch columbiads. Beginning in late 1862, the arsenal's major responsibility was to supply the Army of Tennessee. The factory's percussion caps were sent to Confederate armies all over the South. Josiah Gorgas, chief of the Ordnance Bureau, believed that it was more reliable than its only competitor at Richmond and consequently added to its burden by ordering the wide distribution of its caps.[28]

The Atlanta Arsenal compiled an impressive production and employment record. Between July 1, 1862, and June 30, 1864, the arsenal manufactured more than forty-one million percussion caps for muskets, nearly five million percussion caps for pistols, more than nine million rounds of small arms ammunition, and more than half a million friction primers. It also turned out thousands of saddles, bridles, harnesses, cartridge boxes and belts, canteens, and other ordnance items. In addition, it made and repaired gun caissons and repaired and altered bayonets, rifles, cannon, and pistols. The arsenal employed 5,464 men and women in 1863 and 5,453 in 1864, making it the largest single employer in nineteenth-century Atlanta. On July 5, 1864, its machinery and stores—except for the ammunition and supplies ignited by Confederate troops who fled the city on September 1, 1864—were crated and sent farther south.[29]

Other than the arsenal, Atlanta's most important ordnance pro-

Papers, AHS; Elizabeth Bowlby, "The Role of Atlanta During the Civil War" (M.A. thesis, Emory University, 1939), 26–27.

28. Mallet, "Work of the Ordnance Bureau," 1–6; Frank E. Vandiver, *Ploughshares into Swords: Josiah Gorgas and Confederate Ordnance* (Austin, 1952), 122, 156; Moses H. Wright to Captain J. L. Shields, June 16, 1862, Chap. IV, Vol. 10, and Wright to G. W. Rains, May 4, 1863, Chapter IV, Vol. 11, RG 109.

29. Annual Reports of Colonel Moses H. Wright, 1862–1864, in Compiled Service Records, RG 109 (microfilm copy, GDAH); Moses H. Wright to R. M. Cuyler, July 5, 1864, Chap. IV, Vol. 16, RG 109; OR, Ser. I, Vol. VII, pp. 785–86, Vol. XXIII, Pt. 2, p. 767.

ducer during the Civil War was the Quartermaster's Depot, which was established in August, 1861, under the command of Major G. W. Cunningham. By April, 1863, the depot operated a shoe factory, a steam tannery, and various cloth-making facilities. Its annual production quotas at that time were 130,000 jackets and pants, 175,000 shirts, and 130,000 pairs of shoes. By June 20, 1863, the depot had already exceeded its goals for pants and jackets and was ready to issue more than 30,000 cotton drawers and 3,000 wool hats. The depot's work that year required the services of forty shoemakers, twenty-two tailors, and more than three thousand seamstresses. It was Cunningham's publicly announced intention that his facilities, which rapidly became the chief supply depot for the lower South, should employ poor women, particularly the wives and daughters of Confederate enlisted men. But, according to one observer of Cunningham's work force, "wealthy ladies were doing the government work, and making money rapidly" while poor women "with eager anxious faces" stood in line outside the depot's employment office for days without being hired. [30]

Despite the difficulties at the Quartermaster's Depot, the industrial movement appeared to be quite a success in Atlanta by 1863. Many local businessmen had channeled their entrepreneurial energies into industrial ventures. Merchants had come from behind their counters to work beside the steam engine. Partially because of their inexperience, some former merchants encountered frequent setbacks. Edward N. Spiller, co-proprietor of the pistol factory, had been "bred purely to commercial pursuits," according to one Confederate officer, "and consequently . . . was to a certain extent 'at sea' in manufacturing operations." Other merchants made the conversion more successfully. William McNaught, the leading dry goods merchant in antebellum Atlanta, established a prosperous novelty iron works. James McPherson, formerly a bookseller, founded a match factory, and the products were much in demand. Similar ventures enabled the entire city to maintain a bustling appearance even as its commercial economy faltered. "We hear a great deal of complaint from other cities of their dull and lifeless appearance," remarked one observer in

30. OR, Ser. I, Vol. XXIII, pp. 759, 765–67, 769, Ser. IV, Vol. II, p. 380; Bryan, *Confederate Georgia*, 28; Richard Goff, *Confederate Supply* (Durham, 1969), 72–76; *Daily Atlanta Intelligencer*, August 11 (quotation), October 30, 1862.

January, 1863. "But the very reverse of this is true in Atlanta . . . [which] is destined to be a great manufacturing city."[31]

The industrial economy, however, was not quite as healthy as it appeared in 1863. Local factory owners had displayed great ingenuity in correcting technical difficulties, but some problems defied solution. Two such problems were the shortages of skilled labor and essential raw materials, especially coal and iron. One historian deemed these shortages the Confederacy's "fatal industrial weakness."[32]

The dearth of skilled labor was the most frustrating for local industrialists. Every manufacturing plant suffered for want of craftsmen and skilled mechanics, many of whom returned to their northern hometowns when war broke out. The Quartermaster's Depot, according to an aide of Jefferson Davis, could have doubled its output of boots and shoes with an additional sixty shoemakers. Throughout the war, the Atlanta Arsenal was in dire need of blacksmiths, machinists, and gunsmiths. Colonel Wright also searched as far away as Virginia in 1863 for skilled workers for Spiller & Burr. Skilled slave labor was nearly impossible to find in Atlanta during the war.[33]

Inflation further complicated the labor problem. Skilled workers in wartime Atlanta earned what would have earlier been high wages. Machinists, carpenters, and blacksmiths at the arsenal were paid $4.75 daily in 1863, and a talented gunsmith at the pistol factory earned $500 per month in 1862. Inflation negated these high salaries, however. Although mechanics' wages at the arsenal were raised by 100 to 300 percent between July 1, 1863, and June 30, 1864, Colonel Wright readily admitted that during the same period "many articles necessary for life have advanced 5,000 percent in price."[34]

The widening gap between real wages and prices resulted in a growing sense of class-consciousness among the skilled laboring population. Employers did apparently try to narrow the social gap be-

31. Garrett, *Atlanta*, I, 533; *Daily Atlanta Intelligencer*, January 25, 1863; James H. Burton to Josiah F. Gorgas, December 17, 1862, in Spiller-Burr Papers.
32. Charles B. Dew, *Ironmaker to the Confederacy: Joseph P. Anderson and the Tredegar Iron Works* (New Haven, 1966), 265, 286–87.
33. Mallet, "Work of the Ordnance Bureau," 7; *Daily Atlanta Intelligencer*, April 12, July 7, 1863; Moses H. Wright to Colonel O. H. Oladowski, April 3, 1863, Chap. IV, Vol. 8, and Wright to Oladowski, July 6, 1863, Chap. IV, Vol. 11, RG 109.
34. Samuel P. Richards Diary, November 15, 1962; Moses H. Wright to Captain J. F. Trezevant, April 18, 1863, Chap. IV, Vol. 11, RG 109; Carole E. Scott, "Coping with Inflation: Atlanta, 1860–1865," *GHQ*, LXIX (1985), 536–56; Annual Report of Wright for 1864.

tween owners and workers. The Fulton Mechanics' Association, a workingmen's charitable society organized in 1861, was patronized by both merchants and local industrialists, who donated books for its library. A similar organization founded in 1863, the Atlanta Workingmen's Mutual Benefit Association, included among its officers both skilled workers and such factory owners as John C. Peck and James E. Gullatt. In addition, the Mechanics' Savings Bank was founded by local merchants and factory proprietors in 1863. Nevertheless, skilled workers went on strike sporadically in 1863 and 1864 at the arsenal and local newspaper offices. The threat of immediate conscription ended these strikes. "Wages will not be regulated to suit the idle and the careless—but to suit the times," bluntly wrote the arsenal's commander, after dispatching one of the more recalcitrant strikers to Camp Randolph, Virginia.[35]

An even more serious problem was the shortage of essential raw materials. The arsenal thoughout the war was on the verge of shutting down for want of sheet copper, which was necessary for manufacturing percussion caps. Osnaburgs were always in great demand at the Quartermaster's Depot. Cured leather was scarce and much needed by firms that made shoes, saddles, and harnesses. Lead, for making bullets, was also in short supply. The scarcity of beeswax, used for lubricating bullets, caused great embarrassment at the Atlanta Arsenal in 1863—their bullets stuck in Confederate rifle barrels in Tennessee.[36]

Iron and coal were undoubtedly the most urgently needed raw materials. They were in short supply in the city and nearby counties throughout the war. Iron deposits in Bartow County and in the Coosa Valley at Round Mountain, where Georgia's richest lodes were found, were of poor quality. Iron mined near Chattanooga was insufficient for the demand. As the steam engine became common in Atlanta factories after 1861, coal became more desirable as a fuel. Charcoal made by burning wood was the fuel the antebellum indus-

35. Quotation from Special Order of Moses H. Wright, October 4, 1862, Chap. IV, Vol. 77, RG 109. See also Atlanta *Southern Confederacy*, March 7, 21, 1861; *Daily Atlanta Intelligencer*, May 3, July 2, 1863; Malone, "Atlanta Journalism during the Confederacy," 217–18.

36. *Daily Atlanta Intelligencer*, December 30, 1862; OR, Ser. I, Vol. XXIII, Pt. 2, p. 758; Moses H. Wright to Major N. R. Chamberliss, February 23, 1863, and Wright to Major William R. Hunt, March 14, 1863, Chap. IV, Vol. 10, Wright to Josiah F. Gorgas, May 6, 1864, Chap. IV, Vol. 16, and Wright to Lieutenant J. Pryor, June 23, 1862, Chap. IV, Vol. 77, all RG 109; Charles W. Ramsdell, "The Control of Manufacturing by the Confederate Government," *Mississippi Valley Historical Review*, VIII (1921), 244.

tries used, but wood also became scarce in Atlanta and its environs. By 1863, the arsenal had even denuded the city cemetery of all its trees in a rapacious search for wood.[37]

The shortage of iron and coal had become so desperate by December, 1862, that Confederate authorities and local industrialists in Atlanta held a public meeting. Lemuel P. Grant, at that time a captain in the Confederate Engineers' Bureau, proposed to build a railroad from Rome, Georgia, to Blue Mountain, in the heart of the Alabama coal and iron district. Rome was nearer to Blue Mountain and so was the logical choice as the eastern terminus. Atlanta would have access, however, to Alabama coal and iron because Rome was also on the W & A. At first Colonel J. F. Gilmer, chief of the Engineers' Bureau, and James A. Seddon, secretary of war, endorsed the project as essential to "the great mining industries of the Confederacy." They both lobbied for an act passed by the Confederate legislature on October 2, 1862, which authorized the issue of $1,122,480.92 in bonds to finance construction costs. With Grant as their joint agent, two companies contracted to build the road and were quickly approved by Seddon on behalf of the government.[38]

Prospects for the Rome & Blue Mountain Railroad soured in the spring of 1863. Duff Green, one of the South's craftier politicians and more colorful railroad entrepreneurs, was also the founder of Dalton, Georgia, and an alert guardian of its interests. Green wrote several letters to Jefferson Davis, denouncing the Rome & Blue Mountain since it would benefit Rome at Dalton's expense. Under pressure from Davis, the War Department reneged on its promise to remove iron rails from "unimportant roads" to complete the project. Without rails the road obviously could not be built. Thus passed Atlanta's last hope of obtaining iron and coal to sustain its industrial growth during the war.[39]

Despite all the difficulties, industrialization in wartime Atlanta was impressive. Several private and government manufacturing plants

37. *Daily Atlanta Intelligencer,* July 31, 1861; *Ga. Laws, 1863,* pp. 86–87; CM, March 4, 1864; Moses H. Wright to J. D. Allison, July 19, 1862, Chap. IV, Vol. 12, RG 109.

38. *Daily Atlanta Intelligencer,* December 13, 1862; Ethel Armes, *The Story of Coal and Iron in Alabama* (Cambridge, Mass., 1910), 115, 121–33; J. F. Gilmer to James A. Seddon, May 5, 1863 (quotation), Gilmer to Lemuel P. Grant, October 22, November 28, 1862, A. S. Rivers to Grant, November 19, 1862, and Contract of Georgia & Alabama R. R., January 1, 1863, all in Lemuel P. Grant Papers, AHS.

39. Black, *Railroads of the Confederacy,* 159; J. F. Gilmer to Lemuel P. Grant, April 10, 1863, in Grant Papers.

employed more workers than did other local factories founded during the nineteenth century before or after the war. Even more important was the conversion of so many merchants and community leaders to the industrial gospel. For a lot of them, industrialization had become an essential ingredient in city building.

Quick Growth and Urban Dilemmas

Largely because of the manufacturing plants and government facilities established in the city, Atlanta's population during the Civil War more than doubled the 1860 total. But city institutions could not deliver essential services to so many people. Badly overextended were police and judicial functions. Such a rapid increase in a very short time should have provided valuable lessons about planning for future growth.

The task of maintaining social order in wartime Atlanta was aggravated not only by the tremendous population increase but also by the invasion of disreputable citizens and slaves. While conditions doubtless provided sufficient incentive for many Atlantans to descend to illegal activities, the city's prominence as a Confederate industrial center was definitely a magnet to an astounding variety of undesirable newcomers. Toughs, gamblers, prostitutes, suspected spies, and other unsavory characters labored diligently to reinstate Marthasville's social atmosphere. In addition, slaves were brought to work in local industries and also to avoid capture by invading Federal armies. That rapidly increasing population worried military and civil officials concerned about possible insurrections.

The proceedings of the Mayor's Court, fully preserved for the period from February 18, 1861, to March 16, 1864, document the range of minor social disturbances that plagued the city—gambling, prostitution, firing pistols at all hours of the night, riding horses on sidewalks and occasionally into hotel lobbies, and indecently exposing male bodies "designedly to females." The most frequently prosecuted offense was disorderly conduct: 176 cases in 1861 and 255 cases in 1863—about 60 percent of all the offenses tried in the Mayor's Court in those years—fell into that category. More serious crimes were handled by the Fulton County Superior Court, which indicted at least ten individuals for homicides, forty-two for assault, and seventy-six for larceny. Homicides were frequent enough in 1863 and 1864 to arouse concern for the city's moral condition. "We think that (all things considered) Atlanta is improving very much in the morality of her citizens," sarcastically remarked one newspaper editor in 1863. "There has been only one murder committed this week in the city."[40]

To deal with the disorderly population, local authorities had a small police force, which theoretically could have been assisted by Confederate soldiers stationed in the city. In 1862, Atlanta's entire police force consisted of a marshal, his deputy, chief of police and his lieutenant, station-house keeper, and fifteen privates. Two years later, it still numbered only twenty officers, many of whom were of poor quality because the Confederacy's draft laws had deprived the city of more suitable candidates for the force. The city council heard many complaints about drunk and sleeping police officers, but there was usually no action to take in such cases because able-bodied men could not be found to replace the miscreants. Before the city became the target of Sherman's army in late 1864, there were 534 Confederate soldiers in Atlanta, which was declared a military post on June 1, 1862. These soldiers had the authority (martial law was also imposed in 1862) to police the city, but their willingness and ability to do so were questionable, partially because their commander for most of the war, Major G. W. Lee, was notoriously incompetent and himself a suspected thief.[41]

Despite small numbers and inefficiency, local police and Confederate officials did try to curb disorder. They made a concerted effort in 1862 to crack down on prostitution, but there were simply too many patrons of the Cyprian contingent. A more determined effort to extirpate what many saw as the root cause of social disorder came in 1863 when Major G. W. Lee issued an order outlawing the sale of spirituous liquors in saloons and other public places. Prohibition ultimately failed, however, to cleanse the city of its rowdies and toughs, who also thrived during the war.[42]

Atlanta's growing slave community, however, caused far more

40. Minutes of the Mayor's Court of Atlanta (February 18, 1861–March 16, 1864), August 9, 30, March 21, May 9, September 15, November 14, 1861, July 27, 1863, February 5, March 11, 1864, in AHS; Paul D. Lack, "Law and Disorder in Confederate Atlanta," *GHQ*, LXVI (1982), 178, 188; *Daily Atlanta Intelligencer*, October 25, 1863.

41. CM, January 24, 1862, July 17, September 18, October 9, December 11, 1863, January 1, 24, 1864; OR, Ser. I, Vol. XVI, Pt. 2, p. 754, Vol. XXIII, Pt. 2, pp. 656–57, Vol. XXXII, Pt. 3, p. 740.

42. CM, July 28, 1862; *Daily Atlanta Intelligencer*, September 2, 1862, September 20, 1863; Atlanta *Southern Confederacy*, August 29, 1862, November 24, 1863.

anxiety among local police authorities and the general population. The fear of insurrection was widespread, and officials were eager to punish any slave whose behavior suggested a rebellious spirit. Slaves accused of using "impudent and insolent language" in addressing whites were frequently brought before the Mayor's Court, which routinely imposed a sentence of "39 lashes upon the bare back." Both municipal and Confederate officials rigorously supervised the sale of liquor and renting of horses and carriages to slaves. Arson was the most feared but usually unverified form of slave rebellion. Two female slaves in 1863 "confessed" to setting fire to a boardinghouse owned by banker E. W. Holland and were threatened with execution. The epidemic of robberies that haunted property owners in wartime Atlanta was also attributed mainly to "negroes [brought] from a distance . . . who are too frequently left in the charge of no responsible party."[43]

During the war Atlanta slaves held "Negro balls," ostensibly to raise money for indigent families of Confederate soldiers. These balls, at first regarded favorably but later disapproved of by white authorities, occurred frequently in 1861 at various local hotels. Austin Wright, a slave owned by E. W. Holland, organized three lively balls in December, 1861, which raised $20.00 for soldiers' families and $15.00 for the families of Negro servants attached to Confederate armies. Negro balls—even those supervised by white Atlanta policemen—were nevertheless outlawed by the city council in 1863 as a "public nuisance" and incitement to rebellion. Similar occasions for extralegal frolic were apparently still available after the council's action. There was, for example, a combination cockfight and drinking contest held near the rolling mill in 1864. This latter event, attended by fifteen whites and approximately sixty Negroes, ended with the killing of one slave and the arrest of thirty-two other blacks by city police.[44]

Such gatherings were difficult to suppress because of the city's population growth. Slaves had many new opportunities to escape their masters' eyes. Neither the nighttime slave patrols nor passes

43. Minutes of the Mayor's Court, July 5, October 18, November 8, 1861, February 12, March 25, June 12, 1864; Atlanta *Southern Confederacy*, May 20, 1863; *Daily Atlanta Intelligencer*, September 8, 1862.
44. Atlanta *Southern Confederacy*, December 21, 1861; *Daily Atlanta Intelligencer*, December 13, 18, 1861, August 8, 1863, January 26, 1864.

required of slaves by Confederate soldiers after 1862 appeared to hamper the movement of Negroes about the city. Fifteen runaway slaves were arrested in 1862 not far from the city jail. They were found in an upstairs room of a warehouse, where they had been living for several weeks. Another runaway slave named Henry, owned by John Reed of Pike County, Georgia, was also captured in 1862 near the city's center in a "negro kitchen," his hiding place for nearly eighteen months. To prevent such occurrences, the city council considered in 1863 a "special negro yard" for imprisoning all black visitors in town more than a day, but abandoned the idea as impractical.[45]

The problems local authorities encountered in controlling the slave population were symptomatic of the general breakdown of government in Atlanta during the Civil War. The city was simply growing too fast at a time when both able leadership and material resources were scarce. By 1863, gas lighting for the city's streets was a thing of the past—coal gas was no longer available. Whitehall, Decatur, and other main streets in the business district were barely passable. Not only was rock scarce, laborers were not available to do the paving. These same streets were littered with offal, excrement, and garbage. Lime could not be purchased in sufficient quantities to lessen the stench. The result of these and other problems was a smallpox epidemic, which began in December, 1862, and ended by May, 1863. According to the report of the superintendent of the Smallpox Hospital, this epidemic by February, 1863, had infected more than one hundred persons.[46]

One additional service inadequately maintained by local government was poor relief. Refugees from Kentucky, Tennessee, and elsewhere joined with soldiers' families, the unemployed, and the habitually impoverished to swell the ranks of those in need. The burden of caring for them quickly overwhelmed local societies, and the largest of these organizations, the Voluntary Relief Association, stopped taking subscriptions or contributions when the state of Georgia moved to take up the responsibility of aiding needy families of Confederate soldiers. Prodded vigorously by Governor Joseph E. Brown, the legislature appropriated $16.5 million for poor relief between 1861 and

45. *Daily Atlanta Intelligencer*, January 1, May 15, September 25, 1862; CM, August 28, 1863.
46. *Daily Atlanta Intelligencer*, January 13, June 30, December 12, 1863, July 2, 1864; Atlanta *Southern Confederacy*, February 26, 1863; CM, April 10, 1863.

1864, of which $62,676 was spent in 1863 and 1864 in Fulton County alone.[47]

Pressed hard by those who thought it unpatriotic to ignore needy families of Confederate soldiers, Atlanta's city government spent more during the war for poor relief than ever before. In 1863 the city council devoted 22 percent of its revenues (excluding those spent on paupers' burials) to such care. There was a "city relief store," which sold groceries at cost to deserving families, and in 1864, there were 558 families with approximately 2,200 members registered to buy goods. The needy also were allowed free medical treatment (a privilege denied them during the antebellum era). City physician S. S. Beach reported in 1863 that he had treated 183 charity patients. The city also purchased firewood, paid burial expenses, gave cash handouts, and delivered other benefits to the poor. Although such policies showed that Atlanta's local authorities had become more aware of the plight of the needy, few argued that the combination of private, state, and municipal relief had done more than alleviate a small portion of the want and misery in the city.[48]

Atlanta's city government was, in sum, unable to meet the challenge of imposing order, maintaining physical welfare services, and providing adequate care for the poor. The experience that civic officials had with some of these problems could have been put to use after 1865 when Atlanta's population (especially its black population) also grew rapidly. There is little evidence, however, that knowledge gained from confronting rapid urbanization during the war was constructively used later.

Death of "Old" Atlanta

Atlanta's industrial and population growth made the city an inviting target. As the summer of 1864 approached, the muffled sound of distant artillery fire began to reach the ears of worried residents. Con-

47. *Daily Atlanta Intelligencer*, September 24, 1861; Bryan, *Confederate Georgia*, 62–63; Peter Wallenstein, "Rich Man's War, Rich Man's Fight: Civil War and the Transformation of Public Finance in Georgia," *JSH*, L (1984), 25, 30; Paul D. Escott, "Joseph E. Brown, Jefferson Davis, and the Problem of Poverty in the Confederacy," *GHQ*, LXI (1977), 59–70; *Annual Report of the Comptroller-General of the State of Georgia, 1863* (Milledgeville, 1863), 94; *Annual Report of the Comptroller-General of Georgia, 1864*, pp. 111, 121.

48. CM, August 29, 1862, September 18, 1863, January 1, 1864; Atlanta *Southern Confederacy*, March 25, 1863; *Daily Atlanta Intelligencer*, May 3, 1864. Of the $170,540.11 spent by the city in 1863, funds in the amount of $37,116.44 went for relief and care of paupers at the Smallpox Hospital.

federate authorities and civic leaders did their best to allay the civilians' increasing fears, and through the month of June their efforts appeared successful. "A great many persons are packed up . . . to leave if there is any danger of the enemy capturing the city," wrote an Atlanta schoolgirl confidently on June 1, 1864, "[but] we of course anticipate no such result from the . . . battle."[49]

During the next two months, however, there were unforeseen disasters. In the middle of July, panic-stricken Atlantans learned that Union and Confederate armies had crossed the Chattahoochee River. Foolishly venturing outside the elaborate fortifications that Lemuel P. Grant had designed for the city, John Bell Hood led a series of brave but senseless assaults at the Decatur Road, Ezra Church, and Peachtree Creek. Within nine days in late July, the Confederate Army of Tennessee suffered nearly fourteen thousand casualties.[50]

Even before these assaults, Union guns had begun bombarding Atlanta. Shells hit many private homes and businesses as well as military targets. According to one of Sherman's subordinates, shells fired at least once every five minutes on the night of August 11 crashed "through the houses as if they were so many egg-shells." By the middle of August, another observer reported, almost every building in the city had been struck "by shells or fragments . . . except in the Southern and Southeastern portions of the place." And at least twenty-two people —of whom only two were Confederate soldiers— died as a direct result of the shelling. Survivors lived like animals in the besieged city. Several families took refuge in a large culvert on Houston Street. Many others lived in muddy pits, usually dug about eight feet deep and covered with railroad crossties.[51]

The bombardment finally stopped on September 1, 1864, a day after Hood's army began the evacuation of the city. Since Hood could not remove the vast military ordnance and machinery still in Atlanta,

49. Janice to Mary Lou Yancie, June 1, 1864, in B. C. Yancey Papers, William R. Perkins Library, Duke University, Durham; *Daily Atlanta Intelligencer*, July 6, 1864.
50. Grady McWhiney and Perry D. Jamieson, *Attack and Die: Civil War Military Tactics and the Southern Heritage* (University, Ala., 1982), 17, 21; Richard M. McMurry, *John Bell Hood and the War for Southern Independence* (Lexington, Ky., 1982), 116–51.
51. Quotations from *Daily Atlanta Intelligencer*, August 13, 1864, and John White Geary to My Dearest Mary, August 11, 1864, in John White Geary Papers, AHS; *Daily Atlanta Intelligencer*, August 23, 1864; Charles Fessenden Moore, *Letters Written During the Civil War, 1861–1865* (Boston, 1898), 188–89; Colin Dunlop to My Dear Sister, August 13, 1864, in Colin Dunlop Papers, AHS; John Henderson to W. L. Calhoun, August 6, 1895, in William L. Calhoun Papers, AHS.

a detachment of Confederate cavalry remained behind to destroy as much as they could. They leveled the Atlanta Rolling Mill, 7 locomotives, and 150 railroad cars. During the night of September 1, probably the most tremendous explosion of the entire war, heard over forty miles away, occurred when that detachment ignited more than eighty railroad cars filled with ammunition. The smoke and the resulting fires—partially responsible for the loss of many homes and buildings later said to have been burned by Sherman—were still much in evidence on the following day when Mayor James M. Calhoun formally surrendered the city to Colonel John Coburn, one of Sherman's aides. [52]

Coburn promised to protect the private property of noncombatants in Atlanta. But Colonel Orlando M. Poe of the Corps of Engineers attached to Sherman's army began to methodically destroy the railroad shops and remaining industrial plants on November 14, 1864, and the fires spread. The civilian population had long since been forcibly evicted, and few remained to witness this final conflagration. "The heaven is one expanse of lurid flame. . . [B]uildings covering two hundred acres are in ruins or in flames," wrote one of Sherman's officers who saw the events of the night of November 15. "This city, which next to Richmond, has furnished more material for prosecuting the war than any other in the South, exists no more." Fires started by Poe and his subordinates spread throughout the business district, and vindictive Federal soldiers acting without Sherman's approval torched and pillaged residences. [53]

Those who saw Atlanta after Sherman's departure were astounded. "It would be impossible for me to give you a description of matters in that once flourishing city," wrote former resident and railroad ticket agent James R. Crew on December 1, 1864. "I should judge that at least two thirds have been destroyed." A more precise assessment of the destruction was that of Confederate General W. P. Howard, who visited the city a few days earlier. He made a detailed map and

52. *Daily Atlanta Intelligencer*, September 6, 1864; Charles W. Hubner, "Some Recollections of Atlanta During 1864," *AHB*, I (1928), 5–7; Mary Rawson Diary, August 31, 1864, in Mary Rawson Papers, AHS; Samuel Bachtell to His Dear Wife, September 3, 1864, in Samuel Bachtell Papers, AHS; Affidavit of James M. Calhoun, Mayor of Atlanta as to Facts in Regard to the Surrender of Atlanta, September 2, 1864, in James M. Calhoun Papers, AHS.
53. Diary of Major George Ward Nichols, November 15, 1864, cited by A. H. Guernsey, "Sherman's Great March," *Harper's New Monthly Magazine*, XXXI (1865), 574–75; F. Y. Hedley, *Marching Through Georgia* (Chicago, 1884), 257; William T. Sherman, *Memoirs of William T. Sherman* (New York, 1891), 177.

estimated that four thousand to five thousand buildings within the incorporated limits had been reduced to rubble and ashes. According to Howard, only four hundred buildings were undamaged. All the railroad machine shops, depots, manufacturing establishments, and commercial houses in the business district (with the exception of those on portions of Whitehall and Alabama streets) lay in ruins. Few private homes in any quarter of the city remained untouched. [54]

Obviously, few physical reminders of the city's industrial and population growth were left as Atlanta prepared to enter the New South era. "All that remained to attest to the former existence of great mills and foundries," wrote one visitor to the city in early 1865, "were a few battered brick walls, and an occasional chimney looking grim and gaunt."[55] Nevertheless, wartime industrialization had left an important legacy. Partially because so many plants did not survive after 1865, historians have not properly recognized the connection between the Civil War industrial experience in cities such as Atlanta and the New South urban-industrial creed.

As Atlanta entered the postbellum era its promoters soon discovered to their delight that the Civil War had done no permanent harm to their city. Rebuilding was quick, and the city grew as rapidly as it had before the war. But there had been a significant change in city-building strategy. Industrialization was an important element in urban progress, a recognition that was a direct product of the wartime industrial crusade. In sum, the war only momentarily slowed Atlanta's commercial expansion and opened up possibilities for significant new economic growth.

54. James R. Crew to Jane, December 1, 1864, in James R. Crew Papers, AHS; *Daily Atlanta Intelligencer*, December 20, 1864; Joseph T. Glatthaar, *The March to the Sea and Beyond: Sherman's Troops in the Savannah and Carolinas Campaigns* (New York, 1985), 136–39. Howard's report is reprinted in Garrett, *Atlanta*, I, 653–55.
55. Kennaway, *On Sherman's Track*, 115–16.

5

THE "PHOENIX CITY"
Physical and Economic Resurrection,
1865–1880

This epoch marks a distinctive era in the history of Atlanta. . . .
Old fortunes were swept away, and with them old customs had
to be consigned to the shades of memory. No people were ever
more fully equal to an emergency than were the people of
Atlanta. . . . [S]oon from the debris and smouldering ruins of
the city began to rise, phoenix-like, a more progressive city,
which was destined . . . to be the proud type of the New South.

—*First Annual Report of the Atlanta Chamber
of Commerce* (1886)

Lo scores of visitors and many inhabitants, Atlanta's recovery from the Civil War was miraculous. The war brought as much or more devastation to Atlanta than to any other southern city, but caused only a momentary pause in its growth. Atlanta's 1870 population of 21,789 was more than twice the 1860 total, and the 1880 population of 37,409 nearly quadrupled it (see Table 1 in Appendix A).[1] These figures are only one indication that the war, despite initial appearances, had dealt relatively mildly with Atlanta. Many aspects of the southern economy had not recovered by 1880, and only Richmond and Nashville (besides Atlanta) among the region's larger cities enjoyed significant growth in the fifteen years after 1865.[2] One confirmation of the economic lassitude that characterized especially the older southern seaports is in a study indicating that per capita real estate values in Mobile, Savannah, and Charleston declined precipitously between 1860 and 1870. In Atlanta during the same decade they rose by 40 percent.[3]

Many observers during the nineteenth century and a few historians searched for explanations of Atlanta's not only recovering from wartime destruction but also escaping the severe economic retardation that gripped most of the South in the postbellum era. Some cited the city's railroad connections while others pointed to "the energy, industry, and go-aheadativeness of her people." Still others concluded that Atlanta's prosperity was a "perfect enigma" and defied rational explanation.[4]

1.   Cf. Marion B. Lucas, *Sherman and the Burning of Columbia* (College Station, Tex., 1976).

2.   James L. Sellers, "The Economic Incidence of the Civil War in the South," and Eugene M. Lerner, "Southern Output and Agricultural Income, 1860–1880," both in Ralph Andreano (ed.), *The Economic Impact of the American Civil War* (Cambridge, Mass., 1967), 98–109, 399–416; Howard N. Rabinowitz, "Continuity and Change: Southern Urban Development, 1860–1900," in Blaine A. Brownell and David R. Goldfield (eds.), *The City in Southern History: The Growth of Urban Civilization in the South* (Port Washington, N.Y., 1977), 92–93; Blaine A. Brownell, "Urbanization in the South: A Unique Experience," *Mississippi Quarterly*, XXVI (1973), 110–11; E. Merton Coulter, *The South During Reconstruction, 1865–1877* (Baton Rouge, 1947), 252–60.

3.   Arnold M. Pavlovsky, "Commerce and the Standard of Living in Four Southern Cities, 1850–1880" (Seminar paper, Princeton University, 1971), 45–48, copy in my possession; *Annual Report of the Comptroller-General of the State of Georgia, 1860* (Milledgeville, 1860), 46; *Annual Report of the Comptroller-General of the State of Georgia for 1870* (Atlanta, 1870), 29. Per capita real estate values in Atlanta rose from $288 in 1860 to $404 in 1870.

4.   George Rose, *The Great Country or Impressions of America* (Boston, 1868), 175; Alfred Falk, *Trans-Pacific Sketches: A Tour through the United States and Canada* (Melbourne,

As several historians have said, however, expansion of the region's railroads and the demise of the factorage system promoted the growth of southern interior cities at the expense of older tidewater urban centers. Atlanta happened to be more fortunate in its railroad geography than even most interior cities were. Local businessmen quickly found ways to exploit these advantages. Entrepreneurial successes—becoming the state capital, having the largest hotel south of Louisville, and building the largest cotton factory in Georgia—also stimulated Atlanta's economic boom and attracted migrants to the city.

Whatever its ultimate causes, Atlanta's quick recovery was the most persuasive advertisement for and greatest stimulus to its postbellum population growth. More than its railroad advantages, growing political importance, or any other single factor, Atlanta's "phoenix-like rise from its ashes" convinced outsiders and its own inhabitants that the city was destined for metropolitan status. One observer stressed this point in 1873: the city's physical rebirth gave "Atlanta a great name in . . . [Georgia] and the neighboring states" and so lured "every man, young or old, who had $100 or more to invest . . . [like] the pilgrims to Mecca or Jerusalem." Urban growth attracted "a continuous stream of adventurers."[5]

Commerce and Industry: Recovery and Expansion

Those who arrived to rebuild Atlanta's economy and their own fortunes faced enormous difficulties. Living conditions for returning exiles and new settlers alike were grim for several years after 1865. "A dirty, dusty ruin it is" was merchant Samuel P. Richards' succinct description in August. For almost a year after Sherman's capturing Atlanta, the city was a wilderness of mud, ashes, and rubble. Virtually every warehouse, commercial building, and public facility within its business districts had been destroyed. As late as 1869, in many outlying residential neighborhoods "the walls of houses alone remain, while a heap of charred rubbish occupies the interior." Effie McNaught wrote that "[p]eople live very hard here, corn bread mostly, and seem thankful to get that. . . . Pa does not know whether

1877), 279–80; I. W. Avery, *Atlanta, the Leader in Trade, Population, Wealth, and Manufactures in Georgia* (Atlanta, 1885), 4–5; LaGrange (Ga.) *Reporter* quoted in Atlanta *Daily New Era*, January 31, 1869; Athens *Watchman* quoted in *Daily Atlanta Intelligencer*, January 31, 1869.
    5. Atlanta *Daily Herald*, January 21, 1873.

to let you come South or not, and I don't wonder that he hesitates. . . having no home."[6]

Despite the hardships that awaited them, many prominent settlers went back with amazing haste to the ruined city in 1865 and 1866. "Everyone that can," O. S. Hammond wrote after he had gone back in February, 1865, "is returning as fast as transportation and the roads will permit." Among the first were many members of the mercantile community. The wholesale and retail produce merchants were a few months earlier than the specialists in dry goods, since initially the demand for food exceeded that for shoes, clothes, and related items. Many of these men returned with stocks of goods that had been shipped to safe places in advance of Sherman's army.[7]

Although most of the warehouses and stores had been leveled during the war, many merchants immediately went to work with their own hands to rebuild. Hard labor put 150 stores back in operation in 1865, and two years later an observer counted more than 250 commercial buildings in Atlanta. Frequent complaints about high rents during the late 1860s indicate that even this rate of construction could not keep pace with demand. Rebuilding mercantile houses took precedence: "Immediately after the war our dwelling places were generally put on a plain and cheap plan, while our business houses were on a grander and more costly style," a local newspaper editor wrote in 1870. "This was our true policy."[8]

During the late 1860s and early 1870s, Atlanta's new and rebuilt mercantile houses not only sold their goods rapidly, the volume increased. In 1865 the city's trade, according to one estimate, was already 30 percent greater than it had been during the antebellum period. Atlanta's 1866 trade was valued at $4.5 million, and the approximate total for 1872 was $35 million. By 1873, grocery and produce sales amounted to approximately $11.5 million, dry goods sales to $3.5 million, the tobaccco trade to $2 million, and hardware

6. Diary of Samuel P. Richards, August 10, 1865, in AHS; Alex Rivington, *Reminiscences of America in 1869* (London, 1870), 296; Effie McNaught to Mother, July 14, 1867, in William McNaught–James Ormond Papers, AHS.

7. O. S. Hammond to Mrs. Adair, February 10, 1865, in A. D. Adair Papers, AHS; Ernest Ingersoll, "The City of Atlanta," *Harper's New Monthly Magazine*, LX (1879), 33–35.

8. *Daily Atlanta Intelligencer*, July 25, 1865, June 8, 1870 (quotation); V. T. Barnwell, *Atlanta City Directory 1867* (Atlanta, 1867), 34–35; Atlanta *Constitution*, September 14, 1873; William R. Hanleiter, *Atlanta City Directory for 1871* (Atlanta, 1871), 170; Franklin M. Garrett, *Atlanta and Environs: A Chronicle of Its People and Events* (3 vols.; New York, 1954), I, 675.

sales to $800,000. By 1873, wholesale merchants and jobbers had doubled their market area, which encompassed the territory within a two-hundred-mile radius of the city. Reports in local newspapers of wholesale trade with merchants in Macon, Warrenton, Sparta, Athens, and Milledgeville indicated that Atlantans were invading Savannah's and Augusta's markets as early as 1869.[9]

Several factors enabled Atlanta merchants to rebuild and expand the city's commerce during the late 1860s and 1870s. The quick recovery and changes in the network of railroads terminating in Atlanta aided them tremendously. Despite extensive damage, all those railroads as well as their major connecting lines were in excellent condition by early 1867. In addition, fast freight associations sought to establish through routes for transporting western foodstuffs and cotton to southern Atlantic seaports for export abroad. The Green Line, initially organized in 1868 as a cooperative venture among several railroads connecting St. Louis, Louisville, and Atlanta, was the earliest such association. A more limited version of the Green Line, the Liverpool, Savannah, and Great Western Transportation Line, was established in 1874 to expedite shipments of produce and cotton from St. Louis to Savannah. Although both freight associations had coastal cities as their ultimate southern termini, Atlanta was a natural breaking point in their routes. The city's merchants handled goods brought in by wagon and other feeder railroads, and such items were added to Green Line and Great Western Line freights. Fierce competition later in the 1870s among the Louisville & Nashville, the East Tennessee, Virginia & Georgia, and the Richmond & West Point also benefited Atlanta merchants. All these companies had ambitious schemes for expanding their lines and chose the city as a hub in their respective empires, further consolidating Atlanta's position as a major railroad entrepôt.[10]

Also helping to increase Atlanta's trading territory was the decline

9. Sidney Andrews, *The South Since the War: As Shown by Fourteen Weeks of Travel and Observation in Georgia and the Carolinas* (Boston, 1866), 340; Atlanta *Daily New Era*, October 27, 1866, January 13, 1867, September 25, 1869; William R. Hanleiter, *Atlanta City Directory for 1870* (Atlanta, 1870), 34–35; Atlanta *Constitution*, September 14, 1873; Hanleiter, *Atlanta City Directory for 1871*, p. 170.

10. John H. Stover, *The Railroads of the South, 1865–1900: A Study in Finance and Control* (Chapel Hill, 1955), 58, 233–40; William H. Joubert, *Southern Freight Rates in Transition* (Gainesville, Fla., 1949), 31–33, 35; Atlanta *Constitution*, June 8, 1875; Minutes of the Board of Directors of the Western & Atlantic Railroad (1870–1890), May 23, 1874, in Joseph E. Brown Papers, AHS.

of the factorage system, which disintegrated in the wake of the Civil War. Since factors no longer organized the trade of southern tidewater cities with the interior, cities such as Atlanta were free to expand their market areas considerably. During the 1860s and 1870s, Atlanta cotton brokers succeeded in diverting increasingly larger shipments away from their tidewater competitors for direct rail transport to northern markets. The completion of the Atlanta & Richmond Air Line in 1873 (the only new line added before 1880) provided a new convenient route.[11]

Atlanta's mercantile community and its allies acted aggressively to rebuild and expand all sectors of commerce. Wholesale and retail grocers were especially vigorous in reestablishing and adding trade contacts with western cities. One way to secure produce at lower prices and in greater volume was to send "trade representatives" on extended buying trips through the West. Produce broker Robert F. Maddox, for example, served as a buying agent for several Atlanta firms on his journey through various western cities in March, 1867. The Board of Trade, founded in 1866 by several produce merchants, posted daily market prices of wheat, corn, and other produce in western cities. In addition, the city council seized every opportunity to send delegates to various commercial conventions held in western cities. In 1872, Benjamin E. Crane, a member of Atlanta's richest wholesale produce firm, represented the city at the National Commercial Convention in St. Louis, where he was elected president of the convention. The city council and the Board of Trade also entertained trade delegations from Chicago, Indianapolis, and other cities later in the 1870s.[12]

An inducement for western merchants to trade in Atlanta was the completion of the Kimball House in 1871. Begun as a project of the city's most active promoter, Hannibal Ingalls Kimball, the hotel eliminated complaints that accommodations for visiting merchants were inadequate. The building was six stories high, and its 317 rooms

11.   Stover, *Railroads of the South*, 113; Harold D. Woodman, *King Cotton and His Retainers: Financing and Marketing the Cotton Crop of the South, 1800– 1925* (Lexington, Ky., 1968), 269–84; Thomas D. Clark, *Pills, Petticoats, and Plows: The Southern Country Store* (New York, 1944), 19–23; Jacqueline P. Bull, "The General Merchant in the Economic History of the New South," *JSH*, XVIII (1952), 37–59.

12.   *Daily Atlanta Intelligencer*, February 14, 19, 1867; Atlanta *Constitution*, March 12, 1876; Atlanta *Daily New Era*, August 1, 1869; CM, May 7, 1869, August 18, 1871, April 11, 1876; *Proceedings of the National Commercial Convention Held at Saint Louis, December 11, 12, & 13, 1872* (St. Louis, 1873), 20.

were elaborately furnished with Brussels carpets, gold ornaments, and solid-walnut furniture. Amenities included a French cook, fountains surrounded by tropical plants, three steam-powered elevators, and a steam laundry where clothes could be washed, dried, and ironed in fifteen minutes. Travelers and western newspaper correspondents consistently praised its facilities. Such spacious hotels were, in the words of a writer for the Toledo *Democrat & Herald* in 1875, "a rare thing in Dixie." At that time, the larger hotels in St. Louis, Cincinnati, and Louisville were not as commodious as the Kimball House. Throughout the postbellum period, local newspapers posted daily notices of those who had been drawn to this paradise, together with the names of the firms they represented, for the benefit of Atlanta merchants.[13]

The city's produce trade assumed enormous proportions during the postbellum era. Tonnage reports for the Western & Atlantic, the only railroad that connected Alabama, Georgia, and the Carolinas to sources of western foodstuffs before 1872, indicate that in that year shipments of bacon, lard, corn, oats, and flour to Atlanta were roughly 400 to 500 percent greater than they had been before the war. According to one estimate in 1867, the city's merchants handled between 40 and 50 percent of the freight the W & A brought in. Not all the produce sold in local markets after the Civil War originated in the West, but there are indications that much of it did. One observer reported that most of the corn sold in Atlanta in 1867 came from St. Louis. The W & A's superintendent reported in 1871 that two-thirds of the company's freight earnings were derived from the "Western business." Jonathan Norcross in that year maintained in an address delivered to the local chamber of commerce that the "Western trade had become the most important department of Atlanta's commerce."[14]

Large quantities of produce also came via the wagon trade, which

13. Hanleiter, *Atlanta City Directory for 1871*, p. 170; Robert Somers, *The Southern States Since the War, 1870–71* (New York, 1871), 94, 97; John Stainback Wilson, *Atlanta As It Is* (New York, 1871), 51–58; Arthur Reed Taylor, "From the Ashes: Atlanta During Reconstruction" (Ph.D. dissertation, Emory University, 1973), 73–74; Toledo *Democrat & Herald* quoted in Atlanta *Daily Herald*, April 7, 1875.

14. Table F (facing page 24) in *Second Annual Report of the Officers of the Western & Atlantic Railroad Company, 1873* (Atlanta, 1873); *Daily Atlanta Intelligencer*, February 14, 1867; Atlanta *Daily New Era*, February 10, 1867; *First Annual Report of the President and Superintendent of the Western & Atlantic Railroad Co., 1872* (Atlanta, 1872), 112; Atlanta *Constitution*, July 30, 1871. In 1872, the W & A deposited at Atlanta 114,735,634 pounds of bacon and lard, 385,173 barrels of flour, 3,822,112 bushels of corn and oats, and 741,103 bushels of wheat.

additionally brought thousands of bales of cotton to the city. The wagon trade quickly surpassed its antebellum volume. On a single day in 1866, an observer counted 125 canvas-covered country wagons drawn by four- or six-mule teams and "loaded with various kinds of country produce," in a long line from the intersection of Luckie and Peachtree streets to A. K. Seago's wholesale produce house on Forsyth Street. Another observer reported in 1869 "a large increase in the number of wagons coming into the city." The owners, by their extensive purchases in Atlanta, had made "the retail trade very good" that year.[15]

As they had before the war, Atlanta businessmen and civic leaders offered farmers a number of inducements to trade in the city. The greatest incentive was that produce sold for relatively high prices while dry goods and related items were more readily available and cheaper than at home. And the cash trade was still customary at dry goods, hardware, and clothing stores. These items sold at prices lower than country store and small-town merchants could offer, since they usually sold on credit. Although the public market was shut down in 1866, Atlanta's municipal government afterwards permitted farmers to sell produce on street corners all over the city.[16]

The Georgia State Agricultural Society fairs, held biennially in Atlanta from 1870 to 1881, offered farmers yet another chance to sell their crops and also view the latest in agricultural implements and fertilizers, which were frequently exhibited in the Manufacturers' Hall at the fairs. Benjamin Yancey, president of the society and part-time Atlanta resident, was influential in persuading the society to locate its fairs there. The city council also spent $75,000 to purchase forty-one acres of land, which were donated to the society as a site for its fairs.[17]

Atlanta's burgeoning entertainment industry drew bored farmers

15. Atlanta *Commercial Bulletin*, March 27, 1866; Atlanta *Commonwealth*, December 9, 1874; Edward King, *The Great South* (Hartford, Conn., 1875), 350; Atlanta *Daily New Era*, December 6, 1866, August 11, 1869.

16. Kenneth R. Wesson, "The Southern Country Store Revisited: A Test Case," *Alabama Historical Quarterly*, XLII (1980), 157–66; Henry Jackson (cod.), *The Code of the City of Atlanta* (Atlanta, 1870), 159; Atlanta *Daily Herald*, October 17, 1875. The ledgers of one hardware firm from this period confirm in detail the existence of the cash trade. See Ledgerbook (November 1, 1870–October, 1874), in John R. and Alexander M. Wallace & Co. Papers, AHS.

17. Atlanta *Daily True Georgian*, October 20, 22, 1870; Wallace P. Reed, *History of Atlanta, Georgia* (Syracuse, 1889), 477; John T. Glenn (cod.), *The Code of the City of Atlanta* (Atlanta, 1869), 36–37.

from isolated rural districts into the city by the thousands during the postbellum period. In 1876, there were forty-five saloons. Dan Costello's "model circus," accompanied by Van Armburgh's menagerie (complete with a South American hippopotamus [allegedly discovered in the Amazon], a Bactrian camel, and several "four-horned Patagonian sheep") appeared regularly at Davis Hall in the late 1860s. Bell-Johnson Hall, which could accommodate sixteen hundred, countered with a resident acting troupe, managed by Captain W. H. Crisp and his comely daughter Jennie. Until its departure in late 1867, Crisp's talented company performed such masterpieces as "the mirth-provoking farce of Slasher and Crasher" before lively audiences. In 1875, Laurent DeGive's Opera House, built in 1869 with a seating capacity of two thousand, scored a coup by presenting the city's first cancan show, which was reportedly greeted with "a flutter, a shout, and loud, continued applause."[18]

The nature of such performances and the audiences—often predominantly rural visitors to the city—were acidly criticized. "The method of applauding in vogue among Atlanta audiences is an abomination and a nuisance," one critic complained in 1869. "Whooping, snorting, shrieking, groaning, whistling, stamping, grunting . . . and bellowing out applause is in no wise gratifying."[19] Low-brow cultural offerings nevertheless contributed significantly to the consolidation of the city's trading alliance with farmers.

Those who specialized in cotton increasingly took advantage of the city's marketing and processing facilities. Upcountry cotton farmers' production grew dramatically: the city received only 17,000 bales in 1867 but the total rose to 107,223 by 1880, when Atlanta was ranked as the South's fourth-largest interior port for the receipt of cotton. Railroads were a major incentive for cotton growers to send their crops to the city. Only a few thousand bales were reserved for the city's sole cotton factory, which did not commence operations until 1879. Virtually all the cotton was sent by rail to Savannah or Charleston for export abroad or by the Atlanta & Richmond Air Line to eastern cities.[20]

18. T. M. Haddock, *Atlanta and West End Directory for 1876* (1876; rpr. Atlanta, 1975), 289–90; *Daily Atlanta Intelligencer*, February 13, 1867; Atlanta *Daily New Era*, February 1, 2, 3 (quotation), 19, April 20, 1867; Atlanta *Daily Herald*, March 26, 1875.

19. Atlanta *Daily New Era*, November 26, 1869.

20. David F. Weiman, "The Economic Emancipation of the Non-Slaveholding Class: Upcountry Farmers in the Georgia Cotton Economy," *JEH*, XLV (1985), 71–93; *Commercial*

By 1880, Atlanta had acquired most of the facilities for marketing and processing cotton that were, according to one urban economist, associated with cities destined for metropolitan status in the region. There were four large cotton warehouses and several firms with the national and international connections necessary to sell the crop. The largest of these firms was Samuel M. Inman & Co., which handled more than sixty thousand bales in 1877 alone. Samuel Inman's brother, Hugh, operated the largest cotton press available anywhere—it could compress four thousand bales daily. The Atlanta Compress and Warehousing Company, employing 150 hands, maintained two additional presses, which together could compress two thousand bales daily. The Clarke Seed Cotton Cleaner Manufacturing Company was also available for removing seeds and undesirable material from high-grade cotton. The only facility lacking by 1880 to attract cotton growers was a seed oil mill, which was established two years later. [21]

In addition to offering numerous attractions to farmers to trade in the city, Atlanta wholesale produce and dry goods merchants sent a rapidly growing army of drummers to country stores and small-town merchants. In 1878, more than two hundred drummers covered a market area that extended into the Carolinas, Alabama, Tennessee, and Florida. The wholesale dry goods firm W. A. Moore, E. W. Marsh & Co., which reported sales of more than $1 million in 1870, kept on its payroll ten "travelling jobbers" who regularly patrolled all the towns accessible by railroad in east Tennessee, east Alabama, the western Carolinas, and the upper half of Georgia. Moore, Marsh & Co. also employed several men with "two-horse teams" to visit towns and villages off the railroads. [22]

Such diligent pursuit of customers by local merchants rapidly expanded the city's wholesale merchandise business during the 1870s and early 1880s. The value of Atlanta's jobbing trade in dry goods alone was placed at $3 million in 1876 and at $10 million in 1881.

---

and Financial Chronicle quoted in Atlanta Constitution, September 14, 1880; E. Y. Clarke, Illustrated History of Atlanta (2nd ed., 1879; rpr. Atlanta, 1971), 110.

21. Kenneth Weiher, "The Cotton Industry and Southern Urbanization, 1880–1930," Explorations in Economic History, XIV (1977), 131–33; Atlanta Registry of Merchants, 1873 to 1883 (MS in AHS), 31; Atlanta Constitution, March 16, 1880; Clarke, Illustrated History of Atlanta, 105; Reilly & Thomas [sic], Atlanta, Past, Present, and Future (Atlanta, 1883), 62, 115, 133.

22. Atlanta Constitution, September 5, 1878; Manufacturing and Mercantile Resources of Atlanta, Georgia (Atlanta, 1883), 241–42.

Similar estimates for wholesale produce are not available before 1883, when the jobbing trade was valued at $15 million. In 1881, wholesale firms of all types were reported to have average annual sales between $400,000 and $1.25 million each. To maintain this volume, Atlanta's drummers by that year, according to one source, "travelled regularly over all the country between Richmond and Key West and Charleston and the Mississippi River."[23]

One urban geographer has argued that wholesale trade was the determining factor in the growth of large American cities during the nineteenth century and that the talent of wholesale merchants as entrepreneurs was by no means evenly distributed among the nation's cities. This argument lends credence to boosters' praise of local wholesale dry goods and produce mercantile houses (whose sales constituted the lion's share of the city's wholesale trade) as key factors in Atlanta's commercial growth after the war. Newspaper editors in other cities commented on the ubiquitousness and aggressive zeal of Atlanta drummers in pursuing new customers. "The Atlanta drummer . . . restricts himself to no territory and dreads no competition," remarked the Hawkinsville (Ga.) News in 1882. "He skips with his little sample bag all over the face of the earth from Richmond to New Orleans."[24]

Whether arranging the sale of cotton or wholesaling and retailing dry goods and groceries, Atlanta's mercantile community increasingly acquired an image as more energetic than its competitors in other southern cities. Charleston and Savannah had better access to foreign markets for exporting cotton, but they could not match Atlanta's growing reputation as a citadel of New South enterprise. That reputation was expertly advertised and exploited.

Observers of business life in post–Civil War Atlanta frequently commented on its fast pace. "Atlanta is a devil of a place. . . . The men rush about like mad, and keep up such a bustle, worry, and chatter, that it runs me crazy," wrote one country visitor in 1866. "Everybody looks as if nearly worked to death, and I have not seen a gentleman with a calm, placid face in the whole town." Sidney

23. Atlanta Constitution, September 20, 1876; E. Y. Clarke, History of Atlanta, Illustrated (3rd ed.; Atlanta, 1881), 126; Reilly & Thomas, Atlanta, Past, Present, and Future, 50; Atlanta Constitution, October 5, 1881 (quotation).

24. James E. Vance, Jr., The Merchant's World: The Geography of Wholesaling (Englewood Cliffs, N.J., 1970), 138, 150–59; Hawkinsville News quoted by Atlanta Constitution, December 1, 1882.

Andrews said, "Men rush about the streets with little regard for pleasure or comfort, and yet find the days all too short and too few for the work at hand." Andrews and others who came later would have agreed with the local newspaperman who bragged in 1881 that "a nervous energy permeates all classes of the people and all departments of trade, and the spirit of enterprise never sleeps."[25]

The nervous energy so visible in Atlanta led visitors especially to compare it to northern and western cities. "Atlanta . . . has sprung up a new, vigorous, awkwardly alert city, very similar in character to the mammoth groupings of brick and stone in the North-West," commented Edward King in 1875. "There is little that is distinctively Southern in Atlanta; it is the antithesis of Savannah." The correspondent for a Toledo newspaper wrote, "Excepting that the map and the climate tell me that I am in the heart of Dixie, I would believe this to be a bustling, thriving, growing city of the North and West." James A. Mann, a Kansas City newspaper editor, found the city similar to his hometown: "Both have the same restless energy. If we have a sharp infusion of the orderly business-like Yankee blood, so have you." For local boosters, the highest praise came from a northern merchant in 1868—Atlanta merchants, he said, were "more like New York merchants than any he had met outside the metropolis."[26]

The sharpest contrast that postbellum observers of the city drew was between Atlanta and the region's tidewater cities. Many visitors found that business life in Atlanta after the war differed greatly from what they encountered in "Augusta, Savannah, Mobile, and the rest of the sleepy cotton markets, whose growth, if they have had any, is imperceptible." The most vivid distinctions were penned by a *Constitution* reporter in 1879:

> Many of our leading merchants come to their daily labors at 7 a.m. They continue at it all day, with a short intermission at noon for dinner, and sometimes after dark they are at their business. . . . These men can sell goods cheaper than . . . merchants who come to their houses at 10 a.m. in a fine carriage, smoking an elegant Havana cigar, who go home about four in the evening . . . and spend the balance of the day at dinner, where they entertain a fashionable visitor . . . [with] a

25. *Field and Fireside* quoted in Atlanta *Daily New Era*, October 30, 1866; Andrews, *South Since the War*, 340–41; Clarke, *History of Atlanta, Illustrated*, 129–30.

26. King, *The Great South*, 350; Toledo *Democrat & Herald* quoted in Atlanta *Daily Herald*, April 7, 1875; Mann quoted in Atlanta *Constitution*, January 6, 1880; Atlanta *Daily New Era*, May 7, 1868.

full description of the age of the city, and the pure blood of their ancestors . . . and comments [such as] "d———n Atlanta," "turn a dollar loose on Whitehall street and every man is after it," "the d———d fellows don't know how to dress genteelly," "never wear gloves, sir," "they are crackers, sir, crackers—Georgia crackers."[27]

Visitors from other southern cities often were hostile to Atlanta's social values and business life. A correspondent for a Macon newspaper wrote in 1877 that "Atlanta was inhabited by an alien people . . . and . . . a Georgian [in that city] felt as though he were in the midst of strangers." A Nashville newspaper in 1867 sneeringly referred to the city as "perhaps the 'fastest' little hamlet in the territories." Another Macon newspaper writer rejoiced that his hometown was dominated by "Southern men with Southern principles and instincts" while Atlanta was filled with "itinerant adventurers who come today, swindle somebody . . . and are off tomorrow." Told by an Atlanta acquaintance that he was "trying to make an honest living," a businessman from Columbus, Georgia, retorted that "you ought to succeed admirably . . . because you've got no competition . . . in Atlanta in that business."[28]

The strength of the Radical Republican party in the city during the late 1860s partially accounted for the hostility, but the fundamental cause was Atlanta's successfully invading the trading territory of other cities. Reacting to unfriendly remarks by an Augusta newspaper, a local writer noted in 1869 that Atlanta's trade reached to Augusta, Savannah, Columbus, and Macon, and "there is precisely where the shoe pinches." Since the pace of economic growth in the South was slow during the fifteen years following the Civil War, what one city gained in trade it took away from another—as many of Atlanta's urban competitors correctly perceived.[29]

The worldwide depression that began in 1873 and lasted six years retarded in some areas Atlanta's feverish economic development. Hit hardest were local banks. Ten banks (including private, unincorporated bankers) maintained offices in the city in 1872. Four failed by

27. Ingersoll, "City of Atlanta," 33–34; Atlanta *Constitution*, March 2, 1879.

28. Macon *Telegraph* quoted in Atlanta *Constitution*, September 11, 1877; Nashville *Gazette* and Macon *Telegraph* quoted in Atlanta *Daily New Era*, April 9, May 26, 1867; Columbus *Times* quoted in Atlanta *Constitution*, June 20, 1876.

29. Atlanta *Daily New Era*, September 25, 1869; James G. Doster, "Trade Centers and Railroad Rates in Alabama, 1873–1885," *JSH*, XVIII (1952), 170, 186–87, 192.

1874, and Atlanta's municipal government, trying desperately to compensate for the shortage of negotiable bank notes, issued $50,000 in city scrip. More than one hundred small and large firms also went bankrupt in 1873. The value of the city's trade, estimated at $35 million in 1872, had increased by only a little more than $300,000 in 1875. Real estate values, perhaps the most sensitive barometer of local economic conditions, measured the depression's harshest impact on the city—real estate valued at $11,646,293 in 1873 was worth only $11,647,135 in 1880, an increase of less than $1,000 during a seven-year period. [30]

The depression did not, however, curtail Atlanta's commercial growth altogether. The value of the city's trade in 1878 was estimated at $40 million, a modest increase. According to those who produced the 1878 estimate, wholesale trade showed the most vigor in that year. Some observers claimed that the depression actually helped, since retail merchants in nearby towns had to cut down on travel costs and so purchased goods in Atlanta rather than New York. [31]

Although industrial growth was not as impressive, manufacturing was not entirely neglected. Given that the value of manufactured goods and capital invested in manufacturing in the South declined significantly between 1860 and 1870, the city's postbellum industrial achievements are respectable. By 1880, the amount invested in 196 manufacturing establishments with 3,680 workers was $2,468,456, roughly three times the investment, thirteen times the factories, and twelve times the workers the city had had twenty years earlier. In value of industrial products in 1880, Atlanta ranked only seventy-ninth among the nation's cities, but was ahead of every southern city except New Orleans, Nashville, and Richmond. Virtually all the capital for Atlanta's postbellum industrial growth had come from local sources. [32]

As was true of the city and the region during the antebellum

30. Hanleiter, *Atlanta City Directory for 1871*, pp. 132, 170; Atlanta *Constitution*, September 11, 1875; Atlanta *Daily Herald*, September 6, 27, October 7, November 23, 1873, September 6, 1874; CM, February 6, 1874; *Annual Report of the Comptroller-General of the State of Georgia, 1873* (Atlanta, 1873), 19; *Annual Report of the Comptroller-General of the State of Georgia, 1880* (Atlanta, 1880), 106.

31. Atlanta *News*, August 30, 1874; Atlanta *Constitution*, September 5, 1878.

32. Sellers, "Economic Incidence of the Civil War," in Andreano (ed.), *Economic Impact of the American Civil War*, 84–85; *Report on the Manufactures of the United States at the Tenth Census* (1883), 379–80, 382.

period, relatively large-scale industries were predominant in 1880. Twenty-three industrial establishments in that year employed fifty or more workers, and their combined payrolls represented 63 percent of the city's industrial work force. Most employees were involved in building construction, metals fabrication, paper goods manufacture, or lumber processing. Building construction was the most popular industrial activity in Atlanta, though metals fabrication would have enjoyed that status had not Lewis Scofield's rolling mill, the city's largest industrial employer at the time, become a casualty of the 1870s depression. There were 315 employees when the mill went bankrupt in 1875.[33]

At the same time that manufacturing plants were rebuilt or inaugurated, the pro-industrial ethos born during the Civil War was revived and intensified in Atlanta after 1865. Local urban promoters were keenly aware of the need to couple industrial and commercial growth. "If Atlanta would continue to grow in population . . . as in the past, she will find it necessary to engage extensively in manufacturing ventures," wrote one local newspaper editor in 1869. "It is utterly impossible to concentrate large populations on commercial interests alone." In an enthusiastic address in 1874, Jonathan Norcross listed Atlanta's advantages—among them, cheap labor, excellent railroad facilities, and proximity to plentiful sources of cotton, coal, and iron. "This city must not only enlarge as a commercial center," he concluded, "but must from the nature of things, at no distant day, become a great manufacturing centre."[34]

A number of new organizations were founded in Atlanta to translate Norcross' expectation into reality. The setting for Norcross' speech, the Mechanics' Institute, was established in 1874 to promote "knowledge of the skills of workingmen's trades" and local manufacturing. Industrialists and merchants as well as mechanics enrolled as members of the institute. Three other new associations were created: the Atlanta Agricultural and Industrial Association, organized in 1872 with John B. Gordon as its first president; the German Manufacturing Association, founded in 1875; and the Atlanta Manufac-

33 Atlanta *Daily Herald*, January 10, June 16, 1875. Statistics computed from manuscripts of the 1880 manufacturing census for Fulton County, Georgia, in William R. Perkins Library, Duke University, Durham.
34. Atlanta *Constitution*, January 6, 1869; *Manufacturing Industries: An Address by Mr. J. Norcross before the Mechanics' Institute in Atlanta, Georgia, on the Eligibility of Atlanta as a Manufacturing City* (Atlanta, 1874).

turers' Association, first organized in 1872 with John C. Peck as president.[35]

The Atlanta Manufacturers' Association was the most active of these organizations. One could join by paying a two-dollar initiation fee, and many merchants as well as industrialists did so. The association performed such tasks as collecting statistics on local industries' output, reporting on the potential of various manufacturing schemes, and subsidizing prizes at state fairs for the best display of locally manufactured articles. The association was especially effective at pressuring the city council. In 1873, the council was persuaded to remove all taxes (except for those on real estate) on all existing and future cotton, wool, and iron factories in the city.[36]

Despite the promotional activities of the Atlanta Manufacturers' Association and similar organizations, the city's economy remained predominantly commercial until 1880. In 1870, more of the city's working population (15.3 percent) had commercial jobs, and 9.7 percent were in manufacturing. Ten years later, the proportions were, respectively, 19.0 percent and 14.5 percent (see Table 2 in Appendix A). Both industrial and commercial growth in Atlanta in the fifteen years after the Civil War were impressive, however, in light of the economic paralysis that characterized most southern cities and the region as a whole.

Public and Private Enterprise

Businessmen and public officials organized a variety of entrepreneurial ventures, several of which had a visible impact on Atlanta's growth. An incomplete inventory would include bringing the state capital to Atlanta (1868), attracting the Georgia State Agricultural Society fairs (beginning in 1870), constructing a U.S. customshouse (1875) to encourage overseas trade, a campaign to build Georgia's largest cotton factory, and more than a dozen separate canal and railroad projects.

Before depression conditions caused a revision of Atlanta's charter in 1874 to restrict municipal expenditures and indebtedness, local government contributed substantial sums to several of these enter-

35. Atlanta *Constitution*, October 28, 1874 (quotation), April 18, 1871, January 12, 1872; Atlanta *Daily Herald*, January 8, April 4, 1874, January 6, 1875.
36. William T. Newman (comp.), *Code of the City of Atlanta* (Atlanta, 1875), 105; Atlanta *Constitution*, February 21, March 7, 26, 1873, July 5, August 14, 1874.

prises. It appropriated \$133,000 in city bonds and \$60,000 in cash for construction of the capitol, \$75,000 in bonds for fairgrounds, and \$50,000 in cash to purchase a lot for the customshouse. It also renewed its stock subscriptions to the Georgia Air Line and the Georgia Western railroad projects, which required an additional \$600,000 in municipal bonds. The partnership of municipal government and private entrepreneurs in several of these ventures was an excellent representation of what one economic historian has called the "American system."[37]

There is neither space nor compelling need to describe in detail the plethora of entrepreneurial schemes launched in postbellum Atlanta. Three of them merit brief discussion, since they were effectively turning points in the city's entrepreneurial history. The campaigns to build the Georgia Air Line and the Georgia Western railroads marked the beginning of an era during which community leaders were forced to realize that railroads were being integrated into the national economy and were increasingly beyond local control. The crusade to build the Atlanta Cotton Factory presaged the pro-industrial fervor and industrial expositions of the 1880s, which established the city as a regional center for New South urban-industrial boosterism.

Both the Georgia Air Line and the Georgia Western projects were revived primarily because freight rate discriminations against Atlanta still existed. And businessmen and civic officials held the antebellum view of the rates. "Her railroads are the greatest enemies Atlanta has," wrote one local newspaper editor in 1877. "The envy of would-be rivals to her growth and prominence as a great city . . . would be ineffectual did not the railroads . . . combine against her." Such complaints were justified—southern railroads' rate structures through the 1870s still often reflected proprietary interests of individual cities that had invested heavily in various lines. But Atlanta's continued lack of competing water transportation was probably more significant. Whatever the cause of the discriminatory rates, the city's business leaders decided early in the postbellum era that building locally controlled railroads was the only sure method for eliminating them.[38]

37. Robert A. Lively, "The American System: A Review Article," *Business History Review*, XXIX (1955), 81–96.
38. Atlanta *Tribune*, December 17, 1877; William Z. Ripley, *Railroads: Rates and Regulations* (New York, 1927), 385–86; Maury Klein, "The Strategy of Southern Railroads," *American Historical Review*, LXIII (1968), 1054.

Efforts to revive the Georgia Air Line project began as early as 1866 but did not make much headway until 1868, when local promoters staged a series of public meetings. Speakers argued that the Air Line, a link in a route more direct than that of seacoast railroads and ocean steamships to New York and other eastern cities, would be especially beneficial to dry goods merchants and cotton brokers. During the course of the meetings, Samuel B. Hoyt, Alfred Austell, Jonathan Norcross, and a few other Atlanta businessmen decided to approach A. S. Buford, president of the Richmond & Danville, who was known to be interested in building a chain of railroads between Charlotte and Atlanta.[39]

Upon the invitation of Norcross and his associates, Buford came to Atlanta on November 11, 1868, and addressed a large convocation of local businessmen. "Atlanta should not allow strangers to control the Air Line," Buford warned solemnly. Although local citizens should, preferably, supply the entire amount, Buford added that his company would provide $100,000 of the $500,000 needed to build the first twenty miles of the road north of Atlanta, if local capitalists would raise the remainder. He did not bother to explain just how far local citizens would get "controlling" only twenty miles of the Air Line. Nevertheless, his stirring speech, which stressed the Air Line's potential role in the city's commercial development, elicited $210,000 in private stock subscriptions on the spot. On the same day, Buford also persuaded Atlanta's city council to renew its antebellum pledge of $300,000 in municipal bonds to buy stock in the railroad. A few weeks later, Buford obtained another $240,000 in bonds from the Georgia legislature.[40] This combination of public and private support was more than enough to launch the project.

Actual construction did not begin until February, 1869. The work of laying the track proceeded slowly over rugged terrain, crossing mountains and deep valleys. By May, 1871, the southern portion extended only to Gainesville, Georgia, fifty-five miles from Atlanta. Another section, from Spartanburg, South Carolina, to Charlotte, was nearly finished by that time. Not until August, 1873, was the

39. *Charter of the Atlanta & Richmond Air Line* (Atlanta, 1871); Atlanta *Daily New Era*, November 8, 10, 11, 1868; *Pioneer Citizens' History of Atlanta, 1833–1902* (Atlanta, 1902), 204.
40. Buford quoted in Atlanta *Daily New Era*, November 11, 1868; Glenn (cod.), *Code of the City of Atlanta*, 95; Elizabeth Studley Nathans, *Losing the Peace: Georgia Republicans and Reconstruction, 1865–1871* (Baton Rouge, 1968), 119–20.

entire Air Line completed between Atlanta and Charlotte. Total construction costs were put at $7.95 million, of which sum public and private sources in Atlanta had contributed approximately $500,000.[41]

Although it formed a link with other railroads in a direct line to Richmond, the Atlanta & Charlotte Air Line aroused little enthusiasm when it was completed. There was no local control over the road, and that was due to the relatively modest contribution made by Atlanta's public and private agencies. In 1869, of the nine directors of the Georgia Air Line alone (the portion of the route between Atlanta and Spartanburg), three were from Atlanta and the rest were from outside Georgia. Recognizing belatedly what had happened, Atlanta's city council in that year threatened to repudiate its municipal bond issue but eventually abandoned that idea. Without local control, the railroad was useless as a means of alleviating freight rate discriminations. Complaints about the Atlanta & Charlotte Air Line's discriminating against local merchants were heard soon after the road opened for business in 1874.[42]

The Georgia Western Railroad took even more time to complete than did the Air Line and, like the Air Line, eventually fell prey to corporate interests beyond local control. Proponents of the Georgia Western early in the postbellum period saw the road in combination with other projected lines in Alabama as an alternative to the Western & Atlantic for importing western foodstuffs. They also increasingly saw the project as a prerequisite to industrialization, as its western terminus in Alabama could be located near the rich coal and iron fields in the Coosa and Warrior valleys. Anthracite coal was especially desirable to fuel the steam engines common in Atlanta factories after the war.[43]

Local railroad promoters including Richard Peters, George W. Adair, and Lemuel P. Grant obtained a new charter from the state legislature in 1868 to build the Georgia Western, but soon ran into trouble getting construction under way. A strong advocate of the project before the war, Peters persuaded the city council, of which he

41. Maury Klein, *The Great Richmond Terminal: A Study in Businessmen and Business Strategy* (Charlottesville, 1970), 61–64; General Alfred Austell to Colonel A. S. Buford, March 8, 1872, in "Letters Received by the President of the Atlanta & Richmond Air Line Railway Co., October 14, 1871 to May 23, 1872," Perkins Library, Duke; CM, June 7, 1869; Reed, *History of Atlanta*, 434; *Pioneer Citizens' History*, 204; Atlanta *Constitution*, May 27, 1871, August 26, 1873.
42. CM, June 7, 1869; Atlanta *Daily Herald*, November 10, 1874.
43. *Pioneer Citizens' History*, 107, 202–203.

was a member, in 1868 to renew its pledge of $300,000 in municipal bonds to the railroad, but he could not convince his fellow directors of the Georgia Railroad and Banking Company to reaffirm their $250,000 stock subscription. Peters' associates on the Georgia Railroad's board of directors feared that the Georgia Western would siphon off cotton and trade from Augusta to Atlanta. George Hillyer, another Atlanta resident and Georgia Railroad director, wrote to the city council in 1871 that his company renounced its antebellum subscription. The city clerk disdainfully entered the letter in the minutes under the heading "Georgia Railroad Taking the Back Track." The city council sued the Georgia Railroad and Banking Company but lost the case.[44]

The project then languished for several years. The Georgia Railroad's action discouraged fund-raising efforts, and the construction costs from Atlanta to Jacksonville, Alabama, were estimated at $3.5 million in 1873. When the panic of 1873 arrived, only twenty-seven miles of roadbed were graded and ready for iron. The 1874 revision of Atlanta's municipal charter severely restricted the city's ability henceforth to take stock subscriptions in railroads and canals. Eliminating the possibility of further municipal aid also hindered efforts to recruit private investment.[45]

Events in 1879 and 1880 brought new opportunities to complete the Georgia Western. The Louisville & Nashville and the Nashville, Chattanooga & St. Louis were fighting to create through lines from their respective western terminal cities to the southern Atlantic seaboard. E. W. Cole, president of the Nashville, Chattanooga & St. Louis and co-lessee of the W & A with Joseph E. Brown, made the first move in 1879 by leasing the Central of Georgia Railroad. His system thereby had a through line all the way from St. Louis to Savannah. That action greatly alarmed the L & N's managers, and Atlanta promoters saw a chance to complete the Georgia Western. For $30,000 they sold the Georgia Western's charter to the L & N, believing that the L & N would have to build the road to compete with the Cole-Brown system. Henry Grady, who covered these intricate maneuvers for the Atlanta *Constitution*, visited H. Victor Newcombe, an L & N official, in his hotel suite in New York in 1880 and

44. CM, September 4, December 11, 1868, June 30, July 7, August 4 (quotation), 1871; Atlanta *Constitution*, July 6, August 10, 1871.

45. CM, January 31, 1873; Atlanta *Constitution*, February 22, 1879; Atlanta *Daily Herald*, January 3, 1874.

found a map of the Georgia Western spread out upon a table. "Victor Newcombe is the Moses that leads Atlanta out of bondage" was the wire Grady sent back to his hometown.[46]

To the dismay of Grady and many of his fellow citizens, the L & N soon found a less expensive way to thwart the Cole-Brown interests. In January, 1880, the L & N secretly purchased a majority of the stock of the Nashville, Chattanooga & St. Louis, fired Cole as president, and canceled the lease of the Central of Georgia. Atlanta supporters of the Georgia Western were furious. They had sold the charter with the provision that the road would be completed in sixty days, but the L & N proceeded to ignore this agreement. When Grady asked another L & N official whether his company would surrender the lease to the people of Atlanta, the official arrogantly responded, "Why should we?"[47]

Eventually the L & N relinquished its rights to the Georgia Western to John B. Gordon and a New York syndicate. In a series of Byzantine maneuvers, Gordon's group gave their claim over to the Richmond & West Point, which reincorporated the road as the Georgia Pacific in 1883. This railroad was finally completed in that year from Birmingham to Atlanta, but, like the Georgia Air Line, it was only a minor part of a vast railroad system that did not serve local interests. Atlanta newspapers and the chamber of commerce frequently complained about freight rate discriminations by the Georgia Pacific in the 1880s.[48]

Although the Georgia Pacific and the Atlanta & Charlotte Air Line were important additions to the city's railroad network, neither fulfilled the expectations of its backers in Atlanta. Railroad promoters' experience was part of a larger story: many cities abandoned transportation schemes as a favored form of public and private enterprise. During the 1870s, control of railroads for all but a few cities became impossible because of rising construction costs. The depression that began in 1873 compelled many local governments to recognize this fundamental change in the railroad economy, and they altered state constitutions and municipal charters to prohibit public

46. Maury Klein, *History of the Louisville & Nashville Railroad* (New York, 1972), 153–62; Atlanta *Constitution*, December 18, 1879, January 9, March 16 (quotation), 1880.
47. Atlanta *Constitution*, January 21, 30, February 1, January 24 (quotation), 1880.
48. Stover, *Railroads of the South*, 196–99; Atlanta *Constitution*, April 1, 17, 1886; Minutes of the Atlanta Chamber of Commerce, April 4, 1888, in Atlanta Chamber of Commerce Archives, Atlanta.

financing of railroads and canals. Railroad managers also increasingly looked beyond local interests, and so withdrawing public funding was eminently rational. [49]

Although the completion of the Georgia Pacific and Atlanta & Richmond Air Line did not create freight rates as favorable for Atlanta's businessmen as it did for their counterparts in other cities, several factors minimized that liability by 1880. Competition among the railroads consistently benefited Atlanta shippers. Most southern railroads joined the Southern Railway & Steamship Association created in 1875 to halt "ruinous rate wars" by pooling and dividing freight earnings according to prearranged agreements, but the pool simply did not work. The association's general commissioner stated that 1880 was the first year in which there were no serious violations of the agreements. Atlanta, however, greeted these violations with pleasure since they resulted in low freight rates that the pool's organizers labored fruitlessly to raise. Inaugurated in 1879, the state of Georgia's Railroad Commission acted quickly to equalize freight rates on "short hauls," preventing especially the Central of Georgia and the Georgia from adjusting rates to steer too much traffic away from Atlanta to Augusta and Savannah. [50] The proof that such developments were sufficient to ameliorate Atlanta's freight rate problems is that the city's economic growth greatly exceeded that of cities that allegedly controlled various railroads. A frequent cause of community protest before and after the Civil War and symbol of Atlanta's "oppression" by rival cities, freight rate discriminations had by 1880 little adverse impact on the city's prosperity.

As railroad projects became less fruitful, various schemes to promote industrialization emerged. The focus of the pro-industrial movement in Atlanta before 1880 was the city's first cotton factory, which rapidly turned into a social crusade similar to the southern cotton mill movement in the 1880s. The merchants, industrialists, and public officials who led the movement to build the factory em-

49. See Carter Goodrich, "State In, State Out—A Pattern of Development Policy," *Journal of Economic Issues*, II (1968), 365–83; Goodrich, "Internal Improvements Reconsidered," *JEH*, XXX (1970), 289–311; and Goodrich, "Public Aid to Railroads in the Reconstruction South," *Political Science Quarterly*, LXXI (1956), 407–42.

50. Henry Hudson, "The Southern Railway and Steamship Association," in William Z. Ripley (ed.), *Railway Problems* (Boston, 1907), 98–123; *Circular Letters of the Southern Railway & Steamship Association*, Vol. VII, No. 64, in Perkins Library, Duke; Maury Klein, *Edward Porter Alexander* (Athens, 1971), 165–68; Maxwell Ferguson, *State Regulation of Railroads in the South* (New York, 1916), 95–104.

phasized the enterprise's critical importance. If only one mill were
built, they argued, northern capital would pour into Atlanta for
similar ventures. "If this factory is finished, and successfully operated
for one year, it will be the mother of a dozen factories," maintained
George W. Adair. "There is plenty of money looking for investment
in manufactures now—all it wants is an experiment to justify a
venture."[51]

To supervise the drive, the city's business community turned to its
most flamboyant urban promoter, Hannibal Ingalls Kimball. A native of Maine and a controversial figure in Reconstruction politics in
Georgia, Kimball was involved in almost every important entrepreneurial project in Atlanta during the postbellum period. He had been
a principal in the movement to transfer the state capital to Atlanta,
locate the agricultural society's fairs in the city, and build the grandiose hotel that bore his name. He was also notorious for his ties to
the Radical Republicans, and he participated in several shady deals,
which included receipt of state bonds for railroads that were never
built, the unfinished "Opera House" he supplied for use as a capitol,
and the lease of the state-owned W & A by a private syndicate of
which he was a member. Kimball had fled the state in 1871, barely
escaping prosecution for these and other misdeeds, and was delighted
when he received an invitation three years later to return to Atlanta as
manager of the cotton factory crusade. Kimball saw in this scheme "a
chance to vindicate his name," and the city's business community
saw an opportunity to use his obvious ability as a promoter.[52]

A few months after his return, Kimball went before a large audience, which included the chamber of commerce, the mayor, and
the city council, at the Mechanics' Institute and delivered a speech
entitled "The Manufacture of Cotton in Atlanta." The speech was a
masterpiece, full of statistics and artful rhetoric demonstrating the
city's industrial potential and the cotton factory's feasibility. With
careful calculations, Kimball showed how a cotton mill with twenty
thousand spindles would pay cash dividends of 18 percent per annum. The only thing that might prevent such a moneymaking institution from being completed, according to Kimball, would be
Atlantans' unwillingness to invest in it. "We cannot expect to induce

51. Atlanta *Constitution*, September 19, 1876.
52. H. I. Kimball to R. A. Alston, March 7, 1874, in Felix Hargrett Collection, UGA.
See also Alice E. Reagan, *H. I. Kimball, Entrepreneur* (Atlanta, 1983), 72–76.

the investment of foreign capital among us for any enterprise in which we are not willing to embark ourselves," he intoned. "Let us build the first factory, and prove by its success the truth of our statements and there will be no trouble in procuring capital from outside sources to build a dozen more." Kimball concluded by outlining a plan whereby all parts of the community—from merchants to mechanics—would buy stock in proportion to their income. He set an immediate example, subscribing $10,000 himself. On the basis of his inspiring words and actions, Kimball was promptly elected president of the Atlanta Cotton Factory.[53]

The movement to build the factory was long and drawn-out. Not until July, 1875, was the total stock ($250,000) subscribed. A groundbreaking ceremony was held the same month, but the mill did not open until 1879. Kimball was chiefly responsible for the slow rate of progress. Once again in his career, he was accused of chicanery and fraud. According to his detractors, he subscribed $60,000 of the stock but paid in only $1,200. In 1877, his own board of directors caught him with five carloads of wood and coal (which he was apparently using to heat his house) that were supposed to be on the company's premises. Kimball also negotiated a faulty contract with the Lowell Machinery Company of Massachusetts in 1875, which sent the factory into bankruptcy the following year. There were then several years of expensive litigation.[54]

The Atlanta Cotton Factory finally opened on July 1, 1879. A large crowd gathered for a gala celebration there on the W & A near the city's center. At four o'clock a brass band played "Hail to the Chief," and Kimball strutted through the factory gates, flanked by Governor Alfred H. Colquitt, Mayor William L. Calhoun, and former governors Joseph E. Brown and Benjamin Conley. One florid speech after another praised Kimball's work. The universal sentiment was that only Kimball could have brought the enterprise to completion. And furthermore, Atlanta was on its way to becoming the industrial center of the New South.[55]

53. H. I. Kimball, *Cotton Factory: An Address by H. I. Kimball before the Mechanics' Institute of Atlanta, December 20, 1874, on the Manufacture of Cotton in Atlanta* (Atlanta, 1875), 13; Atlanta *Daily Herald*, December 30, 1874.

54. Atlanta *Daily Herald*, July 7, 1875; Atlanta *Constitution*, November 23, 1876, March 30, April 3, 11, 1882.

55. Atlanta *Constitution*, July 1, 1879; Victor S. Clark, *History of Manufactures in the United States* (2 vols.; New York, 1929), II, 187.

The cotton factory, the first really important manifestation of pro-industrialization in postbellum Atlanta, was a forerunner of the industrial expositions in the 1880s. It also had roots in the past. Industrialization was an extension of the Civil War manufacturing crusade. Other entrepreneurial ventures successfully completed projects begun during the antebellum period. There were many continuities in Atlanta's economic history.

Atlanta was still an upstart interior city engaged in a struggle with older coastal and plantation belt cities for urban supremacy in the Southeast. But the advantage was definitely swinging in favor of interior cities such as Atlanta, and the seaports especially seemed incapable of coping with the situation. Indeed, many fell into genteel decay. While promoters in post–Civil War Atlanta built railroads, a luxurious hotel, a state capitol, and a large cotton factory, Charleston's business community failed to build a resort hotel and to promote an industrial exposition. Mobile's economic elite did little more than celebrate Mardi Gras and then flee to cooler locations when summer arrived.[56] Atlanta boosters' claims that their businessmen were more energetic than were their rivals in the "sleepy, cotton ports" were grounded in reality. How entrepreneurial activities and New South values evolved from Atlanta's social structure and leadership needs closer examination.

56. Don H. Doyle, "Leadership and Decline in Postwar Charleston, 1865–1910," in Walter J. Fraser, Jr., and Winfred B. Moore, Jr. (eds.), *From the Old South to the New: Essays on the Transitional South* (Westport, Conn., 1981), 100–103; Doyle, "Urbanization and Southern Culture: Economic Elites in Four New South Cities (Atlanta, Nashville, Charleston, Mobile) c. 1865–1910," in Orville Vernon Burton and Robert C. McMath, Jr. (eds.), *Toward a New South? Studies in Post–Civil War Southern Communities* (Westport, Conn., 1982), 26–29.

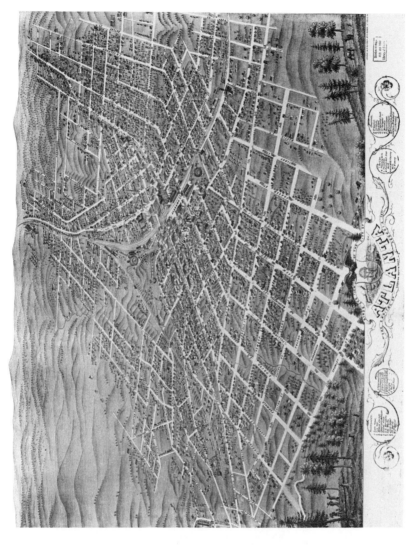

Bird's-eye view of Atlanta, 1871

Peachtree Street, 1865

Pryor Street, 1875

First Kimball House, completed 1871 and destroyed by fire 1883

Atlanta skyline, 1889

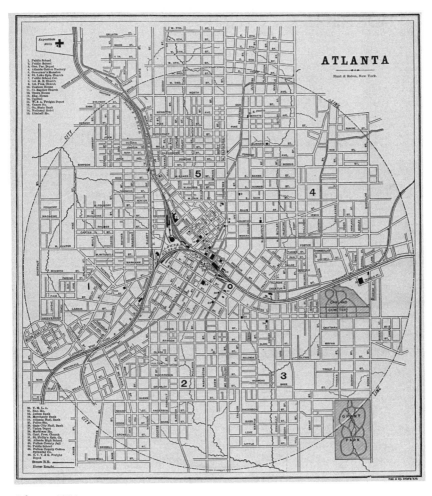

Atlanta, 1886

6

SOCIAL BASES OF "NEW SOUTH" ENTERPRISE
Values, Population Characteristics, and Leadership, 1865–1880

[T]here is no city in this or any other country more free from the domination of *caste*; admission to society being based on character alone. . . . All men are welcomed, and eagerly welcomed to our midst—capitalist or laborer, the seeker after a home or employment—objection being made only to *drones*.

—E. Y. Clarke, *Illustrated History of Atlanta* (1879)

Hang the old customs! They are rags and tatters, and as such are sloughed off with each preceding generation.

—Atlanta *Daily New Era* (1867)

$\mathbf{M}$any observers of postbellum Atlanta were convinced that its societal values and especially its business leadership were different from those prevalent elsewhere in the region. The city had not only recovered remarkably from the war but also accepted enthusiastically Yankee capitalism and rejected the plantation ideal and other fundamentals of Old South culture. The net result was a climate of opportunity that was absent in most southern cities. As one visitor summarized Atlanta's social system in 1875, "the descendant of the time-honored sire could not make his bread . . . [in] this capital, but a fair start was given to energy and ability of either Northern or Southern birth."[1] It was this economic and social democracy that many believed was the underlying cause of the city's economic progress.

Exploring some of these theories can help us gain a better understanding of "New South" Atlanta's social structure and values. The analysis will focus on what was different about social values, economic opportunity, and leadership. And then we can assess what was really "new" about Atlanta during the fifteen years after 1865.

"New South" Values and Population Trends

Confronted with troublesome issues about race relations and Reconstruction, business leaders and public officials adopted a number of policies that were intended to further the city's image as an outpost of progress in a backward region. These policies signaled that the city did not adhere to restrictive Old South social norms and that northern men and capital would be welcome. One historian points out that during early Reconstruction when northerners were often ostracized in Savannah and lowland Georgia, Atlanta boosters were eager to show that such attitudes did not prevail in their city. They were determined to convince outsiders, in sum, that the city was ready for the new age. In this ideological climate, even Sherman was invited back. In 1879 the cranky general was received as cordially as any potential northern investor. There were only a few polite jests about his "carelessness with matches."[2]

1. Columbus *Enquirer* quoted in Atlanta *Daily Herald*, October 6, 1875.
2. C. Mildred Thompson, *Reconstruction in Georgia: Economic, Social, Political, 1865–1872* (New York, 1915), 127–29; Atlanta *Constitution*, January 7, 1879.

Early in the Reconstruction era, Atlanta's business leaders manifested their willingness to rejoin the Union and pursue material progress. Most of the South recoiled in horror at the passage of the Military Reconstruction Acts in 1867, but Atlanta's businessmen and civic leaders mobilized to prepare the city for at least public acquiescence to the demands of Congress. A stormy public meeting chaired by Richard Peters on March 4, two days after Congress passed the first bill, ended with a series of resolutions that "without the least hesitation accept[ed] the plan of restoration" and extended "to our fellow citizens of every state a hearty and cordial invitation to come and settle in our midst."[3]

When Federal troops arrived in Atlanta, community leaders labored diligently to make their stay pleasant. Generals John Pope and George G. Meade, the first two commanders of the Third Military District, the headquarters of which were in Atlanta, were warmly received. A delegation organized by Richard Peters met Pope at the passenger depot on March 31, 1867, and escorted him to the National Hotel, where a lavish banquet was later held in his honor. At that banquet Pope expressed appreciation for his "unexpected" but "kind and friendly welcome." In 1869, a culinary festival staged by local businessmen witnessed the exchange of good-natured toasts between Meade and former general John B. Gordon, Georgia's most celebrated contribution to the Confederate army and a recent arrival in Atlanta. Banquets and receptions for the various commanders of the Federal garrison in the city, McPherson Barracks, were held during and after Reconstruction.[4]

Northern politicians and public figures, such as Radical Republicans Henry Wilson and William D. ("Pig Iron") Kelley, who went on speaking tours in the Reconstruction South, were also given friendly receptions. Most of those who invited men such as Wilson and Kelley to Atlanta were not themselves Radical Republicans. Their motives were economic rather than partisan. A committee consisting of Alfred Austell, James M. Calhoun, Lewis Scofield, and other wealthy citizens welcomed Kelley in 1867. His speech on the South's mineral and industrial resources, which he expected "in the new order of

3. *Daily Atlanta Intelligencer*, March 5, 1867.
4. Atlanta *Daily New Era*, April 13, 1867 (quotation); *ibid.*, January 18, May 30, 1869; *Daily Atlanta Intelligencer*, April 2, 21, 1867; Nellie Peters Black, *Richard Peters* (Atlanta, 1904), 30–31; Wallace P. Reed, *History of Atlanta, Georgia* (Syracuse, 1889), 234; *Pioneer Citizens' History of Atlanta, 1833–1902* (Atlanta, 1902), 111–12.

things would be fully developed," was well received. Wilson's reception committee included Richard Peters, William Markham, and several other prominent Atlanta businessmen. Henry Ward Beecher was also invited to deliver a speech in Atlanta in 1867, but he declined because of prior obligations.[5]

A more controversial project designed to impress northern capitalists was also launched in 1867 with the creation of a "Lincoln Monument Association of Atlanta." Six city council members voted for a resolution that authorized donating ten acres of municipally owned land to the association. None of those councilmen (among them, Richard Peters, banker E. W. Holland, dry goods merchant E. E. Rawson, and brick manufacturer Julius A. Hayden) were Republicans. The association, which Peters helped organize, had as its goal a monument to Lincoln that was to consist of a gigantic stone tower, carved out of Georgia marble, 100 feet thick at its base and 145 feet high. Reverend Wesley Prettyman, an employee of the Freedmen's Aid Society, was appointed principal agent and ordered to raise $1 million as soon as possible.[6]

Although Radical newspaper editor William L. Scruggs argued that completing the monument would bring "thousands of capitalists and businessmen from the North," too many citizens opposed these "sound business principles." The city council later rescinded its offer, and the monument was never built.[7] That such a proposal was ever seriously considered in a Deep South city during Reconstruction was an eloquent testimonial, however, to Atlanta businessmen's determination to placate the North and attract its dollars.

In addition, businessmen and their spokesmen disseminated reams of propaganda calculated to assure potential migrants of the city's political and social harmony. "We . . . extend to all honest and

5. *Daily Atlanta Intelligencer*, May 9 (quotation), 21, 1867; Atlanta *Daily New Era*, February 13, May 10, 19, 1867; Henry Ward Beecher to Joseph E. Brown, July 1, 1867, in Felix Hargrett Collection, UGA.

6. CM, September 20, 27, October 4, 1867; Atlanta *Daily New Era*, June 18, 1867; *Pioneer Citizens' History*, 102–103; Wesley Prettyman to Dear Brother Chalfant, August 28, 1867, in Papers of Freedmen's Aid Society of Methodist Episcopal Church, American Missionary Association Archives, Dillard University, New Orleans. Royce Shingleton maintains that the $1 million was set by Richard Peters and his colleagues to ensure that the monument would never be built (*Richard Peters: Champion of the New South* [Macon, 1985], 155–58). The council minutes, however, state that they voted to donate the land "in accordance with the scale of expenditure viz seven hundred and fifty thousand to one million of dollars proposed in the verbal statement made to council by J. L Dunning, president of the association" (CM, September 27, 1867). Dunning and others argued that such an expenditure would create many jobs.

7. *Daily Atlanta Intelligencer*, October 4, 1867.

enterprising persons a cordial welcome to settle with and join us in building what is destined to be one of the greatest inland cities of the world," wrote the publisher of an Atlanta city directory in 1870. "Come . . . whatever your political and religious credo . . . and have no fear of G. A. R.'s, K. K. K.'s, or anything else." An Atlanta newspaper editor promised a congressional committee investigating civil disorder in the South that "[k]indness and respect" especially awaited northern visitors "when they come on business, or for investment." To emphasize this theme, the editors of the *Constitution* published in 1873 a letter from an Ohio native, living in Atlanta, who denounced as "bosh" the charge that "any bitterness or ill feeling exists towards Northern men."[8]

To supplement advertising efforts, Atlanta's business community and its allies organized several immigration societies—among them, the Immigration Association of the State of Georgia (1871) with its headquarters in Atlanta and Lemuel P. Grant as its president, and the German Immigration Society (1868) led by Charles Rauschenbush. To encourage these societies' efforts, the railroads serving Atlanta agreed in 1869 at a special convention to charge foreign immigrants only one cent per mile for passenger fare. And several ministers in the city's black community founded the Negro Anti-Emigration Club (1876). Its stated goal was to dissuade Negro laborers from joining the "exodusters" migrating to the Southwest in the late 1870s.[9]

It was more difficult to control and project race relations favorably than to organize immigration societies. Especially in early Reconstruction, community spokesmen nevertheless did their best to convince outsiders that the grosser forms of race prejudice were absent from Atlanta. An image of racial violence would probably scare away outside investors. Newspaper editors and others specifically and repeatedly denied the existence of the KKK in the city. Even local blacks testifying in 1871 before the congressional committee appointed to investigate Klan activity supported the editors' claims and maintained that many blacks had come from rural districts to the city principally "to avoid Ku Klux outrages." In fact, only one incident of

8. William R. Hanleiter, *Atlanta City Directory for 1870* (Atlanta, 1870), 29; *House Miscellaneous Documents*, 40th Cong., 3rd Sess., p. 68; Atlanta *Constitution*, July 25, 1873.
9. *Proceedings of a Convention of the Presidents, Superintendents, and Other Officials of Southern Railways, For the Promotion of Immigration to the South, Held in the City of Atlanta, January 4th, 1869* (Atlanta, 1869), 12–13; Atlanta *Constitution*, January 22, 1871, March 10, 1876; Atlanta *Daily New Era*, April 11, 16, 1869.

Klan violence was recorded in the city's postbellum history. In July, 1879, according to an American Missionary Association agent, "three K. K. desperadoes" from an area twelve miles north of Atlanta swept into the city's black neighborhoods "like demons from the lower regions." Although these hooded outlaws invaded several homes, no one was hurt. [10]

Those who contradicted publicly the community consensus about racial peace met a swift and harsh response. When Radical Republican Otto Palmer, owner and editor of the *Deutsche Zeitung*, wrote carelessly in 1871 about "outrages" in the city and his comments were reprinted in several northern newspapers, he soon found himself at the receiving end of a barrage of furious criticism from former business associates and former subscribers. Leaders of Atlanta's German-Jewish community promptly organized a public meeting, and the group passed a number of resolutions censuring Palmer for actions that might discourage "immigration south." These resolutions were signed by Charles Rauschenbush, a former editor of the *Deutsche Zeitung*. Palmer's newspaper went out of business soon thereafter, and he left Atlanta. [11]

Local newspaper editors and community spokesmen made no such efforts to quash reports of physical violence between Atlanta blacks and the Federal soldiers stationed at McPherson Barracks, which at its zenith housed 578 officers and enlisted men. On the night of September 9, 1867, nine white soldiers roamed through Shermantown, a Negro settlement, and pillaged several homes and stores. Shoemaker Festus Flipper, a pillar of Atlanta's black community and father of a son who became the first Negro to graduate from West Point, was among those seized and severely beaten. More than two hundred Shermantown residents promptly armed themselves and prevented thereafter such incidents. Violent squabbles between local blacks and Federal troops took place in other neighborhoods for a variety of reasons in the late 1860s, however. "It is but the beginning of that war between the races . . . which will develop . . . whenever

10. Atlanta *Daily New Era*, March 26, 28, April 16, 1868; *House Reports*, 42nd Cong., 2nd Sess., No. 22, Pt. 6, pp. 11, 212, 700; Simon P. Smith to Reverend E. F. Williams, July 27, 1879, in Simon Smith Papers, American Missionary Association Archives; Allen W. Trelease, *White Terror: The Ku Klux Klan Conspiracy and Southern Reconstruction* (New York, 1971), 50, 79, 319–24, 409–10.

11. *Daily Atlanta Intelligencer*, January 30, 1870; Atlanta *Constitution*, October 18, 19, November 9, 1871.

and wherever attempts are made to force social equality," one newspaper editor concluded.[12] Such commentary contained a plea for understanding from as well as an accusation against the North, which community leaders believed had imposed hypocritical and unreasonable demands in the area of race relations.

Booster propaganda did not fulfill local leaders' aspirations that Yankees and other nonsoutherners would flock to the city. The geographical origins of Atlanta's population during the postbellum period scarcely differed from what they had been in 1850 (see Table 3 in Appendix A). About 92 percent in 1880 were born in the South and the border states, a little more than 4 percent were natives of other states and territories, and the remainder were foreign born (mostly of Germanic or Irish extraction). Atlanta had proportionally fewer foreigners and probably no more nonsouthern natives in its general population than did most other cities in the region by 1880.[13]

These population statistics are somewhat misleading, since they include a large black presence that was not there before the Civil War. None of a sample of black household heads in 1880 were born outside the South, border states, or Washington, D.C. About 75 percent of a sample of white male household heads in the same year were natives of the South or the border states, 11 percent were born elsewhere in the country, and the rest were foreigners. The nonsouthern element in Atlanta's white population was thus more substantial than published census data reveal, but that evidence does not contradict one newpaper editor's conclusion in 1887 that Atlanta was "built by people born and reared within a hundred miles of its streets." According to another writer, the popular belief that Atlanta was "a city of northern people" was "impossible to dislodge from the public mind," but the city could be more accurately described as "the home of the Georgia cracker and his monument."[14]

If nativity patterns in ante- and postbellum Atlanta were virtually identical, two aspects of the population after the war were undeniably new. One was the influx of Negroes from elsewhere in the South.

12.   Returns of Post of Atlanta, Fort McPherson Barracks (1866–1881), in Returns of U.S. Military Posts, 1800–1916, Microfilm Copy no. 617, NA; Henry Ossian Flipper, *The Colored Cadet at West Point* (New York, 1878), 12–13, 17; Atlanta *Constitution*, October 16, November 20, 1868, March 9, 1869; *Daily Atlanta Intelligencer*, September 12, 17 (quotation), 1867.
13.   Lawrence H. Larsen, *The Rise of the Urban South* (Lexington, Ky., 1985), 38, 44–45. *South* here refers to only the eleven states of the Confederacy.
14.   Atlanta *Constitution*, June 17, 1887, September 15, 1889.

Atlanta's 1870 black population of 9,929 was more than five times larger than the 1860 total and the population in 1880 was 16,330 (see Table 1 in Appendix A). Blacks constituted 46 percent of the city's population in 1870 and 44 percent in 1880.

Less obvious but almost as significant was the "newness" of Atlanta's white population. Relatively few of a sample of white male household heads who had lived in antebellum Atlanta were still in the city five years after the war's end. The persistence rate of those household heads from 1860 to 1870 was only 38 percent, the lowest rate of any of the white samples traced for this study (see Table 9 in Appendix A). Priority rates (which involve tracing individuals found in one census back to an earlier one) of the 1870 and 1880 samples confirm that impression. Only 24 percent of the 1870 sample and only 12 percent of the 1880 sample had lived in Atlanta in 1860 (see Table 10 in Appendix A). These statistics—especially the decennial persistence rate of the 1860 sample—may well reflect the loss of life during the Civil War, which by one estimate cost Georgia nearly thirty thousand dead. The only other study of population persistence for a southern community through the Civil War does not show comparable population turnover, but the war did not affect that community as severely as it did Atlanta and its environs.[15]

"New South" Atlanta was thus new in several ways. The city's business and civic leaders were more committed than were many of their competitors to city building, and they were willing to discard various southern ideals and animosity toward Yankees and other outsiders. The population from which the leaders emerged also represented a fresh presence in the city.

Indexes of Opportunity

"The one sole idea in every man's mind is to make money," Robert Somers wrote of Atlanta in 1865. There is no reason to doubt that this blatantly materialistic attitude prevailed among newcomers and long-time residents during the post–Civil War era. More problematic is how many men fulfilled their ambitions. According to the Atlanta Chamber of Commerce, "[A]ny active industrious man may employ his time and capital . . . with a sure guarantee of being

15. Peter Wallenstein, "Rich Man's War, Rich Man's Fight: Civil War and the Transformation of Public Finance in Georgia," *JSH*, L (1984), 38n60; Randolph B. Campbell, *A Southern Community in Crisis: Harrison County, Texas, 1850–1880* (Austin, 1983), 367–95.

crowned with success."[16] No serious student of nineteenth-century American cities would accept this statement as valid, but it is entirely possible that in a rapidly expanding economy, opportunities were greater than they were elsewhere. The allegedly democratic structure of opportunity for southerners and outsiders can best be investigated by means of quantitative indicators such as wealth holding, occupational rank and mobility, and population stability.

Not surprisingly, statistical analysis of real and personal wealth data recorded in the federal census of 1870 suggests that property accumulation was not as easy as the chamber of commerce implied. The distribution of wealth that year was, in fact, no more democratic than it had been before the Civil War (see Table 5 in Appendix A). Only 117 individuals (about 1 percent of the total population twenty-one years of age or older) owned 55 percent of all the wealth listed by the census takers. About 71 percent of adult males and 96 percent of adult females owned no property at all. Further, according to the Gini Index of Inequality, the distribution of wealth was no more equitable than it was elsewhere in the country. The Gini for the total wealth of all property holders and adult males in Atlanta in 1870 was a very high .916. This figure is slightly higher than Gini values based on federal census data in the same year for Milwaukee, Chicago, the South, and the entire country.[17]

Further statistical analysis reveals several distinctive patterns of wealth holding. As expected, race was the factor most associated with poverty. Only 311 black men and 27 black women (about 3 percent of the adult population) owned property, and only 1 had personal and real wealth valued at more than $5,000. This relatively well-heeled man with a total estate of $6,000 was a mulatto barber, Robert Webster (alias Robert Yancey, son of Benjamin Yancey). Webster and other mulatto property holders were richer than were their darker-skinned fellow Atlantans. The mean wealth of mulattoes was about 70 percent greater than that of blacks in postbellum Atlanta.[18]

16. Robert Somers, *The Southern States since the War, 1870–1871* (New York, 1871), 340–41; *First Annual Report of the Atlanta Chamber of Commerce for the Year 1885: Historical, Descriptive, Statistical* (Atlanta, 1886), 68.

17. Lee Soltow, *Wealthholding in Wisconsin Since 1850* (Milwaukee, 1971), 9–10; Soltow, *Men and Wealth in the United States, 1850–1870* (New Haven, 1975), 9, 103, 181; Edward Busbyns, "Nativity and the Distribution of Wealth: Chicago, 1870," *Explorations in Economic History*, XIX (1982), 104.

18. On Webster, see Atlanta *News*, March 7, 1875; and F. Ayer to Reverend Sam Hunt, June 2, 1866, in American Missionary Association Archives. The mean real and personal wealth of black and mulatto property holders in 1870 was, respectively, $429 and $726.

Interestingly, the gap between the mean wealth of mulattoes and blacks was not a function of literacy or occupational advantages. Mulattoes were better paid for the same work and the same educational requirements. A study of the distribution of wealth among Philadelphia Negroes in 1870 reveals that mulattoes had a similar edge, and occupational advantages did not account for it.[19] These findings suggest that skin color contributed in some unknown way to differences in wealth among blacks and mulattoes.

Statistical examination of the white property holders in Atlanta in 1870 reveals other interesting variations involving nativity. Foreigners, about 5 percent of the total population, constituted 16 percent of the white property holders and owned 14 percent of all the wealth recorded by the census takers. Those born in states and territories outside the South accounted for 9 percent of the white property holders, which was roughly their proportion of the total population. Nonsouthern natives held 21 percent of the total wealth, far in excess of their share of the population. Their mean wealth was nearly three times and the mean wealth of foreigners slightly greater than that of white southern natives.[20]

These statistics lead to several conclusions about the distribution of wealth in white Atlanta. Most important, both nonsouthern natives and foreigners fared relatively well in acquiring property, so in a sense boosters were right about the city's receptivity to outsiders. Approximately two-thirds of the foreign property holders were Irish and German. The few available studies of the distribution of wealth elsewhere in the United States during this period show that in Chicago and in Wisconsin in 1870 the mean wealth of Germans, Irish, and other ethnic groups fell well below that of native-born Americans.[21]

The prosperity of foreigners in postbellum Atlanta probably says less, however, about the structure of opportunity than the selectivity

19. Theodore Hershberg and Henry Williams, "Mulattoes and Blacks: Intragroup Color Differences and Social Stratification in Nineteenth-Century Philadelphia," in Theodore Hershberg (ed.), *Philadelphia: Work, Space, Family, and Group Experience in the 19th Century* (New York, 1981), 415–21.

20. Richard J. Hopkins, "Patterns of Persistence and Occupational Mobility in a Southern City: Atlanta, 1870–1920" (Ph.D. dissertation, Emory University, 1972), Table I–1 on p. 9. Nonsouthern natives represented 7.5 percent of the white population in the sample chosen to depict Atlanta's work force in that year. The mean total estates (real and personal property) of white southern, nonsouthern, and foreign property holders in 1870 were, respectively, $6,086, $16,662, and $6,308.

21. Soltow, *Wealthholding in Wisconsin*, 38; Busbyns, "Nativity and the Distribution of Wealth," 101–109.

of immigrant populations. The majority of those foreigners who came to Atlanta after the Civil War had lived in New York and other northeastern cities, and many doubtless acquired capital and occupational skills before undertaking the expensive journey south. Many immigrants feared racial discrimination, which may have scared off most of those who were not financially secure. Similar factors and the South's well-known need for capital and skilled labor may have also drawn nonsouthern natives who were already relatively prosperous.[22]

Unlike the distribution of wealth, which was similar before and after the war, the data on occupational rank give the misleading impression that opportunities for personal advancement declined significantly (see Table 6 in Appendix A). In 1870, those with white-collar occupations were 23 percent of the working population; 42 percent were unskilled laborers. Ten years later, the percentages were about the same. Throughout the post–Civil War era, the percentage in the lowest occupational category was more than three times the antebellum figure, and the percentage in the top category about half.

As Table 6 makes clear, adding the black population to the occupational classifications accounts for this apparent decline in white-collar and increase in unskilled-labor jobs. If slaves could have been included in the antebellum classifications, as freedmen were after the war, the disparities would have been equally obvious. In 1880, only about 3 percent of the black work force had white-collar jobs while 61 percent were unskilled laborers.[23] More than 80 percent of all unskilled and nearly 70 percent of all semi-skilled workers that year were black. Race was, in fact, the only factor that strongly affected occupational rank. Although nonsoutherners and foreigners tended to have slightly higher occupational rankings than did southern whites, the differences were not statistically significant.

Analysis of occupational mobility reveals more complex patterns than does analysis of occupational rank. White male household heads generally enjoyed more occupational mobility than their counterparts did before the Civil War (see Table 8 in Appendix A). In a sample whose careers were followed from 1860 to 1870, there were 22 percent who improved, 13 percent who worsened, and 64 percent

22. Ann Fonvielle Mebane, "Immigrant Patterns in Atlanta: 1880 and 1896" (M.A. thesis, Emory University, 1967), 35; Roland T. Berthoff, "Southern Attitudes Towards Immigration," *JSH*, XVII (1951), 328–60.
23. For data on occupational distribution by age, see William Harris, "Work and the Family in Black Atlanta, 1880," *Journal of Social History*, IX (1976), 320–21.

TABLE 6

Vertical Occupational Distribution
of Atlanta's Working Population
by Race, 1880

Occupational Categories[b]	% of Work Force[a]	
	White	Negro
High white collar	13.2	.9
Low white collar	38.7	2.4
Skilled	29.4	23.8
Semi-skilled	5.0	11.6
Unskilled	13.7	61.3
Total	100.0	100.0
N	802	757

Source: Samples drawn from manuscripts of the
federal population schedules for Fulton County,
Georgia, 1880.

Notes: $\chi^2 = 589.737$ with 4 degrees of freedom.
Significance = .000

Gamma = .807

[a]Includes males and females

[b]All unclassifiable occupations excluded from table

who remained the same.[24] The greatest gains were made by semi-skilled workers, of whom 83 percent advanced to the low-white-collar category. This group included, however, only five men (two farm tenants, a mail guard, a train hand, and a barber) who became, respectively, farmers, a grocer, a bookkeeper, and a proprietor of a tobacco shop. The net gains of the entire sample of household heads were roughly equal to the occupational mobility of male workers in Poughkeepsie and slightly less than that of males in Jacksonville, Illinois, during the same decade.[25]

The work of Richard Hopkins and Steven Hertzberg permits a more comprehensive look at occupational mobility in Atlanta after

24. Because the number in the persistence sample was so small, the findings concerning occupational mobility are not statistically significant and should be regarded as tentative.

25. Clyde Griffen and Sally Griffen, *Natives and Newcomers: The Ordering of Opportunity in Mid-Nineteenth-Century Poughkeepsie* (Cambridge, Mass., 1977), 60; Don H. Doyle, *The Social Order of a Frontier Community: Jacksonville, Illinois, 1825–1870* (Urbana, 1978), 263.

1870. Hopkins found that 22 percent of the native white and 21 percent of the immigrant manual laborers whose careers he followed advanced to white-collar jobs by 1880. Their counterparts in other nineteenth-century cities did less well. Admittedly dealing with a very small group, Hertzberg discovered impressive upward mobility for Jews. Blacks, according to Hopkins, were the only racial or ethnic group on whom Dame Opportunity failed to smile. Of his sample of unskilled black males, 90 percent remained unskilled laborers and only 1 percent attained white-collar jobs by the end of the decade. With this exception, most Atlantans, according to Hopkins and to Hertzberg, had a better chance for occupational progress than they might have had elsewhere. This conclusion is in line with other studies that report high upward occupational mobility rates in cities whose economies were booming and low rates in stagnant or declining urban economies.[26]

The racial characteristics of persistence in postbellum Atlanta further document the difficulties blacks encountered in establishing a satisfactory way of life. Only 30 percent of a sample of black male household heads, compared with 45 percent of a sample of white male household heads, stayed in the city from 1870 to 1880 (see Table 9 in Appendix A). A study of single young black males in Atlanta during the same decade found only a 10 percent persistence rate. Persistence studies generally indicate that the least prosperous residents of nineteenth-century cities were the most likely to depart quickly. A few scholars (including Richard Hopkins) have argued that blacks were as likely or even more likely to persist than were whites in southern cities, but such claims are almost certainly erroneous.[27]

26. Richard J. Hopkins, "Occupational and Geographic Mobility in Atlanta, 1870–1896," *Journal of Social History*, XXXIV (1968), 205–10; Steven Hertzberg, *Strangers Within the Gate City: The Jews of Atlanta, 1845–1915* (Philadelphia, 1978), 254; Michael P. Weber and Anthony Boardman, "Economic Growth and Occupational Mobility in Nineteenth Century America: A Reappraisal," *Journal of Social History*, XI (1977), 52–74.

27. William Harris, "Research Note on Mobility in Atlanta," *South Atlantic Urban Studies*, I (1977), 267–70; Richard J. Hopkins, "Status, Mobility, and the Dimensions of Change in a Southern City: Atlanta, 1870–1910," in Kenneth T. Jackson and Stanley K. Schultz (eds.), *Cities in American History* (New York, 1972), 223–25; Hopkins, "Are Southern Cities Unique? Persistence as a Clue," *Mississippi Quarterly*, XXVI (1973), 121–41; Steven W. Engerrand, "Black and Mulatto Mobility and Stability in Dallas, Texas, 1880–1910," *Phylon*, XXXIX (1978), 203–209; Alwyn Barr, "Occupational and Geographic Mobility in San Antonio, 1870–1900," *Social Science Quarterly*, LI (1970), 396–403. All these studies verified persistence by tracing samples from manuscript censuses to city directories, a practice that can cause problems (see Appendix B).

Black persistence rates were obviously low compared with those of whites, but the geographic stability of white male household heads in Atlanta from 1870 to 1880 is not as high as that comparison indicates. Persistence rates of household heads in eight other American cities during the same decade ranged between 16 and 69 percent.[28] The rate in Atlanta lies at about the mean between those extremes. The implication is that postbellum Atlanta was not a land of exceptional opportunity for adult white males with families to raise.

Multiple Classification Analysis (MCA) was used to determine which social characteristics were the strongest predictors that individuals would remain. Permanence rather than persistence was chosen as the most reliable measure. An individual was deemed permanent in post–Civil War Atlanta if his presence was detected in either an earlier or later census, a verification that he had been in the city for at least ten years. Permanence rates, for obvious reasons, were higher than were persistence rates throughout the nineteenth century (see Table 11 in Appendix A).[29]

Table 7 presents the results of a typical MCA. Possessing property was, not surprisingly, the strongest predictor of a man's likelihood to stay in the city for at least ten years.[30] It was, in fact, the only statistically significant factor, though literacy almost qualified. The swing of twenty-two percentage points in the three property categories meant that those without property had less than a 50 percent chance of remaining for a decade, while those with an estate worth $5,000 or more in nearly seven cases out of ten were likely to stay that long. Despite the clear relationship between property possession and permanence, wealth and the other factors were nevertheless relatively weak predictors of geographic stability.[31]

The relationships among age, occupation, and nativity and permanence of white household heads were more complex and interest-

28. Robert G. Barrows, "'Hurryin' Hoosiers and the American Pattern: Geographic Mobility in Indianapolis and Urban North America," *SSH*, V (1981), 203–204.
29. Tracing for permanence rather than persistence has the advantage of two checkpoints for verifying ten years' residence.
30. Occupational rank, the next most powerful predictor, could not be included with property, since those variables interacted.
31. The beta values for all the independent variables in the table are low. R^2 (measuring the combined effects of all the independent variables on the dependent variable, permanence) is also low. The highest R^2 generated by any MCA of the permanence or persistence of Atlanta's black and white household heads was .077.

TABLE 7

Permanence of White Male Household Heads in Atlanta,
1860–1880 (Grand Mean = .54)

FACTORS	ADJUSTED DEVIATION	N
Age		
Under 30 years	.01	66
30–49 years	.02	191
50 or more years	−.07	64
Property category		
None	−.07	150
$1–4,999	.02	117
$5,000 or more	.15	54
Number of children		
None	.03	80
1–4 children	.00	204
5 or more children	.15	54
Literacy		
Literate	.01	312
Illiterate	−.26	9
Factors	Eta/Beta	
Age	.05/.07	
Property category	.19/.17[a]	
Number of children	.04/.08	
Literacy	.11/.09[b]	
Covariate	Beta	
Household size	.12	
$R^2 = .058$		

SOURCES: Manuscripts of the federal population schedules for Fulton County, 1860–1880.

NOTE: The grand mean represents the percentage of household heads who resided in the city for at least one decade.

[a]Significant at the .004 level

[b]Significant at the .09 level

ing.[32] Nonsoutherners were generally more likely than were southerners to stay in the city. Both young and old (but not middle-aged) nonsouthern household heads were about twice as likely as were southern natives of the same age bracket to remain. Household heads born outside the South with high occupational rank were more than four times as prone as were southerners to reside in the city for at least

32. These relationships were all detected by factor interactions in MCA. Birthplace interacted with age, occupational rank, and property holding.

a decade. These findings suggest that outsiders found lengthy residence in Atlanta to be a more inviting prospect than did southerners. In addition, perhaps, we can conclude that the city's need for skilled labor could be better supplied from outside the South.

The overall picture is highly variegated. Several combinations of factors could affect positively or adversely an individual's likelihood of staying or leaving. No one factor strongly affected persistence or nonpersistence, though property possession came the closest. These conclusions vary slightly from but basically agree with those of Michael Katz and his associates, who argue that "the accumulation of differences" between individuals rather than any single factor determined persistence in nineteenth-century cities.[33]

Statistical analysis of population persistence, wealth holding, and occupational mobility leads to two relevant conclusions. First, the opportunity to gain wealth and climb the occupational ladder in postbellum Atlanta was probably about average for nineteenth-century American cities. Even though success was not as sure as chamber of commerce propaganda asserted, the structure of opportunity may well have been more democratic than were economic and social conditions in the small towns and cities that many new residents left behind. Second, foreigners and nonsouthern natives fared well. Their edge in acquiring wealth and better jobs could have been due to advantages they had before coming to Atlanta, but that possibility should not overshadow recognition that the city was receptive to outsiders. Atlanta was not a place where Yankees and foreigners had to fear ostracism. Boosters' claims about the structure of opportunity, hyperbolic though they were, did have a factual basis.

New South Business Leadership

Henry W. Grady wrote a feature story for the *Constitution* in 1880 entitled "Self-Made Men, Whose Grit Has Made Them." A marvelous expression of New South rhetoric, his essay sketched the careers of thirty-six local businessmen (two-thirds of whom qualified as economic leaders for this study) who came to the city as impoverished young men from respectable but undistinguished families. These men "won fame and fortune by no accident of inheritance . . . but by patient, earnest, heroic work." Grady's self-made men had other

33. Michael Katz, Michael J. Doucet, and Mark Stern, *The Social Organization of Early American Capitalism* (Cambridge, Mass., 1982), 112–27.

characteristics in common. Most were born in rural areas or small towns in the South and had at best grammar school educations. Many of them began as "ploughboys." Upon arrival in Atlanta, these "poor country boys" were typically befriended by local merchants who hired them as junior clerks or drummers. Other refugees from the farm had even less distinguished beginnings. Wholesale dry goods merchant David Dougherty, lumber merchant Frank P. Rice, and planing mill and lumber yard proprietor Anthony Murphy were first employed, respectively, as a city policeman, a newsboy, and a machinist. "Atlanta is full of these self-made men," concluded Grady. "They enrich her blood, quicken her pulses, and give her vitality, force, and power."[34]

Grady's vivid paean is an excellent starting point for an analysis of postbellum Atlanta's economic leadership. No contemporary knew Atlanta's business leaders better than Grady did, and his descriptions therefore deserve serious consideration. More important, Grady's portraits contained fundamental assumptions about the origins of the New South and its leadership. Using Atlanta as a reference point for understanding the New South, Grady assumed that the city's economic growth after 1865 had made possible the rise of a new middle class that was neither descended from nor subservient to the Old South's plantation aristocracy. Atlanta's self-made business leaders, Grady asserted, had their roots in the rural South, but their vision of the region's future involved city building rather than plantation estates. Grady saw Atlanta's economic leaders as pioneers in a social and economic crusade that would bring revolutionary changes to the entire South. To test these and other propositions about the origins and nature of New South Atlanta's leadership, I used several criteria to identify an economic elite for the period from 1865 to 1879.[35] Fittingly for a city whose economy was still predominantly commercial, the majority were merchants and bankers (see Table 12 in Appendix A).[36]

The leaders' geographical origins basically conform to those of Grady's self-made entrepreneurs. About 74 percent were born in the

34. Atlanta *Constitution*, August 15, 1880.
35. See Appendix B. Fourteen members of the antebellum elite still qualified as economic leaders after 1865. Since their social characteristics and behavior were treated in Chapter III, they are not included in the group analyzed in this chapter.
36. The relatively high percentage of bankers was mostly caused by turnover of personnel during the 1870s depression.

South (half of them in Georgia), about 12 percent in northern states, and most of the rest abroad (see Table 15 in Appendix A). Especially compared with the antebellum elite, these leaders were much more southern in their nativity. Compared with business leadership in Alabama and North Carolina after the war, Atlanta's economic elite included, however, proportionately more foreigners and natives born outside the South. [37] As far as can be determined, the birthplaces of Atlanta's economic leaders were also overwhelmingly in rural or small-town settings (see Table 16 in Appendix A). Only one leader born in the United States came from a town with a population of more than 2,500. On the whole, these men were a product of the rural South.

The typical career pattern involved working in a country town before migrating to Atlanta to launch more ambitious ventures. Nearly 60 percent of the leaders whose previous residences are known had lived elsewhere in the South and the majority of them in places that had fewer than ten thousand inhabitants (see Tables 21 and 22 in Appendix A). William A. Moore was born in a small town in east Tennessee, and Edward W. Marsh was a North Carolina native. They owned general stores in La Fayette, Georgia, and Chattanooga before moving to Atlanta in 1865. By 1880, their wholesale dry goods firm was the largest in the city—they had sixty drummers and job-bers, and their annual sales were valued at $1.5 million. Reflecting on the move to Atlanta, Moore made a perceptive remark that under-mined local boosters' assertions about the city's merchants. "I know a good many country merchants," he said, "who are just as good as any in Atlanta, and who, if their lots had been cast here, would have equalled or outstripped the best of us." [38]

Other social attributes of postbellum Atlanta's elite conformed less exactly to Grady's description. Youth, as he implied, was characteris-tic of men such as Moore when they attained elite status—the major-ity were less than fifty years old when they qualified (see Table 17 in Appendix A). [39] On the other hand, their families and educations

37. Justin Fuller, "Alabama Business Leaders: 1865–1900 (Part II)," *Alabama Review*, XVII (1964), 64–65; J. Carlyle Sitterson, "Business Leaders in Post–Civil War North Carolina, 1865–1900," in *James Sprunt Studies in History and Political Science*, XXXIX (1957), 112.

38. R. G. Dun & Co. Credit Reports, Fulton County, Ga., XIV, in Baker Library, Harvard University, Cambridge, Mass.; *Manufacturing and Mercantile Resources of Atlanta, Georgia* (Atlanta, 1883), 241–42; Moore quoted in Atlanta *Constitution*, March 4, 1888.

39. The mean age was 44.3 years; that of white male household heads was 39.3 years.

conform to the letter but certainly not the spirit of the Grady model. His subjects were mostly "poor country boys" who left family farms for mercantile counters. Father's educations and occupations are known for only one-third of the elite. Of this group, 69 percent had no more than grammar school educations, but the remainder had college educations or better, a rare achievement in that era. Most fathers had agricultural occupations (seven were planters and nine were farmers). Only two were manual laborers.[40] Although the city's post–Civil War economic leadership was not predominantly of planter descent, it was far from plebeian in its origins and not poorly educated for its generation.

It is easier to describe their backgrounds than to assess the extent to which their rise was a product of opportunities created by the city's economic expansion. There were examples of impressive occupational mobility. About 15 percent of the economic leaders began their careers as manual laborers (see Table 13 in Appendix A). The ten men in this category included three farm workers and a day laborer on the Georgia Railroad (John Lynch, one of the five Irish brothers who came to Atlanta in 1847). Their elite occupations included banking, wholesale and retail dry goods, and wholesale groceries. Three other manual laborers were David Dougherty, Hannibal Ingalls Kimball (former carriage maker), and Thomas G. Healey, brick manufacturer and president of the Atlanta Gas Light Company, who began his career as a mechanic. The remaining upwardly mobile manual laborers included a railroad conductor, a drayman, and a stonecutter who became, respectively, a wholesale liquor merchant, a lawyer, and a partner in a railroad construction company.

As was true of the antebellum elite, the majority of the post–Civil War economic leaders did most of their occupational climbing before coming to Atlanta. About 94 percent of the elite began their careers in the city as white-collar workers (see Table 14 in Appendix A). Those who started out in Atlanta as manual laborers included David Dougherty, gas fitter Joseph T. Eichberg, millwright Philip Dodd, and stonecutter Thomas Alexander. Dodd and his brother were described by Grady as "poor unmarried boys" who became wealthy wholesale grocers and "whose history reads like a romance." Indicating that there was more romance than reality in Grady's comments, the credit reporter for R. G. Dun & Co. referred to the Dodds

40. The occupations of twenty-three fathers of the postbellum elite were ascertained.

in 1857 as having "small capital," but their father was "a wealthy planter near here & . . . will back them if necessary." The career of Thomas Alexander, on the other hand, was a classic story of poor boy makes good. An English immigrant with little formal education, he had menial jobs all across the country before arriving in Atlanta in 1853 as "a dollar a day" laborer on the Georgia Railroad. Alexander acquired the skill and business connections to become a building contractor shortly before the Civil War. After the war, he made a shrewd decision and joined the railroad construction company of John T. and William D. Grant. His estate was valued at more than $500,000 at the time of his death in 1878.[41]

Although Alexander's career was certainly unusual for men of his class, the data on the capital Atlanta's leaders brought to the city indicate that it was easier for entrepreneurs with small means to gain access to the elite after 1865. There may well have been more opportunities for personal advancement then than was the case during the more restricted frontier trading era. Nearly 30 percent began their careers in Atlanta with less than $1,000, and the majority had less than $10,000 (see Table 19 in Appendix A). Nevertheless, Table 8 shows that those with less than $1,000 took nearly six times as long as those with $50,000 or more to gain access to the elite. In about 44 percent of the cases, the determining factor was how much money a man brought to the city.[42] Those with modest means needed a great deal of perseverance and good luck.

There remain, however, some important questions about mobility into the elite. How many men were like Philip Dodd and how many were like Thomas Alexander? About 41 percent were related by blood or marriage or both (see Table 23 in Appendix A). Marriage was, however, still a means of consolidating wealth as well as acquiring it, and a familial bond did not necessarily mean that an individual could count on financial support.[43] About 37 percent were aided financially by family members or business associates, but those who received such assistance were not necessarily those who began their enterprises with small means (see Table 24 in Appendix A).

41. Atlanta *Constitution*, January 29, 1878; Dun & Co. Credit Reports, Fulton County, XIII; Franklin M. Garrett, *Atlanta and Environs: A Chronicle of Its People and Events* (3 vols.; New York, 1954), I, 950–51.

42. Eta^2 = .444. Thus 44 percent of the differences between the wealth categories in interval times are explained by initial capital.

43. Dun & Co. credit reporters noted occasionally that some wealthy fathers would not be responsible for their sons' debts.

TABLE 8
*Interval Time by Initial Wealth Category
of Economic Leaders, 1865–1879*

INITIAL WEALTH CATEGORY	INTERVAL TIME (YEARS)	N
Under $1,000	17.7	20
$1,000–4,999	12.6	11
$5,000–9,999	7.4	11
$10,000–24,999	10.7	9
$25,000–49,999	9.0	7
$50,000–99,999	3.8	6
$100,000 or more	3.0	4
Eta = .666[a]		
Eta^2 = .444		

SOURCES: See Appendix B.
[a] Significant at the .000 level

Closer inspection of those who started with less than $1,000 reveals that nine had financial backing from a colleague or a relative, which leaves twelve men in the lowest initial wealth category as candidates for adherence to Horatio Alger stereotypes. One of the twelve (banker John H. James) was a planter's son, and four (Dougherty, John Lynch, Alexander, and John Collier) began as manual laborers.[44] There is no record that the remaining seven men got help from friends or relatives in launching their businesses. Probably no fewer than four and no more than eleven men could thus rightly claim to have risen from poverty to become architects of their own fortunes. Although the majority of the postbellum elite were not poor boys made good, it is impressive, nevertheless, that some with modest means became as wealthy and powerful as they did.

Another factor apparently improved individuals' chances of entering the elite—lengthy residence in the city. About 90 percent lived in Atlanta for at least a decade and nearly 80 percent stayed for twenty years or more (see Table 18 in Appendix A).[45] About half (51 percent) of those who became economic leaders after 1865 came to Atlanta

44. On James, see Atlanta *Daily Herald*, April 4, 1875; and Atlanta *Constitution*, October 5, 1881.
45. This statistic refers to any twenty-year period, which began in some cases before and in others after the war.

before that date. There was thus more continuity between the Old and New South than was shown in the persistence rates of the antebellum household heads. Residence in the city was particularly important for those who began their careers with small means. Only two of the twenty men who began with less than $1,000 arrived after the war. An entrepreneur without much money needed to begin his career in pre–Civil War Atlanta if he expected to attain elite status after 1865.

Another representation of an interesting carryover of the Old South into the New was the elite's Civil War record (see Table 26 in Appendix A). About 37 percent were veterans of the Confederate army. Another 27 percent had been members of the state militia, government officials, or southern civilians. None served in the Union army, and only Kimball was a northern civilian.[46] While having supported the Confederate cause was probably not a prerequisite for entering the elite, it was undoubtedly important in deflecting criticism when these men sought during and after Reconstruction to attract northern capital.

Mobility into the elite was, in the final analysis, certainly not as democratic as Grady's success stories implied. But this conclusion should surprise no one. It should be emphasized that not only were the achievements of a few such as Thomas Alexander remarkable, but many also enjoyed truly impressive property mobility. More than half the elite were worth at least $100,000 at the peak of their careers (see Table 20 in Appendix A). Accumulating such wealth would not have been possible in a stagnant urban economy.

Although the career histories of most economic leaders may not read like Horatio Alger novels, the more significant themes in Grady's stories of Atlanta's self-made entrepreneurs were rooted in reality. The city's economic growth after 1865 had made possible the rise of a vigorous leadership. Although they had rural southern roots and a Confederate past, these men generally lacked ancestral and ideological ties to the plantation aristocracy. Carpetbagger Kimball was probably the best known of Atlanta's postbellum economic leaders and was also in many ways representative of their aggressive commitment to the New South urban-industrial creed. Kimball would have been out of place in cities in the plantation districts, but his talent as a promoter was always appreciated in Atlanta.

46. Alice E. Reagan, *H. I. Kimball, Entrepreneur* (Atlanta, 1983), 6–9, 48.

Kimball fitted well into an elite that was becoming increasingly cohesive. Like most of them, he was a Protestant and, as far as can be known, of either British or Irish ancestry (see Table 25 in Appendix A).[47] He also resided in one of the exclusive neighborhoods where men of his class lived in the city at the time.[48] Like several others, he was related by marriage to another member of the elite. While Atlanta's business leaders during this period lacked such institutions as country clubs, the city was still small enough that they could create the personal and financial ties that facilitated organizing urban promotive ventures.

The city that Kimball and others succeeded in raising from its ashes belonged to the New South in several ways. It was "new" in the obvious sense that most of its population, if not its leaders, had come to the city after 1865. While they were a product of the rural South, its business leaders came from outside the planter class. More significant, their well-publicized political stances and social values were a conscious repudiation of the Old South. Even though such attitudes are usually associated with the New South era, the rhetoric and behavior of post–Civil War Atlanta's boosters were natural extensions of antebellum tendencies. Much of what seemed new to some observers about the city after 1865 represented continuities. Although various elements of the population challenged the leaders more often after the war than earlier, New South Atlanta closely resembled the city of prewar days.

47. About 85 percent of those whose affiliations were found were Protestant. The rest were Jewish or Catholic.

48. There were two distinct areas where the postbellum elite resided. One was just north of the conjunction of the Georgia and the Western & Atlantic railroads with a projection north along Peachtree Street. The other was south of those railroads in the section enclosed by Forsyth, Rawson, and Washington streets. Most of these addresses were still within the first half-mile circle of the city.

7

POLITICS AND GOVERNMENT, 1865–1874
Race, Class, and Party

The people, all alike, rich and poor, are deeply interested in the city Government. Property is an interest that deserves to be protected and carefully guarded. But it is not the only object of municipal cares. The poor are to be protected in life and liberty, and consequently they have a right to speak wherever and whenever direction is to be given to public affairs. . . . If there is one class of men who are more deeply interested than all others in the proper management of city affairs, it is those who are without wealth, and have to look to the law for protection.

—Mayor James E. Williams (1867)

The Mayor's reference to the poor . . . [is] all buncombe and stuff.

—George W. Adair (1867)

As they had before the Civil War, Atlanta businessmen believed that the primary role of municipal government was to promote the city's growth. In their judgment, the lion's share of revenues ought to be spent on entrepreneurial projects rather than on poor relief and public schools. They also thought that physical welfare services such as fire protection and street upkeep should benefit mainly the central business district. During the late nineteenth century, businessmen and municipal officials in many other American cities shared these assumptions.[1]

Atlanta's postbellum economic leaders had greater difficulty than their predecessors convincing various elements of the population about their concept of municipal government. Blacks and working-class whites challenged "business priority" in the administration of municipal services and succeeded occasionally in getting something else done. The solution in 1874 to the menace of political action by the have-nots was a new municipal charter. This document severely restricted expenditures for many years, so Atlanta's city government could not extend municipal services to black and white working-class neighborhoods and even had trouble maintaining services to the central business district.

The history of Atlanta politics from the end of the Civil War to the 1874 charter reform divides into three distinct periods. From 1865 to 1867, municipal elections were nonpartisan, and those elected had to deal with the physical destruction and human suffering caused by the war. Beginning in 1868, grass-roots Republican and Democratic organizations catered, respectively, to blacks and working-class whites. As it did in other cities in the Reconstruction South, the Radical Republican party had a dramatic (but, in Atlanta, brief) impact on local politics.[2] Finally, a reform movement backed by the city's

1. Howard L. Platt, *City Building in the New South: The Growth of Public Services in Houston, Texas, 1830–1910* (Philadelphia, 1983); Alan Dawley, *Class and Community: The Industrial Revolution in Lynn* (Cambridge, Mass., 1976), 104–13; Olivier Zunz, *The Changing Face of Inequality: Urbanization, Industrial Development, and Immigrants in Detroit, 1880–1920* (Chicago, 1983), 113–28; Howard N. Rabinowitz, "Continuity and Change: Southern Urban Development, 1860–1900," in Blaine A. Brownell and David R. Goldfield (eds.), *The City in Southern History: The Growth of Urban Civilization in the South* (Port Washington, N.Y., 1977), 111–13.
2. See, for example, the essays by Michael B. Chesson, Howard N. Rabinowitz, and Jerry Thornbery and me in Howard N. Rabinowitz (ed.), *Southern Black Leaders of the Reconstruc-*

newspapers and business leadership emerged in 1873 and attempted to overthrow the "rings and bosses" said to exist in the Democratic party. In the discussion of all three periods, the focus will be on the administration of municipal services. Analyzing street upkeep, fire protection, and gas lines, for example, together with Atlanta's social geography, can depict literally who got what from city hall.

The Aftermath of War

Municipal officials for the first three postwar years faced enormous problems in rebuilding the city and alleviating human misery. There were mountains of rubble to clear from badly neglected streets, bridges to repair, and gullies to fill in. Other services such as fire protection and street illumination had to be recreated. With thousands of poor blacks and whites from all over the South streaming into the city, public relief was needed probably even more than it had been during the war.

In the immediate postwar years, municipal authorities devoted most of their time and money to the public streets. The city council spent 22 percent of its 1866 operating budget alone and issued $412,000 in bonds in less than two years on renovation of the business avenues, which were nearly impassable in the winter of 1865. "We have removed incredible amounts of dirt and rubbish from the principal streets, filled up washes and low places in others, [and have] done a great deal of heavy and expensive work in others," Mayor James M. Calhoun remarked early the following year. By 1867, portions of Broad, Marietta, Forsyth, Peachtree, and Whitehall streets were macadamized, but nowhere did the paving go beyond one-half mile from the city's center. Elsewhere mud or dust was the rule, depending on the season, but Mayor Williams expressed his satisfaction with physical conditions in the business district. "A little over one year has passed, and how changed the scene," he boasted. "The city has been rebuilt, and our thronged streets and active mechanics and businessmen indicate that Atlanta . . . is again on the way to prosperity."[3]

---

tion South (Urbana, 1982). See also Rabinowitz's Race Relations in the Urban South, 1865–1890 (New York, 1978), 257–81.

3. Daily Atlanta Intelligencer, January 10, 1866 (quoting Calhoun), November 15, 1867; Atlanta Daily New Era, February 7, 1867; CM, January 4 (quoting Williams), September 20, October 18, 1867. The city council spent $58,820.09 on streets and bridges in 1866.

The reorganization of the fire department and the municipally owned Atlanta Gas Light Company was completed about the same time as the renovation of the principal business streets. The fire department was in total disarray at the end of the war, and more than two years passed before it could deal effectively with fires in the central business district. Only one broken-down steamer was available to the four volunteer fire companies in 1865, so there was a special bond issue of $20,000 the following year to buy equipment and rebuild the firehouses. To make matters worse, an epidemic of arson swept through the city in 1866. The city council organized a volunteer police force in each ward and appropriated $1,000 as a reward for the arrest of those responsible. Despite these difficulties, the fire companies by 1867 were reasonably well equipped and had managed to dig twelve cisterns. But all the cisterns were within three-quarters of a mile of the city's center. Only the business district and centrally located, mostly upper-class neighborhoods enjoyed fire protection.[4]

Illumination of public streets was even more confined to the city's center. Because of extensive wartime damage, the Atlanta Gas Light Company could not resume operations until September, 1866, and was unable for two years to extend its lines beyond the three-mile network laid during the antebellum period. Gas lamps were scarce even on principal streets in the business district. "Atlanta has probably less gaslight than any other city of equal size in the United States," wrote one observer in 1870. "The scarcity of gaslight affords many convenient dark corners where almost any kind of evil deed . . . [can] be perpetrated."[5]

The physical rebuilding of Atlanta consumed much of the city council's resources and energy, but meeting the needs of impoverished blacks and whites was clearly beyond their capability or sense of responsibility. Municipal authorities were most sensitive about the plight of Confederate widows and orphans—there were 155 women and 294 children in that category, according to a local census in 1867. But there were thousands of other poor people. The most

4. *Pioneer Citizens' History of Atlanta, 1833–1902* (Atlanta, 1902), 94–98; *Daily Atlanta Intelligencer*, June 9, 1865, May 25, September 9, 1867; Atlanta *Daily New Era*, April 16, 1867; John T. Glenn (cod.), *The Code of the City of Atlanta* (Atlanta, 1868), 36–37.
5. Wade Hampton Wright, "Georgia Power Company," *AHB*, III (1938), 195–97; *CM*, April 19, 1867; *Daily Atlanta Intelligencer*, February 6, 1870.

reliable estimate was that of a Freedmen's Bureau official. He characterized 2,200 whites and 1,200 blacks in 1867 as "utterly destitute."[6]

Sympathetic witnesses found it almost impossible to describe the misery of Atlanta's impoverished citizenry in the immediate post–Civil War years. Federal army officials set up segregated camps, which contained one thousand blacks and eight hundred whites in 1865, on opposite sides of the city to provide shelter for the homeless. Families lived in tents supplied by the Freedmen's Bureau or in patched-together huts. All along the railroads toward the outskirts of the city, travelers reported that the poor huddled together in worse circumstances. Some people even sought shelter in pits and crannies they dug in the earthen breastworks abandoned by Confederate armies. "Everywhere were ruins, rubbish, mud, mortar, and misery," an observer wrote in 1866. "Hundreds of the inhabitants, white and black . . . were living in wretched hovels which made the suburbs look like a fantastic encampment of gypsies or Indians."[7]

To make conditions even more miserable, a smallpox epidemic broke out in 1865 and 1866. According to the report of a "Pest House Superintendent" hired by the city council, the disease killed eighty-three people in the first seven months of 1866. Negro deaths were not included. Using a small portion of a $4,000 fund allocated by the city council for "rebuilding purposes," the Atlanta Medical College had maintained a smallpox hospital for freedmen in 1865. When the councilmen heard about the college's "misuse" of public funds, they were outraged, and the resulting furor caused the school to abandon its charitable activities. Late in 1865 the Freedmen's Bureau established a Negro smallpox hospital. It was deliberately located outside the city limits, according to a bureau agent, "to promote harmony among the citizens and this Bureau."[8]

Between December, 1865, and October, 1866, when the epidemic

6. CM, July 27, 1866; V. T. Barnwell, *Atlanta City Directory, 1867* (Atlanta, 1867), 1; John Leonard to Colonel C. C. Sibley, April 9, 1867, in Vol. XCIX, RG 105, NA.

7. *Daily Atlanta Intelligencer*, July 29, August 27, September 1, 1865; John H. Kennaway, *On Sherman's Track* (London, 1867), 110; Sarah Huff, *My Eighty Years in Atlanta* (N.p., 1937), 67; Jerry Thornbery, "Northerners and the Atlanta Freedmen, 1865–69," *Prologue*, VI (1974), 238; J. T. Trowbridge, *A Picture of the Desolated States, 1865–1868* (Hartford, Conn., 1868), 453.

8. CM, July 27, 1866; Gregory Murphy, "The Controversy Between T. S. Powell and the Atlanta Medical College," *GHQ*, XXIV (1940), 236–53; D. C. Poole to Brigadier General Davis Tillson, January 5, 1866, in Vol. XCVIII, RG 105.

was at its worst, ninety-six blacks died in the freedmen's hospital. The facilities there were so primitive and vaccination among blacks so rare that the death toll was considered remarkably low. "Men, women, and children were lying on the ground, suffering in every degree from the mildest symptoms to the most violent," an agent of the American Missionary Association said in February, 1866. "The tents crowded, no fire to make them comfortable, and, worst of all, the poor creatures were almost destitute of wearing apparel." The epidemic ran its course by January, 1867, having claimed nearly two hundred victims.[9]

The destitute turned to a variety of governmental and private agencies for help. Besides operating its hospital until August, 1868, the Freedmen's Bureau dispensed rations to needy blacks and whites from June, 1865, until September, 1867. In its first month in Atlanta, the bureau dispensed 95,000 pounds of breadstuff and of meat to the city's poor. Civic officials and mercantile organizations in St. Louis, Louisville, Cincinnati, and other cities also donated foodstuffs and money for Confederate widows and orphans. The railroad companies whose lines terminated in Atlanta donated firewood. In addition, the American Missionary Association in 1866 founded its Washburn orphanage, which provided for fifty to eighty-five black children annually during Reconstruction.[10]

Local voluntary associations also worked on behalf of the poor. Representing virtually every ethnic group in Atlanta, organizations such as the Hibernian Benevolent Society, the Hebrew Benevolent Society, Saint Andrew's Benevolent Society, the Turn-Verein, and the Concordia Association staged concerts, gymnastic exhibitions, and theatrical productions to raise money. White and black churches held fairs and lecture series. Blacks also established relief societies such as the Sisters of Honor and the Brothers of Aid that supplied needy members of their race with food, clothing, and firewood. Especially popular among white Atlanta females were "calico balls." Women sewed dresses for these dances and afterwards donated both

9. "Monthly Reports of Sick and Wounded Refugees and Freedmen of Freedmen's Bureau Hospital in Atlanta, Georgia from November, 1865 to August, 1868," RG 105; R. M. Craighead to Reverend Samuel Hunt, February 1, 1866, in American Missionary Association Archives, Dillard University, New Orleans.

10. Eugene M. Mitchell, "Atlanta During the Reconstruction Period," *AHB*, II (1936), 20–21; *Daily Atlanta Intelligencer*, July 19, 1865; *Pioneer Citizens' History*, 95–96; E. Merton Coulter, *The Cincinnati Southern and the Struggle for Southern Commerce* (Chicago, 1922), 14; *American Missionary*, XII (1868), 243.

the clothing and the proceeds to Confederate widows. Unfortunately, all these efforts to alleviate the plight of the poor were, in the words of a sympathetic observer in 1867, "no more than a drop in the bucket."[11]

The city council in 1866 spent $29,580.45 on relief, a greater annual expenditure for that item than in any subsequent year in the nineteenth century. This sum still did not match, however, the $32,834.33 collected by local voluntary associations in 1866 for the same purpose.[12] Nor did it exceed what was spent on street improvements.

Public support for high levels of poor relief evaporated early in 1867 when newspaper exposés revealed that city treasurer J. T. Porter had embezzled at least $47,000 in 1866. Porter allegedly had a hidden partnership in a provisions store that the city used for distributing food to needy families. Mayor Williams and the city council were promptly charged with incompetence for not catching Porter, and the city's relief policies were denounced as wasteful and "extravagant."[13]

The Porter scandal developed into a large-scale political struggle between Mayor Williams and his associates who claimed to represent Atlanta's underprivileged and wealthy property holders such as real estate tycoon George W. Adair. A public meeting on January 30, 1867, organized by Adair and other rich Atlantans, was attended by several hundred citizens. The Committee of Ten was appointed to formally request the resignations of the mayor and the city council. Four of the ten councilmen heeded the committee's demand. In the February special elections, which had low turnouts, the voters chose Richard Peters, E. E. Rawson, W. B. Cox, and J. A. Hayden (all rich men). Mayor Williams defiantly refused to resign, and his opponents finally abandoned efforts to oust him when it became clear that they lacked legal grounds for impeachment.[14]

The legacy of the Porter scandal was a rationale for low expenditures for poor relief during the rest of the postbellum period. Although

11.   E. Y. Clarke, *Illustrated History of Atlanta* (2nd ed., 1879; rpr. Atlanta, 1971), 77; *Daily Atlanta Intelligencer*, February 28, March 6, April 6, December 25, 1867; Charles W. Hubner, "Atlanta," *Appleton's Journal of Literature, Science, and Art*, VIII (1872), 378; E. R. Carter, *The Black Side: A Partial History of Business, Religious, and Educational Side of the Negro in Atlanta* (Atlanta, 1894), 38–40, 50–52; Atlanta *Daily New Era*, May 31, 1867.
12.   CM, July 27, 1866, January 25, 1867.
13.   Atlanta *Daily New Era*, January 18, 19, 1867; *Daily Atlanta Intelligencer*, March 10, 1867.
14.   *Daily Atlanta Intelligencer*, January 31, February 5, 8, 1867; Atlanta *Daily New Era*, February 19, 1867

municipal stinginess had other causes than the memory of Porter's misdeeds, the scandal was frequently cited as an outrageous example of the inevitable results of pampering "thriftless and idle citizens." As Mayor John H. James, a banker who participated in the crusade against Williams, declared in 1872: "Idleness is a great source of evil. We should not encourage it in our institutions of charity."[15]

With James's philosophy in mind, Atlanta's municipal government negotiated an agreement with Fulton County in 1867 whereby the city and county would share the cost of caring for the needy. The city's purpose was to shirk its responsibilities (the county eventually ran the Alms House) and to explore methods for transforming the idle poor into useful citizens. The Alms House, located three miles outside the city, beyond the council's immediate attention, consisted of fourteen wood cottages without ceilings or fireplaces and a small farm with six "milch cows" and two cotton looms. All the inmates were required to work the farm, milk the cows, operate the looms, or perform some other useful labor in hopes that the Alms House would become a "paying operation."[16]

Municipal officials were obviously more concerned about the physical rebuilding of the city, an attitude hardly unique to Atlanta. Businessmen in nineteenth-century cities everywhere expected municipal governments to administer services and apportion revenues with economic growth as the overriding goal. Given the success of Peters and his associates in the special elections, the majority of Atlanta's white population shared this philosophy or saw no alternative to it.

Emergence of Partisan Politics

Despite the turmoil of early Reconstruction and the Porter scandal, municipal politics were relatively tranquil. City elections were nonpartisan, and voter turnout was low. But in 1867, Federal troops began registering black voters in Atlanta and the rest of the South. There were no municipal elections that year, and the mayor and the council were retained for another term by order of the commander of the Third Military District. Blacks voted in Atlanta for the first time in 1868.[17]

15. Atlanta *Constitution*, January 6, 1872.
16. CM, January 21, March 28, December 13, 1867; Paul Miller, *Atlanta, Capital of the South* (New York, 1949), 82–83.
17. *Pioneer Citizens' History*, 104.

In preparation for the 1868 presidential election, Radical Republicans and Democrats created executive committees and ward clubs. In accordance with a plan for the party statewide, the Union League of Georgia took the lead in organizing the Republican ward clubs, which were predominantly black. These clubs made their first public appearance during the Fourth of July celebration in 1867. They later nominated council candidates from each ward and combined to select the party's candidate for mayor. The Democrats in 1868 established Seymour ward clubs, which functioned in the same way. The executive committees of both parties coordinated the clubs' activities. In 1871 the Democrats instituted a primary for selecting candidates for mayor and for city council to run in the general elections. These primaries were held every year until 1878.[18]

The Republican party showed impressive strength in Atlanta in 1868 (Grant lost to Seymour by only twelve votes), but played only a minor role in city elections before 1870. Shortly before the 1868 municipal election, the city attorney pointed out that the charter did not recognize black voters. There was not enough time to revise the charter, and the Democrats won in a clean sweep. The next year, the Democrat-controlled city council passed an ordinance requiring that all voters pay a two-dollar poll tax (the Georgia legislature outlawed the tax in 1870). The Republicans abandoned efforts to organize a ticket for the 1869 city elections, though white Radical William Markham ran and was defeated as the "Citizens' Ticket" candidate for mayor. His slogan was "Who votes for Markham . . . votes for free schools, water-works, more light, better streets . . . and good administration throughout." [19]

The Radicals' chances of placing candidates in municipal offices improved dramatically when a new legislature controlled by Republicans passed a law on October 5, 1870, that councilmen be elected by wards rather than on a citywide basis. The Federal army registration

18. *Daily Atlanta Intelligencer*, July 6, 1867; Augusta *Loyal Georgian*, February 15, 1868; Atlanta *Constitution*, August 4, 7, November 11, 1868; Eugene J. Watts, *The Social Bases of City Politics: Atlanta, 1865–1903* (Westport, Conn., 1978), 21–25. For additional details on Atlanta politics, see Clarence A. Bacote, "William Finch, Negro Councilman, and political activities during early Reconstruction," *Journal of Negro History*, XL (1955), 341–64; Bacote, "The Negro in Atlanta Politics, 1869–1955," *Phylon*, XVI (1955), 333–50; and Eugene J. Watts, "Black Political Progress in Atlanta, 1868 to 1895," *Journal of Negro History*, LXIX (1974), 268–86.

19. CM, November 24, 1868; Atlanta *Constitution*, November 5, December 3, 1868; *Pioneer Citizens' History*, 108; Atlanta *Daily New Era*, December 1, 1869. Grant received 2,468 votes and Seymour 2,480 in Atlanta in 1868.

in 1867 had more white than black voters in the city as a whole, but black voters were in the majority in the Third and Fourth wards. And Democrats feared, with good reason, that the Radicals might carry those wards.[20]

With the new election procedures officially in place, the 1870 municipal campaign rapidly developed into a bitter struggle between Radicals and Democrats. The Democrats mobilized their ward clubs in the fall and quickly organized their ticket. After exploring the possibility of a "Citizens' ticket" that would have included a few independents, the Radicals nominated a strictly partisan slate. It consisted of seven white and three black candidates for the council. In a deliberate attempt to attract white working-class voters, the Republicans had a white railroad engineer and a white railroad conductor on the ticket. The Atlanta Workingmen's Union No. 1 had run a candidate for mayor in the previous election, a sign of growing class-consciousness the Radicals hoped to exploit. After Kimball, Markham, and two others turned down invitations to run, the Radicals endorsed an independent, lawyer Dennis F. Hammond, for mayor. A Democrat for many years, Hammond had bolted the party and voted for Markham in 1869.[21]

Tensions were high by the time of the election, December 8. "A desperate effort is being made to saddle a black city government upon us," shrilled one Democratic newspaper. Several days earlier, Democrats charged that Negro voters had been imported from Chattanooga and other places via the "state road" (the Western & Atlantic, an important Radical source of patronage). The city police illegally attempted to collect poll taxes from black voters in the First Ward and arrested a black "imported voter" in the Fifth Ward, where fiery black orator Jackson McHenry had waged a vigorous campaign. A group of about twenty-five black and white sympathizers tried to rescue the prisoner but were thwarted. Later in the day, a mob stormed the police station to free all those who had been arrested, but in the gunfire that halted the mobs, two black bystanders were killed and

20. Bacote, "William Finch," 344. In 1867, army officers registered 181 white and 203 black voters in the Third Ward and 343 white and 521 black voters in the Fourth Ward, the only wards where black voters were in the majority. Citywide registration was 1,765 white and 1,621 black voters. See *Pioneer Citizens' History*, 112–13.

21. Atlanta *Daily New Era*, November 14, 27, 1869; Atlanta *Constitution*, December 4, 1870.

five were wounded. Order finally prevailed when Federal troops, summoned by the mayor, arrived belatedly.[22]

Police harassment of black voters in the Fifth Ward may well have kept the Radicals from gaining a majority on the city council. The Democrats won six of the ten council seats, and the mayor's office was claimed by Hammond. The four Radical council victories came from the Third and Fourth wards. The Republican winners included two blacks, tailor William Finch and carpenter George Graham, whose illiteracy hampered his service. The white Radicals were building contractor Daniel D. Snyder and printer Samuel W. Grubb, who both aspired to political office at the state level and attended council meetings only sporadically.

Despite the liabilities presented by his white Republican colleagues and the Democrats in control of the council, William Finch succeeded in advancing the Radical program. He lobbied effectively for policies beneficial to both blacks and working-class whites and was able to wheel and deal with his Democratic opponents. He also won the good will of the mayor, who appointed Finch to the important committee on streets when the standing council committees were initially organized.[23]

Largely because of Finch's political skill, streets in neighborhoods neglected by previous city councils were improved and repaired. Although one Democratic councilman spoke against "spending money for sewerage on the outskirts when we need a good sewerage system in the business part of the city," the street committee reported in favor of building a rock culvert on Jackson Street, near the property of white Republican William Jennings. The committee also carried successful motions to remove obstructions from Stephens Street in a black neighborhood, build a rock culvert on Markham Street near a black Baptist church, and lay a sidewalk near Bethel African Methodist Episcopal Church. Finch and his allies on the council barely managed to defeat a "street improvement" measure that would have removed "obstructions" on West Mitchell Street. The "obstructions" were a classroom and dormitory building owned by Atlanta Univer-

22. Atlanta *Constitution*, November 26, December 7 (quotation), 8, 9, 1870; Atlanta *Daily True Georgian*, December 8, 1870; Atlanta *Daily New Era*, December 8, 1870.
23. For more detail on Finch and the 1871 council, see James M. Russell and Jerry Thornbery, "William Finch of Atlanta: The Black Politician as Civic Leader," in Rabinowitz (ed.), *Southern Black Leaders*, 309–34.

sity, a black school founded in 1867. Had Mitchell Street been extended to the city limits as white real estate interests and some Democrats wished, the city's only black university would have suffered.[24]

The Radicals on the 1871 council also led the way in reforming police procedures, which Atlanta's black community frequently protested. For the first time, policemen had to wear uniforms. The purposes were to promote professionalism and to minimize the likelihood of violent conflict between officers and civilians. The council abolished the dollar paid for each arrest—critics said that the fee tempted officers to arrest blacks on the slightest pretext. This reform may have had some impact. One student of Atlanta history estimated that of the 949 arrests on a police court docket for the latter part of 1871, only 200 involved Negroes. In accordance with a law the state legislature passed in 1870, the council extended police protection beyond the city's incorporated limits. This measure was welcomed by poor residents of Atlanta's outlying areas, who were often the victims of criminals who lived on the city's perimeter. The most significant reform discussed but not actively promoted by the Radicals was the hiring of black policemen, which local Negroes had requested as early as 1867. To do so, at least one Democrat had to support the reform. Radicals knew that was unlikely.[25]

The Radicals kept alive the two most significant municipal improvements that came up during their tenure, public schools and water works. In 1870, Atlanta voters in referenda had overwhelmingly approved creating public schools and water works, but Democrats on the council dragged their feet. They hesitated to support public schools because they hoped to find some way to avoid the costs of educating black children. Eventually they accepted Finch's resolution to incorporate into the public system two schools owned and operated by the American Missionary Association for black children. The Democrats also refused to attend meetings when matters pertaining to the water works were on the agenda, thereby preventing the council from acting. Opponents feared that building the water works

24. Atlanta *Daily New Era*, June 24, 1871; Atlanta *Constitution*, May 20, 27, June 17, 24, November 11, 1871.

25. *Ga. Laws, 1870*, pp. 159–60, 485; Alexa Wynelle Brown, "Race Relations in Atlanta, 1865–1877" (M.A. thesis, Atlanta University, 1966), 56; Howard N. Rabinowitz, "The Conflict Between Blacks and the Police in the Urban South, 1865–1900," *Historian*, XXXIX (1976), 68–74; Eugene J. Watts, "The Police in Atlanta," *JSH*, XXXIX (1973), 165–72; Atlanta *Daily New Era*, December 24, 1871.

would cost too much and thus undermine entrepreneurial projects such as the Georgia Western Railroad. Their tactics were partially responsible for the long delay in laying water mains, which did not begin until 1875.[26]

Despite Democratic obstructionism, the 1871 council achieved a positive record of municipal improvements. It had taken steps to ensure that blacks would be admitted to public schools and had defeated efforts to sabotage the water works. It had also carried out various reforms in the police department and had extended street and sanitation services to long-neglected neighborhoods. No Radical member of the 1871 council was reelected, however. Nor did the Republican party place any candidate in a municipal office in Atlanta for the remainder of the nineteenth century.[27]

The reasons for that inability are complex. When carpetbagger Rufus Bullock resigned the governor's post in October, 1871, Democrats regained control of the legislature and promptly enacted a law restoring citywide elections in Atlanta. This electoral procedure remained in force for the rest of the nineteenth century, and it deprived blacks of opportunities to exploit their voting strength in individual wards. A city ordinance passed in August, 1873, also required voters to pay all their city taxes before casting their ballots in municipal elections. This ordinance was obviously aimed at the impoverished black community.[28]

These changes do not fully explain, however, the collapse of the Republican party in postbellum Atlanta politics. The Radicals showed impressive strength on two occasions in 1872. A referendum in June led to the defeat (by a vote of 1,470 against and only 331 for) of a proposal to donate $50,000 in municipal bonds to the trustees of Oglethorpe University as an inducement to locate their school in Atlanta. Although white businessmen enthusiastically supported the proposal, Radical Republicans had organized a coalition of black and working-class white voters. "Every laboring man was able to judge for himself whether the appropriation . . . would benefit him . . . [when] we have only half the public schools that are necessary," white Re-

---

26. Atlanta *Daily New Era*, March 25, 1871; Atlanta *Constitution*, May 6, 20, June 3, July 15, 1871, January 6, 1872; John Ellis and Stuart Galishoff, "Atlanta's Water Supply, 1865–1918," *Maryland Historian*, VIII (1977), 5–8.
27. Nor were blacks elected to municipal offices until 1953. See Bacote, "The Negro in Atlanta Politics," 349–50.
28. Bacote, "William Finch," 359–60; CM, August 22, 1873.

publican A. D. Rockafellow remarked about the referendum. And in Atlanta, surprisingly, Grant overwhelmed Greeley in the 1872 presidential election by more than one thousand votes. [29]

These two Republican victories highlighted what the party could not do on other occasions, that is, forge an alliance between black and working-class white voters. Racism, of course, made the coalition impossible in Atlanta and other cities in the Reconstruction South. Wrangling between black and white Republicans over leadership roles and places on tickets in city and state elections also significantly weakened the party. [30]

Although the Radical Republicans ultimately failed for many reasons to control city hall long enough to devise programs that would have benefited a majority of the city's population, their failure was still the most positive chapter in Atlanta's political history during the immediate postbellum years. Certainly they offered more to the city's less prosperous citizens than did the nonpartisan municipal governments during the late 1860s. It is true that a Democratic city council initiated the public school system (but for whites only) and the water works proposal and that Democratic city governments extended some services to working-class white neighborhoods after the Radicals were permanently removed from office. But the 1871 council with its Radical representatives still came closer than any other council to promoting the public welfare in postbellum Atlanta.

Bosses Versus Reformers

Shortly before the onslaught of the 1873 depression, charges began to surface in local newspapers about corruption within the Democratic party. "There are rumors that the city of Atlanta is governed by a ring as insatiable and odious as the late Tammany ring," wrote the editor of the *Daily Herald* in 1872. The members were usually left unspecified, but reporters for the *Herald* and other newspapers occasionally pointed to physician James F. Alexander, lawyers John Tyler Cooper and William F. Newman, and machinist-turned-wholesale-grocer John H. Flynn as "ringmasters." Alexander was chairman of the County Executive Committee of the Democratic party and a long-time member of the Atlanta Board of Health, Cooper was the county

29. Atlanta *Constitution*, June 5, June 8 (quotation), 1872; Atlanta *Daily Herald*, November 7, 1872. Grant received 2,837 and Greeley 1,805 votes.

30. John M. Matthews, "Negro Republicans in the Reconstruction of Georgia," *GHQ*, LX (1976), 145–64; Rabinowitz, *Race Relations in the Urban South*, 282–93.

clerk, Newman the city attorney, and Flynn a six-term council member. The alleged "boss" was a shadowy figure, lawyer Samuel B. Spencer.[31]

Those who led the crusade against Spencer and his colleagues were themselves Democrats. No former Republicans were involved. Besides a number of prominent Atlanta businessmen, the leaders included three editors of the Atlanta *Daily Herald*, Alexander St. Clair-Abrams, Robert Alston, and Henry W. Grady (whose work for the *Herald* marked his journalistic debut in the city). Founded in 1872, the *Herald* was partially financed by John B. Gordon, and it invariably favored Democratic candidates in state and national elections. But its editors bitterly opposed the "regulars" who controlled the party in Atlanta in the early 1870s. The goal of the newspaper and its allies was to reform the party from within.[32]

Newspaper critics and party reformers accused the ring of a variety of evil deeds. The ringleaders frequently negotiated deals to grade streets and lay sewers in various localities so that property values would increase. Complaints focused on an 1871 law that granted "any person or corporation" owning real estate on streets within three-quarters of a mile of the city's center the right to have those streets graded at public expense, if improvements worth $100 or more were made to the property. Such "lavish" street improvements and other services of dubious value, it was charged, had raised the city's expenditures and debt far beyond its resources. Moreover, the ring was accused of having thoroughly corrupted the city police, who were appointed annually by the city council. Policemen were frequently "caught" electioneering for council candidates. These charges appeared more valid in 1872 when R. F. Hoge, a member of the local Democratic Executive Committee and a state legislator, introduced a bill to grant all police officers and city marshals in Atlanta lifetime tenure.[33]

According to spokesmen for the municipal reform movement, the key to the machine's survival was the Democratic ward clubs. Those clubs were, in fact, the building blocks of political power in Atlanta

31. Atlanta *Daily Herald*, October 24, 1872 (quotation), July 15, December 27, 1874; Atlanta *News*, July 11, 12, 1874.
32. Atlanta *Constitution*, April 18, 1880; Franklin M. Garrett, *Atlanta and Environs: A Chronicle of Its People and Events* (3 vols.; New York, 1954), II, 3–6.
33. Atlanta *Daily Herald*, October 25, 1872, September 27, 1873; *Ga. Laws, 1871*, pp. 301–302; Atlanta *Constitution*, August 24, 1872.

during the 1870s. Voters chose the Democratic candidate for mayor in primary elections, which began in 1871, but council candidates were nominated and elected by individual wards. Reformers protested that "ward politicians" controlled the clubs so thoroughly that "the best men do not seek the office of . . . councilmen . . . as they have no taste or inclination for wirepulling and ring forming." Party regulars responded that the clubs represented grass-roots democracy by offering working-class voters a chance to meet in their own neighborhoods at convenient hours to express their political preferences. [34]

The national depression that hit Atlanta in the autumn of 1873 provided the spark that ignited the reformers' efforts to overthrow the ring and its boss. When the crusade against machine rule began, the city's bonded debt was $1,423,900 while its assets amounted to only $1,128,200. The floating debt (interest and principal due on bonds) for 1873 was $269,211.72. The reformers stressed the dangers of municipal indebtedness on this scale and decried the corruption and extravagance that had accompanied its creation. Many involved in the movement, such as commission merchant Robert F. Maddox, banker William M. Lowry, and newspaper publisher Evan P. Howell, represented the cream of the business community. In denouncing the ring for its "extravagance," these men ignored their own role in inflating the city's debt through requests for municipal aid to railroads and other entrepreneurial projects. [35]

The reformers began their assault by touring the ward clubs in October, 1873, when nominations for council candidates were held. They hoped at first to steer the nomination process toward candidates sympathetic to their cause. Party regulars were ready for the reformers, who were greeted in the ward clubs with hisses, fisticuffs, and other hostile demonstrations. Reformer and wholesale grocer Green T. Dodd insisted on carrying a candle to ward club meetings in case the lights were turned off, which occurred on at least one occasion. When the nominations were finally made in late October, the effectiveness of the party regulars' tactics was clear: every candidate endorsed by the municipal reform movement was defeated. [36]

The ward clubs also defeated a decidedly undemocratic proposal,

34. Watts, *Social Bases of City Politics*, 23; Atlanta *Constitution*, October 28, 1871, October 27, 1872; Atlanta *Daily Herald*, September 24, 26 (quotation), 25, October 17, 26, 1873.
35. CM, January 2, 1874; Atlanta *Daily Herald*, May 22, 1874.
36. Atlanta *Daily Herald*, October 8, 11, 1873; Atlanta *Constitution*, October 26, 1873.

first suggested by lawyer Marcus A. Bell and chamber of commerce president Benjamin E. Crane. The plan called for each club to elect delegates who would then select the party's candidates for municipal office. Had the clubs accepted this proposal, the reformers might have captured control of the party's machinery and placed reform candidates on the Democratic ticket. After the rejection of the "delegate plan," the reformers had little choice but to organize an opposition ticket. They asked their sympathizers to support it in the Democratic primary. The *Daily Herald* listed and promoted this reform ticket.[37]

Party regulars responded vigorously. The alleged boss, Samuel B. Spencer, emerged from the shadows to become the regulars' candidate for mayor. He ridiculed the reformers as "haughty capitalists," "delicate-nerved aristocrats," and "the kid glove ticket," and charged the chamber of commerce with the paternity of their platform. The Democratic rank and file reacted enthusiastically to Spencer's demagoguery. To show their support, members of the Seventh Ward Democratic Club bought wool hats and warned that no man would be allowed to vote in that ward unless he wore a wool hat. "Only men who have the best interests of the city at heart are wool-hat boys," read the formal resolution, "and only they should be eligible to hold office."[38]

Such demagoguery helped the regulars in the Democratic primary on October 26, 1873. Spencer won the nomination over the reform candidate, lawyer John Collier, and the entire regular slate for the city council was also victorious. Seven of the fourteen Democratic candidates chosen in the primary were listed on the tickets of both the regulars and the reformers. On the whole, the results favored the regulars, however, since Spencer earned the right to run as the party's candidate for the most important municipal office. Unopposed in the city elections on December 3, 1873, those on the ticket took office in 1874. The reformers were unable to control either municipal government or the party machinery. James F. Alexander, Spencer's ally, retained the chairmanship of the Democratic City Executive Committee until later that year.[39]

Frustrated by their election defeats, the reformers nevertheless

37. Atlanta *Daily Herald*, October 7, 25, 1873.
38. *Ibid.*, October 18, 19, 1873.
39. *Ibid.*, October 26, December 4, 1873; Atlanta *Daily News*, July 12, 1874.

found another way to reach their goals. They succeeded in obtaining a new municipal charter for Atlanta in February, 1874, which restructured the city's government and placed drastic limitations on expenditures and debts. The charter was written by the Committee of Forty-nine, which the city council appointed in November, 1873. The members included several of Atlanta's wealthiest citizens (at least sixteen also belonged to the elite).[40]

The charter gave the mayor veto power over any council resolution involving more than two hundred dollars. It also created the Board of Aldermen, which functioned as a financial watchdog. The board had to approve all the council's expenditures. New municipal bonds required the approval of the mayor, two-thirds of two successive general councils (the city council and the board combined), and the voters in a popular referendum. Finally, the charter created the Board of Police Commissioners with the clear expectation that they would act to curb electioneering by police officers.[41]

The overall intention of those who drew up the 1874 charter was to reduce drastically municipal spending and depoliticize city government. "The chief beauty of the . . . [charter] is the superb remonstrance made against public extravagance," wrote an admirer of the document. "Almost every sentence contains some restriction against the spending of money or the issuing of bonds." It was significant that the charter, introduced in the legislature by two members of the Committee of Forty-nine, was never submitted to a popular referendum in Atlanta. This was not an oversight. Those who drafted the charter feared, with good reason, that the machine might rally the city's voters against the proposed changes. "There are many in Atlanta whose interests would lie against some of these amendments, and who would use every effort to defeat them," one committee member said.[42]

Like the Porter scandal earlier, the 1874 charter marked an occasion when the business elite acted to redirect the policies of city hall. Although the Democratic municipal administrations had not served either working-class whites or blacks especially well, the reformers

40. Incomplete lists of the Committee of 49 appear in Atlanta *Daily Herald*, November 19, 1873; Atlanta *Constitution*, November 18, 19, 1873; and Garrett, *Atlanta*, I, 903. Thirty-eight members can be identified from these sources.

41. *Charter of the City of Atlanta Passed by the General Assembly of the State of Georgia* (Atlanta, 1874), 6, 8, 14–15, 30–33.

42. Atlanta *Constitution*, November 26, 1873; Atlanta *Daily Herald*, February 6, 1874.

designed a government that had to cut back on services to the city's less prosperous citizens.

Municipal Services and the Public Welfare

A review of municipal services on the eve of the charter's implementation shows clearly that Atlanta's city government was not serving the interests of a majority of citizens. The overall administration of both physical and social welfare services reflected the same business priorities that had been evident before the Civil War. All these services were funded by general tax revenues and special bond issues, but the benefits were far from equitably distributed.

To demonstrate who benefited the most from physical welfare services, let us first consider social geography. The city more than doubled its antebellum dimensions in 1866—its incorporated limits were represented by a circle with a one-and-a-half-mile radius. An 1878 land use map shows that especially the western and southern sides of the city more than one mile from its center were sparsely inhabited. West End, separately incorporated in 1868, was the only suburb of any size. It rapidly acquired a reputation as a prestigious upper-class community, though the inhabitants' occupational and racial mix was approximately the same as Atlanta's. Residents commuted either by the Macon & Western line or by a street railway completed in 1871 between West End and downtown Atlanta. A few local businessmen also lived in the nearby town of Decatur and used the Georgia Railroad to commute.[43]

As Maps 4, 5, and 6 reveal, blacks and whites of differing occupational strata had distinctive residential patterns.[44] High-white-collar white males had a north-south residential distribution. The migration of upper-class Atlantans north along Peachtree Street outside the first half-mile circle was just beginning in the 1870s. Most white males with high-status occupations still lived near the city's center. Working-class whites tended to reside outside the first half-mile circle in a generally east-west orientation. Their residential concentrations were along or near Marietta, Elliott, Race Track, and Decatur

43. *Ga. Laws, 1866*, p. 268; CM, October 19, 1866; Garrett, *Atlanta*, I, 751–52; *Daily Atlanta Intelligencer*, February 23, 1867, May 10, 1870; Gerald M. Hopkins, *City Atlas of Atlanta, From Actual Surveys and Records* (Baltimore, 1878).

44. Almost all the residences more than a mile and a half from the city's center could not be depicted because of the scale used.

MAP 4   Residential Distribution of Sample of White Working-Class Males, 1870

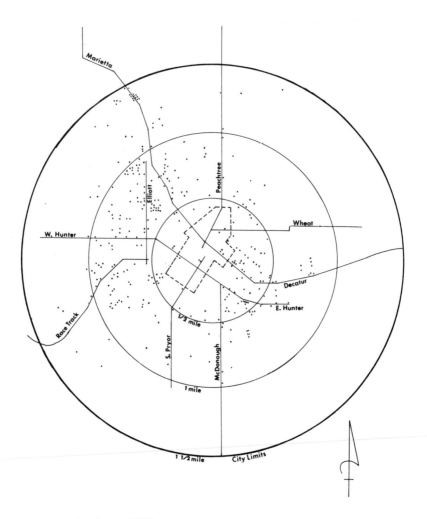

▬▬ ▬▬ Fire limits (1872)
One dot represents one white working-class male

MAP 5   Residential Distribution of Sample of High-White-Collar White Males,
1870

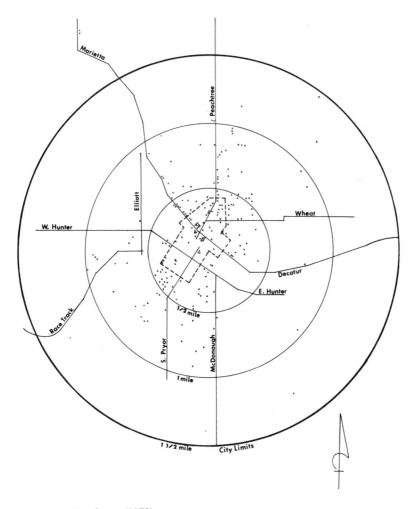

━━━ ━━━ Fire limits (1872)
One dot represents one high-white-collar white male

MAP 6   Residential Distribution of Sample of Black Males, 1876

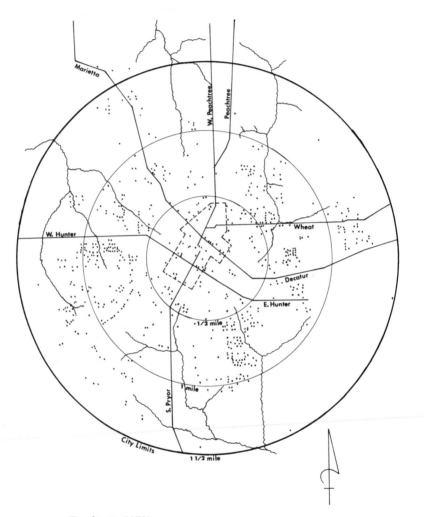

━━ ━━ Fire limits (1872)
One dot represents one black male

streets, which roughly paralleled the three railroads that terminated in Atlanta in 1870. Most of the foundries, machine shops, and other factories that employed many white working-class Atlantans were in close proximity to the railroads. The majority of the white working-class population walked to work. Blacks also tended to live outside the first half-mile circle in distinct neighborhoods—Jenningstown near West Hunter Street, Summer Hill east of South Pryor Street, and Shermantown near Wheat Street. As in other cities in the Reconstruction South, the major determinant of black residential patterns was proximity to streams and rivers, where cheap, low-lying land (subject to flooding) was available.[45]

None of these residential patterns was much affected by the development of Atlanta's street railways, which began in 1871. By 1874, there were only ten and a half miles of streetcar track, which radiated outward from the city's center along Peachtree, Marietta, Decatur, McDonough, and Whitehall streets. Riders were mostly upper-class citizens except on the Marietta line, which was patronized to some extent by working-class whites. Blacks tended to pay the five-cent fare only on Sundays, when they rode in Jim Crow cars for amusement. Streetcars did not affect residential distribution until late in the decade.[46]

One historian has suggested that a pre-industrial residential pattern with the upper class living near the center and the poor on the periphery may have characterized southern cities as late as 1870. Table 9 confirms this theory for Atlanta to a limited degree. About 61 percent of white high-white-collar males resided within the first half-mile circle while only 27 percent of the working-class whites and 16 percent of blacks did. Nearly 59 percent of working-class whites and more than 60 percent of blacks lived between one-half and one mile from the center. Only blacks lived in substantial numbers farther than one mile out, a pattern that conforms to a pre-industrial residential model since blacks were the most impoverished sample group

45. Rabinowitz, *Race Relations in the Urban South*, 115; E. Merton Coulter, *The South During Reconstruction, 1865–1872* (Baton Rouge, 1947), 262; Paul A. Groves and Edward K. Muller, "The evolution of black residential areas in late nineteenth-century cities," *Journal of Historical Geography*, I (1975), 170. Jerry J. Thornbery notes that Jenningstown was an exception, since it was located on high ground ("The Development of Black Atlanta, 1865–1885" [Ph.D. dissertation, University of Maryland, 1977], 20–21). Examination of Map 6 shows that parts of Jenningstown did lie along a stream, however.

46. Jean Martin, "Mule to MARTA, Vol. I," *AHB*, XIX (1975), 1–10; Atlanta *Daily Herald*, May 20, June 13, 1873, September 6, 1874.

TABLE 9
Residential Distribution by Distance from the Center of Atlanta

	0–$\frac{1}{2}$ MILE	$\frac{1}{2}$–1 MILE	1–1$\frac{1}{2}$ MILES	OUTSIDE CITY LIMITS	TOTAL	N
High-white-collar whites (1870)	61.4%	30.7%	2.8%	5.1%	100.0%	215
Working-class whites (1870)	26.7	58.6	14.1	0.6	100.0	326
Blacks (1876)	15.6	60.4	22.0	2.0	100.0	659

SOURCES: Sample data drawn from William R. Hanleiter, *Atlanta City Directory for 1870* (Atlanta, 1870); T. M. Haddock, *Atlanta and West End Directory for 1876* (1876; rpr. Atlanta, 1975).

depicted in the maps. Because systematic analyses of the social geography of other southern cities are not available, one cannot assume that occupational and racial residential patterns in Atlanta were typical of the urban South. Historians have cited, however, descriptive evidence indicating that a center-periphery gradient (with the poor on the outskirts and the rich near the central business district) existed in other cities in the region.[47]

It is true that the homes of blacks, working-class whites, and upper-class whites were scattered all over Atlanta, but the mixed residential pattern of the antebellum commercial city was disintegrating in the 1870s. Atlanta was still a compact "walking city," but working-class and upper-class whites were more spatially separated than they had been before the war. The general tendency of working-class whites and blacks to live farther than upper-class whites from the city's center became crucial as physical welfare services evolved. In Atlanta as in other southern cities (though not necessarily outside the region), fire protection, street upkeep, sewerage, and other municipal services were extended slowly if at all from the central business district toward the perimeter.[48]

47. Zane L. Miller, "The Black Experience in the Modern City," in Raymond A. Mohl, Jr., and James F. Richardson (eds.), *The Urban Experience* (Belmont, Calif., 1973), 45–46; John P. Radford, "Testing the model of the pre-industrial city: the case of ante-bellum Charleston, South Carolina," *Transactions of the Institute of British Geographers*, IV (1979), 392–410; David R. Goldfield, "The Urban South: A Regional Framework," *American Historical Review*, LXXXVI (1981), 1026–27.

48. Rabinowitz, "Continuity and Change," in Brownell and Goldfield (eds.), *The City in Southern History*, 104, 111, 118.

As had been the case before the Civil War, fire protection was generally restricted to Atlanta's core. Maps 4, 5, and 6 show the 1872 fire limits, an area in which wood buildings were prohibited (mainly to protect the business firms and warehouses). Residents of the hotels and homes within this tiny area were assured of fire protection. Even if the fire department responded quickly to alarms (by no means guaranteed—telegraphic alarm bells were not installed until the 1880s), the firemen had to have water. Since all the streams in the city were shallow, water had to come from the fire cisterns. "At present, unless the building is within the immediate area of the cisterns, it burns" was one observer's succinct description in 1872. Atlanta's fire chief admitted that the twenty-three cisterns in 1871 were inequitably distributed. According to the chief's report, the Fifth Ward (which included the increasingly prestigious neighborhoods around Peachtree Street) had eight cisterns while the Third Ward (which encompassed Summer Hill) had only one. Of the twenty cisterns whose locations in 1872 are known, only four were more than one mile from the city's center. When fires erupted in the homes of blacks and working-class whites toward Atlanta's outskirts, the fire engines were useless. Lack of water also meant that buildings owned by upper-class Atlantans could be destroyed by fire. But since they typically lived nearer the city's center where the cisterns were more plentiful, upper-class whites had less to fear in that regard than did blacks or working-class whites. Best protected were, of course, the hotels, industrial plants, and commercial buildings within the central business district.[49]

Street upkeep was even more confined than fire protection to Atlanta's center. "While it is important to keep in good order the main streets in the business parts of the city, those in other parts of the city should not be neglected," Mayor William Ezzard argued in 1870, but to no avail. "Persons in all parts of the city are compelled to pay their proportion of the taxes, and they are always paid more cheerfully when it is believed that the benefits are equally distributed." In 1873 the paved streets were in the central business district, and even there

49. Atlanta *Daily Herald*, December 13, 1872; Atlanta *Daily New Era*, July 15, August 15, 1871; Atlanta *Constitution*, February 1, 1871; Atlanta *Commonwealth*, June 11, 1875. Elizabeth Lyons describes the configuration of Atlanta's central business district between 1878 and 1894 in her "Business Buildings in Atlanta: A Study in Urban Growth and Form" (Ph.D. dissertation, Emory University, 1971), 487, 494–95.

only the principal avenues that led to the railroad depots had been macadamized. [50]

Street conditions elsewhere were deplorable in the early 1870s. For example, a Negro petitioned the city council in 1872 for compensation "for an ox killed by falling into a hole on Markham street." Rains turned the unpaved roads into impassable clay mires that were, an Atlanta resident later remembered, "very intrusive, very sticky, and very red." Hot, dry weather meant dust that was reported in 1870 as "two or three inches deep" in some places. Winds swept the dust into blinding clouds. Predictably, the municipal water carts sprinkled only streets within the central business district. During the mid-1870s a weary pedestrian on an unpaved street at night was unlikely "to find his way lighted through the Red Sea of Mud" by gas streetlamps, which were still scarce outside Atlanta's center. "The want of gas lamps in all sections of the city, remote from the business part of it, is a serious evil," remarked another observer in 1873. [51]

Sewers were as primitive as most streets in the early 1870s. They mostly consisted of rock culverts, which carried fecal matter, industrial by-products, and rainwater away from hotels and factories near the center toward the outskirts of Atlanta. According to one observer, the Hunter Street sewer that drained the W & A's "car shed" and the American Hotel discharged so heavily in 1874 that it "flooded many of the houses in the southern portion of the city." Municipal authorities began to recognize the gravity of the problem in 1873 and established the first standing council committee on sewers and drains. The committee was to "prepare a plan for a general system of sewerage for the city." But any such plan awaited the introduction of water mains. [52]

Often mired in neighborhoods without sewers or paved streets, less prosperous citizens frequently also lacked public schools, health care, and poor relief. Increasingly during the 1870s, these services were inadequately funded. After several years' delay caused by the debate over whether to include blacks in the system, Atlanta's first public schools finally opened in 1872. Initially, there were five white

50. CM, January 8, 1870; Atlanta *Daily Herald*, March 2, August 9, 1873.

51. CM, March 1, 1872; Kate Massey, "A Picture of Atlanta in the Late Sixties," *AHB*, V (1940), 32–36; *Daily Atlanta Intelligencer*, May 18, 1870; Atlanta *Daily Herald*, December 29, 1872, January 25, 1873. See also Hubner, "Atlanta," 377.

52. Atlanta *Daily News*, August 29, 1874; CM, June 13, 1873. See also CM, July 11, 1873, January 1, August 28, 1874.

and two black grammar schools and two high schools for white boys and girls. Although William Finch and other black parents had negotiated with Atlanta University in 1872 to educate black children of high school age for a monthly fee of only three dollars per pupil, the city council and the Board of Education rejected all requests for funding for this arrangement. Blacks did not have a public high school until the 1920s.[53]

From their inception, the public schools failed to educate the majority of the city's black and white populations. The schools enrolled 2,842 children (of whom only 767 were black) in the first year of operation, but an enumeration that school authorities conducted that year listed 9,438 children who were eligible to attend. While some parents elected to send their offspring to private schools or put them to work, public school officials admitted in 1872 that they had sent hundreds of children home because there was not enough space. By 1874, the ratio of enrollments to children entitled to attend and municipal funding of the schools had improved very little. In that year, the cost of operating the schools was $62,597, about $12,000 more than it had been in 1872.[54]

As for public health, the city council appointed five "city physicians" to care for the needy in 1870, but reimbursed them only for medicines and drugs administered to their patients. This policy discouraged impoverished citizens from seeking medical assistance, for which they would be financially responsible. Despite repeated protests, there was no public hospital in the city. "Indigent persons die here every week for the want of such conveniences and comforts as they could have in a hospital," wrote one angry observer in 1869. Partially because of inadequate health services, mortality rates for both races in Atlanta were, in fact, astronomical. The crude death rate per 1,000 in 1873 was 33.6, about four times higher than what it was in the city one hundred years later.[55]

53. Minutes of Atlanta Board of Education, September 26, November 29, December 26, 1872, in Atlanta Board of Education Administrative Building; CM, September 13, 20, 1872; C. T. Wright, "The Development of Public Schools for Blacks in Atlanta, 1872–1900," AHB, XXI (1977), 115–28.

54. Annual Report of the Atlanta Board of Education for . . . 1872 (Atlanta, 1872), 18, 23; Atlanta Daily Herald, November 3, 1872, October 14, 1873, October 4, 1874.

55. CM, December 23, 1870; Bettye Collier Thomas, "Race Relations in Atlanta, from 1877 to 1890" (M.A. thesis, Atlanta University, 1966), 40–44; Garrett, Atlanta, II, 257–58; Atlanta Daily New Era, August 22, 1869 (quotation); Joe Taylor, "Atlanta Mortality Trends, 1853–1873," AHB, XX (1976), 114.

Those needy citizens who managed to survive despite Atlanta's woefully inadequate public health facilities received neither sympathy nor much tangible assistance from the city council's relief committees during the early 1870s. In 1873, municipal expenditures on poor relief were only $4,983.43, which mostly represented the obligatory contribution to the Fulton County Alms House. In that year the Alms House provided wretched lodging and board for only forty-three whites and eighteen blacks. Private relief organizations reported many other cases of poverty-stricken people who were never assigned to the Alms House. The president of the Dorcas Society in 1873 led a reporter to a one-room apartment that was ten by seventeen and housed a family of fourteen. Other black and white families endured dreadful conditions in tenements on one-eighth-acre lots all around the city's perimeter, especially toward the south around Rawson Street. "The man who forms his notion of poverty by the beggar on the street corner, has no notion of the matter," one observer wrote in 1873. "There is a stratum of squalor, of disease unchecked, of loathsomeness and despair."[56]

The reluctance of Atlanta's municipal government to allocate adequate funds for social welfare services and to deliver physical welfare services to poor neighborhoods was duplicated in most other American cities during the postbellum period. The central-city focus was more characteristic of southern cities, since outlying upper-class suburbs were relatively uncommon. In Detroit and Milwaukee during the late nineteenth century, for example, water mains, sewers, and paved streets were installed in middle- and upper-class suburbs on the perimeter but not in ethnic and working-class neighborhoods closer to the central business district.[57] In Atlanta and most of urban America during the postbellum period, business priority dominated the administration of municipal services—a clear reflection of the political power of the entrepreneurial class.

The white working-class and black populations of postbellum Atlanta lacked political mechanisms to challenge effectively business leaders' domination of municipal government. There were more manual laborers on the city council during the period from 1865 to

56. CM, January 2, 1874, June 20, 1873; Atlanta *Daily Herald*, January 22, 23 (quotation), 29, 1873.
57. Platt, *City Building in the New South*, 29; Zunz, *Changing Face of Inequality*, 113–28; Roger D. Simon, *The City-Building Process: Housing and Services in New Milwaukee Neighborhoods, 1880–1910* (Philadelphia, 1978).

1873 than at any other time in the nineteenth century, but their presence did not significantly alter policies. Unlike other late-nineteenth-century cities outside the South with large ethnic populations, Atlanta lacked a real political "machine" that might have organized working-class citizens to force city hall to be more sympathetic. Given the city's population characteristics and the failure of Reconstruction, the Radical Republican party had no real chance for survival as a significant political weapon for local blacks.

The city's working-class whites and blacks were divided by racism, which also prevented a political alliance that might have drastically altered the situation. Students of Atlanta politics and government in the mid-twentieth century have noted that that schism allowed business leaders to assume control of municipal affairs.[58] The 1874 charter was a dramatic illustration of those leaders' power and a controlling factor in Atlanta politics and government for the next ten years and beyond.

58. Edward C. Banfield, *Big City Politics* (New York, 1965), 18–36; Floyd Hunter, *Community Power Structure: A Study of Decision Makers* (Chapel Hill, 1953).

8

POLITICS AND GOVERNMENT, 1874–1890
Retrenchment and Revival

There is a tendency in all cities to create public debt, especially where there are few or no charter restrictions upon the municipal authorities. This arises in a great part from the importunities of the citizens themselves for subscription to this or that enterprise on account of alleged public interest or utility. . . . The citizens of Atlanta . . . had detected the accumulation of city indebtedness, and becoming alarmed, set about devising means to save the city from future bankruptcy. . . . No event of more vital consequence ever occured [*sic*] in the governmental policy of Atlanta. . . . It is true that the severe restrictions of the charter will not permit any very general system of improvements at present, but any inconvenience from this cause will be cheerfully borne, in view of the steady reduction of the public debt, and the new stimulus infused into every feature of the city's prosperity.

—E. Y. Clarke, *Illustrated History of Atlanta* (1879)

The history of Atlanta politics and government from 1874 to 1890 encompasses two sharply contrasting periods. An era of retrenchment in municipal expenditures and political apathy followed the panic of 1873 and persisted well into the early 1880s. Its severity threatened the delivery of even minimal services. As the city's economy and tax base grew substantially in the later 1880s, interest in local politics increased dramatically and municipal services were significantly expanded. A similar progression from cutbacks and apathy to expansion of services and political reawakening occurred in many other American and especially southern cities during the same period.[1]

If the level of political activity and the extent of municipal services varied during the 1870s and 1880s, the purpose of Atlanta's municipal government as expressed in the statements and actions of its public officials remained constant. That purpose was to promote growth, not to make the city a better place for the majority of its citizens to live. Both physical and social welfare services were still administered with the city's economic growth as the overriding concern during the 1870s and 1880s.

Retrenchment and Apathy

The trend represented in the 1874 charter was paralleled in many other cities and states reeling from the 1870s depression. According to one estimate, the value of annual bond issues by state and local governments dropped from about $64 million in 1874 to a little more than $6 million in 1880.[2] For several years after 1873, public officials in Atlanta and many other American cities obviously put a premium on retrenchment in expenditures. In Atlanta this effort resulted in the virtual emasculation of municipal government, which partially explained the political apathy. So lacking in power, city hall was not worth capturing.

1. Howard N. Rabinowitz, "Continuity and Change: Southern Urban Development, 1860–1900," in Blaine A. Brownell and David R. Goldfield (eds.), *The City in Southern History: The Growth of Urban Civilization in the South* (Port Washington, N.Y., 1977), 98, 102–104; Howard L. Platt, *City Building in the New South: The Growth of Public Services in Houston, Texas, 1830–1910* (Philadelphia, 1983), 43–64.
2. Ernest S. Griffith, *The Modern Development of City Government* (London, 1927), 62–82; Platt, *City Building in the New South*, 49.

One immediate casualty of the 1874 charter was the use of municipal funds to subsidize entrepreneurial ventures. Subscriptions to various railroad projects were a cause of the city's high bonded debt on the eve of the 1873 panic. Although numerous such projects were organized in Atlanta during the 1870s and 1880s, none received municipal funds after 1874. This withdrawal of public funds for railroad construction as a consequence of the depression was characteristic of other cities and states, especially in the South, where government revenues were scantier than they were elsewhere.[3]

The reluctance in Atlanta to devote municipal revenues to entrepreneurial ventures extended beyond railroads and persisted even after the depression began to subside in 1879. The famous International Cotton Exposition held in Atlanta in 1881 received no municipal support. Not until 1886 did city authorities spend money on an urban promotive project—they agreed to donate $2,500 annually for twenty-five years to persuade the trustees of the Georgia Institute of Technology to locate their school in the city. This action did not require a bond issue.[4] The depression obviously had a strong and lasting impact on Atlanta's public officials and economic leaders and their concept of local government's proper role in promoting urban growth.

More crucial to the everyday life of most Atlanta residents was the impact of the charter and the depression on the delivery of municipal services. The charter as originally passed by the Georgia legislature in 1874 required that one-half the real estate tax, the city's principal revenue source, be set aside each year to create a sinking fund to pay off the floating debt. The following year, local authorities had to ask the legislature to lower that proportion to one-fourth. Since the city's tax base stubbornly refused to grow, even though the population and the need for services increased during the hard times of the 1870s, Atlanta public officials successfully petitioned the legislature in 1879 for a further reduction to one-eighth. Even with that reduction, the city still devoted 52 percent of its revenue in 1879 and in 1880 to debt

3. See Carter Goodrich, "State In, State Out—A Pattern of Development Policy," *Journal of Economic Issues*, II, (1968), 365–83; Goodrich, "Internal Improvements Reconsidered," *JEH*, XXX (1970), 289–311; and Goodrich, "Public Aid to Railroads in the Reconstruction South," *Political Science Quarterly*, LXXI (1956), 407–42.
4. CM, October 1, 1886; Robert C. McMath *et al.*, *Engineering the New South: Georgia Tech, 1885–1985* (Athens, 1985), 25–35.

repayment alone.[5] Not until 1881, when the value of real estate started to increase again, did the city begin to accumulate sufficient funds to provide more than minimal physical welfare services for just the central business district.[6]

Every branch of Atlanta's government in the lean years before the mid-1880s was strained to the breaking point in maintaining adequate services. Poor relief virtually stopped, and most of the burden was thrust upon either voluntary organizations or the county government, whose financial situation was even worse than was city hall's. City officials managed in 1877 to turn over to the county the entire responsibility of administering the Alms House. Even street upkeep was seriously hampered. To save money, the city council decided in 1876 to turn off all streetlights outside the fire limits, an area roughly equivalent at that time to the central business district. This policy remained in effect for the next three years despite repeated protests from residents of outlying neighborhoods.[7]

The financial restraints of the era effectively crippled those municipal services initiated at the beginning of the 1870s or shortly thereafter. These services included the public schools, the municipally owned water works, and the sewerage and sanitation "systems."

More than any other part of Atlanta's municipal government, the public schools struggled to survive repeated assaults led by wealthy citizens either to curtail sharply or dismantle entirely their operations. Several attempts to reduce expenditures came close to eliminating the boys' high school and the higher grades in the grammar schools. The Board of Education in 1878 rejected by a single vote a resolution introduced by Alfred Austell, a determined foe of "higher education," to abolish the high school and the superintendent's office. A $5,000 cut in 1875 from the council's 1874 appropriation for

5. *Ga. Laws*, 1875, p. 153; *Ga. Laws*, 1879, pp. 255–57. In 1879 the city spent $178,986.06 of its $343,642.25 on debt repayment. In the following year, $200,776.49 of the total revenue of $387,273.98 went for the same purpose. *Annual Report of the Officers of the City of Atlanta for . . . 1879* (Atlanta, 1880), 8; *Annual Report of the Officers of the City of Atlanta for . . . 1880* (Atlanta, 1881), 20–22. These and successive annual reports will hereinafter be cited as *Annual Report of City Officers*, with the appropriate year.

6. The value of Atlanta real estate in 1885 ($21,912,930) was nearly double the 1880 figure ($11,647,135). *Annual Report of the Comptroller-General of the State of Georgia, 1874* (Atlanta, 1874), 19, 29; *Annual Report of the Comptroller-General of the State of Georgia, 1881* (Atlanta, 1881), 106, 111, 116; I. W. Avery, *Atlanta, The Leader in Trade, Population, Wealth, and Manufactures* (Atlanta, 1885), 7.

7. *Ga. Laws*, 1877, p. 313; *Annual Report of City Officers*, 1879, p. 20.

education necessitated shortening the school year by a month. Another cut in 1877 forced the school board to charge tuition for three months. Teachers' salaries were also lowered, and blacks replaced two white teachers at Storrs school (originally operated by the American Missionary Association and absorbed into the public school system in 1872). Northern white teachers there were suspected of harboring dangerous ideas about racial egalitarianism, but the school board was also trying to lower operating costs.[8]

The municipal water works did not have to rely entirely on the annual appropriations of Atlanta's parsimonious local government. It was financed by $300,000 in municipal bonds issued in 1870 and revenues earned from users. The city government had to accumulate a sinking fund to pay off the principal while the water works had to devote six months' revenue to the annual interest payment on the bonds. If revenues during that time period were insufficient, then the city government was legally obligated to pay the interest as well.[9]

Despite its relative financial independence, the Board of Water Commissioners (popularly elected in 1870, when the water bonds were issued) encountered serious problems. Until well into the 1880s, the board had pipe laid very slowly. The water works did not begin laying pipe until 1875, starting along the principal business avenues with the intention of eventually reaching the city's outskirts. An 1878 land use map that depicts the location of fire hydrants shows that none of the mains extended more than a mile from the city's center. The board laid no pipe at all in 1877 and 1879 and, by 1882, had only about seventeen miles of mains in service (not even a mile more than it had six years earlier).[10]

In addition to the depression, a combination of legal, economic, and technological difficulties, as well as errors in judgment, explained the poor performance of the water works. Its progress in the early 1870s was slowed by several suits against the Board of Water

8. Atlanta *Daily Herald*, November 19, 1875; Atlanta *Constitution*, July 10, 11, 1878; *Annual Report of the Atlanta Board of Education for . . . 1877* (Atlanta, 1878), 9; Howard N. Rabinowitz, *Race Relations in the Urban South, 1865–1890* (New York, 1978), 175.

9. *Charter, By-Laws, Rules, Regulations, and Water-Rates Governing the Atlanta Water Works* (Atlanta, 1875).

10. John Ellis and Stuart Galishoff, "Atlanta's Water Supply, 1865–1918," *Maryland Historian*, VIII (1977), 5–9; Gerald M. Hopkins, *City Atlas of Atlanta From Actual Surveys and Records*, (Baltimore, 1878); *Third Annual Report of the Board of Water Commissioners for . . . 1877* (Atlanta, 1878), 17, hereinafter cited as *Report of the Board of Water Commissioners*, with appropriate year; *Report of the Board of Water Commissioners, 1879* (Atlanta, 1880), 35–38; *Report of the Board of Water Commissioners, 1883* (Atlanta, 1884), 3–6.

Commissioners brought by a canal company that had a legislative charter to supply Atlanta with water for manufacturing purposes. When the works finally began operation in 1875, the water was so muddy that it was immediately necessary to construct an expensive standpipe. Moreover, the pumps furnished by the Holly Manufacturing Company of Massachusetts were inadequate and required several costly modifications and additions.[11]

The rate schedule that the board initially adopted was complicated and did not generate enough money to pay for laying more pipe. Residential customers paid a yearly rate of $5 to $28, depending on the front footage of their property and how many stories their houses had. Hotels paid according to front footage and number of rooms. Only large manufactories were charged according to use. The natural consequence of this rate schedule was that residential users wasted water, which was estimated in 1877 at 50 percent of total volume. According to the water works' superintendent, most waste occurred during the summers when homeowners sprinkled dusty streets in front of their houses. This practice kept the fire department from obtaining water pressure sufficient to extinguish a disastrous fire that destroyed the Kimball House in 1883. Water meters were not introduced until 1884 and people protested vociferously.[12]

The water works, despite obvious trouble getting much beyond the planning stage, caused municipal authorities to consider more thoroughly the city's sewerage problems. The council's standing committee on sewers, first established in 1873, acted in 1876 to appoint a Sanitary Commission. After lengthy consideration of Atlanta's waste disposal procedures and extant sewers (mostly open culverts whose foul contents polluted the air and soil), the commission issued two conflicting reports. Both contained serious misconceptions that were nevertheless typical of late-nineteenth-century sanitary engineering. The minority report, written by Dr. Charles Rauschenberg, recommended "combined sewers" (designed to carry off both rainwater and sewage) and extensive use of water closets. Rauschenberg proposed that the sewers empty into Atlanta's five principal streams, which flowed away from the city's center. Like many other reformers, Rauschenberg mistakenly believed that running water would purify

11. Ellis and Galishoff, "Atlanta's Water Supply," 6–7; *Report of the Board of Water Commissioners, 1877*, p. 3.

12. *Charter, By-Laws, Rules, Regulations, and Water-Rates*, 21–23; *Report of the Board of Water Commissioners, 1884* (Atlanta, 1885), 8–9.

sewage. He also believed that the water works could supply enough water during dry seasons to keep the streams flowing. The majority report recommended "dry wall privies" (concrete vaults) where most of the solid waste could be collected and regularly removed by scavenger carts. The waste from water closets was to flow into small-diameter and relatively inexpensive "sanitary sewers" (for sewage but not rainwater) and discharge outside the city limits. Other liquid waste, according to the report's erroneous conclusion, could be safely ignored, since Atlanta's soil and hilly terrain would absorb it. Elements of both plans were unfortunately parts of the sewerage system that evolved later.[13]

The Sanitary Commission's reports did, however, have redeeming features that would have benefited the city. But minuscule appropriations delayed until the late 1880s putting any plan into effect. By 1884, Atlanta had only 13.9 miles of sewers. None had reached the city limits, and several that carried off waste from hotels and industrial facilities in the city's center terminated in densely populated neighborhoods. One sewer emptied into a meadow on Baker Street where cows grazed, and another spewed across a sidewalk on Decatur Street. Moreover, most water closets discharged into street gutters. An 1877 city ordinance required permission from municipal authorities before water closets were connected to sewers, because of fears that there was not enough water to keep the sewers flowing freely. "Atlanta has woefully neglected her sewerage," an observer correctly stated in 1884.[14]

Sewerage problems led directly to consideration of the need for sanitation service, which local authorities acted upon for the first time in the late 1870s. After the terrible yellow fever epidemic in Memphis in 1878, the city council decided to create sanitary districts and provide for emptying privies and collecting refuse. The districts (then identical to the fire limits) encompassed the central business district and upper- and middle-class white neighborhoods contiguous to the city's core. Four "scavenger" and four "night-soil" carts were

13. *Sanitarian*, XV (1877), 424–27; *Proceedings & Reports of the Sanitary Commission of the City of Atlanta, Georgia, 1876* (Atlanta, 1877); Joel A. Tarr, "The Separate vs. Combined Sewer Problem: A Case Study in Urban Technology Design Choice," *JUH*, V (1979), 308–39.

14. CM, August 6, 1877; *Annual Report of City Officers, 1884* (Atlanta, 1885), 50–51, 78–80; Atlanta *Constitution*, June 27, August 20, 1879; Richard Hopkins, "Public Health in Atlanta, 1865–1879," *GHQ*, LIII (1969), 298; CM, January 7, 1884.

responsible for servicing this area twice weekly. There were only two sanitary inspectors to make sure that the carts did their duty, and observers had frequent complaints. Those within the sanitary districts with water closets and those with privies initially paid, respectively, one dollar and two dollars per annum. In all, 763 privies (only one-fifth of all those in the city) were serviced in 1880, the first full year of the new department's operation.[15]

A critical problem ignored in the 1879 ordinance that created the sanitary districts was disposal. Atlanta, like most other American cities, accumulated incredible amounts of garbage toward the end of the nineteenth century. Until late in the 1880s, Atlanta's scavenger and night-soil carts had no official disposal site for their cargoes of human and animal waste. Their usual practice was simply to empty their carts on vacant lots outside the sanitary districts, often in close proximity to crowded working-class white and black neighborhoods. The station master at the water works complained in 1879 that the city carts had deposited dead horses, hogs, cows, and offal on the high ground above the reservoir.[16] It is thus debatable whether Atlanta's sanitation service helped or harmed the general population during this era.

The argument that Atlanta residents got what they paid for in the delivery of municipal services is generally false. It is true that property owners within the sanitary limits were taxed and those who lived outside that area paid nothing. Rate payers also paid for water, but the initial outlay for pumping machinery, reservoir construction, and main pipe was from a municipal bond issue financed by all taxpayers. Moreover, unlike most American cities, Atlanta did not tax owners of property adjacent to sewers and street-paving projects before the 1880s. This policy meant that such services were financed by all tax-payers, even if sewers and macadamized streets never graced their neighborhoods. The overall pattern of financing did not change later in the 1880s. The exceptions were street paving and sewer construction. The property holders who received those services bore two-

15. Hopkins, "Public Health in Atlanta," 291–96; Atlanta *Constitution*, March 19, April 5, 1879; *Annual Report of City Officers, 1880*, pp. 55–56. The original limits for the sanitary districts were only slightly smaller than those in 1886 (see Map 11).

16. Martin V. Melosi, *Garbage in the Cities: Refuse, Reform, and the Environment, 1880–1980* (College Station, Tex., 1981); Report of Lakewood Station Master (1878 to 1882), July, 1879, in AHS.

thirds of the cost after 1881.[17] But, on the whole, a regressive tax structure and patently unfair financing of services was the rule during the nineteenth century.

Protests about municipal services or about any other matter were virtually nonexistent before the political reawakening that began in 1884. There were occasional meetings during the late 1870s and early 1880s about environmental conditions, especially in the Second and Fifth wards, where the Loyd Street and Mineral Springs sewers were a perennial problem.[18] But the result was not a political campaign identified with a particular candidate or party in municipal elections. Excessive tranquillity characterized the political arena.

A complex array of factors accounted for the political apathy. The financial restraints imposed in 1874 and the slow growth of the tax base made many doubt the efficacy of protests about limited municipal services. The erosion of the two-party system also dampened interest in local politics. Haunted by persistent quarrels between black and white party members over patronage and nominations for office, the Republicans lost their influence over municipal politics. There was also evidence of depoliticization in the Democratic party. Confident of its ability to defeat Republicans and independents, the party did not even bother to hold primary elections after 1877. More significant, the Democratic leadership showed no interest in building a political machine that would cater to working-class whites. In addition, black voters' importance was declining. Blacks still voted and represented between 19 percent and 39 percent of registered voters in Atlanta from 1875 to 1891. But the most significant deterrent to black political power was the frustration engendered by the citywide election procedure established in 1871. Black candidates for the city council after that date carried in their own wards but were unable to win across the city. White politicians thus had little reason to fear or heed black voters.[19]

17. *Ga. Laws, 1880–1881,* pp. 358–65. Before January 1, 1890, property owners paid construction costs of branch sewers only. Taxation of property adjacent to the more expensive trunk sewers was made possible by a law passed in 1889 (*Ga. Laws, 1889,* pp. 956–58).

18. Atlanta *Constitution,* January 1, 1877, June 1, 2, 3, 1878, June 3, 1879.

19. Ruth Currie McDaniel, "Black Power in Georgia: William A. Pledger and the Takeover of the Republican Party," *GHQ,* LXII (1978), 225–39; Eugene J. Watts, *The Social Bases of City Politics: Atlanta,1865–1903* (Westport, Conn., 1978), 24–25; Watts, "Black Political Progress in Atlanta, 1868 to 1895," *Journal of Negro History,* LXIX (1974), 268–75; Jerry J. Thornbery, "The Development of Black Atlanta, 1865–1885" (Ph.D. dissertation, University of Maryland, 1977), 240–42.

The exception was the 1878 municipal elections in which the Greenback-Labor party was prominent. The mayoralty election attracted 4,570 votes, the second highest total in the history of municipal contests in Atlanta through 1890. There was, in 1878, the prospect of an alliance between black and white working-class voters.

The Greenback-Labor platform offered a wide variety of promises selected to appeal to businessmen, working-class whites, and blacks. It stressed lowering taxes and the salaries of municipal officials and also replacing the extant tax structure with one that "taxed alike all kinds of property owned by individuals or corporations." Greenback candidates for the city council stood for expanding the public school system, free textbooks, and a public hospital. In an obvious attempt to attract black voters, Greenbackers emphasized educational issues. [20]

The result was less than a resounding victory. The Democrats were so badly divided by the appearance of the Greenback-Labor party that they never officially chose a slate of candidates. Yet Democrats swept the races for mayor, the Board of Aldermen, and council seats from the Second, Fourth, and Fifth wards. The only successful Greenbackers were railroad engineer Edward A. Baldwin and printer James K. Thrower, council candidates from the First and Third wards, respectively. The key may well have been the Greenbackers' inability to sustain the support of black voters. At the last moment, black grocer Mitchell H. Bird ran as an independent in opposition to the Greenbackers' nominee for Fourth Ward councilman. [21]

Political action by the city's less prosperous citizens during the late 1870s and early 1880s to obtain power and a fairer distribution of municipal services was, in sum, a complete failure. The only consolation for the have-nots was that municipal revenues were so scarce that businessmen's traditional preoccupation with administering city government—using municipal resources to promote Atlanta's growth—suffered setbacks as well.

Political Reawakening, 1884–1890

Apathy began to dissipate in 1884. A political scandal and then the city elections marked the beginning of a new method of organization

20. Atlanta *Constitution*, July 23 (quotation), September 24, November 22, December 1, 6, 1878.
21. Atlanta *Constitution*, December 5, 6, 1878; Thornbery, "Development of Black Atlanta," 243–44.

that characterized municipal campaigns during the remainder of the decade. "Citizens' committees" selected in "mass meetings," rather than the Democratic ward clubs, nominated candidates for municipal office. Local newspaper editors praised this "reform" as a means of enrolling Atlanta's "best citizens" (a synonym for wealthy businessmen) in and excluding "back-alley politicians" from local government. The prohibition issue was also raised dramatically in the 1880s and drew more voters than did any political contests in the nineteenth century. Blacks and, to a lesser extent, working-class whites, inspired by their participation in those campaigns, sought payoffs from their allies in both the pro- and antiprohibition forces in the municipal elections during the 1880s. The most dramatic campaign was in 1888. The mayoralty election attracted 4,768 votes, more than did any other municipal election in Atlanta's history to 1890. There was also the promise of an alliance between black and white working-class voters. [22]

The scandal involved the commissioner of streets and sewers, Michael E. Maher, and shaped the 1884 municipal campaign. Maher was accused of graft. The city council appointed a special committee to investigate. The chairman was lawyer John Tyler Cooper, identified frequently in local newspapers as a member of the local Democratic ring. Predictably, Cooper read the majority report that asserted Maher's innocence. A minority report written by insurance agent Harry C. Stockdell disagreed. Later, one of the councilmen who had preferred charges against Maher, planing mill operator Benjamin F. Longley, was himself accused of profiteering in the sale of lumber to the fire department's Engine House No. 1. The charges against Longley, later a prominent member of the reform movement, were also dismissed and widely interpreted as an attempt at revenge by Cooper and other ring politicians. These events were sufficient to convince newspaper editors and leading businessmen that political reform was long overdue. [23]

The reform movement eventually led to a nonpartisan "Citizens' ticket" for the mayoralty, aldermanic board, and city council that was chosen in a series of mass meetings. The object "was to interest the

22. Watts, *Social Bases of City Politics*, 26–30; John Hammond Moore, "The Negro and Prohibition in Atlanta, 1885–1887," *South Atlantic Quarterly*, LXIX (1970), 38–57; Atlanta *Constitution*, December 16, 1888.

23. CM, October 20, December 22, 1884; Atlanta *Constitution*, September 28, December 16, 1884; Atlanta *Journal*, October 19, 1884.

best people of all classes in good municipal government and prevent rings and cliques from taking the city's affairs into their own hands." The meetings were carefully staged, and reform leaders had obviously been diligent in their planning. A nominating committee of thirty-seven drew up the ticket, which represented a compromise between those who wished to retain and those who wanted to eliminate the ward nomination system. One meeting divided itself into groups according to wards and elected five men to represent each ward. To these thirty men were added seven others appointed by the chairman of the mass meeting.[24]

All the nonpartisan movements dominated by businessmen later in the decade adopted the organizational techniques pioneered during the 1884 municipal campaign. The organizers tried to keep power in the hands of chairmen and nominating committees and away from the ordinary voters who attended the mass meetings. At a later meeting, someone pointed out that in presenting a ticket to the assembled voters, the nominating committee had omitted the word *rejection* from its report. "Oh, that's all right," reformer and future Progressive governor Hoke Smith said. "[T]he ticket is here for ratification only." Such attitudes were typical of the reformers, who feared that professional politicians could easily manipulate Atlanta's less prosperous citizens. The reformers' bête noire was the Democratic ward clubs. Many working-class voters preferred that the clubs nominate candidates. Meetings were closer to their neighborhoods than were the reformers' mass meetings, which invariably took place at city hall or some other downtown location.[25]

The "Citizens' ticket" in 1884 dominated the elections but was not without opposition. At one of the reformers' meetings, H. M. Cramer, a self-styled inventor, complained that no workingmen were included on the ticket. His protest "called forth the most deafening cheering on the part of the laboring men in the body." Later in the campaign, another mass meeting attended mostly by working-class voters and traditional Democrats nominated a "People's ticket" for mayor, Board of Aldermen, and city council. Only one candidate on the ticket, John Tyler Cooper, who was running for the board, won in the election. That poor showing was said to be the fault of black voters,

24. Atlanta *Constitution*, August 6 (quotation), August 8, 10, 1884.
25. Smith quoted in Atlanta *Constitution*, November 20, 1889; Eugene Watts, "Characteristics of Candidates in City Politics: Atlanta, 1865–1903" (Ph.D. dissertation, Emory University, 1969), 173–80.

who reportedly sided in 1884 as they did in subsequent elections with the city's business elite.[26]

Less than a year later, prohibition entered Atlanta's political scene and remained at or near center stage for the next five years. The election that established prohibition in Fulton County in 1885 drew 4,927 votes from the city. After fears had been aroused that prohibition would harm Atlanta's economy, an election that attracted 7,041 city voters repealed it in 1887. No other issue in nineteenth century Atlanta—not even secession—elicited such widespread and sustained interest. Not surprisingly, the debate carried over into every municipal campaign of the late 1880s.[27]

The most significant result was the renewed importance of black voters. White politicians and community leaders on both sides of the prohibition question courted and offered numerous promises to Atlanta's black citizens. White leaders invited black politicians and preachers—among them, William Finch, Jackson McHenry, Bishop Henry M. Turner, and William A. Pledger (prominent in the state Republican party)—to appear alongside white speakers at integrated public rallies. Many participants said that the social intermingling at those rallies was remarkable. "Whoever expected to see white and colored people mixed up as they are in Atlanta, where more color prejudice existed for years than anywhere else in the South," Bishop Turner, later known nationally for advocating a back-to-Africa movement, said in 1887. Those black leaders and their followers who joined forces with whites in the crusades for or against prohibition made it clear at the outset that they expected rewards in municipal government.[28]

Both working-class whites and blacks worked diligently to acquire political power and representation on the various municipal tickets during the late 1880s. Both constituencies scored a few victories that were limited in scope, primarily because the leaders (invariably, prominent businessmen) discovered that they could win elections by offering minor (if any) concessions to one group and ignoring the other.[29] Blacks thus demanded and got representation on the Com-

26. Atlanta *Constitution*, August 15 (quotation), December 4, 1884.
27. Atlanta *Constitution*, November 26, 1885, November 27, 1887; Moore, "The Negro and Prohibition," 39, 40–48; Rabinowitz, *Race Relations in the Urban South*, 315–18.
28. Atlanta *Southern Recorder*, October 8, 29, 1886, November 25 (quotation), 1887.
29. No blacks and proportionately fewer white manual laborers were elected to municipal office between 1874 and 1890 than was true during any previous period in the nineteenth

mittee of Fifty, which nominated the successful "Citizens' Fusion ticket" (equally divided between prohibitionists and antiprohibitionists) in 1886. Black antiprohibitionists Moses Bentley and A. W. Burnett and prohibitionists Reverend Wesley J. Gaines and Reverend E. R. Carter served on the committee. Blacks, however, were denied representation on the fusion ticket, as were members of Atlanta's white working-class. The Mutual Aid Brotherhood (the political arm of the Knights of Labor, which claimed to have more than four thousand members in Atlanta) together with a few disgruntled white antiprohibitionists organized a people's ticket in 1886. It included two white manual laborers but no Negroes. Its defeat was caused, it was said, by black voters' supporting the fusion ticket. Once again (as they had done in 1884), black Atlantans had joined with the city's business elite to overwhelm a political organization that catered to the white working-class. In 1887 the business community was divided between prohibitionists and antiprohibitionists. And the leaders put a white manual laborer on their tickets, but no blacks.[30]

The political tensions among blacks, working-class whites, and businessmen-reformers erupted in the municipal campaign of 1888. Leading businessmen put together a conservative ticket that was equally balanced between wets and drys. No black or white manual laborer appeared on that ticket. The conservatives urged those attending their meetings to put aside questions about representation or "any of these little side issues" and, as Henry W. Grady urged, "work with conservative men for the good of the whole city."[31]

Having supported "good government" tickets several times, and to no avail, many blacks in the early stages of the 1888 campaign were hostile to the conservatives. At the meeting that approved the Committee of Seventy to select the ticket, several Negroes heatedly denounced the lack of black representation and the conservatives' unwillingness to promise that blacks would be on the ticket. "Not a Negro will vote for the ticket of this committee," declared Smith Easley, a black from the Fourth Ward. "We don't want to be the tail end of anything." Subsequently, Moses Bentley and other black pol-

century. See my "Elites and Municipal Politics and Government in Atlanta, 1847–1890," in Orville Vernon Burton and Robert C. McMath, Jr. (eds.), *Toward a New South? Studies in Post–Civil War Southern Communities* (Westport, Conn., 1982), 44–45.

30. Atlanta *Constitution*, March 14, October 27, 1886; Watts, "Characteristics of Candidates," 187–88.

31. Atlanta *Constitution*, September 29, October 5 (quotation), 1888.

iticians advocated reviving the Republican party and organizing a ticket that would include Negroes. This possibility, explored several times during the campaign, was opposed by many white Republicans who favored the conservatives. [32]

In response to the conservative ticket, Mutual Aid Brotherhood leaders, white antiprohibitionists, and several influential Democrats such as Julius L. Brown and John B. Goodwin organized an anti-conservative movement. They put together a people's ticket in 1888 aimed at uniting working-class white and black voters. The Committee of Seventy, which still dominated the people's ticket, included eighteen blacks, though three (including Jackson McHenry) quickly withdrew. Nevertheless, Atlanta's black community was better represented on the committee than in any similar political organization during the period. The final version of the ticket listed two white manual laborers but no blacks. Three men (two of them manual laborers) had withdrawn earlier because their employers threatened to fire them if they did otherwise.

Fiery demagogic lawyer Walter R. Brown and others on the people's ticket ran a bitterly class-conscious campaign, which included the most specific, biting commentary about inequities in municipal services nineteenth-century Atlanta had ever heard. Brown, the anti-conservatives' candidate for mayor, sneered at his opposition as the "Peachtree ticket" and made much of the fact that the only water line extended to the city limits by 1888 paralleled that affluent street. Brown and others made promises to working-class whites and blacks: a separate Negro fire company; more public schools; free textbooks; better streets and sewers in working-class white and black neighborhoods; and abolition of the street tax. Brown also hinted that he would not oppose the hiring of Negro policemen. [33]

The people's ticket was totally defeated in the city elections. Several poll watchers reported that blacks had voted heavily in favor of the conservatives. One reason may have been the gap between what blacks asked for and what they got. Black members of the Committee of Seventy had requested but were denied pledges to appoint four blacks—two detectives and two drivers—to the police force, four

32. Atlanta *Constitution*, September 29 (quotation), October 11, 20, 23, 28, November 27, December 1, 1888; Watts, "Characteristics of Candidates," 202–203.
33. Atlanta *Constitution*, October 17, 21, 30, November 2, 3, 11, 14, 15, 16, 20, 22, December 2, 6, 7, 1888.

blacks to the Board of Education, two Negro clerks in the county courthouse, and a black candidate for city council.

More significant was that many blacks distrusted white working-class members of the anticonservative movement and that several prominent black leaders opted for a continued alliance with the city's business elite. At one conservative mass meeting, Jackson McHenry, who had fleetingly supported the people's ticket, referred publicly to the anticonservatives as "the hardest crowd he had ever seen." "He did not like to vote for democrats, but . . . the conservative ticket was the best thing in sight," a reporter paraphrased McHenry's comments. "He would support it because he wanted to go on record as voting with the best people of Atlanta."[34]

In subsequent municipal campaigns, McHenry and other black political leaders found reasons to regret their decision to vote with Atlanta's "best people." Blacks' militant demands in 1888 led to a white backlash that significantly eroded their political power.

The public's overwhelming support for continuing the citizens' reform movement resulted in another movement in 1889. A petition signed by more than one thousand voters led to a mass meeting attended by more than two thousand citizens. They elected a hundred-member committee to compose a slate of candidates for municipal office. The resulting citizens' ticket of 1889 listed the names of three white manual laborers (a printer, a master car builder, and a gardener). The printer and candidate for alderman, James G. Woodward, had several months earlier dismissed the outspoken H. M. Cramer as "an old fossil" and a "disgrace to the Knights of Labor." Reform-minded members of the business community and the white working-class had obviously made their peace in 1889 in an effort to prevent the class-conscious politics associated with earlier campaigns.[35]

The organizers of the 1889 citizens' ticket ignored Atlanta blacks. No Negroes were on either the nominating committee or the ticket. Walter R. Brown, who had joined his former enemies, introduced a resolution at one meeting that called for reinstating the white Democratic primary. This resolution was voted down, but only because the organizers wanted white Republicans to feel free to vote for it. A prominent white Republican was, in fact, on the ticket. He was opposed by

34. Atlanta *Constitution*, October 19, December 7, November 28 (quotation), 1888.
35. Atlanta *Constitution*, May 9 (quotation), November 12, 13, 15, 1889.

an independent candidate, but the citizens' ticket swept the municipal elections. Color, class, and party lines were closing Atlanta politics to blacks.[36]

When the city's black community prepared for one last effort in 1890 to gain control of or at least be represented in city hall, whites took steps to crush their political ambitions permanently. The Democratic City Executive Committee seized the initiative and arranged the election of another hundred-member committee to select a ticket. Several new political organizations immediately protested. The 1890 Club, primarily a prohibition group, drew up its own ticket, which was soon opposed by one from the Citizens' Conservative Club (which was dominated by leading businessmen). The Liberals, an antiprohibition organization, also opposed the 1890 Club and collected fifteen hundred signatures on a petition calling for "the reformation of city politics and methods." Another group formed a citizens' ticket that contained the names of manual laborers, workers not represented on any other ticket. The eventual result was a decision by the City Executive Committee to hold a white primary on November 21, 1890. White voters were allowed to select candidates for the city council by wards; candidates for mayor and the Board of Aldermen were chosen by citywide elections. In the primary, the conservatives won handily.[37]

Negro political leaders drew up an all-black municipal ticket after the primary and kept it secret, hoping to catch white Atlantans napping on election day. Word of this "anti-primary ticket" was leaked to local newspapers the day before, and white voters turned out in force and defeated every black candidate. This debacle began the final march toward the elimination of black political power in Atlanta. The white primary was a persistent feature of Atlanta politics from 1892 until the mid-twentieth century, a period that witnessed the nadir of black political activity in the city.[38]

Battles over moral and political issues and class and racial conflicts characterized Atlanta politics during the ten years that led to the destruction of black political power. Prohibition was an issue through-

36. Atlanta *Constitution*, November 15, December 5, 1889; Watts, "Characteristics of Candidates," 207–208.
37. Atlanta *Constitution*, October 10, November 4, 7, 8, 15, 19, 20, 1890; Watts, "Characteristics of Candidates," 209–11.
38. Atlanta *Journal*, December 3, 1890; Watts, "Black Political Progress," 282–84; Clarence A. Bacote, "The Negro in Atlanta Politics 1869–1955," *Phylon*, XVI (1955), 337–43.

out most of the period, as was the principle of ward representation (even during the 1889 campaign, which was otherwise harmonious among whites). The outstanding failure was the inability of working-class whites and blacks to unite, a repetition of events during Reconstruction and a prelude to the same thorny problem that overwhelmed the Populist party in the South. Their mutual distrust resulted in the triumph of political organizations that disregarded them both.

Municipal Services and the Public Welfare

Given the political defeats during the 1880s, it is hardly surprising that the administration of municipal government reflected what was important to the business elite. The validity of this generalization can be demonstrated in a final survey of welfare services in Atlanta around 1890.

Although the city remained relatively compact in 1890, it had expanded legally and spatially since the early 1870s. Its incorporated limits were extended in 1889 to include the area within the one-and-three-quarter-mile radius from the city's center and also a bulge on its eastern side that represented Inman Park, a planned suburban community. Areas toward the city's perimeter that had been sparsely populated in the 1870s had filled up by 1890. [39]

Especially as streetcar lines were added during the 1880s, neighborhoods at or just beyond Atlanta's legal limits and various suburbs grew rapidly. The working populations there mostly commuted to the city. By 1890, the city had four streetcar companies (two horse-drawn and two electric) with 51.84 miles of track. They carried 6,026,054 passengers annually. The lines radiated from the city's center in all directions to and beyond its limits and, together with the existing steam railroads, made possible the dispersal of substantial numbers of people toward the perimeter. Richard Peters and George W. Adair, co-proprietors of the largest streetcar concern (the Atlanta Street Railroad Company), were both heavy investors in real estate on the city's perimeter and dedicated salesmen of suburban property. [40]

39. *Ga. Laws, 1889*, p. 815; Rick Beard, "From Suburb to Defended Neighborhood: The Evolution of Inman Park," *AHJ*, XXVI (1982), 113–40. Inman Park is represented on Maps 12 and 13. A Sanborn Fire Insurance Company map of Atlanta in 1886 (on microfilm in the Robert R. Woodruff Library, Emory University) depicts land use.
40. U.S. Bureau of the Census, *Report on Transportation Business in the United States at the Eleventh Census: 1890. Part I. Transportation by Land* (1895), 683, 705; Don L. Klima, "Breaking Out: Streetcars and Suburban Development, 1872–1900," *AHJ*, XXVI (1982), 67–82; Jean Martin, "Mule to MARTA, Vol. I," *AHB*, XIX (1975), 11–29.

Atlanta's suburbs and peripheral neighborhoods were diverse in character. Some—Reynoldsville to the east, Red Row to the west, and Miles City to the south—were predominantly black. West End was still the only incorporated town besides Decatur, which was a marginal suburb because of its distance from the city.[41] West End had its own schools, gas mains, and street maintenance force, but no sewers, water lines, or fire department. Inman Park was within the city limits and was the only really exclusive peripheral neighborhood—there were paved streets, gas mains, water lines, and sewers. Lots in Inman Park cost between $5,000 and $8,000, and houses had to be at least thirty feet from the street and appraised at no less than $3,000. The South Atlanta Land Improvement Company, organized in 1887 by white businessman Campbell Wallace, planned to create an exclusive Negro suburb on the city's south side beyond Clark University. This project had not gotten far off the drawing board by 1890, however.[42]

Table 10 shows that despite the suburban movement, white males with white-collar occupations in 1888 were still more than twice as likely as were working-class (manual laborers) whites and blacks to live near the city's center. The percentages of high-white-collar and low-white-collar white males are almost the same, an interesting example of a tendency of the latter to live near high-status workers (even if living there imposes severe strains on family budgets).[43] Blacks and working-class whites in 1888 were still more likely than were white-collar whites to reside between one and one and a half miles from the city's center. On the other hand, roughly the same proportions of the various groups lived outside the city limits. Suburbanization was not solely an upper-class phenomenon in late-nineteenth-century Atlanta.

41. *First Annual Report of the Atlanta Chamber of Commerce, for the Year 1885: Historical, Descriptive, Statistical* (Atlanta, 1886), 38; Atlanta *Constitution*, June 7, 1886, February 13, March 9, October 6, 1887, March 15, 30, April 6, 27, September 9, 1890. The Atlanta *Post Appeal*, November 16, 1882, reported, however, that 150 Atlanta businessmen resided in Decatur. In 1889, there were fourteen passenger trains that ran every day between Decatur and Atlanta (Atlanta *Constitution*, March 15, 1889).

42. Atlanta *Journal*, February 22, December 15, 1890; Atlanta *Constitution*, May 10, June 21, 1889, February 26, 1890; Timothy J. Crimmins, "West End: Metamorphosis from Suburban Town to Intown Neighborhood," *AHJ*, XXVI (1982), 33–50. Census takers in 1890 estimated the population of the area encompassed by a one-quarter-mile extension from the city limits at 13,980 (Atlanta *Constitution*, July 27, 1890).

43. Otis Dudley and Beverly Duncan, "Residential Distribution and Occupational Stratification," *American Journal of Sociology*, LV (1955), 493–503.

TABLE 10

Residential Distribution by Distance from the Center of Atlanta, 1888

	0–½ MILE	½–1 MILE	1–1½ MILES	OUTSIDE CITY LIMITS	TOTAL[a]	N
High-white-collar whites	37.9%	36.5%	15.1%	10.5%	100.0%	285
Low-white-collar whites	36.2	38.0	17.0	8.7	99.9	629
Working-class whites	16.8	43.9	25.6	13.6	99.9	784
Blacks	10.0	48.4	33.3	8.4	100.1	682

SOURCE: Sample data drawn from R. L. Polk & Co., *Atlanta City Directory for 1888* (Atlanta, 1888).

[a]Percentages do not sum to 100 because of rounding errors.

Maps 7, 8, 9, and 10 reveal more detail about Atlanta's social geography in 1888.[44] High-white-collar whites still maintained a residential concentration near the city's center on the south side, but their migration north along prestigious Peachtree and West Peachtree streets was noticeable. Low-white-collar whites displayed similar patterns. Working-class whites continued their east-west residential orientation and mostly lived near railroads, where many of the largest industrial plants were still located. As was characteristic of Negro residential patterns in other southern cities, Atlanta's black population still lived in peripheral and low-lying neighborhoods near streams. Land in these areas became increasingly unhealthy as the city's sewerage system evolved.[45]

These residential trends were closely related to physical welfare services. Municipal revenues more than tripled between 1880 and 1890, making possible significant growth of street-paving programs, sanitation service, and the sewer system. But extending these services beyond the central business district (the boundaries of which remained about the same from the late 1870s to the early 1890s) did not significantly improve the quality of life in black and working-class

44. Many of those in the "Outside city limits" category in Table 10 had addresses that could not be plotted on the maps because of the scale used.

45. John Kellogg, "Negro Urban Clusters in the Postbellum South," *Geographical Review*, LXVII (1977), 315–17; Kellogg, "The Evolution of Black Residential Areas in Lexington, Kentucky, 1865–1887," *JSH*, XLVIII (1982), 21–52.

MAP 7   Residential Distribution of Sample of High-White-Collar White Males, 1888

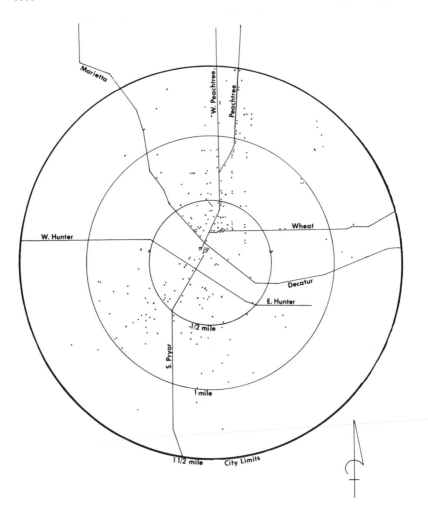

One dot represents one high-white-collar white male

MAP 8   Residential Distribution of Sample of Low-White-Collar White Males, 1888

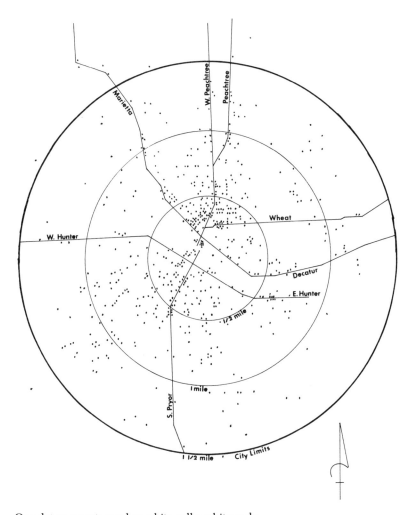

One dot represents one low-white-collar white male

MAP 9   Residential Distribution of Sample of White Working-Class Males, 1888

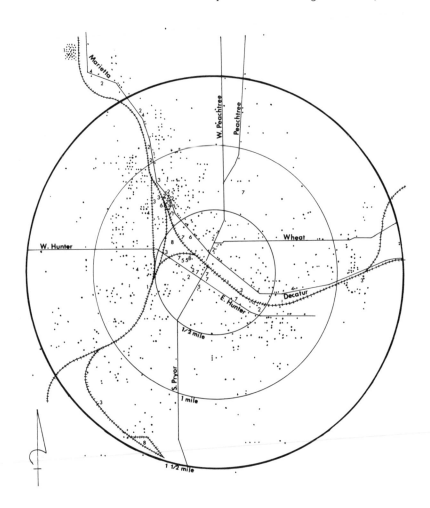

One dot represents one white working-class male

Key to Manufacturing Plants

1 Cotton mills & related
2 Foundries & metalworks
3 Lumber & building supplies
4 Furniture & woodwork

5 Book & paper goods
6 Utilities (gas & electric)
7 Miscellaneous
8 Railroad & machine shops

MAP 10   Residential Distribution of Sample of Black Males, 1888

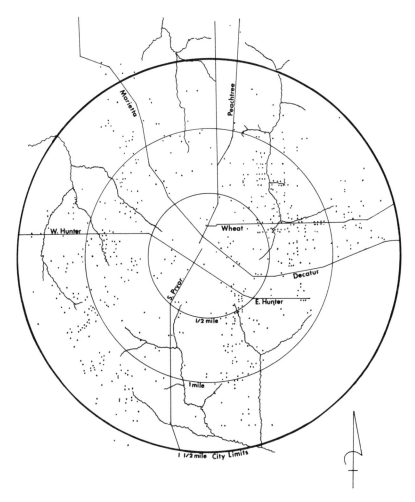

One dot represents one black male

white neighborhoods.[46] The expansion of physical welfare services during the 1880s generally and not unexpectedly followed the residential movement of white-collar whites.

Street maintenance, still the largest item in the city's budget, remained oriented toward Atlanta's core during the 1880s.[47] By 1890, there were 32.89 miles of paved streets (about 14.5 percent of the total), and most were in the central business district. Although a considerable improvement over conditions ten years earlier, this percentage was lower than those of thirty-eight of the nation's fifty largest cities that year. William A. Hemphill, mayor in 1890, argued against "the policy of paving outside [beyond the business district] streets" unless all homeowners along those streets requested it (an impossible prerequisite). John T. Glenn, mayor in 1889, admitted that such attitudes led to nearly impassable streets on the city's outskirts. "The condition of Marietta street between Hunnicutt street and the city limits is such that waggons [sic] are broken in passing over it," Glenn confessed. Occasional protests about such conditions went unheeded.[48]

Street illumination was also still confined to Atlanta's central districts. In 1887 the city began converting from gas to electric streetlamps and had 167 "arc lights" and 436 "series lights" in use three years later. According to the report of a city council committee, all the larger arc lights were either in "the business portions of the city" or on main thoroughfares leading from the center to the corporate limits. The committee's chairman cautioned against "indiscriminate placing of the large arc lights [where they] would be of no public good." As protests from residents of various wards during the late 1880s helped make clear, this statement was intended to justify the lack of streetlights in peripheral neighborhoods.[49]

Sanitation service was only slightly less restricted to Atlanta's core.

46. Elizabeth Lyons, "Business Buildings in Atlanta: A Study in Urban Growth and Form" (Ph.D. dissertation, Emory University, 1971), 487, 494–95. Total revenues were $395,693.18 in 1880 and $1,264,594.50 in 1890 (Annual Report of City Officers, 1880, pp. 20–22; Annual Report of City Officers, 1890 [Atlanta, 1891], 101).

47. In 1890, the city spent $299,716.54 (24 percent of its revenues) on street upkeep (Annual Report of City Officers, 1890, p. 101).

48. Melosi, Garbage in the Cities, 44–46; Atlanta Constitution, February 4, 1888; Atlanta Journal, February 22, 1886; Annual Report of City Officers, 1890, pp. 23–24 (quoting Hemphill), 111, 126–27; Mayor John T. Glenn to Richard Peters, March 26, 1889, in Mayor Glenn's Letterbook, 1889, AHS.

49. Annual Report of City Officers, 1890, pp. 32–33; Atlanta Constitution, January 29, 1888.

Map 11 indicates that the extension of sanitary services took a north-south direction.[50] Comparison with the residential distribution maps verifies that this trend favored white-collar white neighborhoods over those of blacks and working-class whites.

Within the sanitary limits, conditions had definitely improved by 1890. An 1887 city ordinance required that all water closets inside those limits empty into sewers rather than street gutters. Since all but 84 of the 2,944 water closets in Atlanta were within this area, the ordinance virtually eliminated one persistent nuisance. The chief sanitary inspector in 1890 also reported that about two-thirds of the city's privies were serviced by night-soil carts, which now numbered twelve. The chairman of the council committee on sanitation in 1890 admitted, however, that nothing was done about "many thickly settled localities in the city."[51]

Other than the limited sanitary districts, Atlanta's greatest sanitation problem in 1890 was still the disposal of waste. Night-soil and scavenger carts collected 1,902,940 bushels of "excrementious matter" that year. The total did not include the carcasses of large animals, which were donated to a glue factory during part of the year (the scavenger carts had to get rid of 3,036 dead animals in 1889). Not until 1885 did municipal authorities arrange to create a dumping ground outside the city, but people also chose other areas. One unofficial site was on West Simpson Street near a white working-class neighborhood. The municipal facility's location (three miles west of Atlanta) tempted citizens—especially those who lived outside the sanitary districts—to dump their refuse on the nearest vacant lot. By 1890, there were obviously compelling reasons, of which Board of Health officials were well aware, for building a crematorium and extending the sanitary limits over the entire city. In 1893, collection of human waste (but not garbage) took place throughout the city, and the following year Atlanta's first crematorium was built.[52]

50. Sanitary limits in 1886 are described in John B. Goodwin (comp.), *Code of the City of Atlanta* (Atlanta, 1886), 348. The fire limits in 1888 are specified in Goodwin and James A. Anderson (comps.), *The Code of the City of Atlanta, containing the Charter of 1874* (Atlanta, 1891), 235. The fire limits remained unchanged through 1890. Although the enclosed area of the sanitary districts remained the same through 1890, individual streets were added after 1886. Almost all were in north Atlanta or in a section to the southwest (which coincided with an area of low-white-collar white residences).

51. Goodwin and Anderson (comps.), *Code of the City of Atlanta*, 256–57; *Annual Report of City Officers, 1890*, pp. 53–54 (quotation), 162, 199.

52. *Seventh Annual Report of the Atlanta Board of Health* (Atlanta, 1886), 79; *Eleventh Annual Report of the Atlanta Board of Health* (Atlanta, 1890), 6; CM, June 18, 1888; *Annual*

MAP 11   Fire and Sanitary Limits

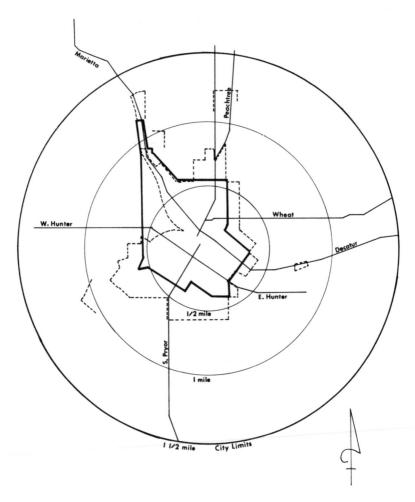

━━━━━━ Fire limits (1888)
━━ ━ ━ Sanitary limits (1888)

The superintendent of the water works reported in 1890 that slightly more than forty miles of pipe had been laid and that 3,759 residential and commercial subscribers were entered in the "tap book." But, as Map 12 shows, the extension of water mains beyond the central business district had taken a decidedly north-south direction in conformity with the residential distribution of white-collar workers.[53] The only water lines that extended to the city limits followed Peachtree Street to the north and Pryor Street to the south (the path of the main pipe from the reservoir). Few working-class whites and even fewer blacks lived near water mains. Municipal authorities spent $10,000 in 1885 to dig an artesian well near the junction of Peachtree and Marietta streets. It was hoped that mains could be laid from this well to "low lying portions of the city that are thickly inhabited by the poorer classes." This scheme was declared a "palpable failure" in 1888, when it was discovered that surface rainwater had carried sewage into the well.[54]

Even those who obtained their water from the municipal works had cause by 1890 to be concerned about pollution. The reservoir was fed by the South River and two streams, both of which originated outside the city limits. By 1887, Todd branch had 774 homes along its watershed and received all their washings and drainage. So, in 1888, Todd branch was cut off from the reservoir, which was thereafter replenished only by rainwater, the South River, and Harden branch (an insufficient supply). Harden branch was farther south of Atlanta than was Todd branch, and it was in a sparsely populated area. It was relatively unpolluted until 1890, when a fire destroyed a refinery, which spewed cottonseed oil into its headwaters. Municipal authorities began looking for a purer and more plentiful source of water north of the city along the Chattahoochee River. This project

Report of City Officers, 1890, pp. 163, 165, 206; John H. Ellis, "Businessmen and Public Health in the Urban South during the Nineteenth Century: New Orleans, Memphis, and Atlanta," *Bulletin of the History of Medicine*, XLIV (1970), 356–57.

53. *Report of the Board of Water Commissioners, 1890* (Atlanta, 1891), 10–12. The earliest extant map of water mains in Atlanta is attached to the board's 1898 report. Most of the water mains drawn in Map 12 were listed in the commissioners' annual reports, which are virtually intact for this period. A few of the reports did not specify the location of mains added during certain years. Newspaper accounts filled in those gaps for 1875 and 1888 (Atlanta *Daily Herald*, May 12, 1875; Atlanta *Constitution*, February 2, 1888). There were probably a few additional mains that could not be plotted for want of information.

54. Atlanta *Journal*, April 14, 1887 (quotation); *Tenth Annual Report of the Atlanta Board of Health* (Atlanta, 1889), 19–30 (quotation); Atlanta *Constitution*, March 16, 1886; H. G. Saunders, *Guide to the City of Atlanta* (Atlanta, 1889), 51.

MAP 12   Water Mains and Incidence of Fires

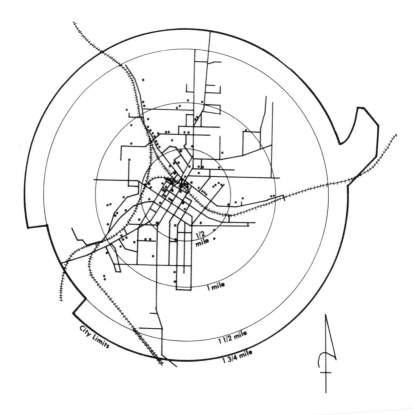

City Limits

1/2 mile
1 mile
1 1/2 mile
1 3/4 mile

Water main (1890)
One dot equals one fire (1888)

was finally completed in 1893, raising the hopes of the Board of Water Commissioners that with abundant water "the time is not distant when every city street will be traversed by a sewer and a water main." Ten years later, more than two-thirds of Atlanta's population still lacked piped-in water, however.[55]

The majority of Atlanta's homes did not have safe drinking water, and these residences also risked destruction by fire at any moment. The area served by the fire department (paid since 1882) was no longer identified with the fire limits but was defined by access to water mains. Map 12 shows that nearly all the 118 fires to which the fire department responded in 1888 were close to water mains.[56] The fire chief's reports earlier in the 1880s occasionally mentioned that the fire engines had answered alarms and found fires "out of reach of water mains." The usual policy was to ignore such fires, an eminently practical approach. The fire engines did respond in 1887 to a call at Spelman University in a black neighborhood, but watched helplessly as the school's Union Hall burned to the ground "because of the deficiency of water."[57]

Atlanta's sewerage system was virtually useless to the city's less prosperous citizens. Interest in improving the system picked up in 1888. Municipal authorities hired noted sanitary engineer Rudolf Hering to study the existing sewers and make recommendations. Unfortunately, most of his recommendations were enthusiastically adopted. His detailed report repeated critical errors in judgment committed by the Sanitary Commission twelve years earlier. Hering urged completion of the trunk sewers beyond the city limits, where he believed they could safely spew their contents on the ground. Much of this land was pasture where cows grazed, and their milk became contaminated. He also recommended continued work on the sanitary sewers, which he thought should terminate in the city's streams at points where they broadened sufficiently. Like the authors of the

55. *Report of the Board of Water Commissioners, 1887* (Atlanta, 1888), 9–10; *Report of the Board of Water Commissioners, 1889* (Atlanta, 1890), 7; *Report of the Board of Water Commissioners, 1890*, p. 9; *Report of the Board of Water Commissioners, 1891* (Atlanta, 1892), 3; Ellis and Galishoff, "Atlanta's Water Supply," 12.

56. The locations of fires in 1888 were specified in an unpaginated table in the city officials' annual report. The four fires in the southwestern section of the city that appear to be distant from mains may not have been. The mains along those streets are shown on the map that was part of the water commissioners' 1898 report.

57. Atlanta *Southern Recorder*, July 8, 1887.

1876 report, Hering erroneously believed that running water could purify raw sewage. [58]

In the two-year period after the adoption of Hering's report, about 14.8 miles of sewers were laid according to his recommendations, expanding the system to a total of 34.71 miles by 1890. But, as Map 13 shows, Atlanta's sewerage system was far from complete and had serious imperfections. [59] Neither trunk sewers nor sanitary sewers extended beyond the city limits, and vast areas of the city were totally deprived of sewerage. The city's largest sewer, the Loyd Street sewer, terminated in 1890 on the premises of a Jewish orphanage. This sewer and the Butler Street sanitary sewer, which emptied into a stream running through densely populated Negro neighborhoods, were denounced vehemently by the Board of Health in 1889 as "a constant menace to the health of the city." That stream and the ones that collected the filth from the Mineral Springs sewer and the Jail sewer polluted the drinking water of the mostly black neighborhoods through which they coursed. Dumping raw sewage into these streams continued until 1911, when Atlanta finally acquired its first sewage treatment plant. Typhoid death rates in the city, especially for blacks, consequently remained among the highest in the nation until that date. [60]

If they managed to survive the lack of pure drinking water, fire protection, and other physical welfare services, Atlanta's less prosperous citizens found city hall no more eager to supply social welfare services such as public education and poor relief. These services were still low on the agenda of municipal authorities.

As the financial restraints imposed by the 1870s depression eased, more but not enough money became available for the public schools. A month was, in fact, dropped from the school year in 1882, and teachers had to work a month without pay in 1883. In 1887 the Board of Education decided to hire only black teachers (provided they had

58. Hering's report can be found in *Annual Report of City Officers, 1890*, pp. 279–87.
59. *Annual Report of City Officers, 1890*, pp. 108–110. Map 13 was drawn mostly on the basis of data in the Hering report. Two maps of trunk and sanitary sewers that appeared in newspapers are also helpful (Atlanta *Journal*, March 11, 13, 1890). The city officers' annual reports list every sewer built during this era, but the descriptions of sewer locations are too vague for mapping purposes. The reports did yield some information about the longer branch sewers, however.
60. Quotation from *Eleventh Annual Report of the Atlanta Board of Health*, 105; Atlanta *Journal*, March 13, 1890; Stuart Galishoff, "Triumph and Failure: The American Response to the Urban Water Supply Problem, 1860–1923," in Martin V. Melosi (ed.), *Pollution and Reform in American Cities, 1870–1930* (Austin, 1979), 49–51.

MAP 13   Sewer Network, 1890

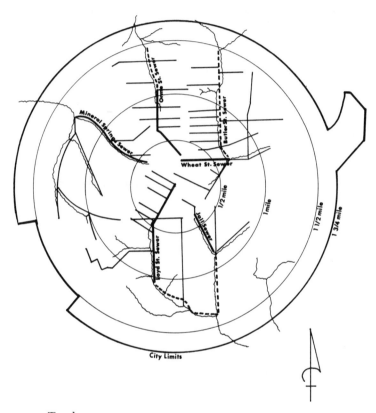

———— Trunk sewer
▬ ▬ ▬ Sanitary sewer
———— Branch sewer
〰〰〰 Stream

graduated from southern institutions) for the city's Negro grammar schools. The decision generally pleased local black leaders, but it was mainly a cost-cutting measure—black teachers' salaries were low. By 1890, Atlanta had twelve white and four Negro public grammar schools and two white high schools. An 1888 enumeration of the school-age population found 12,794 eligible children. But in 1890, Atlanta's public schools enrolled only 8,413 pupils. School officials admitted that at least 1,000 children would have willingly attended school had there been room for them. [61]

Municipal authorities were even less generous to Atlanta's poor. In 1890, city hall spent a grand total of $8,700 on poor relief (less than 1 percent of its total budget). About $1,000 went for burying paupers and transporting undesirables away from the city. Most of the rest went for medical assistance to the needy and support of orphans and destitute women. Black patients in 1890 were treated at the Ivy Street Hospital, and white patients went to the King's Daughters Hospital. Both hospitals were privately owned and did not accept all charity patients. The municipal appropriation for treating paupers at these institutions ranged between $.75 and $1.00 per day, and the hospitals were understandably reluctant to care for all those in need. There was no public facility until Grady Hospital was completed in 1892. White orphans and destitute women were sent to the Home of the Friendless and the Women's Christian Association Mission School, which received both public and private support. The municipal appropriation for people at these two facilities was $.25 per day for children and $.30 per day for adults. There were no public funds bestowed on black orphans, who fortunately were taken in at a private institution founded in 1890 by Mrs. Carrie Steele Logan, a black stewardess at the train depot. The city did allow this orphanage to use municipally owned land rent free, but offered no other support. [62]

While it is perhaps understandable that there was no great outcry about the city's relief policies, the relative lack of complaints about public education, sewerage, sanitation, and other municipal services is harder to account for. Political defeats doubtless bred futility

61. *Annual Report of the Atlanta Board of Education for . . . 1884* (Atlanta, 1885), 8; *Annual Report of the Atlanta Board of Education for . . . 1890* (Atlanta, 1891), 7–11, 13–14, 16–17, 23; C. T. Wright, "The Development of Public Schools for Blacks in Atlanta, 1872–1900," *AHB*, XXI (1977), 124–26.

62. *Annual Report of City Officers, 1890*, pp. 51, 220–24; *Annual Report of City Officers, 1889* (Atlanta, 1890), 35; Atlanta *Constitution*, December 1, 1887; Atlanta *Journal*, February 12, 1889; Rabinowitz, *Race Relations in the Urban South*, 144.

among blacks and the white working class, but that alone does not explain why there were not more protests. Both constituencies had opportunities to express their views. A referendum was held in 1890 on whether to issue $250,000 in municipal bonds to lay more water mains and $100,000 in bonds to extend the trunk sewers. Neither was approved, because the minimum number of voters (two-thirds of the total vote in the previous municipal election) did not go to the polls. Some Atlantans living in outlying neighborhoods and suburbs believed that healthful air meant they did not need sewers and sanitation. They had yet to learn about the germ theory of disease. Residents of West End in 1889 rejected annexation. It took a serious fire in 1894 to make them realize they needed the city's fire department.[63]

As the spirit of New South urban boosterism swept through Atlanta during the 1880s, the city's economic growth had made possible substantial improvements in some physical welfare services. But a philosophy that frowned on adequate services for the majority of the city's population still dominated Atlanta's municipal government in 1890.

63. Atlanta *Constitution*, April 24, 30 1890; Crimmins, "West End," 43–44.

9

NEW SOUTH, NEW CITY
Atlanta During the 1880s

Atlanta has every appearance of being the legitimate offspring of Chicago. There is nothing of the Old South about it, and all the traditions of the old-time South . . . have no place . . . in the young and thriving Gate City. . . . The young men are not the dawdling pale-faced, soft-handed effeminates which were so often visible in the nurslings of the slave. . . . They bear unmistakable signs of culture, but it is the culture that comes with self-reliance. . . . The best vigor of the South with the best vigor of the North seem to have met here on the same mission, and the new Atlanta is the Queen of Beauty among Southern cities.

—A. K. McClure, *The South* (1886)

The 1880s were pivotal years in Atlanta's history. By the decade's close, the population had reached 65,533, nearly doubling the total ten years earlier and enabling the city to surpass long-time rivals Memphis, Charleston, and Savannah. Only New Orleans, Richmond, and Nashville among southern cities still had populations larger than Atlanta's in 1890.[1] More important, Atlanta by that time had achieved a national reputation as an embodiment of the New South creed and had consolidated its position as the commercial and industrial center of the Southeast. The foundations for the city's continued and rapid growth during the twentieth century had been firmly laid.

Although much of what happened in Atlanta during the 1880s represented a continuation of urban promotive activities, there was also a great deal that was new. Its economy was still predominantly commercial in 1890, but commerce had expanded significantly and was balanced by industrial growth. The industrial crusade begun during the Civil War reached a crescendo during the 1880s and resulted in far more industrialization than occurred in any other decade in the nineteenth century.[2] Partially because of these developments, there were also significant changes in the city's economic leadership and general population. According to some historians, the year 1880 was a watershed in southern history, as it marked the beginning of a takeoff in southern urbanization and consequently the rise of a "new middle class."[3]

New South Enterprise

Entrepreneurial activities in Atlanta during the 1880s in some cases introduced important changes. Railroad promotion was more than ever before a popular pastime among local boosters. Enthusiasts organized literally dozens of projects to further commerce and indus-

1. Atlanta ranked forty-second in population among American cities in 1890. New Orleans was twelfth; Richmond, thirty-fourth; and Nashville, thirty-eighth. See *Compendium of the Eleventh Census, Part III* (1897), 40–41.

2. In 1890, Atlanta had $9,508,962 invested in manufacturing and the value of products of local industries was $13,074,037. Ten years later, the respective figures were $16,045,156 and $16,707,027. See *Twelfth Census of the United States, Manufactures, Part II* (1902), 134.

3. Don H. Doyle, "New Men, New Cities, New South: Charleston, Mobile, Atlanta, Nashville, 1865–1915" (Paper presented at the Fourth Citadel Conference on the South, April 12, 1985).

try. The International Cotton Exposition (1881) and subsequent expositions and conventions were in the tradition of the agricultural and state fairs. But the expositions and other promotions in the 1880s generally had a greater economic and psychological impact. And, because of the 1874 charter, private funds were used exclusively (with the exception of municipal support for the Georgia Institute of Technology) to finance urban promotion during the 1880s. The city's economic leadership and private institutions such as the chamber of commerce and the manufacturers' association matured sufficiently to undertake a variety of promotive activities that would not have been possible earlier without public funding and supervision.

More than any other event during the 1880s, the International Cotton Exposition put Atlanta on the national map as the headquarters of the New South movement. Those who labored to organize the exposition (which in its early stages especially involved Evan P. Howell, Henry W. Grady, and others associated with the Atlanta *Constitution*) had many purposes: to further sectional reconciliation, to improve agricultural techniques in the South, and to promote Atlanta as an interior marketing center for cotton. But, above all else, they wished to offer a clear signal that Atlanta's economic leaders were more than ready to worship the Yankees' industrial gospel as a means of engineering urban growth. It made no difference that the original suggestion came from gruff Boston textile mill magnate Edward L. Atkinson—or that his intention was to educate southern cotton farmers about ginning techniques so that cleaner bales would be sent north. Atkinson's opposition to southern industrialization was simply brushed aside as plans for the South's first world's fair took shape.[4]

To ensure the success of the exposition, the planners once again turned to Hannibal Ingalls Kimball. He was chosen as chairman of the executive committee of the International Cotton Exposition Association in late February, 1881, and invited to put his famed powers of persuasion to work. Less than six hours after the subcription books opened on March 15, local businessmen had pledged to buy more than $36,000 worth of stock. Kimball shrewdly relayed news of this

4. Jack Blicksilver, "The International Cotton Exposition of 1881 and Its Impact upon the Economic Development of Georgia," *Atlanta Economic Review*, VII, no. 5 (May, 1957), 2–3; Marshall B. Dalton, *Edward Atkinson (1827–1905): Patron of Engineering Science and Benefactor of Industry* (New York, 1950), 7–11; Patrick J. Hearden, *Independence and Empire: The New South's Cotton Mill Campaign, 1865–1901* (De Kalb, Ill., 1982), 92–93.

dazzling success to newspapers across the country. The remainder of the stock was purchased mostly in New York, Boston, Cincinnati, and Philadelphia. Accompanied by influential cotton merchant Samuel M. Inman, Kimball went on a whirlwind tour through these and other northern cities after Atlanta subscribers promised to buy at least one-third of the association's stock. Kimball reportedly had little trouble finding Yankee capitalists willing to finance the exposition.[5]

When the exposition opened on October 5, attendance lagged initially because hotel facilities were thought inadequate. The executive committee built a three-hundred-room hotel adjoining the fairgrounds and sought out residents willing to house visitors. In response, leading citizens promptly opened their elegant residences along Peachtree Street. Attendance increased, and more than 350,000 people came to the exposition before it ended on December 31. What these visitors saw in the 1,113 exhibits from thirty-three states and seven foreign countries were mostly items involved in cotton cultivation or textile manufacturing. But some exhibits showed outsiders the South's timber and mineral resources for industrialization.[6]

Although it is impossible to assess precisely its impact on Atlanta's economy, the exposition at the very least vigorously stimulated the industrial crusade. One manufacturing establishment was a direct consequence of the exposition. After the exposition closed, twenty-five local capitalists gathered in the mayor's office and pledged $10,000 each to found a second cotton mill. It was housed in the main exhibit hall of the exposition. With Hugh T. Inman as president, Exposition Cotton Mills began operations in 1882 with more than five hundred employees. They spun more than fifty million yards of yarn during the remainder of the decade.[7] Local promoters justifiably hailed this factory as an indication of the city's sincere adherence to New South industrial values.

Later there were the National Commercial Convention (1885) and the Piedmont Exposition (1887). These ventures lacked the drama

5. *Report of the Director-General, H. I. Kimball, International Cotton Exposition, Atlanta, 1881* (New York, 1882), 87–92; Alice E. Reagan, *H. I. Kimball, Entrepreneur* (Atlanta, 1983), 93–94.
6. Blicksilver, "International Cotton Exposition of 1881," pp. 5–11; Mary Roberts Davis, "The Atlanta Industrial Expositions of 1881 and 1895: Expressions of the Philosophy of the New South" (M.A. thesis, Emory University, 1952), 7–10.
7. *Exposition Cotton Mills Co., Seventieth Anniversary, 1882–1952* (Atlanta, 1952); Atlanta *Constitution*, February 26, 1882; Ledger Book of the Exposition Cotton Mills (1883–1890), in possession of Mr. Emory Cocke, Atlanta.

and the impact of the 1881 exposition, but they helped to publicize the city's growing commercial importance in the region and its industrial ambitions and achievements. Many of the same business leaders involved in 1881 also worked on planning and staging these events.[8] These men and others were determined that the impetus given the city's growth by the International Cotton Exposition would not falter or be overlooked within or outside the South.

The idea of holding a commercial convention in Atlanta was first broached during an informal meeting at the chamber of commerce in December, 1884. Samuel Inman and others voiced reservations, partially because only one such convention had taken place in the South since the end of the Civil War (in New Orleans in 1869). But the always effusive Kimball declared that "Atlanta was the best place for anything." It was agreed that the city first needed a hotel to replace the Kimball House, which had been destroyed in a fire the previous year. Kimball, who had gone to Chicago after the International Cotton Exposition and had come back only recently to superintend the construction of the new hotel, assented. Within a year, a second Kimball House, one story higher and 117 rooms larger than its predecessor, stood ready to admit guests. Led once again by Kimball, the city's business elite completed arrangements for the convention within a matter of weeks.[9]

The convention, which lasted from May 19 to May 21, attracted fourteen former governors and delegates from thirty states. Those in attendance discussed the leading commercial issues of the day, including silver coinage and railroad regulation. Henry W. Grady delivered one of his stock but eloquent invocations to sectional reconciliation. He said that "fifty feet from where we stand . . . our streets rang with the clamor of battle." But he assured his listeners that "not the slightest trace of bitterness has survived that fearful struggle . . . and . . . that the people of Atlanta . . . welcome you in the best way as friends and brothers." The *Nation*'s editors applauded this rejection of "sectionalism in trade" and remarked that the convention's success demonstrated that Atlanta was "beyond question the most enterprising place in the whole South."[10]

The Piedmont Exposition in 1887 was not national in scope (as was

8. Davis, "Atlanta Industrial Expositions of 1881 and 1895," p. 46; Reagan, *Kimball*, 118.
9. Kimball quoted in Atlanta *Journal*, December 29, 1884; Reagan, *Kimball*, 114–20.
10. *Proceedings of the National Commercial Convention of 1885, held in Atlanta, May 19, 20 and 21* (Atlanta, 1885), 1–7; *Nation*, XL (1885), 412.

the commercial convention), and it was more modest than was the 1881 exposition. Grady (a staunch prohibitionist) was the chief architect of this exposition, which he conceived as a counter to the impression that prohibition had slowed Atlanta's economy and divided the city's business leaders so badly that they had lost their initiative. The exposition opened October 9 and for two weeks displayed examples of southern manufacturing prowess to thousands of visitors who were mostly from the South. The high point was President Grover Cleveland's visit on October 18. It served to put the stamp of national approval on New South industrialization. Cleveland, whom Grady had personally invited, was greeted by huge crowds and was wined and dined elegantly at the Gentlemen's Driving Club. Rain dampened some spirits during the president's visit and on several other days, but one resident summed up the attitude of the city's business elite: the venture was "a wonderful success notwithstanding the rains and wind."[11]

Railroad ventures in Atlanta during the 1880s received far less national attention than did the industrial expositions but aroused intense interest among local businessmen. Countless articles and editorials in local newspapers described a veritable plethora of schemes. Whether the promise was a shorter connection with the Atlantic coast, a speedier route to sources of western foodstuffs, or access to coal and iron fields in Alabama, all these prospective roads were deemed essential to Atlanta's economy by their backers. Few were ever built, however. The Atlanta & Florida illlustrated the problems involved in local financing and why railroads no longer could be realistically expected to serve as effective instruments of urban imperialism.

The drive to build the Atlanta & Florida began in April, 1886, with a meeting at the chamber of commerce called by the editors of the *Constitution* and attended by more than three hundred local businessmen. Evan P. Howell suggested that a line should run to the coast at Brunswick, since managers of the railroads already serving Atlanta continually threatened—whenever protests arose about freight rate discriminations—"that if we do not keep quiet the coast

11. Henry W. Grady to Daniel S. Lamont, July 15, 1887, Henry W. Grady Papers, Robert R. Woodruff Library, Emory University, Atlanta; Franklin M. Garrett, *Atlanta and Environs: A Chronicle of Its People and Events* (3 vols.; New York, 1954), II, 145–55; Harold E. Davis, "Henry W. Grady, Master of the Atlanta Ring—1880–1886," *GHQ*, LXIX (1985), 2; Diary of Sarah Huff, October 22, 1887, in AHS.

cities will be turned into our [trading] territories and will ruin us." With a locally controlled outlet to the sea, Atlanta merchants, Howell argued, could turn the table on their seaboard rivals and also be advantageously positioned for exporting grain and cotton to Liverpool and other foreign ports. Howell's argument was persuasive, and local businessmen planned to incorporate the Atlanta & Hawkinsville, chartered by the Georgia legislature later that year. The strategy was to build the road south from Atlanta one leg at a time rather than immediately aim for the seaboard. The project's backers, aware of the history of the Georgia Western and the Atlanta & Charlotte Air Line, did not want to risk loss of local control by extending their resources too far too fast.[12]

Local control was briefly maintained. The Atlanta Improvement Company, with wholesale grocer Aaron Haas as president, raised $250,000 in stock subscriptions and about $500,000 in cash. This amount of private capital was the largest ever raised for a railroad project in Atlanta. But after the road was completed to Hawkinsville in 1887, financial problems began to erode the dream of an important, locally controlled line. Rechartered in 1887 as the Atlanta & Florida, the railroad was to end at some point along the Georgia-Florida boundary. Still under the control of local capitalists, the road was extended by June, 1888, to Fort Valley, 105 miles south of Atlanta, where construction halted abruptly because of lack of capital. In 1889, half of the company's stock passed into the hands of the Americus Investment Company, which promised to extend the road farther south to Cordele but had not done so by 1890. The company still had its headquarters in Atlanta, and ten of its twelve directors and its president, Robert F. Maddox, were residents. The Atlanta & Florida in 1890 was one of the region's fifteen railroads more than one hundred miles long that were still owned by southerners.[13]

In 1895, however, the Atlanta & Florida became part of J. P. Morgan's Southern Railway empire. The road eventually reached Thomasville (just north of Florida) and crossed several railroads that ran to the Atlantic seaboard at Brunswick and Savannah.[14] But local

12. Atlanta Constitution, April 14, 1886 (quotation), April 4, 6, 18, 1887; Ga. Laws, 1886, pp. 102–105.

13. Ga. Laws, 1887, pp. 238–39; Atlanta Constitution, July 31, 1888, March 27, May 14, 1889, August 14, 1890; John F. Stover, The Railroads of the South, 1865–1900: A Study in Finance and Control (Chapel Hill, 1955), 208.

14. Stover, Railroads of the South, 262.

control had been eliminated, and the route to the coast was too indirect to be of much use to Atlanta merchants interested in trading overseas. The road became little more than another means of bringing south Georgia's cotton crop to the city.

Atlanta businessmen had tried their best to control a potentially significant railroad but had been defeated by a shortage of capital. One of Atlanta's oldest citizens and a veteran railroad promoter, Jonathan Norcross had seen the problem coming in 1886 and had proposed that the chamber of commerce seek a legislative charter for the Atlanta Railroad Buying and Leasing Association. Norcross had suggested an initial capitalization of $5 million, which might have given the association sufficient financial clout to buy an existing railroad or build a new, important line.[15] But that much private capital was beyond the capacity of the city's business community. In an era of high construction costs, increasing consolidation, and takeover of railroads by northern capitalists, Norcross' proposal was an anachronism.

Although members' investment capital was not sufficient for railroad ventures, the Atlanta Chamber of Commerce helped local entrepreneurs organize urban promotive activities during the 1880s. It became a lively forum for ideas about the city's needs and prospects. Restructured in 1883, the chamber of commerce saw its membership grow from 137 to more than 600 in 1890. Numerous committees dealt with matters of concern to local businessmen, such as transportation, manufacturing, and commerce. An entertainment committee staged an annual banquet and other social events to foster collegiality. The chamber thus made a major contribution to a sense of purpose and unity among local businessmen. As a correspondent from New York concluded in 1889, "an important factor in the city's prosperity is its chamber of commerce."[16]

Also effective in promoting industrial growth was the Atlanta Manufacturers' Association, which was reorganized in 1883. The association kept statistics on local industries and published occasional pamphlets for distribution to manufacturers interested in the city's potential. A precursor of industrial parks was the association's 1887 purchase for

15. Atlanta *Evening Capitol*, March 4, 1886; Atlanta *Journal*, March 1, 1886.
16. *First Annual Report of the Atlanta Chamber of Commerce for the Year 1885: Historical, Descriptive, Statistical* (Atlanta, 1886), 8–17; Atlanta Chamber of Commerce, *Annual Report of Officers, 1889* (Atlanta, 1889), 3–6; Atlanta *Constitution*, June 22, 1890; New York *Commercial Bulletin* quoted in Atlanta *Constitution*, November 13, 1889.

$100,000 of a large tract on the Central of Georgia Railroad near the city's outskirts, which was divided into 282 inexpensive sites for future plants. The association claimed a membership of two hundred companies in 1887 and to have attracted eight new concerns representing an aggregate capital of $250,000. The association frequently pressured railroad companies for lower freight rates and the city council for tax relief on local industries.[17] Such actions encouraged manufacturing in Atlanta.

Urban promotion, though hardly a new phenomenon in Atlanta, reached new levels of intensity and achievement as the manufacturers' association, the chamber of commerce, and other organizations were strengthened. The city's business leaders used these institutions wisely and found other ways to develop a dedication to city building and a cohesiveness that outsiders admired and sometimes envied. One of the city's wealthier citizens, lumber merchant Frank P. Rice, remarked in 1889 that "Atlantans . . . have built up the city themselves, and they are always ready to put their own money into any local enterprise that promises good for the community at large." He correctly added, "That is one secret of our prosperity." The same could not be said of less vibrant business elites in Charleston and Mobile, for example.[18]

Perhaps local boosters' greatest skill and most durable product was advertising Atlanta's image as a progressive urban center. "Few southern cities have made more rapid progress in wealth and population," a Richmond newspaper correspondent wrote in 1890, "and this largely in consequence of its determination to leave no opportunity unutilized to advertise the advantages which it has to offer." A Massachusetts newspaper commented that "Atlanta has become one of the best advertised cities in the United States."[19] These tributes described best what the International Cotton Exposition and similar enterprises had achieved.

17. Wallace P. Reed, *History of Atlanta, Georgia* (Syracuse, 1889), 468–72; M. M. Welch to Charles E. West, May 24, 1887, in Hobbs-Mendenhall Papers, Southern Historical Collection, University of North Carolina, Chapel Hill; Atlanta *Journal*, May 9, 1887.
18. Rice quoted in Atlanta *Constitution*, December 15, 1889; Don H. Doyle, "Urbanization and Southern Culture: Economic Elites in Four New South Cities (Atlanta, Nashville, Charleston, Mobile) c. 1865–1910," in Orville Vernon Burton and Robert C. McMath, Jr. (eds.), *Toward a New South? Studies in Post–Civil War Southern Communities* (Westport, Conn., 1982), 22–24, 26–28, 30–31.
19. Richmond *Times* quoted in Atlanta *Constitution*, February 21, 1890; Worcester (Mass.) *Home Journal* quoted in Atlanta *Constitution*, July 7, 1886.

Economic Growth and Change

Although it could not be attributed solely to such promotional ventures as the expositions and national commercial convention, Atlanta's economic growth during the 1880s was as dramatic and impressive as were those events. The city's trading area kept expanding, and industrialization became far more significant.

By 1890, Atlanta's commerce had roughly tripled its 1880 volume and had assumed regional dominance in some areas. The estimated value of commerce that year (excluding locally fabricated manufactures) was $115 million. Cotton receipts in 1889 totaled 270,000 bales, a record that showed the city had overtaken traditional cotton ports such as Charleston.[20] Atlanta's trade "embraced the entire territory from the Potomac to the Rio Grande." A more conservative source specified an area defined by a two-hundred-mile radius from the city.[21]

Atlanta's major wholesale and retail firms acquired impressive financial power and resources. According to an R. G. Dun & Co. report in 1885, one firm (the wholesale and retail dry goods concern of W. A. Moore, E. W. Marsh & Co.) was worth almost $1 million, three others were worth between $500,000 and $750,000, and another ten were estimated to be worth between $200,000 and $500,000. Some had branches in other cities (the cotton brokerage house of Samuel M. Inman & Co. established one in Houston during the 1880s), and several employed as many workers as did some manufactories (John Keely's wholesale and retail dry goods company had seventy-five people on its staff in 1884). By 1890, the city had in all forty-six wholesale and retail dry goods firms, nine wholesale and retail hardware houses, and twenty-eight wholesale and retail grocery businesses, and their commercial horizons extended far beyond Atlanta.[22]

The city's 410 industries in 1890 had an aggregate capital nearly four times as large and employed more than twice as many workers as their predecessors had ten years earlier. Nearly 30 percent of the

20. Atlanta *Constitution*, August 31, 1890. Charleston in 1887 and 1888 received 450,000 bales (see Jamie W. Moore, "The Lowcountry in Economic Transition: Charleston since 1865," *South Carolina Historical Magazine*, LXXX [1979], 160).

21. Atlanta Manufacturers' Association, *Atlanta, The Capital of Georgia and the Coming Metropolis of the South* (Atlanta, 1889), 54; Atlanta *Constitution*, August 28, 1886.

22. R. G. Dun & Co., *Mercantile Agency Reference Book*, LXVII (January, 1885); Howard L. Platt, *City Building in the New South: The Growth of Public Services in Houston, Texas, 1830–1910* (Philadelphia, 1983), 80; Atlanta *Constitution*, November 23, 1884; R. L. Polk & Co., *Atlanta City Directory for 1890* (Atlanta, 1890), 1213, 1218–19, 1220, 1223–29.

working population had industrial jobs in 1890, about twice as many as had been similarly employed in 1880.[23] These figures were striking evidence that manufacturing had emerged as an important part of the city's economy.

Although large-scale concerns were still dominant in 1890, there was a noticeable shift away from metals fabrication toward cotton goods. Three cotton mills together employed 1,092 workers: the Exposition Cotton Mills (16,000 spindles), the Atlanta Cotton Factory (19,304 spindles), and the Fulton Cotton Spinning Company (14,000 spindles). The most successful was the Fulton Cotton Spinning Company, which established retail sales outlets in Kansas City and New Orleans during the 1880s. Other large industrial plants included Elias Haiman's Southern Agricultural Works, which specialized in steel plows and other implements, and the Atlanta Bridge & Axle Company. Haiman employed 225 in 1886, and the bridge company 325 men in 1887. Other firms with large payrolls manufactured fertilizers, beer, and patent medicines.[24]

Several factors accounted for Atlanta's rapid commercial and industrial growth during the 1880s. Besides the Atlanta & Florida, three new lines opened new transportation arteries into the city's hinterland. Local merchants continued to use aggressive trading practices to capture the territory of rival cities. Manufacturers found ways to obtain sufficient capital and other resources to establish their plants.

As Map 14 shows, Atlanta was well supplied with railroads by 1890. The three new roads were the Georgia Pacific, the East Tennessee, Virginia & Georgia, and the Marietta & North Georgia. The Georgia Pacific came to Atlanta in 1883 and gave the city its long-sought connection with the coal and iron fields in Alabama. The E.Tenn., Va. & Ga. in 1882 united a string of roads from Bristol, Virginia, to the Georgia coast at Brunswick. The Marietta & North Georgia was completed between a community a few miles north of Atlanta and Murphy, North Carolina, by 1887.[25]

23. Atlanta had 8,684 industrial workers in 1890 (see *Report on Manufacturing Industries in the United States at the Eleventh Census: 1890, Part II* [1895], 38–41). Percentage computed from that report, and total of employed workers (1890) given in *Report of the Population of the United States at the Eleventh Census, 1890* (1895), 634–35.

24. Atlanta *Constitution*, January 15, 1882, January 31, 1883, October 23, 1886; Minutebook of Fulton Cotton Spinning Co., October 26, 1889, and clipping from *Milling Production* (August, 1946), both in Fulton Cotton Mills Scrapbook, Fulton Cotton Mills Archives, Georgia Institute of Technology, Atlanta; Reed, *History of Atlanta*, 461.

25. Garrett, *Atlanta*, II, 23; Stover, *Railroads of the South*, 196–203; Reed, *History of Atlanta*, 435.

MAP 14   Railroads Terminating in Atlanta, 1890

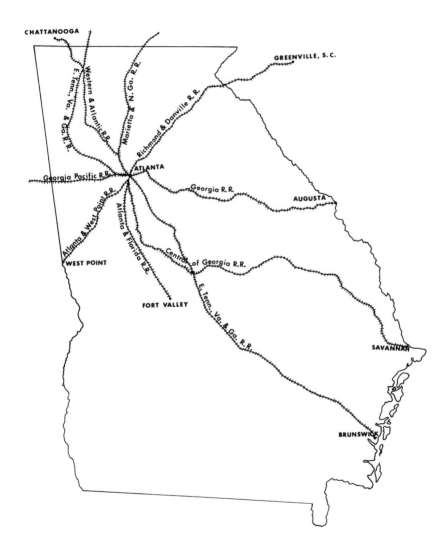

Only two other railroads were ever built to Atlanta. The Seaboard Air Line (1892) consisted of a through line with numerous branches from Portsmouth, Virginia, into Savannah, and on to Florida. Some Atlanta capitalists, led by Hoke Smith and Charles A. Collier, largely financed part of the system. This road was the Georgia, Carolina & Northern, which linked Atlanta with Monroe, North Carolina. The investment, though, hardly gave Atlanta businessmen much voice in the Seaboard's affairs. The last railroad to come to the city was the Atlanta, Birmingham & Coast (1908), which stretched from Birmingham to Brunswick. It was eventually absorbed into the Atlantic Coast Line system controlled by northeastern capitalists. [26] These two additions did not substantially improve the city's railroad network. In 1890, railroads penetrated every corner of the countryside and provided excellent through lines to sources of western foodstuffs and northern manufactures.

Atlanta businessmen nevertheless complained about freight rates. Costs per ton per mile were, in fact, higher from Louisville and other western cities to Atlanta than they were from the same points to Savannah, Augusta, and other urban centers south of Atlanta. Correspondingly, rates on dry goods shipped from New York to Atlanta were still greater than those from the same point to Augusta and other cities south of Atlanta. [27] Particularly galling to wholesale grocers in 1885 was the Southern Railway & Steamship Association's bestowing and revoking "reshipping privileges" within a six-week period. Those privileges (which applied only to western freights and which mer-

---

26. Garrett, *Atlanta*, II, 252–53, 520–23; Stover, *Railroads of the South*, 263–74; Atlanta *Constitution*, September 24, 1886; Atlanta *Journal*, January 16, March 11, 1890; Hoke Smith to General R. F. Hoke, December 3, 1886, in Hoke Smith Letterbooks, UGA.

27. According to Jonathan Norcross, *Atlanta, Northern Georgia, and the Great Southern Railroad Pool* (Atlanta, 1886), 14, freight rates per ton per mile from Louisville were:

	Class B (meats, lard, etc.)	Class C (meal & flour)	Class D (grain & hay)
Atlanta	$1.61	$1.38	$1.21
Augusta	1.23	1.07	.94
Savannah	.86	.48	.54

Rates on first-class goods shipped from New York per one hundred pounds to Atlanta, Augusta, and Macon were, respectively $.94, $.76, and $.89 (New York *Times* quoted in Atlanta *Constitution*, August 29, 1882).

chants in other southern cities enjoyed) meant that wholesalers could forward produce purchased from western dealers to points south of their own city at the through rate rather than the more expensive local rate. The reason for that loss and for other instances of discrimination was still Atlanta's lack of competing water transportation. As Albert Fink, general manager of the Southern Railway & Steamship Association, tactlessly explained to outraged Atlanta businessmen in 1886, the city's "high and dry" location was "unfortunate."[28]

Efforts by Atlanta businessmen during the 1880s to counteract the association's arrogant and harmful policies generated only further frustration. "Merchants' pools"—that is, placing all the city's through freight on one line (usually the E. Tenn., Va. & Ga.)—gained only temporary advantages. The chamber of commerce, angered by the railroad pool, protested to the association in 1888 that "well might Atlanta be termed the Orphan City . . . [as] she alone seems to be without a friend in your body to further her interests." Another critic remarked that without the railroad pool "Atlanta would now be a town of 100,000, instead of 65,000."[29]

These complaints ignored significant improvements in freight rate structures that affected Atlanta and the city's substantial growth. Rate discriminations were not in fact crippling its commerce and industry. In an 1886 case brought by wholesale grocers Aaron Haas and John N. Dunn, the Georgia Railroad Commission ruled that it had the right to regulate rates on freight originating outside but going through Georgia. This decision led to reduced rates on western produce transported to Atlanta, and the rates were more competitive with those enjoyed by Augusta and Savannah. Without pressure from any regulatory agency, the Southern Railway & Steamship Association decided in 1880 that freight rates for western produce shipped to Chattanooga and Atlanta would be identical. The latter city thus gained a tremendous competitive advantage over its rival.[30]

Perhaps the most telling statement from Atlanta's business com-

28. Atlanta *Constitution*, July 10, 1885, December 22, 1889, June 6, 1886.
29. Minutes of the Atlanta Chamber of Commerce, April 4, 1888, in Atlanta Chamber of Commerce Archives, Atlanta; Norcross, *Atlanta, Northern Georgia, and the Great Southern Railroad Pool*, 22.
30. Railroad Commission of Georgia, *Eleventh through Fourteenth Semi-Annual Reports* (Atlanta, 1886), 14–17; *Circular Letters of the Southern Railway & Steamship Association*, "Record of the Ninth Session of the Rate Committee, Atlanta, March 25, 1880," VII (1880), in Perkins Library, Duke.

munity came in 1887, when the newly appointed members of the Interstate Commerce Commission visited the city to gather testimony about southern railroads. Representing the Atlanta Chamber of Commerce, its secretary M. M. Welch joined several southern railroad officials in asking that the commission not enforce the "long haul–short haul" rule, which stated that railroads could not charge more per ton per mile for a short haul on a through line than they did for the entire route. This rule did not take into account competing water routes and, if strictly enforced, would benefit merchants in smaller cities. In cooperating with the railroads in this instance, Atlanta businessmen showed that they realized at least at that time that rate discrimination had become inconsequential, in view of the city's growing importance as a railroad center.[31]

Railroads helped far more than hindered Atlanta's commercial development during the 1880s. Wholesale merchants increasingly relied on trains to expand their trading territory. The value of Atlanta's wholesale trade rose to an estimated $80 million by 1890, and much of it was conducted via railroads. Wholesale grocers A. C. Wyly and B. F. Wyly reported in 1886 that their drummers no longer went into territory within fifty miles of the city but instead pursued "the bulk of their business between seventy-five and two hundred miles of Atlanta." Prominent dry goods merchant John Silvey never sent a drummer less than fifty miles from Atlanta, and his firm advertised extensively in newspapers in Asheville, North Carolina (roughly 175 miles away via the Richmond & Danville). The wholesale and retail dry goods firm operated by E. P. Chamberlin and Henry S. Johnson supplied retail merchants in Montgomery (168 miles from Atlanta) by railroad in 1885. Farmers still brought cotton and produce to Atlanta via the wagon trade during the 1880s, and the city's wholesale merchants still sent two-horse teams to country stores off the railroads. But, as Atlanta's wholesale trade expanded, its practitioners preferred to use transportation that promised maximum returns.[32]

Atlanta's commercial economy showed other signs of increasing sophistication. Merchants built larger stores, went on more ambitious buying trips, and found other ways besides simple part-

31. Atlanta *Constitution*, April 28, 1887; Gabriel Kolko, *Railroads and Regulation, 1877–1916* (Princeton, 1965), 49–52, 68–69, 193–94.

32. Atlanta *Constitution*, April 14, 1885, August 28, 1886 (quotation), August 31, 1890; Atlanta *Post Appeal*, October 6, 1882.

nerships to finance their enterprises. Chamberlin & Johnson, which had begun in 1865 in a small store twenty-five by one-hundred, was housed twenty years later in a six-story building with thirteen thousand square feet on each floor. There were hydraulic elevators powered by gas engines, electric paging devices, and other modern conveniences. The wholesale and retail dry goods house of Morris Rich, which became one of the South's largest department store chains, placed a permanent representative in Frankfurt, Germany, in 1887 to purchase the latest in carpets, lace and linen, and similar goods. Other firms also sent their buyers to European countries. At least three stores—the Atlanta Provision Company and the retail hardware firms of Lewis H. Beck and William A. Gregg and the King Hardware Company—were joint stock companies that had impressive capital at their disposal. By 1890, these three had issued about $400,000 worth of stock.[33]

Atlanta's wholesale and retail merchants maintained that one cause of their increased business during the 1880s was their reliance on the cash trade. The retail grocery firm of Samuel B. Hoyt and Charles C. Thorn, which claimed to be the largest in the South, stated that they could thus "save any lady 20% on groceries." Surviving ledgers of John R. Wallace and Alexander M. Wallace, wholesale and retail hardware merchants, confirm that at least one local business during the 1880s did operate largely on the cash basis. The available evidence supports Atlanta merchants' contention that the cash trade helped them deal in large volume and sell goods at low prices. A committee appointed by farmers' cooperative stores in Carroll County, Georgia, visited the city in 1886 and found that prices for flour were 20 percent, for syrup 35 percent, and for coffee 25 percent lower than they were anywhere else in the state.[34]

The expansion of Atlanta's commerce and industries during the 1880s was well supported by its banking institutions, which increased in number and financial resources. Even if the city's merchants preferred not to extend credit to their customers, local banks had sufficient capital to make generous loans to upstanding businessmen

33. Atlanta *Constitution*, December 13, 1885, April 25, 1886, November 27, 1887; Minute Book of Beck & Gregg Hardware Company (1883–1941), April 7, 1883, in possession of Beck & Gregg Hardware Company, Atlanta; Minute Book of the King Hardware Co. (1887–1928), May 21, 1890, in possession of King Hardware Company, Atlanta.

34. Atlanta *Constitution*, June 26, 1887; Ledgerbook (1880–1887), in John R. and Alexander M. Wallace & Co. Papers, AHS; *Carroll County Free Press* quoted in Atlanta *Journal*, January 1, 1887.

when necessary. By 1890, Atlanta had eighteen private or joint stock banking institutions whose combined capital stock issue exceeded $2.5 million and whose net deposits during the year amounted to about $60 million. Their outstanding loans and discounts stood at $6.7 million and deposits on hand at $6 million on May 1, 1890.[35] Per capita banking deposits in the South averaged only $5.09 in 1880, about one-twentieth of what they were in Atlanta ten years later.[36] These statistics do not include the city's twenty-one building and loan associations, whose combined capital exceeded $4 million and loans exceeded $1.25 million in 1890. There seems little reason to question one local banker's assessment that Atlanta was well on its way to becoming "the financial center of the South."[37]

Excellent railroad connections and adequate banking resources aided Atlanta manufacturers in their efforts to secure essential raw materials and sufficient capital to build and improve their physical plants. In addition, local manufacturers had no serious difficulty obtaining another prerequisite for industrialization, a docile labor force.

Although there were repeated overtures to Yankee investors, the available evidence indicates that Atlanta's industrial growth during the 1880s was largely financed by local capital. The stock of the city's only brewery, of the Southern Agricultural Works, and of a wagon factory founded in 1886 were entirely owned by Atlanta residents. As was characteristic of the cotton mill movement, the initial capitalization of Atlanta's textile plants was also local. All the Exposition Cotton Mills' initial stock issue of $250,000 and the Atlanta Cotton Factory's $142,000 were subscribed by city residents. The Fulton Cotton Spinning Company's initial stock issue was $100,000, and 52 percent was in the hands of men who lived in the city. Even if Yankee dollars did not flow into the city, local manufacturers found it far easier during the 1880s to accumulate enough capital to start various enterprises.[38]

35. Atlanta *Constitution*, May 11, 1890. The sources are not precise about the geographic origins of the capital, but there are indications that most of it was probably local.

36. Per capita bank deposits in Atlanta in 1890 were $91.56 (see John A. James, "Financial Underdevelopment in the Postbellum South," *Journal of Interdisciplinary History*, XI [1981], 443).

37. Atlanta *Constitution*, April 3, 1887, October 6, 1889 (quotation), March 27, 1890.

38. Minutes of the Atlanta City Brewing Company (March 1, 1876–November 25, 1905), March 1, 1876, in AHS; Atlanta *Journal*, March 14, 1885; Atlanta *Constitution*, April 6, 1886; Minutes of the Board of Directors (1881–99), February 21, 1881, in Fulton Cotton Mills

Local manufacturers had easy access to all essential raw materials, with the exception of high-grade iron ore. The closest deposits were in Bartow County in north Georgia and yielded inferior ore. Pig iron was fifty cents per ton cheaper in Birmingham than it was in Atlanta during the 1880s, so metals fabrication became an important industry in the former city. On the other hand, cotton was easily obtained in Atlanta. Samuel M. Inman's cotton brokerage house alone handled more than 250,000 bales in 1886. It was not coincidental that Hugh T. Inman became president of Exposition Cotton Mills and his uncle Walker P. Inman acquired nearly one-third of that company's stock.[39]

Coal, used to fuel the steam engines that most Atlanta factories had, was readily and cheaply obtained from Joseph E. Brown's coal mines, consolidated as the Georgia Mining, Manufacturing and Investment Company in 1889. Most of Brown's mines were in Dade and Walker counties in northwestern Georgia, and access to Atlanta was via the Western & Atlantic. Brown adjusted freight rates on the W & A (of which he was president and principal lease-holder) and prices to encourage delivery to Atlanta. The coal was not popular for home heating because it did not kindle well, but it was adequate as "steam coal" for local factories and was widely used.[40]

Easily managed, inexpensive labor for local industries was readily available. An Exposition Cotton Mills ledger indicates that labor costs ranged between 54 and 58 percent of expenses from 1885 to 1890. Daily wages in 1889 for laborers were $1.00, and varied between $1.25 and $3.50 for skilled workers. Women, who were the majority of the work force in the textile mills, earned from $1.50 to $10.00 for a six-day week and an average of eleven hours per day. The Atlanta Cotton Factory employed 125 women in 1885 whose weekly earnings were between $1.85 and $7.20 for thirteen-hour workdays. Exposition Cotton Mills and the Fulton Cotton Spinning Company offered their workers cheap housing as a slight compensation for their low wages. Monthly rentals for cottages at the Exposition Mills ranged from $2.50 to $4.00, and all 425 of its workers in 1888 lived

Archives, Georgia Institute of Technology; Broadus Mitchell, *The Rise of the Cotton Mills in the South* (Baltimore, 1921), 215–76.

39. Atlanta *Constitution*, February 26, 1882, October 15, 1886, June 16, 1887.

40. "Statement of the Properties, Betterments and Earnings of the Georgia Mining, Manufacturing and Investment Company: Historical Sketch," in Julius L. Brown Papers, AHS; Atlanta *Constitution*, July 24, December 2, 1880.

there. Cottages at the Fulton Cotton Spinning Company were $1.50 monthly, but only half its work force could be housed in them.[41]

Despite the city's poor industrial wage scale and labor unrest elsewhere in the country, strikes were rare in Atlanta. In 1885, weavers went on strike at the Fulton Cotton Spinning Company and at the Atlanta Cotton Factory, both actions caused by a wage reduction. Since jobs in the southern textile industry required little skill or experience, such strikes were doomed to failure. An 1886 boycott of the Constitution Publishing Company organized by the Atlanta Typographical Union, which sought an increase in wages, fizzled, even though the union was regarded as the city's strongest, and printers were skilled workers. The chamber of commerce observed that "the fungous [sic] growth of communism and similar isms have never found a genial soil in this climate."[42]

Although industrial entrepreneurs succeeded in controlling their labor force and acquiring capital and raw materials, Atlanta was not destined to be a large manufacturing city. The lack of concentrated urban markets in the South, freight rates for southern manufactures shipped by rail to northern cities, and several other factors ruled out that possibility. On the other hand, while the South's proportion of the nation's capital invested in manufacturing and share of factories actually declined between 1860 and 1904, the city experienced substantial industrial growth during the 1880s.[43] Coupled with Atlanta's commercial expansion, industrial development gave substance to New South rhetoric and unleashed forces that led to substantial changes in the city's social structure and leadership.

Population Change and Leadership

Atlanta's economic growth during the 1880s strongly affected the stability and composition of the general population and also the nature of the economic leadership. Commercial and industrial prog-

41. Ledger of the Exposition Cotton Mills (1883–1890); Atlanta Manufacturers' Association, *Atlanta, Capital of Georgia,* 53; Atlanta *Constitution,* November 22, 1885, April 8, 1888, August 4, 1889.

42. "Comment" by Mary J. Oates on paper by Leonard A. Carlson in *JEH,* XLI (1981), 72–73; Atlanta *Constitution,* November 8, 26, 1885, March 12, 1886; *First Annual Report of the Atlanta Chamber of Commerce,* 68.

43. C. Vann Woodward, *Origins of the New South, 1877–1913* (Rev. ed.; Baton Rouge, 1971), 140, 312–17; David M. Potter, "Historical Development of Eastern-Southern Freight Rate Relationships," *Law and Contemporary Problems,* XII (1947), 416–48.

ress acted like a magnet to keep people in the city and to attract and facilitate the rise of a new economic elite. As was true in other nine-teenth-century cities experiencing substantial economic growth, Atlanta's population was relatively stable. Decennial persistence rates were the highest in the city's history—about 51 percent of white and 59 percent of black male household heads in Atlanta in 1880 were still there ten years later (see Table 9 in Appendix A). The rates for white household heads in Waltham, Massachusetts, St. Louis, and Indianapolis ranged between 36 and 71 percent, and the rate for black household heads in Dallas was 66 percent for the 1880s.[44]

Although the persistence rates are probably inflated, the decennial priority rate of white household heads in 1880 confirms the overall impression of population stability (see Table 10 in Appendix A). More than 40 percent had been residing in Atlanta ten years earlier, a rate much higher than those for previous samples. In addition, it should be noted, only about 12 percent had been there twenty years earlier. Atlanta's white population in 1880 thus represented a New South generation in the sense that it lacked personal knowledge of the antebellum city.

Economic growth and change had a measurable impact on the city's leaders as well. Those who qualified as members of the economic elite for the first time during the prosperous 1880s were reluctant to leave Atlanta (see Table 18 in Appendix A). Only fourteen members failed to stay in the city for at least ten years, and one of them died. And the occupational structure changed. About 41 percent of the elite were manufacturers, 13 percent were bank officers, 20 percent were engaged in commercial pursuits, and the remainder were in other categories (see Table 12 in Appendix A).

Like the city's general population, the elite represented a new generation in several ways. Only twenty members selected during the 1880s lived in Atlanta before the end of the Civil War. Almost as many (nineteen men) arrived after 1879. Moreover, the majority of economic leaders identified before 1880 no longer qualified as such after that date, even though most of them still lived in Atlanta.[45] The

44. Robert G. Barrows, "'Hurryin' Hoosiers and the American Pattern: Geographic Mobility in Indianapolis and Urban North America," *SSH*, V (1981), 203. Rate for blacks computed from Table 1 in Steven W. Engerrand, "Black and Mulatto Mobility and Stability in Dallas, Texas, 1880–1910," *Phylon*, XXXIX (1978), 205.
45. The leaders selected before 1880 are not included in the analysis. About 59 percent of the pre-1880 elite no longer qualified as such after that date.

men admitted to the elite during this decade thus generally had no ties to the city's antebellum past.

If the occupational composition and membership of Atlanta's economic elite changed noticeably after 1880, local boosters' and visitors' descriptions of its characteristics did not. Philadelphia *Times* publisher A. K. McClure, for example, wrote of the city's youth, the fortuitous intermingling of energetic southerners and northerners, and especially the "culture of self-reliance." As in the past, boosters heavily emphasized the opportunities for individuals steeped in this cultural ideal. The president of the Atlanta Chamber of Commerce, Junius G. Oglesby, told a delegation of northern capitalists and public officials invited to the city in 1890 that "a notable feature of Atlanta's glory is the fact that she is a home-made city by self-made men."[46]

The validity of such generalizations can best be investigated by reference to the elite's actual characteristics and experiences. As was discovered in earlier analyses of economic leadership in Atlanta, there were gaps between rhetoric and reality.

Age and nativity characteristics differ somewhat but not substantially from those of the earlier postbellum elite. Atlanta's 1880s elite was slightly younger and less southern in its origins (see Tables 15 and 17 in Appendix A). The percentage of nonsouthern natives was greater than that among the general population. Especially noticeable was the number of foreigners who were economic leaders. Nearly half were German Jews, and four men of this ethnic background were manufacturers, an occupation perhaps still more appealing to them than to native white southerners despite the strength of the New South industrial gospel. Nevertheless, Atlanta was still "a home-made city": about 64 percent of the elite were born in the South, and most of them were Georgians. Like the majority of nineteenth-century cities and as it had in the past, Atlanta drew most of its economic leaders from its own region.[47]

The native-born leaders for whom information is available were mostly born in towns of under 2,500 (see Table 16 in Appendix A). Only about 4 percent were born in larger American towns and cities.

46. Oglesby quoted in Atlanta *Constitution*, February 14, 1890.
47. Edward J. Davies, "Regional Networks and Social Change: The Evolution of Urban Leadership in the Northern Anthracite Region, 1840–1880," *Journal of Social History*, XVI (1982), 51; Frederic Cople Jaher and Jocelyn Maynard Ghent, "The Chicago Business Elite: 1830–1930: A Collective Biography," *Business History Review*, L (1976), 297–98.

Atlanta's economic elite thus still had predominantly rural southern antecedents.

Most leaders whose prior residences are known had lived and worked elsewhere in the South before coming to Atlanta (see Table 21 in Appendix A). These men were not, however, as likely to have lived in villages of less than 2,500 inhabitants prior to their arrival in Atlanta. About 19 percent came from cities of 10,000 or more (see Table 22 in Appendix A). This trend reflected the rapid increase in the number of secondary urban centers in the South after 1880.[48] Nevertheless, the move to Atlanta was still a journey from a smaller to larger city where there were more chances for personal advancement.

Joseph M. High, for example, a wholesale and retail dry goods merchant, was a Georgia native who had been associated with a firm in Madison, Georgia, before coming to Atlanta in 1880 at the age of twenty-four. According to a credit reporter for R. G. Dun & Co., High had "started trading at the age of 17, made money, and at a recent dissolution drew out $11,500." In Atlanta he began with $10,000 in capital and increased it within nine years to $85,000. In 1889 he joined the prestigious Capital City Club. In 1890 he was planning to build a "$100,000 dry goods emporium" with five stories, which would be "one of the handsomest and most convenient in the South." He said, "We believe that in a few years we will have one of the largest retail businesses in America. Why shouldn't we?" In the same year, High was profiled in a newspaper story with the headings "By Hard Work Success has Come" and "The City's Success is Due to the Young Men Who have Given it Dash."[49] Clearly, High was one of Atlanta's entrepreneurs who so impressed A. K. McClure, always a cheerleader for the New South's business leaders.

High's meteoric career raises questions about the structure of opportunity and the kind of men who flourished during the 1880s. Case histories of other economic leaders present a complex picture. John Keely and Jacob Elsas generally conform to self-help stereotypes, but John W. Grant is in a different category.

Wholesale and retail dry goods merchant John Keely was an Irishman who arrived in the United States with very little education and

48. T. Lynn Smith, "The Emergence of Cities," in Rupert B. Vance and Nicholas J. Demerath (eds.), *The Urban South* (Chapel Hill, 1954), 28–29.
49. R. G. Dun & Co. Credit Reports, Fulton County, Ga., XIV, in Baker Library, Harvard University, Cambridge, Mass.; Garrett, *Atlanta*, II, 216–17; Atlanta *Constitution*, March 23, May 18, 1890.

no capital. He came to Atlanta in 1858 by way of New York at the age of nineteen and took a job as a clerk. Three years later, he was a second lieutenant in the Confederate army, where he earned a reputation for courage. He returned to Atlanta at the end of the war and, after several months' convalescence (he had a severe leg wound), became a clerk to dry goods merchant John N. Gannon. When Gannon went bankrupt in 1869, Keely bought the stock for $2,000 and launched his own company. In 1872, he married the daughter of John Neal, a wealthy banker whose three sons were dedicated Confederate army officers. After his marriage, Keely's business grew enormously and rapidly. His firm was worth at least $150,000 by 1888, when he retired. He then assumed the responsibility of managing the Neal Loan & Banking Company.[50] His marriage was obviously the key to his success.

Jacob Elsas was a German Jew, and his family for generations had been weavers. He arrived from Europe virtually penniless and lived in Cincinnati with his uncle, who was a merchant. Elsas came to Atlanta in 1869 from Cartersville, Georgia, where he had been in "the junk trade" for three years. He was a rag dealer and junk trader until 1874, when, having accumulated some capital and with a little help from his uncle, he founded a paper bag manufactory. Seven years later, he abandoned this concern, having increased its annual sales to nearly $400,000 in twelve states and its work force to one hundred men. His new venture was the Fulton Cotton Spinning Company, which he and seven other men capitalized. This mill was the most successful in Atlanta, and it survived for more than a century. Elsas became a respected figure in the community and a leader in the movements that brought the Georgia Institute of Technology to Atlanta and founded Grady Hospital.[51]

John W. Grant was the son of immensely wealthy railroad contractor William D. Grant, who made his millions using convict labor. At the age of twenty-one, young Grant became president of Gate City Loan, Saving, and Banking Company and thus qualified for admission to the economic elite. His grandfather John T. Grant, also a railroad contractor and bank president, helped him obtain the presidency. The grandson married the daughter of Hugh T. Inman, who

50. Atlanta *Constitution*, April 1, 1888; Thomas H. Martin, *Atlanta and Its Builders: A Comprehensive History of the Gate City of the South* (2 vols.; Atlanta, 1902), II, 670; Dun & Co. Credit Reports, Fulton County, XIII.
51. Dun & Co. Credit Reports, Fulton County, XIII–XIV; Garrett, *Atlanta*, I, 807–809.

gave him the Kimball House as a wedding present. Grant became a fixture in high society and was active in both the Piedmont Driving and the Capital City clubs. [52]

What do the careers of Joseph M. High, John Keely, Jacob Elsas, and John W. Grant say about opportunity and the city's social environment? Which career was typical? These questions can be answered only by examining collectively the occupational histories and other pertinent social characteristics of Atlanta's economic leaders during the 1880s.

Only about 11 percent are known to have begun as manual laborers (see Table 13 in Appendix A). Of the ten men in this group, two are especially convincing examples of upward mobility. Retail grocer John J. Falvey lost his father at an early age and was forced to take a job as a drayman to support his family. Then he clerked for an older merchant who befriended him. Later Falvey launched a successful business on his own. Descended from a poor New England family, Frank P. Rice was a newsboy in antebellum Atlanta and after many years' effort became a wealthy lumber merchant. Two other cases are questionable. James W. English, eventually a building contractor and Atlanta's mayor, spent several years as a carriage maker. His father was, however, a Louisiana planter who died in his son's infancy and allegedly left his family very little. Cotton gin manufacturer Edward Van Winkle first worked in a foundry in Patterson, New Jersey. His father was, however, "a well known builder of cotton machinery," and his son's first job may have been some sort of apprenticeship. [53] The remaining six manual laborers—two farm workers, two carpenters, and two machinists—became planing mill proprietors, two manufacturers, a hardware merchant, and a wholesale and retail dry goods merchant.

Like previous elites, the 1880s leaders did most of their occupational climbing before they arrived in Atlanta. Only 8 percent began as manual laborers in the city; all the rest were white-collar workers (see Table 14 in Appendix A). The seven included Falvey, English, and Rice. The other four began as a drayman, a carpenter, a machinist, and a wagonmaker and became, respectively, a building contractor, a planing mill owner, a lumber dealer, and a lawyer. Lumber

52. Garrett, *Atlanta*, II, 488–89, 511, 576.
53. Atlanta *Constitution*, May 18, 1890; *Pioneer Citizens' History of Atlanta, 1833–1902* (Atlanta, 1902), 335–43; Reed, *History of Atlanta*, 23–27, 140–41 (quotation); Dun & Co. Credit Reports, Fulton County, XIV.

dealer Anthony Murphy, a native of Ireland whose forebears were peasants, first worked as a machinist in Trenton, New Jersey, and later for the Western & Atlantic. He became one of Atlanta's most respected citizens. He was twice elected to the city council, led the movement to establish the municipal water works, served on the Committee of Forty-nine, which drafted the 1874 municipal charter, and was involved in several railroad projects. [54]

Such cases indicate that it was possible to rise from obscurity to membership in Atlanta's economic elite during the 1880s, as had been true in the past. Only a few enjoyed such extraordinary mobility, but even fewer came from distinguished family backgrounds. Although the father of just one man is known to have been a manual laborer, only five men besides English had fathers who were planters. Men such as English were as rare as ever in Atlanta. This finding about the economic leadership of a southern interior city that was still relatively young is hardly surprising.

While the occupational histories of Atlanta's economic elites throughout the nineteenth century followed the same basic patterns, there were signs that attaining elite status during the 1880s was easier than ever before for men with small means. About 24 percent began their careers with less than $1,000 in capital, and nearly 65 percent started with less than $10,000 (see Table 19 in Appendix A). Table 11 also implies that the race for wealth and economic power was more open in the 1880s. The time lag between arrival in the city and entry into the elite could be explained by the amount of initial capital in only 17 percent of the cases. [55] These findings do not mean that undercapitalized entrepreneurs could easily acquire elite status, but they do confirm impressions that economic expansion had encouraged a vigorous, new generation of business leaders.

Another perspective on mobility is how the leaders used familial and social networks. Some (like Keely) married into the elite. Others (like Elsas) had help from a relative not in Atlanta or (like Falvey) from a former employer or business associate. Nearly half of the 1880s elite are known to have received some financial assistance (see Table 24 in Appendix A). This percentage is larger than that of any previous elite in the city's history. It affirms the maturity of the elite's support and business connections in and outside the city. Those who

54. *Pioneer Citizens' History*, 303–306.
55. Eta^2 = .167. Thus 17 percent of the differences between the capital categories in interval times are explained by initial capital.

TABLE 11

Interval Time by Initial Wealth Category
of Economic Leaders, 1880–1890

INITIAL WEALTH CATEGORY	INTERVAL TIME (YEARS)	N
Under $1,000	21.1	22
$1,000–4,999	17.2	18
$5,000–9,999	11.5	18
$10,000–24,999	17.4	16
$25,000–49,999	12.0	7
$50,000–99,999	4.3	4
$100,000 or more	3.0	1
Eta = .408[a]		
Eta^2 = .167		

SOURCES: See Appendix B.
[a]Significant at the .02 level

received such help were not, however, necessarily short on capital when they began their working lives.

Focusing on the twenty-three men who had no more than $1,000 in initial capital narrows the search for self-made men among the 1880s elite. Eight (including Falvey) were given various degrees of financial assistance. Except for Falvey and hardware merchant Calvin W. Hunnicutt, who was blessed with a wealthy father-in-law, all were aided by other economic leaders in the city—three had generous relatives and three had generous employers. The remaining fifteen men are not known to have received financial aid from anyone. Even if these fifteen individuals were the only truly self-made men, their achievements were nevertheless impressive evidence that a rapidly expanding urban economy could still offer personal rewards to some entrepreneurs with small means.

In a review of the social characteristics of Atlanta's economic leaders and the dynamics of their ascent during the 1880s, the continuities with earlier economic elites are conspicuous—the familial background with only shallow roots in the planters' South, the nativity distribution, the previous work experience and occupational histories. There were also cases of upward mobility—Elsas and Murphy, for example—that were as striking and about as frequent as they were during the antebellum period and immediately after the war.

The leaders were also a cohesive group. They lived in much the same neighborhoods as had the earlier postbellum elite, though more of them had migrated north along Peachtree and West Peachtree streets. Most of them were still Protestants and 27 percent were related by blood or marriage or both (see Table 23 in Appendix A).[56] More than in the past, Atlanta's economic leaders during the 1880s used institutions such as the chamber of commerce and the manufacturers' association to carry out joint enterprises. The Capital City Club (1883) and the Piedmont Driving Club (1889) were signs that the city's economic leadership during this era was on the verge of acquiring a greater sense of class identity. Nearly half the elite belonged to one or both of these increasingly exclusive and prestigious social clubs.[57]

If many characteristics represented continuity with the past, that should not disguise the fact that both the elite and their city had changed as the spirit of New South urban boosterism reached new heights in Atlanta during the 1880s. The city's population, economic leadership, and economic structure were new in fundamental ways. Most of the changes served notice to the rest of the South and the country that Atlanta had come of age. A new generation of leaders had acquired the ability to mobilize men and capital with ease and speed, as exemplified in the successful stock subscriptions for the International Cotton Exposition and Exposition Cotton Mills.

The meaning of these changes and achievements was not lost on the city's business community. "Atlanta is beginning to see her destiny clearly," wrote one local newspaper editor in 1890. "She is to be the metropolis of the most magnificent section of the United States, the . . . southeast."[58] Beneath this booster rhetoric was a valid assumption that accomplishments in the 1880s had prepared Atlanta well for metropolitan stature in the near future.

56. Of those whose religious affiliations could be verified, about 88 percent were Protestants. The rest were Jews or Catholics.

57. About 47 percent of the elite belonged to one or both of these clubs. Membership lists appear in *Officers, Members, Constitution and Rules of the Capital City Club of Atlanta, Georgia* (Atlanta, 1892), 10–23; and *By-Laws and Rules of the Piedmont Driving Club of Atlanta, Georgia with List of Membership* (Atlanta, 1903), 8–17.

58. *Atlanta Journal,* September 18, 1890.

EPILOGUE

The city was adapting itself, with remarkable rapidity, to the new order of things. . . . The soil of the country, for many miles in all directions is poor, but . . . the people were infected with the mania of city-building.

—Whitelaw Reid, *After the War* (1866)

I have never been able to sing "Dixie". . . . If Dixie were Atlanta or Atlanta Dixie, I could sing "Dixie." Not that Atlanta is what it ought to be or what it could and must be, but because Atlanta has come a long way . . . I know from my travels that Atlanta is not the typical South. It is better.

—Benjamin E. Mays quoted in Bradley R. Rice and Richard M. Bernard (eds.), *Sunbelt Cities* (1983)

As the nineteenth century neared its end Atlanta's history, according to many contemporaries, presented several noticeable contrasts with that of the region as a whole. These men believed that Atlanta was not typical of the South, just as prominent black school official Benjamin E. Mays claimed later. Much of what observers perceived as "different" were contrasts between Atlanta's business leadership and social life and those of the rural South and the older coastal and plantation belt cities. But nineteenth-century Atlanta's story was actually less exceptional than many realized. It was the opening (though no doubt the most important) chapter in the history of southern interior cities, where significant social and economic changes occurred.

One easily discernible theme was continuity between the Old South and the New. The Civil War may have been an important dividing line in the history of the region generally and many of the older urban centers, but it did not mark a sharp break in Atlanta's. The war caused a significant population turnover and intensified interest in industrialization but did not fundamentally change the direction of Atlanta's development. The city entered the New South era with a reservoir of values and city-building ideas that had already coalesced. Those who guided Atlanta's destiny after 1865 had much in common with their predecessors, who successfully bypassed the culture and economic institutions of the plantation South.

Another "different" aspect is implied in Whitelaw Reid's comments. Unlike most of the South, Atlanta before and after the war experienced sustained economic and population growth. Whether the cause was entrepreneurial talent, as Reid and others suggested, or location, the social consequences are important. Atlanta's economic prosperity attracted entrepreneurs from all over the region and elsewhere, and they grew wealthy as the city itself rapidly increased in population and in economic significance. Growth bred a dynamic business community whose values and outlook differed from those of competitors in more stagnant urban centers. The old southern seaports did not match Atlanta's dedication to appeasing northern capitalists during Radical Reconstruction, so eloquently expressed in the attempt to build a monument to Abraham Lincoln. And it is difficult to imagine Hannibal Ingalls Kimball as a leader in Charleston or Savannah during the postbellum era.

Some were sure that Atlanta's progress was a positive influence on the region. "Such a city in the heart of the South is a perennial stream of progress," wrote a Philadelphia *Times* correspondent.[1] Such observers were confident that Atlanta's success was a model of what hardworking entrepreneurs, imbued with modern capitalistic values, could achieve in other southern cities, which regrettably had for generations lacked such men and ideas.

The unfortunate truth, however, was that Atlanta's act was hard for much of the urban South to follow in the late nineteenth century. In 1860 only 10 percent of the South's population lived in cities, and it had risen to only 18 percent by 1900. In the northeastern states in the same years, the percentages were 36 and 59.[2] Many of the South's older cities failed to grow significantly and some lapsed into genteel decay. As Table 12 shows, Mobile and Charleston were conspicuous examples of urban decline. Savannah fared a little better, mostly because it became a target during the 1880s of various railroad systems that linked the West and the southern Atlantic seaboard. Augusta and Montgomery had generally kept pace with Savannah. But these cities, which had roughly equaled or surpassed Atlanta's 1860 population, were later left far behind.

As the data in Table 12 also indicate, Atlanta's population growth rate was matched (though generally on a smaller scale) by several other southern interior cities. Birmingham and Chattanooga—though hampered by their dependence on an iron industry that was second to the Northeast's—enjoyed impressive growth after 1880. Nashville, with a more balanced economy, was nearly as large as Atlanta at the end of the nineteenth century. By 1900, cities in the Southwest, such as Houston, Dallas, and San Antonio, had the foundation for their phenomenal population explosions in the modern Sun Belt era.

Clearly, the late nineteenth century witnessed a dramatic change: the locus of urban growth in the South moved from the seacoast to the interior. Although the region's ten largest cities in 1860 were ports, Atlanta, Nashville, San Antonio, and Houston of the top ten in 1900 were located in the interior, and Dallas and Birmingham ranked eleventh and twelfth. Although there were some individual varia-

1. Philadelphia *Times* quoted in Atlanta *Journal*, February 14, 1885.
2. Eric E. Lampard, "The Evolving System of Cities in the United States: Urbanization of Economic Development," in Harvey S. Perloff and Lowdon Wingo, Jr. (eds.), *Issues in Urban Economics* (Baltimore, 1968), 108.

TABLE 12

Population Growth of Selected Southern Cities, 1860–1900

	POPULATION (1,000s)			GAIN	
	1860	1880	1900	1860–80	1880–1900
Savannah	22	31	54	38%	77%
Charleston	41	50	55	23	12
Mobile	29	29	38	− .4	32
Augusta	12	22	39	75	80
Montgomery	9	17	30	89	82
Columbus, Ga.	3	10	18	229	74
Macon	8	13	23	52	83
Atlanta	10	37	90	292	140
Nashville	17	43	81	155	87
Birmingham	—	3	38	—	1,145
Chattanooga	3	13	30	307	134
Charlotte	1	7	18	431	155
Houston	5	17	45	241	170
Dallas	—	10	43	—	312
San Antonio	8	21	53	150	159

SOURCES: *Population of the United States in 1860* (1864); *Report on the Social Statistics of Cities. Part II, The Southern & Western States* (1887); and Donald B. Dodd and Wynelle S. Dodd (comps.), *Historical Statistics of the South* (University, Ala., 1973)

tions, the rise of such interior cities was mostly attributable to the demise of the factorage system, the disruption of the plantation system, the transformation from self-sufficiency to cotton agriculture in the upcountry, and especially the southern railroad systems.[3]

The social and cultural changes spawned by the emergence of these interior cities were more significant than were the population growth rates. C. Vann Woodward recognized that even with the contributions of cities such as Atlanta, "the sum total of urbanization in the South was comparatively unimportant" by 1900 and also that industrialization in the region had not kept pace with industrial growth in the Northeast. But he also argued that "changes of a profound and subtle character in the southern ethos—in outlook, institutions, and

3. Howard N. Rabinowitz, "Continuity and Change: Southern Urban Development, 1860–1900," in Blaine A. Brownell and David R. Goldfield (eds.), *The City in Southern History: The Growth of Urban Civilization in the South* (Port Washington, N.Y., 1977), 92–93.

particularly in leadership—*did* take place in this period."[4] These changes were most noticeable in the interior towns and cities.

Although Atlanta businessmen believed that their leadership was unsurpassed elsewhere in the urban South, boosters in other interior cities used the same language and duplicated many of their entrepreneurial activities. Birmingham promoters boasted that their city "was not typically southern" and was a "wide-awake town" with "none of the lazy-going southern spirit." In 1897, Nashville held an extravaganza that rivaled Atlanta's International Cotton Exposition (1881). In South Carolina's upcountry during the postbellum period, merchants and professional men who were mostly natives founded dozens of towns and small cities that specialized in manufacturing textiles. These "town people" mobilized their newspapers, chambers of commerce, and local governments in much the same ways their Atlanta counterparts did.[5]

The most important social change symbolized in such activities was the emergence of an urban middle class that was about to assume the political and economic leadership of the postbellum South. While Atlanta may have had the most visible of these New South business communities, it was not the only southern city to possess one. New men had come forth in many urban centers in the southern interior, and city-building ideals rather than King Cotton and plantation agriculture had captured their imagination.

Victims of the "city-building mania" in postbellum Atlanta tended to express their understanding of these changes by offering a progressive interpretation of the city's history. According to this version, Atlanta began as a democratic outpost of entrepreneurial talent and had to survive vigorous assaults led by agents of the aristocratic, plantation South. The city next had to contend with wartime devastation and still later with railroad monopolies. But whether the enemy was the planter South or the railroad corporations, Atlanta's enemies inevitably lost and virtuous enterprise prevailed again and again. The city's leadership could not be defeated by opponents of progress.

This outlook is one of the most durable features of Atlanta's history and it has persisted to the present day. Sloganeering and image fab-

---

4. C. Vann Woodward, *Origins of the New South, 1877–1913* (Rev. ed.; Baton Rouge, 1971), 139–40.
5. Carl V. Harris, *Political Power in Birmingham, 1871–1921* (Knoxville, 1977), 38; Don H. Doyle, *Nashville in the New South, 1880–1930* (Knoxville, 1985), 144–56; David L. Carlton, *Mill and Town in South Carolina, 1880–1920* (Baton Rouge, 1982), 13–81.

rication are still extremely popular in Atlanta. The Forward Atlanta campaign of the 1960s was not to be deterred by racial unrest. Atlanta became the city "too busy to hate." In the 1980s the white business elite has adapted quite well to blacks running city government and has confidently joined with them to work toward establishing Atlanta as an international city.[6] No matter what the threat to growth, Atlanta's business leaders seem prepared to adopt the right slogan and program. The city's history of overcoming challenges helped to breed a sense of confidence that is even more omnipresent than Coca-Cola. The Atlanta spirit thus has deep roots in the city's past and is constantly regenerated by it.

One final shared characteristic of nineteenth- and twentieth-century Atlanta is the domination of city government by white business elites. They have sometimes had significant opposition and have lost some local battles, but they have exercised remarkable control over city hall until recently. The election of black lawyer Maynard Jackson as mayor in 1973 inaugurated the first real deviation from this pattern, but even the continued presence of blacks in city hall does not seem to have upset significantly the plans and policies of the white business community. It is too much to argue, as does one student of the city's power structure, that there has been an overwhelming continuity in Atlanta's political history in the form of a "family succession" of power elites.[7] On the other hand, white business elites have been repeatedly successful in controlling the direction of municipal government's policies and programs. The same generalization would probably accurately sum up the political histories of many other American cities, but the trend may be more pronounced in Atlanta.

Perhaps the most compelling message of Atlanta's history besides its continuities is that there is no solid South. Historians often write of the diversity wrought by time, geography, and other factors, but just

6. Bradley R. Rice, "If Dixie Were Atlanta," in Rice and Richard M. Bernard (eds.), *Sunbelt Cities: Politics and Growth Since World War II* (Austin, 1983), 32, 50–53.

7. Floyd Hunter, *Community Power Succession: Atlanta's Policy Makers Revisited* (Chapel Hill, 1980). Hunter found quite a few family connections between power elites he identified in 1950 and 1973. He also wrote that many were descendants of families that had been prominent in nineteenth-century Atlanta. However, only four of the forty-four surnames on his 1950 list and only three of the fifty-three surnames on his 1973 list are shared by men who were members of Atlanta's economic elite identified in my study. Moreover, of the thirty-eight "historically powerful families" Hunter specified, only seven had representatives in the economic elite (see pp. 29–65).

as frequently they seem to lapse into generalizations that assume a monolithic South. While Atlanta's physical location and people in many ways were indisputably part of the region, the city's history is a reminder that there were and are "other Souths."[8]

8. Carl N. Degler, *The Other South: Southern Dissenters in the Nineteenth Century* (New York, 1974).

APPENDIX A

TABLES 1–26

TABLE 1
Population of Atlanta, 1850–1890

	TOTAL	WHITE	NEGRO	% WHITE	% NEGRO	% INCREASE
1850	2,572	2,060	512[a]	80	20	
1860	9,554	7,615	1,939[b]	80	20	271
1870	21,789	11,860	9,929	54	46	128
1880	37,409	21,079	16,330	56	44	72
1890	65,533[c]	37,416	28,098	57	43	75

SOURCES: *Seventh Census of the Population* (1853), 366; *Population of the United States in 1860, Eighth Census* (1864), 74; *The Statistics of the Population of the United States . . . 1870* (1872), 102; *Report on the Social Statistics of Cities, Part II* (1887), 157; *Report on the Population of the United States: 1890* (1895), 454.

[a]Includes 19 free Negroes and 493 slaves

[b]Includes 25 free Negroes and 1,914 slaves

[c]Includes, in addition to whites and Negroes, 18 Chinese and 1 Indian

TABLE 2
Horizontal Occupational Distribution of Atlanta's Working Population, 1850–1880

	% of Work Force			
	1850	1860	1870	1880
Primary				
Agriculture	2.9	1.8	.6	1.5
Extractive	—	.3	—	.3
	2.9	2.1	.6	1.8
Secondary				
Manufacturing	16.3	15.4	9.7	14.5
Construction	22.8	21.1	15.6	10.6
Labor[a]	5.5	11.0	21.0	12.2
	44.6	47.5	46.3	37.3
Tertiary				
Commerce[b]	31.3	21.7	15.3	19.0
Transportation	11.2	13.4	10.9	9.2
Domestic service	—	.4	19.4	21.8
Professional	5.3	6.7	2.9	3.5
Education & gov't service	2.2	4.5	2.6	3.8
Other	2.4	3.8	1.9	3.6
	52.4	50.5	53.0	60.9
Combined totals[c]	99.9	100.1	99.9	100.0
N	544	783	1,590	1,561

SOURCES: Manuscripts of federal population censuses for De Kalb and Fulton counties, 1850–1880.

NOTES: Horizontal Occupational distributions reflect the economic rather than class structures of cities. The scheme used here was adapted from Theodore Hershberg et al., "Occupation and Ethnicity in Five Nineteenth-Century Cities: A Collaborative Inquiry," Historical Methods Newsletter, VII (1974), 174–216.

All Ns are samples (of both male and female workers) except for 1850, when all who listed occupations in the census were counted. All unclassifiable occupations were excluded.

[a]The percentages of laborers in 1850 and 1860 are relatively low because slave populations were excluded.

[b]Includes banking

[c]Percentages do not sum to 100 because of rounding error.

TABLE 3
Geographic Origins
of Atlanta's Population

	% OF POPULATION	
BIRTHPLACE	1850[a]	1880
South	91.9	90.8
Border states	.4	1.2
New England	1.1	1.2
Middle Atlantic	2.5	1.8
Middle West	—	1.0
West	—	.1
Other U.S. [b]	.1	.2
Foreign	4.0	3.8
Total[c]	100.0	100.1
N	2,030	37,409

SOURCES: Ruth Blair, "Federal Census of Atlanta, 1850," *AHB*, VII (1942), 16–82; *Compendium of the Tenth Census, 1880* (1884), 40–41.

NOTE: South = eleven Confederate states; Border states = Del., Ky., Md., Mo., W.Va.; New England = Conn., Mass., Vt., N.H., Me.; Middle Atlantic = N.J., N.Y., Pa.; Middle West = Ill., Ind., Iowa, Kan., Mich., Minn., Ohio, Wis.; West = Calif., Ore.

[a]The 1850 population statistics are for whites only and do not include forty-two individuals whose birthplaces could not be determined.

[b]Includes those born in U.S. territories and at sea on ships carrying U.S. flag

[c]Percentages do not sum to 100 because of rounding error.

TABLE 4

Distribution of Real Wealth in Atlanta, 1850

VALUE OF REAL PROPERTY	NO. OF OWNERS
$1–999	68
$1,000–1,999	44
$2,000–4,999	30
$5,000–9,999	4
$10,000 or more	10
Gini Index of Inequality	
among owners	.599
among owners and all males 18 or older	.914
among owners and males and females 18 or older	.950

SOURCE: Manuscripts of the federal population schedules for De Kalb County, 1850.
NOTE: Real Wealth refers to real estate, the only form of wealth listed in the 1850 census.

TABLE 5

Distribution of Wealth in Atlanta, 1870

WEALTH CATEGORY	NO. OF OWNERS
$1–1,999	1,045
$2,000–4,999	359
$5,000–9,999	213
$10,000–19,999	139
$20,000–49,999	79
$50,000–99,999	25
$100,000 or more	13
Gini Index of Inequality	
among owners	.74
among owners and all males 21 or older	.916
among owners and males and females 21 or older	.957

SOURCE: Manuscripts of the federal population schedules for Fulton County, 1870.
NOTE: Wealth refers to both personal and real wealth.

TABLE 6

Vertical Occupational Distribution of Atlanta's Working Population, 1850–1880

	% OF WORK FORCE			
	1850	1860	1870	1880
High white collar	17.2	13.9	7.1	7.2
Low white collar	22.9	24.0	15.9	21.0
Skilled	50.6	44.1	28.3	26.7
Semi-skilled	2.8	6.8	7.1	8.2
Unskilled	6.5	11.2	41.7	36.8
Total[a]	100.0	100.0	100.1	99.9
N	494	783	1,582	1,559

SOURCES: Manuscripts of federal population censuses for De Kalb and Fulton counties, 1850–1880.

NOTES: Vertical Occupational categories depict the hierarchy or ranking of occupations. The categories used here were adapted from Hershberg *et al.*, "Occupation and Ethnicity," 174–216.

All Ns are samples except for 1850, when all who listed occupations in the census were classified. All those occupations that could not be classified in one of the five categories are excluded.

[a]Percentages do not sum to 100 because of rounding error.

TABLE 7
Occupational Mobility of Household Heads in Atlanta, 1850–1860

Occupation, 1850	Occupation, 1860						Mobility			N
	%High White Collar	%Low White Collar	%Skilled	%Semi-Skilled	%Unskilled	%Unclassifiable	%Up	%Down	%Stable	
High white collar	69	23	4	0	0	4	—	28	72	26
Low white collar	20	60	0	10	0	10	22	11	67	20
Skilled	4	16	71	0	2	7	21	2	77	56
Semi-skilled	0	0	50	0	50	0	50	50	0	2
Unskilled	0	33	33	0	17	17	80	—	20	6
Unclassifiable	0	40	40	0	10	10	=	=	=	10
			Total				19	12	69	

SOURCES: Manuscripts of the federal population schedules for Fulton and De Kalb counties, 1850, 1860.

NOTES: Mobility does not include unclassifiable occupations.
  Total means the percent of cases of all occupational categories combined.

TABLE 8
Occupational Mobility of Household Heads in Atlanta, 1860–1870

OCCUPATION, 1860	OCCUPATION, 1870						MOBILITY			N
	%High White Collar	%Low White Collar	%Skilled	%Semi-Skilled	%Unskilled	%Unclassifiable	%Up	%Down	%Stable	
High white collar	77	23	0	0	0	0	0	23	77	17
Low white collar	26	58	10	0	3	3	27	13	60	31
Skilled	4	13	69	4	9	0	17	13	69	45
Semi-skilled	0	83	0	17	0	0	83	0	17	6
Unskilled	0	14	0	14	57	14	<u>33</u>	<u>0</u>	<u>66</u>	7
Total							22	13	64	

SOURCES: Manuscripts of the federal population schedules for Fulton County, 1860, 1870.
NOTES: Mobility does not include unclassifiable occupations.
Total means the percent of cases of all occupational categories combined.

TABLE 9
Persistence Rates of Household Heads
in Atlanta, 1850–1890

	WHITE		BLACK	
	N	%	N	%
1850–1860	268	44.8	—	
1860–1870	279	38.0	—	
1870–1880	321	44.9	302	29.5
1880–1890	447	51.2	328	58.5

SOURCES: Manuscripts of the federal population censuses for De Kalb and Fulton counties, 1850–1880; city directories for 1879–1881 and 1889–1891.

TABLE 10
Priority of White Household Heads in Atlanta, 1850–1880

	N	% PRIOR ONE DECADE	% PRIOR TWO DECADES
1860	279	14.0	—
1870	321	24.3	5.0
1880	447	40.3	11.9

SOURCES: Manuscripts of federal population censuses for De Kalb and Fulton counties, 1850–1880.

TABLE 11
Permanence of White Household Heads in Atlanta, 1850–1890

	N	% PERSISTENT OR PRIOR ONE DECADE
1860	279	43.7
1870	321	53.9
1880	447	68.2

SOURCES: Manuscripts of federal population censuses for De Kalb and Fulton counties, 1850–1880; city directories for 1889–91.

NOTE: Permanence refers to those who either were persistent in Atlanta one decade or who resided in Atlanta one decade before selection in a sample group.

TABLE 12

Occupations of Economic Leaders, 1847–1890

	ELITE GROUP		
	1847–64	1865–79	1880–90
Commerce	48.4%	48.5%	20.0%
Banking & finance	6.5	26.5	13.3
Manufacturing	9.7	7.4	41.1
Construction	3.2	2.9	6.7
Transportation	9.7	5.9	6.7
Utilities	—	—	5.6
Professional	12.9	5.9	5.6
Other	9.7	2.9	1.1
Total[a]	100.1	100.0	100.1
N	31	68	90

SOURCES: See Appendix B.

NOTE: Elite Group refers to year of initial qualification as an economic leader.

[a]Percentages do not sum to 100 because of rounding error.

TABLE 13
Initial Occupations of Economic Leaders, 1847–1890

		ELITE GROUP	
	1847–64	1865–79	1880–90
Professional	9.7%	1.5%	5.6%
Merchant	3.2	2.9	3.3
Banker	—	2.9	1.1
Planter or farmer	3.2	2.9	3.3
Manufacturer	—	—	5.6
Railroad official & related position	—	—	2.2
Other high white collar	3.2	2.9	—
Low white collar	12.9	26.5	15.6
Skilled	9.7	5.9	5.6
Semi-skilled	6.5	2.9	1.1
Unskilled	9.7	5.9	4.4
Unknown	41.9	45.6	52.2
Total[a]	100.0	99.9	100.0
N	31	68	90

SOURCES: See Appendix B.

NOTE: These first jobs were usually not in Atlanta.

[a]Percentages do not sum to 100 because of rounding error.

TABLE 14

Initial Occupations in Atlanta of Economic Leaders, 1847–1890

	ELITE GROUP		
	1847–64	1865–79	1880–90
Professional	12.9%	8.8%	6.7%
Merchant	41.9	38.2	18.9
Banker	3.2	17.6	5.6
Planter or farmer	—	2.9	1.1
Manufacturer	6.5	2.9	26.7
Railroad official & related position	6.5	5.9	1.1
Other high white collar	3.2	5.9	7.8
Low white collar	22.6	11.8	24.4
Skilled	3.2	4.4	4.4
Semi-skilled	—	1.5	3.3
Total[a]	100.0	99.9	100.0
N	31	68	90

SOURCES: See Appendix B.

[a]Percentages do not sum to 100 because of rounding error.

TABLE 15
Birthplaces of Economic Leaders, 1847–1890

	ELITE GROUP		
	1847–64	1865–79	1880–90
South	51.6%	73.5%	64.4%
Border states	—	—	1.1
New England	22.6	8.8	2.2
Middle Atlantic	9.7	2.9	4.4
Middle West	—	2.9	3.3
Foreign	12.9	8.8	16.7
Unknown	3.2	2.9	7.8
Total[a]	100.0	99.8	99.9
N	31	68	90

SOURCES: See Appendix B.
NOTE: Regions defined in same manner as in Table 3.
[a]Totals do not sum to 100 because of rounding error.

TABLE 16
Population of Birthplace of Economic Leaders, 1847–1890

NUMBER OF INHABITANTS	ELITE GROUP		
	1847–64	1865–79	1880–90
Under 2,500	54.8%	48.5%	35.6%
2,500–9,999	3.2	1.5	3.3
10,000–49,999	—	—	1.1
Born in Atlanta	—	—	3.3
Foreign	12.9	8.8	16.7
Unknown	29.0	41.2	40.0
Total[a]	99.9	100.0	100.0
N	31	68	90

SOURCES: See Appendix B.
[a]Percentages do not sum to 100 because of rounding error.

TABLE 17
Age of Economic Leaders, 1847–1890

	ELITE GROUP		
	1847–64	1865–79	1880–90
20–29 years	9.7%	4.4%	5.6%
30–39 years	45.2	25.0	31.1
40–49 years	19.4	36.8	32.2
50–59 years	19.4	22.1	16.7
60 or more years	3.2	8.8	5.6
Unknown	3.2	2.9	8.9
Total[a]	100.1	100.0	100.1
N	31	68	90

SOURCES: See Appendix B.

NOTE: The categories give estimated age at time of selection as economic elite.

[a]Percentages do not sum to 100 because of rounding error.

TABLE 18
Permanence of Economic Leaders in Atlanta, 1847–1890

	% RESIDING FOR ONE DECADE	% RESIDING FOR TWO DECADES	N
1847–64	89.7	81.5	31
1865–79	89.6	78.9	68
1880–90	84.3	—	90

SOURCES: See Appendix B.

NOTE: All permanence rates were corrected for death.

TABLE 19

Initial Wealth of Economic Leaders, 1847–1890

	ELITE GROUP		
	1847–64	1865–79	1880–90
Under $1,000	12.9%	29.4%	24.4%
$1,000–4,999	16.1	16.2	20.0
$5,000–9,999	6.5	16.2	20.0
$10,000–24,999	25.8	13.2	17.8
$25,000–49,999	12.9	10.3	7.8
$50,000–99,999	19.4	8.8	4.4
$100,000 or more	6.5	5.9	1.1
Unknown	—	—	4.4
Total[a]	100.1	100.0	99.9
N	31	68	90

SOURCES: See Appendix B.

NOTE: Initial wealth is estimated wealth at the time economic leaders arrived in Atlanta.

[a]Percentages do not sum to 100 because of rounding error.

TABLE 20
Peak Wealth of Economic Leaders, 1847–1890

	ELITE GROUP		
	1847–64	1865–79	1880–90
Under $10,000	—	2.9%	7.8%
$10,000–24,999	19.4%	7.4	15.6
$25,000–49,999	25.8	8.8	25.6
$50,000–99,999	16.1	26.5	17.8
$100,000–499,999	32.3	44.1	24.4
$500,000–999,999	6.5	7.4	2.2
$1,000,000 or more	—	2.9	1.1
Unknown	—	—	5.6
Total[a]	100.1	100.0	100.1
N	31	68	90

SOURCES: See Appendix B.

NOTE: The research for this study ended while most of the elite selected after 1879 were in mid-career. The data in this table consequently underestimate the peak wealth of those individuals in some cases.

[a]Percentages do not sum to 100 because of rounding error.

TABLE 21
Prior Place of Economic Leaders, 1847–1890

	ELITE GROUP		
	1847–64	1865–79	1880–90
South	87.1%	58.8%	42.2%
Border states	—	—	2.2
New England	—	3.0	—
Middle Atlantic	—	3.0	7.8
Middle West	—	2.9	3.3
West	—	—	—
U.S. territories	—	—	1.1
Unknown or foreign	12.9	32.4	33.3
Born or raised in Atlanta	—	—	10.0
Total[a]	100.0	100.1	99.9
N	31	68	90

SOURCES: See Appendix B.
NOTE: Regions defined in same manner as in Table 3.
[a]Percentages do not sum to 100 because of rounding error.

TABLE 22
Population of Prior Place of Economic Leaders, 1847–1890

NUMBER OF INHABITANTS	ELITE GROUP		
	1847–64	1865–79	1880–90
Under 2,500	74.2%	35.3%	25.6%
2,500–9,999	6.5	11.8	10.0
10,000–49,999	3.2	13.2	7.8
50,000–99,999	—	—	1.1
100,000 or more	—	—	10.0
Born or raised in Atlanta	—	—	10.0
Unknown or foreign	16.1	39.7	35.6
Total[a]	100.0	100.0	100.1
N	31	68	90

SOURCES: See Appendix B.
[a]Percentages do not sum to 100 because of rounding error.

TABLE 23
Kinship Status of Economic Leaders, 1847–1890

	ELITE GROUP		
	1847–64	1865–79	1880–90
Related by marriage	35.5%	13.2%	6.7%
Related by blood	3.2	22.1	14.4
Related by marriage & blood	3.2	5.9	5.6
Unknown or unrelated	58.1	58.8	73.3
Total	100.0	100.0	100.0
N	31	68	90

SOURCE: See Appendix B.

TABLE 24
Financial Backing of Economic Leaders, 1847–1890

	ELITE GROUP		
SOURCE OF AID	1847–64	1865–79	1880–90
Business associate in elite	3.2%	7.4%	4.4%
Non-elite business associate	6.5	4.4	8.9
Elite family	—	8.8	15.6
Non-elite family	19.4	16.2	15.6
None or unknown	71.0	63.2	55.6
Total[a]	100.1	100.0	100.1
N	31	68	90

SOURCES: See Appendix B.
[a]Percentages do not sum to 100 because of rounding error.

TABLE 25
Ancestry of Economic Leaders, 1847–1890

	ELITE GROUP		
	1847–64	1865–79	1880–90
English	29.0%	7.4%	11.1%
Irish	3.2	8.8	8.9
Scottish	6.5	7.4	2.2
Scotch-Irish	6.5	5.9	4.4
German	3.2	2.9	11.1
Other foreign	3.2	—	—
Unknown	48.4	67.6	62.2
Total[a]	100.0	100.0	99.9
N	31	68	90

SOURCES: See Appendix B.

[a]Percentages do not sum to 100 because of rounding error.

TABLE 26
Civil War Experience of Economic Leaders,
1847–1890

	ELITE GROUP		
	1847–64	1865–79	1880–90
Confederate army	16.1%	36.8%	35.6%
Confederate gov't	3.2	2.9	—
Georgia militia	6.5	7.4	5.6
Southern civilian	45.2	16.2	6.7
Unionist	3.2	5.9	—
Union army	—	—	2.2
Northern civilian	—	1.5	1.1
Deceased or underage	9.7	—	23.3
Unknown	16.1	29.4	25.6
Total[a]	100.0	100.1	100.1
N	31	68	90

SOURCES: See Appendix B.

[a]Percentages do not sum to 100 because of rounding error.

APPENDIX B
Quantitative Sources and Methodology

The quantitative data analyzed in this study fall into three categories: samples and population groups drawn from the manuscripts of the federal population censuses for De Kalb County (1850) and Fulton County (1860–1880); residential samples for occupational and racial groups collected from Atlanta city directories (1859–1860, 1870, 1876, 1888); and biographical information taken from a variety of sources for the city's economic leaders from 1847 to 1890.

Samples were drawn from the censuses and the city directories to measure occupational and geographic mobility, horizontal and vertical occupational structures, and residential patterns. (The information on wealth holding did not involve sampling, since information on all property holders was collected.) The sampling issues that arose included sizes and methodology.

Concerning sizes, it is important to keep in mind the questions being investigated statistically and the degree of confidence in the results the investigator is willing to accept. A mistake was originally made in taking 10 percent samples of the various quantitative sources. One should not take a 10 percent sample of a universe, since the size of the universe has very little to do with the reliability of the statistical analysis.[1]

What matters is the size of the sample itself and the results of the statistical analysis. Unfortunately, the results of analysis cannot be known, of course, until long after the sample is collected. A rule of thumb suggested by some is to opt for about one thousand when dealing with categorical data (numbers that are not precise—such as height or weight—but that represent an ordered hierarchy).[2]

For several reasons, I decided to take smaller samples. Having to

1. See Charles M. Dollar and Richard Jensen, *Historian's Guide to Statistics: Quantitative Analysis and Historical Research* (New York, 1971), 11–15.
2. Richard Jensen, "Categories of Errors and Mistakes" (Paper available from the Newberry Library, Chicago).

trace both priority and persistence through several censuses made it desirable to work with as small samples as were justifiable. Moreover, the breakdown of the results for the dependent variable for the acceptable confidence interval (the degree of certainty that the sample truly represents the population from which it is taken) made larger samples unnecessary. The persistence and priority samples yield results that have a confidence level of about 80 percent (with a possible variation of about plus or minus three percentage points).[3] This confidence interval would be unacceptable in a presidential preference poll, but it is reasonable in a historical study. Confidence levels in the horizontal and vertical occupational samples are much higher.

The method of taking samples from both the censuses and the city directories was systematic rather than random. Some have recently argued that historians should use random sampling methods, but this did not seem necessary given that the populations sampled for this book were ethnically homogeneous.[4] Further, I was warned that random numbers have a tendency to cluster, and that might present problems in working with manuscript censuses.

The main purpose in taking samples from the censuses was to analyze population persistence and priority. Richard J. Hopkins has dealt with occupational and geographic mobility in Atlanta from 1870 to 1920. Partially because of record linkage difficulties in his studies, it seemed advisable to duplicate some of his work for the period after 1870, with one exception. I did not attempt to survey occupational mobility in Atlanta after 1870, because geographic mobility was more relevant to the organizing themes of this study. So my original findings concerning occupational mobility cover the years before 1870.

All Hopkins' subjects were traced from either censuses or city directories to directories one or more decades later. This fairly common method of studying persistence and occupational mobility is fraught with serious defects that only recently have come under scrutiny.

Directories do not give enough information about individuals for us to be sure that they are the same people whose names were drawn

3. Since occupational mobility was not a central concern, the confidence intervals for those data do not approach this level. The formula for determining confidence intervals is discussed in Hubert M. Blalock, *Social Statistics* (Rev. ed.; New York, 1979), 208–18.
4. R. Christian Johnson, "A Procedure for Sampling the Manuscript Census Schedules," *Journal of Interdisciplinary History*, VIII (1978), 515–30.

from the censuses earlier. As an example, take the case of Tandy Steagall. In the 1870 census for Fulton County, I found a Tandy Steagall who was a white "pattern maker" (a railroad craft). According to an 1880 city directory, a white "car maker" (another railroad craft) with the same name was still in Atlanta. Checking the 1880 population census led to the discovery, however, that the Tandy Steagall in Atlanta that year was the nephew of the other man. The older Steagall was no longer in the city. Given the unusual nature of the person's name, one would not anticipate such duplication.[5] Name duplication is a serious record linkage problem, especially with blacks, who tended to have more common names.[6]

Fortunately, censuses alone could be used to trace the persistence and the priority of white male household heads for the period from 1850 to 1880 in Atlanta. This was possible because of a resource that Hopkins apparently did not discover in his work. Franklin Garrett compiled meticulous indexes of all white males over various ages (and white female family heads) in the censuses for De Kalb County (1840–1880) and for Fulton County (1860–1880). These indexes are available in the archives of the Atlanta Historical Society. The page references correspond to numbers Mr. Garrett put in his own bound copies of photostats of the censuses. It is possible to devise a system for relating his pagination to the numbers the census takers used. Since Mr. Garrett kindly put those volumes at my disposal, I used them for much of my work, however. It was easy to place them next to each other and, by checking an individual's age (often wildly inconsistent between censuses), his family size and composition, birthplace, and other characteristics, be reasonably sure that he was or was not the same man.[7]

Unfortunately, the same procedures were not possible with blacks' persistence or with white male household heads' persistence from

5. I performed a few random checks, using city directories for record linkage before abandoning the directories when I could.

6. Gerald Bouchard and Christian Pouyez, "Name Variations and Computerized Record Linkage," *Historical Methods Newsletter*, XIII (1980), 119–25; Christian Pouyez, Raymond Roy, and François Martin, "The Linkage of Census Name Data: Problems and Procedures," *Journal of Interdisciplinary History*, XIV (1983), 129–52.

7. The 1850 Atlanta census, with a complete index, is in *AHB*, VII (1942), 16–82. Garrett's indexes for Fulton County include the following: 1860, heads of families and males over twenty years of age; 1870, heads of families and males over twenty; and 1880, heads of families and males over eighteen. On the census and individuals' ages, see Peter R. Knights, "Accuracy of Age Reporting in the Manuscript Federal Censuses of 1850 and 1860," *Historical Methods Newsletter*, IV (1971), 79–83.

1880 to 1890. In those cases, it was necessary with one exception to use city directories. Since I have less confidence in these data, I did not attempt a statistical analysis of the samples. The exception was black persistence from 1870 to 1880. The existence of a soundex index for 1880 makes it possible to use census records.[8] I found to my surprise, however, that the soundex was a very incomplete record of Atlanta's population in 1880. Numerous black males with relatively unusual names who were selected from the 1870 census did not show up in the soundex but did appear in city directories covering the period from 1879 to 1881, often with identical or very similar occupations.[9] Using the soundex, I found that the persistence rate of black male household heads from 1870 to 1880 was only 16 percent; using city directories, I came up with 46 percent. I discovered through the soundex that about 8 percent of the sample found in the city directories were cases of name duplication. Another 9% with fairly common names found in the directories were also discarded because of the possibility of name duplication. It did not seem reasonable to leave out all the remaining directory traces not found in the soundex. I therefore counted as persistent those black males found in the directories who had relatively uncommon surnames and good occupational matches. This decision may have resulted in an inflated persistence rate, but any overestimate is probably minuscule.

The major issue not discussed in the text concerning the residential distribution maps and tables is the use of city directories. That was necessary because only the 1880 census included addresses. I did attempt to construct a residential map using this census, but the census takers' meanderings were too erratic—they returned to some alleys and streets on three separate occasions (separated by several census pages) to gather information.

City directories have been criticized because they tend to under-enumerate blacks and lower-class individuals. However, John P. Kellogg tested city directories against the manuscript censuses and found that the former were adequate to map black residential patterns

8. See Charles Stephenson, "The Methodology of Historical Census Record Linkage: A User's Guide to the Soundex," *Prologue*, XII (1980), 151–53; and Stephenson, "Tracing Those Who Left: Mobility Studies and the Soundex Indexes to the U. S. Census," *JUH*, I (1974), 73–84.

9. In tracing persistence, I used directories for the year before and the year after as well as for the ten- or twenty-year terminal date. This was to compensate for possibly incomplete listings.

in Lexington, Kentucky, in the mid-1880s. I see no reason to doubt his contention that directories usually include sufficient numbers of less prosperous individuals and so are useful for displaying occupational and racial residential patterns.[10]

The directories used to gather the data depicted in the maps were chosen for several reasons. Only one city directory survives for the antebellum period. The 1870 city directory is as good as any from that period. It contains, however, the names of few blacks. The 1876 directory is one of the earliest to include large numbers of blacks and has conveniently been reprinted. The 1888 directory is the most thorough for the entire period up to 1890. It is accompanied by the best map of the era, and its authors made a determined effort to clarify Atlanta's street-numbering "system." Street numbers were so irregular during the 1880s that it would be very difficult to plot addresses without this directory.

The biographical sources for Atlanta's economic leadership are too numerous to cite in full but the most useful can be described. A great deal of information was garnered from the manuscript censuses. The local histories by Thomas Martin, Wallace P. Reed, and the Pioneer Citizens' Society all contain biographical sections. Franklin Garrett's three-volume history contains many valuable tidbits on white Atlanta businessmen during the nineteenth century, and the index is comprehensive. His history is a year-by-year account, and most chapters have a "local death roll" for the year. Newspapers also contained a wealth of data in the form of obituaries and miscellaneous articles on the city's business leaders. The Georgia Department of Archives and History maintains a Confederate citizens' file, wherein one can look up the names of male Georgia citizens during the Civil War. The file refers the researcher to microfilm copies of Confederate records from the National Archives that are available at the GDAH. Much biographical information was also obtained from the credit reports of R. G. Dun & Co., housed in the Baker Library at Harvard University. This information must be used carefully, however, since it often contains inaccuracies.[11] Finally, most of the data on wealth holding

10. Peter R. Knights, "City Directories as Aids to Ante-Bellum Urban Studies: A Research Note," *Historical Methods Newsletter*, II (1969), 1–10; John P. Kellogg, " The Evolution of Black Residential Areas in Lexington, Kentucky, 1865–1887," *JSH*, XLVIII (1982), 26–28n17.

11. See James H. Madison, "The Credit Reports of R. G. Dun & Co. as Historical Sources," *Historical Methods Newsletter*, VIII (1975), 128–31.

was collected from county and city tax digests, which are almost complete for the entire period.

The tax digests were an important resource for identification and study of the economic elites. There is a full record of individuals' property holdings. Although much property was doubtless concealed from the assessors, much was revealed also. The variety of property taxed locally was extensive. In addition to poll taxes, taxes on free persons of color, professional and business licenses, revenues were collected, according to the Fulton County Tax Digest (1854), from taxation of slaves; amount of money and solvent debts; capital invested in shipping; capital invested in stocks of any kind and manufactories; household and kitchen furnishings (above a $300 deductible); merchandise; real estate; and all other property except plantation and mechanical tools, annual crops, and provisions.

The estimated worth given by the Dun credit reporters were almost always based on data in the tax digests. They simply went down to the county courthouse or city hall and looked up the names of their targets. I preferred in most cases not to accept the reporters' numbers, since it was obvious to me that they did not represent a full inventory of the property of wealthy individuals. One problem is that, though the tax digests were arranged alphabetically, the order is not exact. The name of Joseph E. Brown, for example, might appear in several places under B. Also, counties were divided into several tax districts ("North Atlanta," "South Atlanta," "Blackhall," etc.), and it is necessary to search them all, since wealthy men tended to have dispersed investments in real estate. Finally, prosperous businessmen were likely to share ownership, and the property could be listed under the last name of any one of the partners. This necessitated arbitrary decisions about the division of such property. Tax digests are, in sum, a rich source, but using them requires much care and patience.

The criteria for selecting Atlanta's economic leaders were designed to reflect the nature of the city's economy, which was predominantly commercial throughout the era (the tax digests are especially useful for detecting commercial wealth). Many studies of nineteenth-century economic elites focus on directors of incorporated companies, whose names can be found easily in city directories. However, Atlanta's business leaders during my period were mostly merchants whose firms were rarely incorporated. The criteria (which included both positional and wealth-holding standards) I employed to identify the city's economic leadership were appropriate, since the names that surfaced were the ones I found in newspaper articles and other sources concerning railroad ventures, the industrial expositions, and similar urban promotive ventures. Specifically, I used: president, superintendent, or director of any existing railroad; president or cashier of any bank; president of any locally owned insurance company, street railway, utility, or building and loan association; president of the chamber of commerce, board of trade, or manufacturers' association; proprietor of any manufacturing concern that employed at least fifty in 1880 (according to the 1880 federal manuscript census of manufacturing); president of any incorporated company with a capital stock issue of at least $50,000 from 1881 to 1885 and $100,000 or more from 1886 to 1890; any male with at least $10,000 in property (according to the 1850 census) and $50,000 (according to the 1870 census); and males whose total property holdings met a minimum that rose from $33,000 in 1847 to $90,000 by 1890 (determined from the tax digests).

BIBLIOGRAPHICAL ESSAY

The less well known primary sources and secondary literature on nineteenth-century Atlanta will be the principal targets of my commentary. Some readers may also want to consult the fuller bibliography in my "Atlanta, Gate City of the South, 1847 to 1885" (Ph.D. dissertation, Princeton University, 1972). Three publications offer a partial guide to the primary sources: Richard T. Eltzroth, "The Atlanta Historical Society: Its Archival and Library Holdings," *Georgia Archive*, I (1972), 3–14; Louise D. Cook (comp.), *Guide to the Manuscript Collections of the Atlanta Historical Society* (Atlanta, 1976); and Dale A. Somers, Timothy J. Crimmins, and Merl E. Reed, "Surveying the Records of a City: The History of Atlanta Project," *American Archivist*, XXXVI (1973), 353–59. A useful survey of secondary literature is James C. Starbuck's *Historic Atlanta to 1930: An Indexed, Chronological Bibliography* (Monticello, Ill., 1974).

The best primary source for the historical investigation of any city is its newspapers. Although nineteenth-century newspapers were usually partisan and biased in various ways, no other source offers such a comprehensive review of the lives of a city's inhabitants. Those interested in Atlanta history are fortunate to have rich newspaper resources, except for the pre–Civil War era. U. B. Phillips early in this century used a complete file of the Atlanta *Intelligencer* for the antebellum period, which he cited as in the possession of Joseph M. Brown. This newspaper began as a weekly in 1849, became a daily in 1854, and continued publication until 1870. Guides to newspaper collections list only scattered issues of this paper before 1857. All my efforts to locate the file that Phillips used met with failure. No member of the Brown family whom I contacted about the matter was aware of the newspaper's existence. The earliest continuous run of any local newspaper that I read was that of the Atlanta *Daily Examiner* for 1857 (which merged with the *Intelligencer* in that year). I filled the gap left by the loss of the *Intelligencer* for the period before 1857 with other Georgia newspapers that quoted excerpts from Atlanta papers. Newspapers read for this purpose included the Augusta *Constitutionalist*, the Augusta *Daily Chronicle and Sentinel*, the Athens *Banner & Watchman*, the Columbus *Enquirer*, the Macon *Telegraph*, the Milledgeville *Southern Recorder*, and the Savannah *Republican*.

Recently, I learned from Professor David Weiman of the Department of Economics at Yale University that a portion of the *Intelligencer* file that may have once been in U. B. Phillips' possession is now in the Beinecke Rare Book Room in Yale's Sterling University Library. Now available are a run of the weekly from 1851 to 1853 and another run of the daily from 1854 to 1856. This should be an invaluable source for students of the antebellum Georgia upcountry as well as Atlanta. There was no other newspaper published in the upcountry during this period whose issues have survived to this extent. Unfortunately, I learned of this resource too late to make use of it here.

There is no shortage of local newspapers for the era of the Civil War and the remainder of the nineteenth century, though the best papers for various periods are not necessarily the most famous ones. Three provide good coverage of the wartime era: the Atlanta *Gate City Guardian* (1861); the Atlanta *Southern Confederacy* (1861–1864); and the *Daily Atlanta Intelligencer*. The Atlanta *Daily New Era* (1866–1869) offers a valuable Radical Republican perspective on local news after the war. The Atlanta *Constitution* began publication in 1868, but is less comprehensive than several other papers before the late 1870s. The Atlanta *Daily Herald* (1872–1876) is the best for the early 1870s, though the Atlanta *Daily News* (1874) has additional detail on politics and race relations. For the period after the *Herald's* demise, the *Constitution* is usually the best paper. The Atlanta *Journal*, which began publication in 1883, and a Democratic organ published by Julius L. Brown, the Atlanta *Evening Capitol* (1885), need to be consulted, however.

Several other papers, though less useful, are worth looking at: the *Daily True Georgian* (1870); the Atlanta *Daily Sun* (1870–1872); the Atlanta *Daily Evening Commonwealth* (1874–1875); the Atlanta *Times* (1876); the Atlanta *Telegram* (1877); the Atlanta *Tribune* (1877–1878); and the Atlanta *Post Appeal* (1882). Scattered issues of various other newspapers are also available for the same period. Unfortunately, very few exist that give the black perspective on local news. There are a few issues from 1881 of a black newspaper, the Atlanta *Weekly Defiance*. A weekly black church newspaper, the Atlanta *Southern Recorder*, has interesting material on the prohibition campaigns and school affairs. Edited by Bishop Henry M. Turner, this paper covers the period from 1886 to 1888.

Three guides give the locations and other useful data about all the cited newspapers: Winifred Gregory, *American Newspapers, 1821– 1936: A Union List of Files Available in the United States and Canada* (New York, 1937); Rabun Lee Brantley, *Georgia Journalism of the Civil War Period* (Nashville, 1936); and Ruth Feldman, "A Checklist of Atlanta Newspapers, 1846–1948" (M.A. thesis, Emory University, 1948).

Next to newspapers, the most useful primary sources were local and federal government records. The bulk of this material is still unpublished, though some valuable municipal and federal government publications are extant.

Despite Sherman, there is a wealth of municipal and county source material. The Minutes of the Atlanta City Council are available on a continuous basis from the city's founding in 1847 through the nineteenth century. Beginning in 1874, the Minutes of the Atlanta Board of Aldermen are also extant. Both are at the Atlanta Historical Society. Numerous other unpublished municipal records are housed there: Atlanta Ordinance Book (April 25, 1851–August 31, 1860); Atlanta City Tax Digests (1858–1862); Minutes of the Mayor's Court (February 8, 1861–March 16, 1864); Report of Lakewood Station Master (1878 to 1882); and West End Council Minutes (1868–1893). The Minutes of the Mayor's Court is particularly useful for information on law and disorder in Confederate Atlanta. The minutes of the Atlanta Board of Education are extant from 1869 on and are kept in the office of the secretary of the board. The only county records consulted extensively were the tax digests, which are available for Fulton County beginning in 1854 and for De Kalb County in 1846 and even earlier. These digests are extant on an almost annual basis for the entire period. They were mainly used in gathering financial data on the elite and are in the Georgia Department of Archives and History.

Federal government primary sources were not as crucial (with the exception of the manuscript censuses), but some provided information that could be found nowhere else. Except for the censuses for De Kalb and Fulton counties from 1850 to 1880 (available in many places on microfilm) and the 1880 manufacturing census for Fulton County (deposited in the William R. Perkins Library, Duke University, Durham), all the federal government primary sources were in the National Archives. Indispensable for following the history of manufacturing in wartime Atlanta were the plentiful records of the Atlanta Arsenal in Record Group 109. Especially helpful was the Contract Book of the Atlanta Arsenal (January 9, 1862–June 14, 1864), which contains information on production expectations. Also useful for Unionist activities were the Fulton County folders in the records of the Southern Claims Division, Record Group 217. Valuable information on race relations and social issues during Reconstruction can be found in the correspondence of Freedmen's Bureau agents stationed in Atlanta. This correspondence and the "Monthly Reports of Sick and Wounded Refugees and Freedmen of Freedmen's Bureau Hospital in Atlanta, Georgia from November, 1865 to August, 1868" are in Record Group 105.

Published primary documents of local and national governments often contain maps, charts, and numerical data not available in the unpublished records. For municipal government, the most comprehensive is the *Annual Reports of City Officers*, available for every year after 1878. They are scattered, though, in the holdings of the Atlanta Historical Society, the Library of Congress, and the New York Public Library. In addition to the best collection of those reports, the New York Public Library has an almost complete collection of *Annual Reports of the Board of Water Commissioners* (from 1876 through the 1890s). Attached to these reports is the *Charter, By-Laws, Rules, Regulations, and Water-Rates Governing the Atlanta Water Works* (Atlanta, 1875), an important source on the rate structure and finances of the water works. Also in the New York Public Library is the *Proceedings & Reports of the Sanitary Commission of the City of Atlanta, Georgia, 1876* (Atlanta, 1877). This 276-page book is crucial for understanding the evolution of Atlanta's sewerage system. A synopsis of the commission's recommendations appeared in *Sanitarian*, XV (1877), 424–27.

Other published municipal records include annual reports from the Atlanta Board of Education and the Atlanta Board of Health. The first is available from 1872 on an annual basis, and the second on the same basis beginning in 1878. They are located in the administrative buildings of the respective municipal departments in Atlanta. The legal history of Atlanta's government is fully documented in various collections of city ordinances. The earliest, Marshall J. Clarke's *Acts of Incorporation and Ordinances of the City of Atlanta* (Atlanta, 1860), is in the Atlanta Public Library. All other city codes for the nineteenth century are in the library of the Atlanta Historical Society.

Relevant published records of state and federal government were fewer in number. The *Acts of the General Assembly of the State of Georgia*, extant for the entire period, are in the Georgia Department of Archives and History. In the State Law Library in Atlanta are the *Annual Reports of the Comptroller-General of the State of Georgia*, also complete for the era. They contain estimates of the value of various kinds of property in every county. An indispensable federal publication is *The War of the Rebellion: A Compilation of the Official Records of the Union and Confederate Armies* (130 vols.; Washington, D.C., 1880–1901).

Personal papers and collections were frustrating sources. Frequently, there was only one letter of any interest. However, such letters often provided an interesting insight or colorful comment on a topic inadequately covered elsewhere.

Some manuscript collections were relatively rich in relevant material, more so for the antebellum and Civil War periods than later. The Governors' [of Georgia] Letterbooks in two volumes (1821–1829 and 1835–1840) contain a great deal of information on railroad developments. They are in the Georgia Department of Archives and History. One of the best collections is the Lemuel P. Grant Papers in the Atlanta Historical Society. There are three diaries, twelve letterbooks, several boxes of loose correspondence, and various materials relating to the Civil War fortifications of Atlanta and Augusta he designed. Most of Grant's correspondence concerns various railroad projects, but it also touches on other entrepreneurial projects such as the Atlanta Bank and an agricultural fair. Also housed at the Atlanta Historical Society, the William McNaught–James Ormond Papers are good for coverage of antebellum business. McNaught was the president of the city's first chamber of commerce. In addition, the collection includes the Minute Book of the Fulton County Export & Importing Company, a blockade-running company headquartered in Atlanta. The Atlanta Historical Society also has the diary of Samuel P. Richards, which covers the Civil War period and early Reconstruction. Richards wrote well, and his diary has interesting tidbits on life behind the lines. The only collection for the postbellum period that has more than a few letters of interest is the Felix Hargrett Collection at the University of Georgia in Athens. Although more valuable to students of state politics than of Atlanta history, it contains some interesting letters from Henry W. Grady, Hannibal Ingalls Kimball, Joseph E. Brown, and others.

There is also a massive collection of letters written by American Missionary Association personnel stationed in Atlanta after the Civil War, which is kept in the association's archives at Dillard University in New Orleans. On the whole, this collection focused on educational and ecclesiastical concerns, but I did find a few items on race relations generally.

Few diaries and letters have been published. But one was helpful on Atlanta in its infancy. Edited by William Stafford Irvine, it appeared in the *Atlanta Historical Bulletin*, III (1937), as "Diary and Letters of William N. White, a Citizen of Atlanta Written 1847" (pp. 35–50).

Not many records of local nineteenth-century business have survived. Those that are extant made possible limited investigations of such topics as the sources of local manufacturing capital and the importance of the cash trade.

Industrial records are scarce. Emory Cocke of Atlanta has an Exposition Cotton Mills ledger dating from 1883. It contains production totals and data on expenditures not available for any other industry. The Georgia Institute of Technology has recently acquired the Fulton Cotton Mills Archives. The most valuable items were a scrapbook, the Inventory Book (1883–1898), and the Minutes of the Board of Directors (1881–1899). The minute book of the Atlanta City Brewing Company (dating from 1876) is at the Atlanta Historical Society.

Mercantile records with two exceptions are at the Atlanta Historical Society. The exceptions are the Minute Book of the King Hardware Co. (1887–1928) and the Minute Book of the Beck & Gregg Hardware Co. (1883–1941), which are kept by the respective companies. The Atlanta Historical Society has the minute book of the Atlanta Hardware Association (May 24, 1875–April 16, 1880). The most valuable source on the cash trade and credit practices is also in the society's archives, the John R. and Alexander M. Wallace & Co. Papers. Wallace & Co. was a hardware firm. Its ledgers, which date back to 1870, are in the collection.

Railroad records, considerably better preserved than are those of local industries and mercantile houses, were searched mainly for freight rate discriminations. The Western & Atlantic Railroad Archives in the Georgia Department of Archives and History are voluminous, but I read only a small portion of the correspondence for information on the location of Atlanta. The published annual reports of the superintendents and the officers were more useful and are intact (1844–1869) at the State Law Library. Three other W & A annual reports (1872–1874) are in the Ilah Dunlap Little Memorial Library, University of Georgia. A minute book of the Board of Leasees of the W & A (1870–1890) is in the Joseph E. Brown Collection at the Atlanta Historical Society. The Central of Georgia annual reports (1838–1885) are in the Robert R. Woodruff Library, Emory University, Atlanta. Incomplete files of the annual reports of the Georgia, Macon & Western and the Atlanta & West Point are in the State Law Library and in the Bureau of Railway Economics Library, American Association of Railroads Building, Washington, D.C.

Other business records used for this study include those of the Atlanta Chamber of Commerce and R. G. Dun & Co. The Chamber of Commerce Archives in Atlanta has a minute book that begins in 1883. Two published chamber of commerce reports, one for 1885 and the other for 1889, are in the New York Public Library. The *First Annual Report of the Atlanta Chamber of Commerce for the Year 1885: Historical, Descriptive, Statistical* (Atlanta, 1886) contains an interesting historical sketch of the city and a separate history of the chamber itself. The credit reports of R. G. Dun & Co., contained in Volumes XIII and XIV for Fulton County (1847–1880), were by far the most valuable source for biographical information on Atlanta businessmen. They are housed in the Baker Library at Harvard University in Cambridge, Mass. Dun & Co. reports must be used with care and seemed especially inaccurate about the estimated worth of individuals. Their most essential contribution was information about the familial and support networks of the elite.

Two convenient guides for locating contemporary books and pamphlets are: Marcia Shufelt, "A Checklist of Atlanta Imprints, 1846 to 1876" (M.A. thesis, Catholic University of America, 1956); and Ella May Thornton, *Finding List of Books and Pamphlets Relating to Georgia and Georgians* (Atlanta, 1928).

The pamphlets and books with the broadest variety of information were: George White, *Statistics of the State of Georgia* (Savannah, 1849); White, *Historical Collections of Georgia* (Savannah, 1854); John Stainback Wilson, *Atlanta As It Is* (New York, 1871); Reilly & Thomas [*sic*], *Atlanta, Past, Present, and Future* (Atlanta, 1883);

Manufacturing and Mercantile Resources of Atlanta, Georgia (Atlanta, 1883); Atlanta Manufacturers' Association, *Atlanta, The Capital of Georgia and the Coming Metropolis of the South* (Atlanta, 1889); and I. W. Avery, *Atlanta, The Leader in Trade, Population, Wealth, and Manufactures* (Atlanta, 1885). These works are in the Atlanta Historical Society, the State Law Library, and Robert R. Woodruff Library, Emory University.

Two other contemporary publications are worth noting. A sketch of antebellum Atlanta by Green B. Haygood is invaluable. It appears in *Williams' Atlanta City Directory for 1859–1860* (Atlanta, 1860) and is also reprinted in *De Bow's Review*, XXVII (1859), 462–68. The best biographical information on Atlanta blacks is in E. R. Carter, *The Black Side: A Partial History of Business, Religious, and Educational Side of the Negro in Atlanta* (Atlanta, 1894). Both sources are available in the library of the Atlanta Historical Society.

Travelers' accounts often contained quotable passages and had the advantage of offering more objective perspectives on Atlanta's development than did those of local boosters. Three guides contain brief synopses of these works and information on which libraries have them: Thomas D. Clark (ed.), *Travels in the Old South* (3 vols.; Norman, Okla., 1956–59); Clark (ed.), *Travels in the New South* (2 vols.; Norman, Okla., 1962); and E. Merton Coulter (ed.), *Travels in the Confederate States: A Bibliography* (Norman, Okla., 1948).

The most perceptive accounts date from the postbellum period. Among the best were: Whitelaw Reid, *After the War: A Tour of the Southern States, 1865–1866* (1866; rpr. New York, 1965); Sidney Andrews, *The South Since the War: As Shown by Fourteen Weeks of Travel and Observation in Georgia and the Carolinas* (Boston, 1866); John T. Trowbridge, *A Picture of the Desolated States, 1865–1868* (Hartford, Conn., 1868); John H. Kennaway, *On Sherman's Track* (London, 1867); Robert Somers, *The Southern States Since the War, 1870–1871* (New York, 1871); Edward King, *The Great South* (Hartford, Conn., 1875); A. K. McClure, *The South: Its Industrial, Financial, and Political Condition* (Philadelphia, 1886); and M. B. Hillyard, *The New South* (Baltimore, 1887).

Three articles in contemporary journals are also worth reading: A. H. Guernsey, "Sherman's Great March," *Harper's New Monthly Magazine*, XXXI (1865), 571–89; Charles W. Hubner, "Atlanta," *Appleton's Journal of Literature, Science, and Art*, VIII (1872), 376–

78; and Ernest Ingersoll, "The City of Atlanta," *Harper's New Monthly Magazine*, LX (1879), 30–43.

Historiography on Atlanta has increased noticeably in the past twenty years, except for broad studies that are generally quite old. The most recent and most comprehensive urban biography is Franklin M. Garrett's *Atlanta and Environs: A Chronicle of Its People and Events* (3 vols.; New York, 1954). It is meticulously researched and reprints a good deal of primary material. One of its best features is a thorough index. The most interpretative work is Paul Miller's *Atlanta, Capital of the South* (New York, 1949). There are four earlier histories: Wallace P. Reed, *History of Atlanta, Georgia* (Syracuse, 1889); Thomas H. Martin, *Atlanta and Its Builders: A Comprehensive History of the Gate City of the South* (2 vols.; Atlanta, 1902); *Pioneer Citizens' History of Atlanta, 1833–1902* (Atlanta, 1902); and E. Y. Clarke, *History of Atlanta, Illustrated, 1881* (3rd ed.; Atlanta, 1881). The third edition is the most comprehensive of Clarke's books. Cherokee Press reprinted the second edition (originally published in 1879) in 1971, and it is usually cited in the notes, since it is the most accessible. Like all the early histories, it contains a good deal of primary source material. Walter G. Cooper's *Official History of Fulton County* (Atlanta, 1934) also contains quite a bit of primary material.

Of the various topics in Atlanta history, the best developed is politics and government. The only book-length study in this area is Eugene Watts's *The Social Bases of City Politics: Atlanta, 1865–1903* (Westport, Conn., 1978). Watts's book is narrowly conceived and does not provide good coverage of municipal campaigns. Those interested in those issues also need to consult Watts's "Characteristics of Candidates in City Politics: Atlanta, 1865–1903" (Ph.D. dissertation, Emory University, 1969). Black politics has received the most attention from scholars. See Eugene J. Watts, "Black Political Progress in Atlanta, 1868 to 1895," *Journal of Negro History*, LXIX (1974), 268–86; Clarence A. Bacote, "The Negro in Atlanta Politics, 1869–1955," *Phylon*, XVI (1955), 333–50; Bacote, "William Finch, Negro Councilman, and political activities during early Reconstruction," *Journal of Negro History*, XL (1955), 341–64; John Hammond Moore, "The Negro and Prohibition in Atlanta, 1885–1887," *South Atlantic Quarterly*, LXIX (1970), 38–57; and James M. Russell and Jerry Thornbery, "William Finch of Atlanta: The Black Politician as Civic

Leader," in Howard N. Rabinowitz (ed.), *Southern Black Leaders of the Reconstruction South* (Urbana, 1982), 309–34. Two articles on Atlanta politics and government from the perspective of white elites and the working class are my "Elites and Municipal Politics and Government in Atlanta, 1847–1890," in Orville Vernon Burton and Robert C. McMath, Jr. (eds.), *Toward a New South? Studies in Post–Civil War Southern Communities* (Westport, Conn., 1982), 37–70, and "Politics, Municipal Services, and the Working Class in Atlanta, 1865 to 1890," *Georgia Historical Quarterly*, LXVI (1982), 467–91.

Some studies of twentieth-century politics and government provide valuable perspectives on the earlier period. The most useful were: Edward C. Banfield, *Big City Politics* (New York, 1965), 18–36; Floyd Hunter, *Community Power Structure: A Study of Decision Makers* (Chapel Hill, 1953); and Hunter, *Community Power Succession: Atlanta's Policy Makers Revisited* (Chapel Hill, 1980).

Some articles provide details about various municipal departments during the nineteenth century. An excellent essay on the water works by John Ellis and Stuart Galishoff, "Atlanta's Water Supply, 1865–1918," is in *Maryland Historian*, VIII (1977), 5–22. Richard Hopkins covers public health, welfare, and sanitation services in "Public Health in Atlanta, 1865–1879," *Georgia Historical Quarterly*, LIII (1969), 287–305. More can be found in a two-part article by John H. Ellis, "Businessmen and Public Health in the Urban South during the Nineteenth Century: New Orleans, Memphis, and Atlanta," *Bulletin of the History of Medicine*, XLIV (1970), 197–212, 346–71. On police affairs, see Eugene J. Watts, "The Police in Atlanta," *Journal of Southern History*, XXXIX (1973), 165–82. Specific details can be found in Howard N. Rabinowitz's "The Conflict Between Blacks and the Police in the Urban South, 1865–1900," *Historian*, XXXIX (1976), 62–76.

Of the various governmental services, public education has received the most attention. The most comprehensive study is Philip Racine's "Atlanta's Schools: A History of the Public School System, 1869–1955" (Ph.D. dissertation, Emory University, 1969). Two articles provide additional information: Meta Barker, "Atlanta's First Public School," *Atlanta Historical Bulletin*, I (1930), 31–39; and C. T. Wright, "The Development of Public Schools for Blacks in Atlanta, 1872–1900," *ibid.*, XXI (1977), 115–28. Clarence A. Bacote's *The Story of Atlanta University* (Atlanta, 1969) describes the early history of the American Missionary Association grammar schools that were eventually absorbed into the public school system. An institution of higher learning that received some municipal aid is thoroughly covered in Robert C. McMath *et al.*, *Engineering the New South: Georgia Tech, 1885–1985* (Athens, 1985).

Black history apart from politics and education has received less attention from scholars, but there are still some useful studies. The most comprehensive is Jerry J. Thornbery's "The Development of Black Atlanta, 1865–1885" (Ph.D. dissertation, University of Maryland, 1977). In addition, see his "Northerners and the Atlanta Freedmen, 1865–69," *Prologue*, VI (1974), 236–51. Edward F. Sweat's "Free Blacks in Antebellum Atlanta," *Atlanta Historical Bulletin*, XXI (1977), 64–71, is the only study of black Atlanta for that period. An interesting article is William Harris' "Work and the Family in Black Atlanta, 1880," *Journal of Social History*, IX (1976), 319–30. Two theses focus on the black aspect of race relations: Alexa Wynelle Brown, "Race Relations in Atlanta, 1865–1877" (M.A. thesis, Atlanta University, 1966); and Bettye Collier Thomas, "Race Relations in Atlanta from 1877 to 1890" (M.A. thesis, Atlanta University, 1966). There is also a wealth of information in Howard N. Rabinowitz's superb book, *Race Relations in the Urban South, 1865–1890* (New York, 1978).

Social and geographic mobility and physical development are well-developed topics in Atlanta historiography. Most of the work on mobility has been done by Richard J. Hopkins. His most comprehensive treatment is "Patterns of Persistence and Occupational Mobility in a Southern City, Atlanta, 1870–1920" (Ph.D. dissertation, Emory University, 1972). His published works include the following: "Occupational and Geographic Mobility in Atlanta, 1870–1896," *Journal of Southern History*, XXXIV (1968), 200–214; "Status, Mobility, and the Dimensions of Change in a Southern City, Atlanta, 1870–1910," in Kenneth T. Jackson and Stanley K. Schultz (eds.), *Cities in American History* (New York, 1972), 216–29; and "Are Southern Cities Unique? Persistence as a Clue," *Mississippi Quarterly*, XXVI (1973), 121–41. Hopkins' work came under sharp criticism on methodological grounds from William Harris in "Research Note on Mobility in Atlanta," *South Atlantic Urban Studies*, I (1977), 267–70. For Jewish mobility patterns in Atlanta, see Steven Hertzberg, *Strangers Within the Gate City: The Jews of Atlanta, 1845–1915* (Philadelphia, 1978).

Atlanta's physical history has been studied from several viewpoints. For a geographical and topological explanation of Atlanta as the antebellum junction of several railroads, see Raymond Stanley Wallace, "The Railroad Pattern of Atlanta" (M.A. thesis, University of Chicago, 1947). On the impact of streetcars and the automobile, see Jean Martin, "Mule to MARTA, Vol. I," *Atlanta Historical Bulletin*, XIX (1975), 1–112; Howard L. Preston, *Automobile Age Atlanta* (Athens, 1979); and Don L. Klima, "Breaking Out: Streetcars and Suburban Development, 1872–1900," *Atlanta Historical Journal*, XXVI (1982), 67–82. The entire issue of the *Atlanta Historical Journal*, XXVI (Summer/Fall, 1982), is devoted to spatial themes. See especially Rick Beard, "From Suburb to Defended Neighborhood: The Evolution of Inman Park"; Dana F. White, "The Black Sides of Atlanta: A Geography of Expansion and Containment, 1870–1970"; and Timothy J. Crimmins, "West End: Metamorphosis from Suburban Town to Intown Neighborhood." There is also material on suburban planning in Atlanta in Dana F. White and Victor A. Kramer (eds.), *Olmstead South: Old South Critic/New South Planner* (Westport, Conn., 1979). For information about racial and ethnic residential patterns, see Dorothy Slade, "The Evolution of Negro Areas in the City of Atlanta" (M.A. thesis, Atlanta University, 1946); Ronald H. Bayor, "Ethnic Residential Patterns in Atlanta, 1880–1940," *Georgia Historical Quarterly*, LXIII (1979), 435–47; and John Kellogg, "Negro Urban Clusters in the Postbellum South," *Geographical Review*, LXVII (1977), 310–21. For a description of the architecture and limits of the city's business district, see Elizabeth Lyons, "Business Buildings in Atlanta: A Study in Urban Growth and Form" (Ph.D. dissertation, Emory University, 1971).

The economic history of Atlanta is surprisingly underdeveloped. There is some useful literature on the industrial expositions: Jack Blicksilver, "The International Cotton Exposition of 1881 and Its Impact upon the Economic Development of Georgia," *Atlanta Economic Review*, VII, no. 5 (May, 1957), 1–5, 11–12, and VII, no. 6 (June, 1957), 1–5, 11–12; and Mary Roberts Davis, "The Atlanta Industrial Expositions of 1881 and 1895: Expressions of the Philosophy of the New South" (M.A. thesis, Emory University, 1952). A brief statement concerning the impact of boosterism on Atlanta's development can be found in Dana F. White and Timothy J. Crimmins, "How Atlanta Grew: Cool Heads, Hot Air, and Hard Work," in Andrew M. Hamer, Jr. (ed.), *Urban Atlanta: Redefining the Role of the City* (Atlanta, 1980), 25–44. Two articles by Charles Paul

Garofalo assess boosterism in a later period: "The Sons of Henry Grady: Atlanta Boosters in the 1920s," *Journal of Southern History*, XLII (1976), 187–204; and "The Atlanta Spirit: A Study in Urban Ideology," *South Atlantic Quarterly*, LXXIV (1975), 34–44. Garofalo's comments apply very well to its earlier counterpart in the city.

In the absence of more studies of economic factors and institutions, some information can be derived from biographies of local entrepreneurs. The best works are: Alice E. Reagan, *H. I. Kimball, Entrepreneur* (Atlanta, 1983); and Royce Shingleton, *Richard Peters, Champion of the New South* (Macon, 1985). Raymond B. Nixon's *Henry W. Grady, Spokesman of the New South* (New York, 1943) is a dated biography in need of replacement, but it is still useful. Biographical detail on one member of nineteenth-century Atlanta's economic elite is available in Georgia Bar Association, *A Memorial of Logan E. Bleckley* (1909; rpr. Macon, 1982). The man who introduced electric streetcars to Atlanta and the principal developer of Inman Park is the subject of Sarah Simms Edge's *Joel Hurt and the Development of Atlanta* (Atlanta, 1955).

The Civil War period has attracted the most attention. Two books cover the siege and destruction of Atlanta, but both lack footnotes and are of limited use to scholars: A. A. Hochling, *Last Train from Atlanta* (New York, 1958); and Samuel Carter III, *The Siege of Atlanta, 1864* (New York, 1973). A more comprehensive account is Ralph Benjamin Singer, Jr., "Confederate Atlanta" (Ph.D. dissertation, University of Georgia, 1973). A good summary of the military engagements around Atlanta from the Confederate viewpoint is presented in Richard M. McMurry, "The Atlanta Campaign of 1864: A New Look," *Civil War History*, XXII (1976), 5–15. Two studies deal with Confederate Atlanta's economy: Elizabeth Catherine Bowlby, "The Rôle of Atlanta During the Civil War" (M.A. thesis, Emory University, 1937); and Carole E. Scott, "Coping with Inflation, 1860–1865," *Georgia Historical Quarterly*, LXIX (1985), 536–56. Social problems are dealt with by Paul D. Lack's "Law and Disorder in Confederate Atlanta," *ibid.*, LXVI (1982), 171–95.

There are several dissertations and theses on various topics. Two general studies are worth consulting: Arthur Reed Taylor, "From the Ashes: Atlanta During Reconstruction" (Ph.D. dissertation, Emory University, 1973); and Grigsby Hart Wotton, Jr., "New City of the South: Atlanta, 1843–1873" (Ph.D. dissertation, Johns Hopkins University, 1973). Two other theses have valuable information on immigrants: Ann Fonvielle Mebane, "Immigrant Patterns in Atlanta: 1880 and 1896" (M.A. thesis, Emory University, 1967); and Carol Louise Hagglund, "Irish Immigrants in Atlanta, 1850–1896" (M.A. thesis, Emory University, 1968).

Anyone working on Atlanta history is a practitioner of southern urban history. There have been a good many publications in recent years in this field, which can no longer be described as in its infancy. The starting point for an understanding of the field is Blaine A. Brownell and David R. Goldfield (eds.), *The City in Southern History: The Growth of Urban Civilization in the South* (Port Washington, N.Y., 1977). Goldfield has issued a provocative summons to a new approach to southern urban history, which calls for understanding southern urban development in the context of regionalism. See his *Cotton Fields and Skyscrapers: Southern City and Region, 1607–1980* (Baton Rouge, 1982). This work contains the most up-to-date and comprehensive bibliography of the field.

Several publications have come out since then that were useful. A book that provides hard data on the contrasts between the urban South and North is William H. Pease and Jane H. Pease, *The Web of Progress: Private Values and Public Styles in Boston and Charleston, 1828–1843* (New York, 1985). Detail on antebellum Charleston's elite can also be found in Frederic Cople Jaher's *The Urban Establishment: Upper Strata in Boston, New York, Charleston, Chicago, and Los Angeles* (Urbana, 1982). Don H. Doyle's *Nashville in the New South, 1880–1930* (Knoxville, 1985) gave me a perspective on Atlanta. The most comprehensive account of racial residential patterns in any postbellum southern city is John P. Kellogg's "The Evolution of Black Residential Areas in Lexington, Kentucky, 1865–1887," *Journal of Southern History,* XLVIII (1982), 21–52. A good account of the evolution of public services is presented in Howard L. Platt's *City Building in the New South: The Growth of Public Services in Houston, Texas, 1830–1910* (Philadelphia, 1983). An informative, brief survey of economic and political developments in Atlanta's post–World War II history is Bradley R. Rice, "If Dixie Were Atlanta," in Rice and Richard M. Bernard (eds.), *Sunbelt Cities: Politics and Growth Since World War II* (Austin, 1983), 31–57. A general survey of southern urban history has organizational problems but also some useful data. See Lawrence H. Larsen, *The Rise of the Urban South* (Lexington, Ky., 1985).

INDEX

Government: 1847 municipal charter, 72; Marthasville town commissioners, 72; 1874 municipal charter and railroad subscriptions, 135, 200; 1874 charter and municipal expenditures, 170, 199–201; Board of Aldermen created, 186; General Council created, 186; 1874 charter revised (1879), 185–86, 201; tax structure, 205; 1874 charter and public enterprise, 234. *See also* Politics, municipal

Grady, Henry W.: on Jonathan Norcross, 53; involvement in postbellum Georgia Western project, 135; role in reform movements, 183, 211; at National Commercial Convention, 236; mentioned, 2, 5, 7, 136, 160, 162–64, 167, 234, 237

Grady Hospital, 230, 254

Grant, John T., 55, 165

Grant, John W., 253–54

Grant, Lemuel P.: and Southern Central Agricultural Society, 52; western railroad interests of, 55–56; and antebellum crusade for Georgia Western, 56–57; early career of, 86; and Rome & Blue Mountain, 107; designs wartime fortifications of Atlanta, 113; and postbellum immigration, 150; mentioned, 50, 134

Graves, John W., 51

Green, Duff, 107

Green Line, 120

Gregg, William, 100

Gregg, William A., 247

Haas, Aaron, 238, 245

Haiman, Elias, 242

Hambleton, James P., 92

Hammond, Dennis F., 178–79

Hayden, Julius A., 83, 149, 175

Healey, Thomas G., 95, 164

Health: antebellum, 64; postbellum, 195; need for public hospital, 195. *See also* Smallpox epidemics

Helme, William, 59–60

Hemphill, William A., 222

Hering, Rudolf, 227–28

Hertzberg, Steven, 157

High, Joseph M., 253

Hoge, R. F., 183

Holland, E. W., 64, 110, 149

Home of the Friendless, 230

Hood, John Bell, 113

Hopkins, Richard, 157–58

Howell, Evan P., 184, 234, 237

Hoyt, Samuel B., 133

Hunnicutt, Calvin W., 257

Industrial gospel: during antebellum era, 48–49; during war, 91, 100–101; after war, 130

Inflation, during Civil War: and blockade, 96; and currency issue, 98; and speculators, 98–99; extent of, during war, 105

Inman, Hugh T., 235, 249, 254

Inman, Samuel M., 125, 154, 235–36, 241, 249

Inman, Walker P., 249

Inman Park, 215–16

International Cotton Exposition: organization of, 234–35; exhibits and attendance at, 235; impact on Atlanta, 235; mentioned, 200, 234, 236, 258, 263

Interstate Commerce Commission, 246

Ivy Street Hospital, 230

Jackson, Maynard, 264

James, John H., 166, 176

Johnson, Henry S., 246–47

Keely, John, 241, 253, 256

Kelley, William D., 148–49

Kimball, Hannibal Ingalls: and Kimball House, 121; sketch of, 138; and crusade for cotton factory, 138–39; and local Republican party, 178; and International Cotton Exposition, 234–35; mentioned, 164, 167–68, 236, 260

Kimball House: built after war, 121–22; destroyed by fire (1883), 203; rebuilt, 236

King Hardware Co., 247

King's Daughters Hospital, 230

Knights of Labor, 211, 213

Ku Klux Klan, 150–51

Ladies Union Benevolent Society, 64

Lee, G. W., 109

Lincoln monument, 149, 149n6, 260

Liverpool, Savannah, and Great Western Transportation Line, 120

Location of Atlanta: liabilities of, 14, 29; site selected, 20

Logan, Mrs. Carrie Steele, 230

Long, Henry, 71

Long, Stephen H., 25

Longley, Benjamin F., 208

Longstreet, Augustus Baldwin, 72

INDEX

Wealth: distribution of, in antebellum era, 74–75; distribution of, by nativity (1850), 75–76; distribution of, in 1870, p. 154; distribution of, by race in 1870, pp. 154–55; distribution of, by nativity (1870), 155
Webster, Robert, 154
Welch, M. M., 246
West End, 187, 216, 231
Western & Atlantic: plans for, and Indian removal, 17–18; building of, 19–21; machine shops in antebellum era, 46; performance during war, 97; machine shops during war, 102; leased in 1871, p. 138; and Republican party, 178; and coal for Atlanta industries in 1880s, p. 249
Western foodstuffs: and antebellum South's self-sufficiency, 21; local trade in, before war, 43; revival of local trade in, following war, 121–22
Wiener, Jonathan, 3, 6, 7
Williams, James E., 169, 171, 175–76
Wilson, A. N., 64
Wilson, Henry, 148–49
Winkle, Edward Van, 255
Winship, Joseph, 46, 82, 86
Women's Christian Association Mission School, 230
Woodward, C. Vann, 2–3, 7, 262–63
Wright, Austin, 110
Wright, Moses H., 103, 105
Wyly, A. C., 45, 246
Wyly, B. F., 246

Yancey, Benjamin C., 71, 123, 154